Farm Journal's
Best-Ever
Vegetable
Recipes

Farm Journal's
BEST-EVER
VEGETABLE
RECIPES

A fresh approach

to main dishes, appetizers and snacks,

soups, salads and desserts—

with 400 never-fail recipes

By the Food Editors of Farm Journal

Alice Joy Miller, Editor
Ronnie J. Fulvi, Associate Editor
Joanne G. Fullan, Assistant Editor
Margaret C. Quinn, Home Economist

Farm Journal, Inc.
Philadelphia, Pennsylvania

Distributed to the trade by
Doubleday & Company, Inc.
Garden City, New York

OTHER FARM JOURNAL COOKBOOKS

Farm Journal's Country Cookbook
Homemade Bread
Farm Journal's Homemade Snacks
Farm Journal's Best-Ever Recipes
Farm Journal's Great Dishes from the Oven
Farm Journal's Freezing and Canning Cookbook
Farm Journal's Friendly Food Gifts from your Kitchen
Farm Journal's Choice Chocolate Recipes
Farm Journal's Complete Home Baking Book
Farm Journal's Meal & Menu Planner Cookbook
Farm Journal's Speedy Skillet Meals
Farm Journal's Best-Ever Cookies
Farm Journal's Best-Ever Pies
Farm Journal's Picnic & Barbecue Cookbook
Farm Journal's Complete Cake Decorating Book

Book design: Michael P. Durning
Photography: Ken Bronstein/Mel Richman Inc.
Consulting Art Director/Photography: Alfred A. Casciato
Illustrations: Gwen Brodkin

Library of Congress Cataloging in Publication Data
Farm journal's best-ever vegetable recipes.
    Includes index.
    1. Cookery (Vegetables)
    I. Farm journal (Philadelphia, Pa.: 1956)
TX801.F25   1984   641.6'5   82-46053
ISBN O-385-18849-8

Contents

Introduction   vii

1 / Vary the Vegetable   1
Basic information on more than 40 vegetables, including seasonality,
selection, storage, preparation and yield, with a microwave chart.

2 / Incredible Edibles   47
Elegant, easy garnishes made from raw vegetables, plus directions
for a whole bouquet of garnishes to arrange into a centerpiece.

3 / Fresh Beginnings   59
Appetizing tidbits such as Shrimp-filled Snow Peas, Oven-fried Broccoli
Flowerets, New Potato Canapés, and dips both hot and cold.

4 / Country Soups   71
For first courses, lunches and suppers: chowders, hot and cold cream
soups, vichyssoise and borscht, plus a savory vegetable stock.

5 / Spectacular Salads   97
Layered, marinated, molded or simply mixed, such choices as Hot
Spinach Salad, Jicama Salad, Carrot Mousse and classic potato salads.

6 / Satisfying Main Dishes   117
Soufflés, quiches, casseroles and stews, some with an ethnic heritage:
Chinese Pepper Steak, Pasta Primavera, Russian Pie, and more.

7 / Side by Side   159
Complement main dishes with the colors, flavors and textures of Basil
Beans and Tomatoes, Sweet-Sour Red Cabbage or Potatoes Anna.

8 / Seasonings, Sauces and Salad Dressings   209
Basic white sauce, classic Béarnaise and Hollandaise sauces, herb
butters, spicy sauces and dozens of dressings, with a seasoning chart.

9 / Goodies with Goodness   231
Aromatic tea breads, rolls, muffins, cakes and cookies, including
Raised Corn Muffins, Pumpkin-Raisin Cookies and Sweet Potato Pie.

10 / After Your Garden Grows   251
Recipes for preserving summer's bounty as pickles, relishes, marmalade,
chutney and sauces, with a chart for blanching and freezing.

Index   265

CHARTS

Microwaving Fresh Vegetables   pages 39-45

Seasonings for Vegetables   pages 210-213

Blanching and Freezing   pages 254-255
   Vegetables

COLOR PHOTOGRAPHS

Appetizer Tray   facing page 86

Braised Leeks and Carrots;   following page 86
Sautéed Tomatoes and Anise

Sampling of Vegetable Breads   following page 86

Garnish Basket   facing page 87

Creamy Cucumber-Dill Dressing;   facing page 182
Pesto Butter;
Blender Hollandaise Sauce

Vegetable-filled Dutch Pancake;   following page 182
Carrot Ravioli with Spinach Filling

Meatball and Pasta Soup   following page 182

Pickles and Relishes   facing page 183

Introduction

You've probably noticed that produce sections in supermarkets are a lot bigger and better than they used to be. Vegetables that were once grown mainly in home gardens—sugar snap peas, Jerusalem artichokes, spaghetti squash and a seemingly unlimited variety of lettuce and greens—are available right in your local market.

Until recently it was almost impossible to buy fresh green beans in the dead of winter. Now, it's second nature to plan on using them in a stir-fry dinner even on a snowy evening. Because of technical advances in growing, storage and refrigeration, many other seasonal vegetables are now available year 'round, just like onions, carrots and potatoes.

All across the country, cooks are preparing fresh vegetables every day of the week, as more people discover what country cooks have known all along: that vegetables are good, wholesome foods, high in fiber, generally low in calories and rich in vitamins and minerals. Today's vegetables even seem to look and taste better, because we've learned to treasure their fresh flavor and to cook them just until they're tender-crisp. Vegetables are so versatile, too. Even their colors are varied—snow-white cauliflower, pastel-green leaf lettuce, golden-yellow corn, fiery-red tomatoes and crimson beets.

The 400 recipes in this cookbook reflect the know-how of experienced country cooks on ranches and farms around the country, some of whom maintain vegetable gardens that were started by their grandparents. These women, and men, generously shared their tried-and-true vegetable recipes—their best-ever. We added a few of our own favorites, then retested and double-checked each recipe in Farm Journal's Test Kitchens.

Whether you gather fresh vegetables from your own garden or from the produce bins of a big city supermarket, we hope you'll enjoy using these recipes and discovering just how versatile vegetables can be.

ALICE JOY MILLER
Food Editor

1

Vary
the Vegetable

Even those of us who have vegetable gardens often find ourselves standing in front of the produce counter at our supermarket, trying to select fresh vegetables for the week ahead. What we're interested in comes down to this: Which vegetables are at their best right now? The most nutritious? The most versatile? Which ones are the best buy? If I take advantage of this week's special, how much will I need to feed my family? How long will it keep, and how am I going to cook it?

This chapter is a cook's handbook of useful information that will help you eliminate the guesswork in choosing and preparing more than 40 vegetables.

Many vegetables included here are family favorites that you probably enjoy often. Others, like jicama, kohlrabi or Jerusalem artichokes, may seem unfamiliar to you. It's not that you haven't seen these unusual ones; you probably have, but passed them up just because you hadn't a clue as to what to do with them once you got them home. In the pages that follow, you'll find out exactly how to take advantage of their natural goodness.

The 44 vegetables in this chapter are arranged alphabetically to make them easy to find, and there's a brief description of each one. Information about seasonality is included, too—whether a vegetable is generally available in supermarkets year 'round, or just for a certain few months.

Basic cooking directions are included for every vegetable, and a chart on pages 39-45 tells how to microwave fresh vegetables.

If you have questions about how to select or serve some vegetables, look in this chapter for the answers, whether you want to know how to choose fresh okra or how to tell the difference between summer and winter squash; how to store fresh-picked corn; how long to cook celeriac; how many servings you can get from a pound of green beans; how to grow your own sprouts; how to serve sugar snap peas; or even how to roast pumpkin seeds.

With this basic information about vegetables—from licorice-flavored anise to turnips and their leafy greens—you'll be well equipped to take full advantage of the abundant versatility of vegetables as part of just about any dish you serve, from snacks to desserts.

ANISE

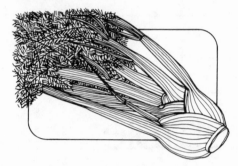

Also called fennel or finocchio, anise is a member of the parsley family. It looks like celery and can be used either raw or cooked. Anise is prized for its mild licorice flavor.

Its feathery tops look like dill; its broad stalks overlap at the stem, forming a bulbous base. Both the tops and bulb are edible.

Anise is a good source of vitamins A and C.

SEASONALITY: Available October through March.

SELECTION: Choose firm, greenish-white bulbs and stalks with green, feathery tops. Avoid stalks with wilted tops and soft bulbs with brownish bases or deep cracks.

STORAGE: Refrigerate, unwashed, in plastic bag 3 to 5 days. Anise does not freeze well.

PREPARATION: Rinse under cold running water, and remove dry outer leaves. Cut off stalks 1″ above bulbous base.

Use the trimmings—stalks and edible leaves—for flavorings or garnish. Use the bulb sliced or chopped.

YIELD: For 4 servings, allow 2 lb.; 1 bulb with tops (1 lb.) yields about 3 c. sliced or chopped.

COOKING: Boil, blanch, steam, braise, sauté, stir-fry, bake, deep-fry or microwave.

To boil: In 2-qt. saucepan over high heat, bring ½″ salted water to a boil. Add 2 lb. anise, sliced, and let water return to a boil. Reduce heat to low. Cover and simmer 10 to 20 minutes or until fork-tender. Drain.

SERVING: Use raw anise in salads. Cooked anise can be used in soups, main and side dishes.

ARTICHOKES

Many times this splendid vegetable is overlooked because it seems too complicated to cook. But it's quite simple to prepare and fun to eat—leaf by leaf!

Globe artichokes are the fleshy, leafy buds of a thistle-like plant—not to be confused with Jerusalem artichokes, which are totally different plants.

To enjoy the nut-like flavor of an artichoke, pull off the leaves, one by one, and dip the fleshy ends in melted butter or a creamy herb sauce. Then pull the fleshy ends through your teeth and eat the pulp.

The most savored part of an artichoke is the tender heart. To eat the heart, remove the fuzzy "choke." Then cut the heart into bite-size pieces and dip in melted butter.

Artichokes are high in fiber and a good source of vitamin A.

SEASONALITY: Available year 'round; the peak season is March through May.

SELECTION: Choose plump, compact artichokes heavy in relation to their size, with thick, tightly closed green leaves. Size is not an indication of quality, but avoid artichokes with blemishes or spreading leaves.

STORAGE: Refrigerate, unwashed, in plastic bag with a few drops of water 2 to 3 days. Artichokes freeze well; just blanch and freeze.

PREPARATION: Rinse under cold running water. Cut off stem end. With serrated knife cut 1″ from top of artichoke, cutting straight across. Remove any loose leaves from bottom of artichoke and use scissors to snip thorny tips from leaves.
Use whole, or halved. Whole artichokes can be stuffed.

YIELD: For 1 serving, allow 1 artichoke.

COOKING: Boil, steam, braise, bake, deep-fry, microwave or pressure-cook.
To boil: In 4-qt. Dutch oven over high heat, bring 1″ salted water to a boil. Place 4 whole artichokes upright in Dutch oven and let water return to a boil. Reduce heat to low. Cover and simmer 30 minutes or until a leaf can be pulled out easily. Drain.

SERVING: Cooked artichokes and hearts can be used as appetizers or in salads, main and side dishes or for pickles.

ASPARAGUS

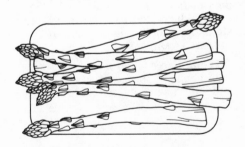

You'll know that it must be spring when asparagus is in season. This aristocratic-looking vegetable has a delicate yet distinctive flavor. Asparagus ranges in color from bright green to snow white, and in shape from thin to thick. It takes especially well to sauces.

Asparagus is low in sodium, high in fiber, and an excellent source of vitamins A and C.

SEASONALITY: Available in spring; the peak season is March through May.

SELECTION: Choose straight, round spears that are rich green almost the entire length of the stalk; the spears should be at least two-thirds green. Top buds should be closed and compact. Avoid spears that have open or spreading buds, as well as those with large, woody white bases.

STORAGE: Refrigerate, unwashed, in plastic bag or crisper 1 to 2 days. Asparagus freezes well; just blanch and freeze.

PREPARATION: Holding base of stalk in one hand, bend stalk until it breaks. The white area of the stem is tough and can be used in long-cooking soups. Trim scales if gritty.
Use whole, sliced or chopped.

YIELD: For 1 serving, allow ½ to ¾ lb., or 6 to 8 spears; 1 lb. asparagus, trimmed and cut into 1″ pieces, yields about 3 c.

COOKING: Boil, blanch, steam, braise, sauté, stir-fry, bake, deep-fry or microwave.
To boil: In 12″ skillet over high heat, bring ½″ salted water to a boil. Add 1 lb. asparagus, trimmed, and let water return to a boil. Reduce heat to low. Cover and simmer 5 to 7 minutes or until tender-crisp. Drain.

SERVING: Cooked asparagus, hot or cold, can be used in appetizers, soups, salads, main and side dishes.

BEANS

Green beans that just pop when snapped are the ones you most often think of when someone mentions fresh beans, but there are other common types, too.

Snap beans have long, slender edible pods. They're often called string beans, but this is a misnomer because they've been cultivated to be almost string-free. Their pale yellow close relatives, wax or yellow beans, are handled and cooked the same way as snap beans.

Lima beans or *butter beans* are a favorite vegetable throughout America. They grow in light to dark green pods about 3 to 4″ long. They're not easy to shell, but like fresh peas, they're well worth the effort. There are two types: small, thin baby limas and the larger and thicker lima beans, sometimes called Fordhook.

Fava, broad or *horse beans* are similar to limas, but they have larger pods, ranging from 6 to 12″ long, with bigger beans. Use them as you would limas; just cook them a little longer. You'll see these in the market in the late spring and summer.

For more bean information, see Dried Beans.

Both snap and lima beans are good sources of vitamins A and C.

SEASONALITY: Snap and wax beans are available year 'round; the peak season is April through August. Lima beans are available July through September.

SELECTION: Choose smooth, crisp but tender beans that snap easily and are free of blemishes and soft spots. Pods should be well shaped, with very small seeds. Avoid pods that are flabby, wilted, discolored, blemished or thick.

Choose lima beans with fresh, dry, well-filled pods. Shelled limas should be light green to green, with tender skins. Avoid tough, hard pods with overmature beans.

STORAGE: Refrigerate all beans, unwashed, in perforated plastic bag or crisper 2 to 3 days. Beans freeze well; just blanch and freeze.

PREPARATION: Trim both ends of snap or wax beans. Rinse under cold running water. Use whole; or snap or cut beans into 1 to 2″ pieces. To French-cut, simply slit beans lengthwise into thin strips.

For lima beans: Rinse pods under cold running water. Snap off one end of pod and open to push out beans. If the pods do not snap open easily, cut a thin strip from the inner edge of pod and push out beans.

YIELD: For 4 servings, allow 1 lb. snap or wax beans; 1 lb. yields about 4 c.

For 2 to 3 servings, allow 1 lb. lima beans; 1 lb. unshelled beans yields about 1½ c. beans.

COOKING: Snap, wax and lima beans can be boiled, blanched, steamed, braised, sautéed, stir-fried, baked, deep-fried or microwaved. Lima beans can be pressure-cooked.

To boil snap or wax beans: In 2-qt. saucepan over high heat, bring 1″ salted water to a boil. Add 1 lb. whole or cut beans and let water return to a boil. Reduce heat to low. Cover and simmer 5 to 10 minutes or until tender-crisp. Drain.

To boil lima beans: In 2-qt. saucepan over high heat, bring 1″ salted water to a boil. Add 1 lb. shelled lima beans and let water return to a boil. Reduce heat to low. Cover and simmer 20 to 30 minutes or until tender. Drain.

SERVING: Use cooked snap, wax or lima beans in soups, salads, main and side dishes or for pickles.

BEETS

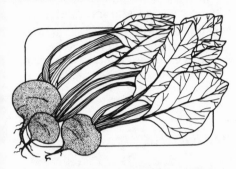

Widely appreciated for their sweet, earthy flavor and ruby-red color, beets can complement many foods. Many of us are all too familiar with canned beets, but it's well worth cooking fresh beets to experience their distinctive deep flavor and crisp texture, which are often lost in the canning process. Don't throw away the tops—these tender leaves and stems make a great side dish and can be added to soups and stews.

Beets are a good source of vitamins A and C. Beet greens are high in vitamin A and iron.

SEASONALITY: Available year 'round; the peak season is June through August.

SELECTION: Choose richly colored red beets, small to medium in size, with round shapes and smooth, firm flesh. Avoid spotted, pitted beets with scales and very large or flabby beets. Choose a bunch of beets equal in size so they'll cook evenly.

The greens should be thin-ribbed and the leaves fresh-looking and crisp. (For more information, see Greens later in this chapter.)

STORAGE: Cut off greens. Refrigerate beets, unwashed, in plastic bag or crisper 5 to 7 days.

To store beet greens: Cut tops 1 to 2" from crowns and refrigerate, unwashed, 1 to 2 days.

Beets and tops freeze well; just blanch and freeze.

PREPARATION: Cut off tops and root ends. Scrub beets with a soft brush under cold running water. Peel. (If boiling beets, peel after cooking; it's much easier.)

Use whole, sliced, cubed or shredded.

For greens: Rinse under cold running water to remove dirt and sand. Trim bruised leaves and tough stems. Cut tops and stems into 2" pieces. Spin dry in salad spinner or pat dry with paper towels.

YIELD: For 3 to 4 servings, allow 1 lb. beets; 1 lb. yields about 2 c. sliced.

For 2 to 3 servings, allow 1 lb. beet greens; 1 lb. yields about 8 c. chopped.

COOKING: Both beets and greens can be boiled, blanched, steamed or microwaved. Beets also can be baked and pressure-cooked. Greens can also be sautéed and stir-fried.

To boil beets: In 2-qt. saucepan over high heat, bring 1" salted water to a boil. Add 1 lb. small whole beets and let water return to a boil. Reduce heat to low. Cover and simmer 30 to 60 minutes or until tender. Drain and cool slightly, then peel.

Cook 1 lb. peeled, sliced beets 20 to 30 minutes.

To boil greens: In 4-qt. Dutch oven over high heat, bring 1/4" salted water to a boil. Add 1 lb. chopped beet greens and let water return to a boil. Reduce heat to low. Cover and cook 5 to 10 minutes or until tender. Drain.

SERVING: Use raw beets in salads. Cooked beets and greens can be used in soups, main and side dishes.

BELGIAN ENDIVE

heat to low. Cover and simmer 15 minutes or until endives are tender-crisp but still intact. Drain.

SERVING: Use raw endive in appetizers and salads. Cooked endives can be served hot or cold as a side dish.

BROCCOLI

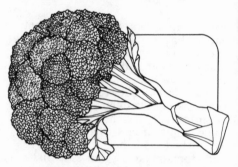

Also called French endive, Belgian endive is a member of the humble sunflower family. Its woody roots are called root chicory and are used as a coffee substitute.

Endive is grown underground in dark, warm places so that the developed vegetable will have white bleached leaves. It has a pointed, cylindrical shape with yellow-tipped leaves. Endive has a crisp texture and a slightly bitter taste.

Belgian endive is a good source of minerals.

SEASONALITY: Available fall through spring; the peak season is November through April.

SELECTION: Choose 5 to 6″ firm, tightly closed heads that are creamy white with light yellow tips. Avoid endives with loose, soft, bruised or wilted leaves.

STORAGE: Refrigerate, unwashed, in plastic bag or crisper 1 to 2 days. Endive does not freeze well.

PREPARATION: Rinse leaves under cold running water. Trim and cut out bitter center core.

Use whole, sliced or chopped. Whole leaves may be stuffed.

YIELD: For 1 serving, allow 1 medium endive; 1 lb. equals about 5 endives.

COOKING: Boil, steam, braise, sauté, stir-fry or microwave.

To boil: In 2-qt. saucepan over high heat, bring ½″ salted water to a boil. Add 1 lb. whole endives and let water return to a boil. Reduce

The Italian word *brocco*, meaning arm or branch, gave this vegetable its name. Its thick stem branches into clusters of flower buds, and it's closely related to cauliflower.

Broccoli is high in fiber, an excellent source of vitamin C, and a good source of minerals and vitamin A.

SEASONALITY: Available year 'round; the peak season is October through March.

SELECTION: Choose heads with firm, compact clusters of deep or purple-green flowerets with tender, firm stalks. Avoid bruised, wilted and flabby broccoli or heads with yellow flower buds.

STORAGE: Refrigerate; unwashed, in plastic bag or crisper 1 to 2 days. Broccoli freezes well; just blanch and freeze.

PREPARATION: The secret of cooking broccoli is to peel the stems. Trim away the tough part of stems. Remove leaves. For more even cooking, cut slits in stalks lengthwise 2 or 3 times. Rinse well under cold running water.

For flowerets: Cut about 2½" below the top of flowerets, or where stalk branches into small stems. Then peel stems and cut into 2½" pieces.

Use whole, cut into flowerets or chopped.

YIELD: For 2 servings, allow 1 lb.; ½ lb. yields about 2 c. chopped.

COOKING: Boil, blanch, steam, sauté, stir-fry, deep-fry or microwave.

To boil: In 4-qt. saucepan or Dutch oven over high heat, bring 1" salted water to a boil. Add 1 lb. broccoli, cut into flowerets, and let water return to a boil. Reduce heat to low. Cover and simmer 7 to 10 minutes or just until tender-crisp. Drain.

SERVING: Use raw broccoli as appetizers with a dip or in salads. Cooked broccoli can be used in soups, stews, main and side dishes.

BRUSSELS SPROUTS

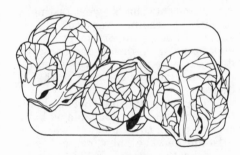

Often served at Thanksgiving in the East, these little cabbages carry the name Brussels because they were first grown in Belgium. As elite members of the cabbage family, they're prized for their miniature shape and mild cabbage flavor.

The smaller the sprout, the better the flavor; sprouts should be about the size of your thumbnail, compact and bright green.

Brussels sprouts are high in vitamins A and C.

SEASONALITY: Available September through April; the peak season is October through February.

SELECTION: Choose small, firm, bright green sprouts with compact heads that are free from blemishes. Avoid soft, wilted, puffy sprouts with loose or yellow leaves.

STORAGE: Remove yellow leaves. Refrigerate, unwashed, in plastic bag 1 to 2 days. Sprouts freeze well; just blanch and freeze.

PREPARATION: Remove any yellow leaves and trim stems. Cut an X in stem ends to allow for fast, even cooking. Rinse sprouts under cold running water.

Use whole or halved.

YIELD: For 2 to 3 servings, allow a 1-pt. container (about 10 oz.); 1 lb. yields 3 to 4 servings.

COOKING: Boil, steam, braise, sauté, stir-fry, bake, deep-fry or microwave.

To boil: In 2-qt. saucepan over high heat, bring 1" salted water to a boil. Add 1 lb. Brussels sprouts, trimmed, and let water return to a boil. Reduce heat to low. Cover and simmer 8 to 10 minutes or until tender. Drain. (Do not overcook or they will become soggy and strong-flavored.)

SERVING: Cooked Brussels sprouts can be used in main and side dishes.

CABBAGE

Cousin of collards, broccoli and Brussels sprouts, cabbage has long been a mainstay of American as well as European cuisine. The Germans are famous for their pickled cabbage, sauerkraut, and the Russians know the secret of braising cabbage in soups and stews.

Cabbage is a popular vegetable because it's easily grown in varied climates. It's an economical vegetable with a strong flavor and crisp texture.

Most cabbage is green, but there are red and purple varieties, too. There are even heads of cabbage with curly, crinkled leaves; these are called Savoy. Heads can vary in size from round to oval and be firm or loose.

The most common are the smooth-leaved green or white varieties that have a compact round head with many thick, overlapping leaves.

Cabbage is high in fiber and an excellent source of vitamin C.

SEASONALITY: Available year 'round; the peak season is October through March.

SELECTION: Choose firm heads that are heavy in relation to their size. Outer leaves should be crisp, with a fresh green or red color. Savoy has a softer, loose head but should have firm, crisp, crinkly-edged leaves. Avoid heads that are too white or soft with blemished and discolored leaves.

STORAGE: Refrigerate, unwashed, in plastic bag or crisper 1 to 2 weeks. Cabbage does not freeze well.

PREPARATION: Remove and discard any wilted or discolored outer leaves. If using whole, core and trim stem end.

For wedges: Cut cabbage in half and then in quarters, trimming core from each wedge.

To slice, shred or chop: With knife, slice, shred or chop wedges.

Use whole, quartered, sliced, shredded or chopped.

YIELD: For 4 servings, allow 1 small head (about 1 lb.); 1 small head (about 1 lb.) yields 4 to 5 c. sliced or 4 c. shredded.

COOKING: Boil, steam, braise, sauté, stir-fry, bake or microwave.

To boil: In 4-qt. Dutch oven over high heat, bring 1" salted water to a boil. Add 4 cabbage wedges. Reduce heat to low. Cover and simmer 10 to 15 minutes or until tender-crisp. Drain.

Cook 1 lb. cabbage, shredded, 3 to 6 minutes or just until tender-crisp. (Overcooking will produce a strong odor and flavor.)

SERVING: Use raw cabbage in appetizers and salads. Leaves can be stuffed and cooked for main dishes. Cooked cabbage can be used in soups, main and side dishes.

CARROTS

Any vegetable that's sweet-tasting, brightly colored and versatile enough to be an important part of appetizers, main dishes and desserts deserves a four-star rating—even if it's a vegetable as common as the carrot.

These long, tapering root vegetables sometimes are available as baby carrots just 2 to 3" long.

Of all the vegetables, carrots are the richest in vitamin A. They also are a good source of vitamin C and minerals.

SEASONALITY: Available year 'round.

SELECTION: Choose firm, smooth, clean, well shaped, bright orange carrots with fresh green tops.

STORAGE: Cut off tops. Refrigerate, unwashed, in plastic bag or crisper 1 to 2 weeks. Carrots freeze well; just blanch and freeze.

PREPARATION: Scrape with knife or peel with vegetable peeler. Rinse under cold running water. Some cooks prefer to simply scrub carrots with a stiff vegetable brush and do not peel.

Use whole, cut lengthwise into halves or quarters, chopped, sliced, shredded or grated.

YIELD: For 3 to 4 servings, allow 1 lb. carrots; 1 lb. carrots yields about 3 c. sliced or 3 c. grated or shredded.

COOKING: Boil, blanch, steam, braise, sauté, stir-fry, bake, deep-fry, micro-wave or pressure-cook.

To boil: In 3-qt. saucepan over high heat, bring 1″ salted water to a boil. Add 1 lb. whole carrots. Reduce heat to low. Cover and simmer 20 minutes or until tender-crisp. Drain.

Cook 1 lb. carrots, sliced, 8 to 12 minutes.

SERVING: Use raw carrots in appetizers, salads or as garnishes. Cooked carrots can be used in soups, sauces, baked goods, main and side dishes or for pickles.

CAULIFLOWER

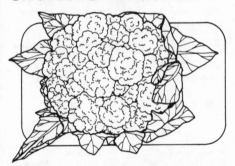

Like broccoli, cauliflower is a member of the cabbage family. It has a single stalk bearing a large, round, tightly packed mass of white or creamy-white flower buds, also called curd. There are several varieties of cauliflower, including ones with green and purple heads.

Cauliflower is high in fiber and a good source of vitamins A and C.

SEASONALITY: Available year 'round; the peak season is September through January.

SELECTION: Choose clean, firm, white to creamy-white heavy heads with compact flower buds and firm green leaves around the base. Avoid those with flower buds that are spreading, spotted or discolored.

STORAGE: Refrigerate, unwashed, in plastic bag or crisper 1 to 5 days. Cauliflower freezes well; just blanch and freeze.

PREPARATION: Rinse under cold running water. Trim off tough outer leaves and core.

Use whole, cut into flowerets or chopped.

YIELD: For 4 servings, allow 1 medium head (about 1 lb.); 1 medium head yields about 3 c. chopped.

COOKING: Boil, blanch, steam, braise, sauté, stir-fry, deep-fry or micro-wave.

To boil: In 3-qt. saucepan over high heat, bring 1″ salted water to a boil. Add 1 head cauliflower, flower-side up, and let water return to a boil. Reduce heat to low. Cover and simmer 10 to 15 minutes or just until fork-tender. Drain.

Cook 1 lb. cauliflower, cut into flowerets, 5 to 8 minutes.

SERVING: Use raw cauliflower in appetizers and salads. Cooked cauliflower can be used in soups, stews, main and side dishes or for pickles.

CELERIAC

A variety of celery that's grown for its enlarged roots rather than its stalks and leaves, celeriac tastes much like celery, only stronger, with a smoky flavor. It has an irregular globe-like shape and is 2 to 4″ wide, with a rough brown skin and white interior.

Celeriac is high in fiber and potassium.

SEASONALITY: Available October through April.

SELECTION: Choose small, firm, clean roots heavy in relation to their size. Avoid large, woody ones with soft wilted roots and deep crevices or knobs on the skin. Smooth skin can be deceiving, so press the top of the root to be sure it's firm—soft spots indicate internal decay.

STORAGE: Trim root fibers and leaves. Refrigerate, unwashed, in plastic bag or crisper 1 to 7 days. Celeriac does not freeze well.

PREPARATION: Celeriac darkens when peeled and cut. To prevent darkening: In medium bowl stir together 3 c. water and 1 tblsp. vinegar. Peel celeriac. Cut into slices and immediately place in vinegar mixture until ready to use. Drain.

Use sliced, cubed, chopped or shredded.

YIELD: For 2 to 3 servings, allow 1 lb.; 1 lb. yields about ¾ lb. peeled flesh, or about 4 c. shredded.

COOKING: Boil, steam, braise, sauté or stir-fry.

To boil: Do not peel. In 2-qt. saucepan over high heat, bring 1″ salted water to a boil. Add 1 lb. whole celeriac and let water return to a boil. Reduce heat to low. Cover and simmer 20 to 30 minutes or until fork-tender. Drain and cool slightly, then peel and slice.

Cook 1 lb. celeriac, peeled and sliced, 3 to 10 minutes.

SERVING: Use raw celeriac in salads. Cooked celeriac can be used in soups, main and side dishes.

CELERY

There are many varieties of celery, but the two basic types are green and golden. Green celery also is called Pascal celery; golden celery is blanched or grown in darkness to change the typical green color to light white or golden bunches with yellow-green leaves. Bunches of celery sold in markets are trimmed to an average length of 12 to 16″.

Celery is high in fiber, low in calories, and a good source of vitamins and minerals.

SEASONALITY: Available year 'round.

SELECTION: Choose crisp, firm, medium-size bunches that are compact, light green and have fresh green leaves. Avoid ones with rubbery, brown or cracked ribs and wilted or yellow leaves.

STORAGE: Refrigerate, unwashed, in plastic bag or crisper up to 1 week. Celery freezes well; just blanch and freeze.

PREPARATION: Trim base and cut off leaves. Reserve leaves for garnishes, soups or stews. Rinse bunch under cold running water; drain well.

Use whole or break into ribs. Use ribs whole, sliced or chopped.

YIELD: For 4 to 6 servings, allow 1 large bunch celery.

COOKING: Boil, blanch, steam, braise, sauté, stir-fry or microwave.

To boil: In 12" skillet over high heat, bring 1" salted water to a boil. Add 1 bunch celery, cut lengthwise into quarters, and let water return to a boil. Reduce heat to low. Cover and simmer 4 to 6 minutes or until tender-crisp.

Cook 1 lb. celery, sliced, 3 to 4 minutes.

SERVING: Use raw ribs of celery, as appetizers or in salads. Cooked celery can be used in soups, stews, main and side dishes.

CHINESE CABBAGE___

Long appreciated for its delicate flavor and crisp texture, Chinese cabbage has been cultivated since before the Christian era.

The two most popular varieties, bok choy and Pe-tsai, are both called Chinese cabbage, and they're also known by other names.

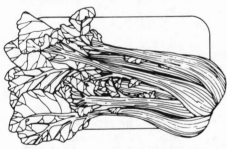
Bok Choy

Bok choy (also called Chinese chard and Chinese mustard) has clusters of thick, greenish-white stalks from 10" to 20" long, with broad, dark green leaves. It has a delicate flavor and a very crisp texture.

Pe-tsai (also called Chinese cabbage, celery cabbage or Napa) belongs to the Napa cabbage family. It looks very much like romaine lettuce, but its leaves are pale green. The leaves are somewhat crinkled and have broad ribs and strong veins. The white heart of the head is a real delicacy. Pe-tsai is crisp,

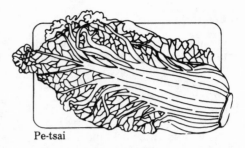
Pe-tsai

and has the most delicate flavor of all cabbages.

Chinese cabbage is high in fiber and a good source of vitamins A and C.

SEASONALITY: Both varieties are available year 'round.

SELECTION: Choose bok choy with long, smooth, firm white heads and dark green tops. Avoid limp, yellow leaves and cracked or discolored stalks.

Choose Pe-tsai with crisp, tightly crinkled, light yellow heads and no discoloration. Avoid ones with limp leaves. Very large heads may have a strong flavor.

STORAGE: Refrigerate, unwashed, in plastic bag 1 to 3 days. These cabbages do not freeze well.

PREPARATION: Rinse under cold running water. Cut bottom from base and separate into stalks or leaves.

Use leaves whole, sliced, shredded or chopped.

YIELD: For 4 servings, allow 1 lb.; 1 lb. yields 6 to 7 c. chopped.

COOKING: Both bok choy and Pe-tsai can be boiled, steamed, braised, sautéed, stir-fried or microwaved.

To boil: In 3-qt. saucepan over high heat, bring 1" salted water to a boil. Add 1 lb. cabbage, shredded, and let water return to a boil. Reduce heat to low. Cover and simmer 5 to 10 minutes or until tender-crisp. Drain.

SERVING: Use raw bok choy or Pe-tsai in salads. Use cooked bok choy or Pe-tsai in soups, side dishes and Chinese-style main dishes.

CORN

The only cereal that's native to this country, corn is probably our most popular vegetable, next to tomatoes.

Corn actually is a type of grass; its proper name is maize, a word of Indian origin. Early settlers learned how to dry corn and grind it into meal, and corn meal found its way into many of our favorite recipes— such as muffins, hush puppies and johnnycakes.

When kernels of corn are treated with a lye solution, they puff up and become hominy; when hominy is dried and ground, it's called grits.

Many varieties of sweet corn are introduced each year, and nowadays, fresh corn on the cob is available year 'round.

Corn is high in fiber and a good source of vitamins B_1 and A.

SEASONALITY: Available year 'round; the peak season is May through August.

SELECTION: Choose medium-size ears with bright green husks and dark brown silks. Kernels should be shiny, plump and slightly firm. Ears should be filled with kernels all the way to the tips. Avoid ears with very large, deep yellow kernels. Dry or yellow husks indicate age, and ears should be free of decay.

STORAGE: It's best to cook corn as soon as you pick it or bring it home, but it can be wrapped in damp paper towels and refrigerated, unhusked, 1 day. Corn toughens and loses its sweetness in storage.

Corn freezes well; just blanch and freeze.

PREPARATION: Peel husk and remove silk. Use a soft vegetable brush to remove any remaining silk. Rinse under cold running water.

To remove the fresh kernels, use a sharp knife to cut lengthwise through the center of each row. Scrape the ear with the back of the knife to extract the juice.

Use whole ears or kernels.

YIELD: For 1 serving, allow 1 to 2 ears; 1 ear yields about ½ c. whole-kernel corn.

COOKING: Boil, steam, braise, sauté, stir-fry, bake, microwave or grill.

To boil whole ears: In large sauce-pot over high heat, bring 1″ unsalted water to a boil. Add 4 ears corn and let water return to a boil. Reduce heat to low. Cover and simmer 3 to 5 minutes. Drain. (Do not overcook, or corn will become tough.)

To cook kernels: In 2-qt. saucepan over high heat, bring 1″ unsalted water to a boil. Add 2 c. kernels and let water return to a boil. Reduce heat to low. Cover and simmer 5 to 8 minutes or until tender. Drain.

SERVING: Cooked whole kernels can be scraped off the cob and used in soups, salads, baked goods, main and side dishes.

CUCUMBERS

Cucumbers are actually fruit, but they're used as vegetables. Their vines are prolific, as gardeners know: one vine can yield as many as 125 cucumbers.

Often cucumbers come to market waxed to slow the rate of spoilage, and these should be peeled.

Cucumbers are high in fiber and are a good source of vitamins and minerals.

SEASONALITY: Available year 'round; the peak season is May through August.

SELECTION: Choose firm, well shaped dark green cucumbers of medium size. Avoid yellow, soft, puffy or very large, dull-colored cucumbers. Smaller ones are good for pickling.

STORAGE: Refrigerate, unwashed, in crisper 1 to 5 days.

Cut cucumbers give off a strong odor that other foods may absorb, so wrap them tightly in plastic wrap or aluminum foil; refrigerate 1 to 4 days.

Cucumbers do not freeze well.

PREPARATION: Rinse well under cold running water. If cucumbers are lightly waxed, rinse well under very hot water; otherwise, peel.

Use sliced, chopped or grated.

YIELD: For 2 to 3 servings, allow 1 medium cucumber; 1 medium cucumber yields about 2 c. sliced.

COOKING: Boil, steam, braise, sauté, stir-fry, deep-fry or microwave.

To sauté: In 10″ skillet over medium heat, melt 2 tblsp. butter or regular margarine. Add 1 medium cucumber, peeled and sliced. Cook, stirring often, 2 to 3 minutes or until tender-crisp.

SERVING: Use raw cucumbers in appetizers, salads, soups, or for pickles and relishes. Cooked cucumbers can be used in side dishes.

DRIED BEANS, PEAS AND LENTILS

The Egyptians cooked with them, the Romans gambled with them and American cowboys made them a staple range food.

Dried beans, peas and lentils are inexpensive but rich in nutrients. They're available in many different varieties: black or turtle, black-eyed, Great Northern, lima, marrow, pinto and pink; red and white kidney beans; green and yellow split peas; and red and green lentils, to name just a few.

Basically, they're all cooked the same way, and many varieties can be substituted for another—pinto and pink beans for kidney beans, and split peas for lentils. Experiment to learn your own preference.

Dried beans, peas and lentils are high in protein and fiber, and are good sources of vitamins and minerals.

SEASONALITY: Available year 'round.

SELECTION: Choose beans that are clean and uniform in size. Avoid ones that are shriveled, cracked, blemished and ones with pinholes, which indicate insect damage.

STORAGE: Dried beans keep almost indefinitely in store-bought packages or in containers with tight-fitting lids.

Cooked beans may be refrigerated, covered, about 4 days, and frozen up to 6 months.

PREPARATION: Discard any shriveled beans and stones. Rinse beans well under cold running water.

Dried beans and whole peas require soaking before cooking; lentils and split peas do not.

To soak beans overnight: In bowl place 1 c. beans and cover with 3 c. water. Let soak, loosely covered, overnight or at least 12 hours at room temperature.

To quick-soak beans: In 2-qt. saucepan over high heat, bring 1 c. beans and 3 c. water to a boil. Boil 2 minutes; remove from heat. Let stand, covered, 1 hour.

YIELD: For 1 serving, allow about ½ to ¾ c. cooked beans; 1 lb. dried beans yields 2 c. raw or about 6 c. cooked.

COOKING: Boil, bake, microwave or pressure-cook.

After soaking, do not drain. In 2-qt. saucepan place 1 c. soaked beans and their liquid; add 1 tsp. salt. (For each cup of dried beans, add 1 tsp. salt). Over high heat bring to a boil; reduce heat to low. Cover and simmer the amount of time indicated (see chart).

Wine, vinegar, tomatoes, lemon juice, ketchup and other acidic ingredients slow the cooking of beans. These ingredients should be added during the last half-hour of cooking.

To prevent foaming when cooking Great Northern, pinto beans or whole peas, add 1 tblsp. vegetable oil for each cup of dried beans.

Cooking Time
for Dried Beans, Peas and Lentils

1 c. soaked	Cooking Time
Black beans	2 hr.
Black-eyed beans (peas)	25-30 min.
Chick peas (garbanzo beans)	2-2¼ hr.
Great Northern beans	1-1½ hr.
Kidney beans	1½ hr.
Lentils (no soaking needed)	25-30 min.
Lima beans	1 hr.
Navy beans	1½ hr.
Peas, split (no soaking needed)	45 min.
Peas, whole	1 hr.
Pink beans	2 hr.
Pinto beans	2 hr.
Red beans	2 hr.
Soybeans	1½ hr.

SERVING: Use cooked beans, peas and lentils in soups, stews, salads, main and side dishes.

EGGPLANT

An eggplant is really a big berry. Its glossy skin may be white, reddish or even striped as well as dark purple, and its pulp may be either white or yellow. A mature eggplant may be as large as 12″ or as small as 2″ long.

Since it's more than 90% water, eggplant is low in calories.

SEASONALITY: Available year 'round; the peak season is August through September.

SELECTION: Choose a glossy eggplant with a smooth, taut skin and bright green cap. It should be heavy in relation to its size. Avoid oversized, rough or spongy-skinned eggplant with brown blemishes.

STORAGE: Refrigerate, unwashed, in plastic bag 1 to 2 days. Eggplants are highly perishable. Be sure to use quickly; longer storage may result in soft spots and a bitter flavor.

PREPARATION: Rinse under cold running water. Trim stem end. If skin is tough, peel. Eggplant darkens quickly, so cut it just before using.

If an eggplant is fresh and not too large, it shouldn't have a bitter flavor. Taste a piece of the flesh; if it's bitter, salt will remove the bitter flavor. Cut eggplant in half or slice and sprinkle with about 1 tsp. salt. Drain, flesh-side down, on paper towels 20 to 30 minutes. Brush off salt and pat dry.

Use halved for stuffing, or sliced, cut into chunks or chopped.

YIELD: For 3 to 4 servings, allow 1 medium eggplant (1½ lb.).

COOKING: Boil, steam, braise, sauté, stir-fry, bake, deep-fry, microwave or grill.

To boil: In 2-qt. saucepan over high heat, bring 1″ water (and ¼ tsp. salt, if eggplant has not been pre-salted) to a boil. Add 1 medium eggplant, cut into 1″ cubes, and let water return to a boil. Reduce heat to low. Cover and simmer 3 to 5 minutes or until tender. Drain.

SERVING: Use cooked eggplant in appetizers, salads, main and side dishes.

GARLIC

It's been claimed that garlic has the medicinal powers to heal dog bites, remedy skin diseases and even cure the plague. It's also been said that a garland of garlic will ward off evil spirits and even vampires. One thing is certain: Garlic's unique odor and flavor can play an important role in seasoning just about any food.

Like chives, onions, leeks and shallots, garlic is a member of the lily family. Its compact bulb has a varied number of white or purplish-colored almond-shaped segments called cloves, each one wrapped in its own papery skin.

Often braided in garlands when harvested, garlic is stored a couple of weeks so that its skin dries. It is also processed into flakes, powders and salts.

SEASONALITY: Available year 'round.

SELECTION: Choose firm, dry bulbs with skins that are dry and unbroken. Avoid soft, dirty or sprouted bulbs with broken skins.

STORAGE: Place bulbs in small open basket or custard cup. Store in a cool, dark, well ventilated place 1 month. Do not refrigerate.

Cloves may be peeled and refrigerated in vegetable or olive oil up to 2 months.

PREPARATION: If using a garlic press, separate cloves, but do not peel. Place a clove flat against the holes in the press and crush.

To crush cloves with a knife, place an unpeeled clove on cutting board. Place flat side of a knife on top of clove and press with heel of hand. Then remove skin.

Use peeled cloves whole, sliced or minced.

YIELD: One bulb yields about 8 to 12 cloves.

COOKING: Rarely served by itself, garlic is used as an ingredient in many recipes—boiled, steamed, braised, sautéed, stir-fried, baked, microwaved or grilled.

When you sauté garlic, be sure not to overcook; it may become bitter.

SERVING: Use raw garlic in appetizers, salads, salad dressings and sauces. Cooked garlic can be used just as you use dry onions, in soups main and side dishes or for pickles and relishes.

GREEN ONIONS

Any young onion, pulled from the ground while its top is still green and its bulb not fully matured, is a green onion or scallion. These mild-flavored onions are edible from their crisp tops to their tender white bulbs.

Green onions are a good source of minerals and vitamins A and C.

SEASONALITY: Available year 'round; the peak season is May through July.

SELECTION: Choose clean bunches of green onions with firm, white bulbs and crisp, bright green tops. Avoid ones with browned roots and wilted tops.

STORAGE: Refrigerate, unwashed, in plastic bag 1 to 2 days. Green onions do not freeze well.

PREPARATION: Rinse well under cold running water. Peel off outer top leaves and trim root.

Use whole, sliced, chopped or minced. Do not chop green onions in a food processor; they will become bitter.

YIELD: For 2 servings, allow 1 bunch; 1 lb. yields about 2 c. chopped.

COOKING: Boil, steam, braise, sauté, stir-fry, bake or microwave.

To boil: In 12″ skillet over high heat, bring 1″ salted water to a boil. Add 1 lb. whole green onions, trimmed, and let water return to a boil. Reduce heat to low. Cover and simmer 5 to 7 minutes or until tender-crisp. Drain.

SERVING: Use raw green onions as an appetizer or in dips, salads, salad dressings and sauces. Cooked green onions can be used just as you use dry onions.

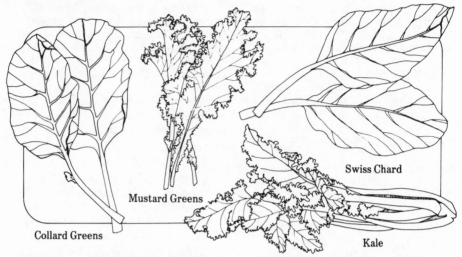

Swiss Chard

Mustard Greens

Collard Greens

Kale

Leafy green vegetables such as broccoli di rape, collards, dandelion greens, kale, mustard greens and Swiss chard are abundant, inexpensive and versatile.

Serve them just as they are or cook them quickly, and you'll be rewarded with a fresh taste and a distinctive flavor.

Young, tender greens can be sautéed; the more mature benefit from slow simmering in water or a broth.

For information about other greens, see Beets, Spinach and Turnips in this chapter.

Broccoli di rape is a medium-sharp, cabbage-flavored green that's also known simply as rape. Its dark, bluish-green edible stems range from 6 to 8″ long with small bud clusters. Use this green as you would cabbage and kale.

Collards are cabbage-like greens with smooth, dark green leaves that can be either broad and thick or curly. Often these greens are confused with kale. They're grown in the South and are usually cooked with bacon or salt pork.

Dandelion greens, though often regarded as weeds, are fresh-tasting and pungent. They're grown commercially, but in the spring you can pick them right from your lawn. Be

sure to get there early; the older the dandelion, the more bitter its flavor. Young, tender leaves can be eaten raw in salads. To cook them, treat them as you would spinach.

Kale, another member of the cabbage family, has large leaves with curly or crimped edges. There are two common varieties: Scotch kale has curly, bright green to greenish-yellow leaves; blue kale has deep green to bluish leaves that are plume-like with frilled edges.

Mustard greens vary in size and texture, but all have the same pleasantly pungent and bitter taste. There are three varieties: One has large, smooth, broad oval leaves with thick, white ribs; another has wider, bright yellow-green leaves that are curly at the tips; and the third has large, smooth leaves with narrow ribs.

Swiss chard, a member of the beet family, is grown for its leaves. Its crisp, broad leaves may be smooth or crinkled, and may vary in color from yellowish to dark green — or even red. The ribs may be white or red.

The delicate flavor of Swiss chard is similar to spinach, with a beet-like aftertaste. The leaves can be cooked alone, combined with other vegetables or substituted for other greens.

Most greens are high in fiber and iron, and are good sources of vitamins A and C.

SEASONALITY: Available year 'round; the peak season is December through April.

SELECTION: Choose fresh young greens with crisp leaves. Avoid oversized leaves.

STORAGE: Refrigerate, unwashed, in plastic bag or crisper 1 to 2 days. Greens freeze well; just blanch and freeze.

PREPARATION: Rinse greens under cold running water to remove dirt and sand. Trim bruised leaves and tough stems. Spin dry in salad spinner or pat dry with paper towels.
Use chopped or shredded.

YIELD: For 3 to 4 servings, allow 1 lb. greens.

COOKING: Boil, steam, braise, sauté, stir-fry or microwave.
To boil: In 4-qt. Dutch oven over high heat, bring ¼″ salted water to a boil. Add 1 lb. greens, chopped, and let water return to a boil. Reduce heat to low. Cover and simmer 5 to 10 minutes or until tender. Drain. (Like spinach, greens cook down to one-quarter of their fresh volume.)

SERVING: Use raw, tender greens in salads. Cooked greens can be used in soups, main and side dishes.

JERUSALEM ARTICHOKES

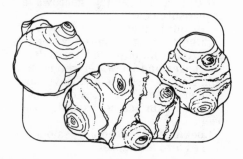

Knobby and gnarled, these little roots offer no clue to the flavor of their firm white flesh—delicate, nutlike and slightly sweet.

Jerusalem artichokes have nothing to do with Jerusalem, or even with globe artichokes. They're native to this country, and they're actually the tubers of a sunflower that produces brilliant yellow flowers. It's thought that the Italian word for sunflower, girasole, gave them their name. A better name might be sunflower artichokes; so American suppliers often call them sunchokes.

SEASONALITY: Available October through March.

SELECTION: Choose firm Jerusalem artichokes that are heavy in relation to their size and free from spots and blemishes. Avoid ones that are soft or shriveled.

STORAGE: Refrigerate, unwashed, in plastic bag 5 days. Jerusalem artichokes do not freeze well.

PREPARATION: Scrub with a soft vegetable brush under cold running water. Peel. (If boiling Jerusalem artichokes, peel after cooking; it's much easier.)
Jerusalem artichokes darken when peeled and cut. To prevent darkening: In medium bowl stir together 3 c. water and 1 tblsp. vinegar. Peel artichokes. Cut into slices and immediately place in vinegar mixture until ready to use. Drain.
Use whole, sliced or chopped.

YIELD: For 3 servings, allow 1 lb.; 1 lb. yields about 2½ c. sliced.

COOKING: Boil, steam, braise, sauté, stir-fry, bake, deep-fry, microwave or pressure-cook.

To boil: In 2-qt. saucepan over high heat, bring 1″ salted water to a boil. Add 1 lb. unpeeled Jerusalem artichokes and let water return to a boil. Reduce heat to low. Cover and simmer 10 to 15 minutes or until tender. Drain and cool slightly; then peel.

Cook peeled, sliced Jerusalem artichokes 5 to 8 minutes.

SERVING: Use raw Jerusalem artichokes in appetizers and salads. Cooked Jerusalem artichokes can be used in soups, main and side dishes or for pickles.

JICAMA

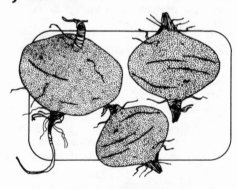

Above the ground, this plant is a high-climbing vine with showy flowers; its delicately flavored roots have the shape of a turnip, a skin with the texture of a sweet potato, and a crisp, snow-white interior.

Its flavor is slightly sweet, and because it tends to absorb more dominant flavors, jicama blends well with many other ingredients.

Most jicama is grown in Mexico; it's high in fiber.

SEASONALITY: Available year 'round; the peak season is September through April.

SELECTION: Choose the smallest jicama you can find, because the larger ones tend to be woody. Avoid jicama that are cut, soft or blemished.

STORAGE: Refrigerate, unwashed, in crisper 1 to 2 weeks. Wrap cut jicama tightly in plastic wrap, refrigerate, and use as soon as possible. Jicama does not freeze well.

PREPARATION: Peel deeply enough to remove fibrous, creamy inner skin.

Use sliced, cubed, chopped or shredded.

YIELD: For 4 servings, allow about 1 lb.

COOKING: Braise, sauté, stir-fry or microwave.

To sauté: In 10″ skillet over medium heat, melt ¼ c. butter or margarine. Add 1 lb. jicama, peeled and sliced. Cook, stirring often, 3 to 5 minutes or until tender-crisp.

SERVING: Use raw jicama in appetizers and salads. Use cooked jicama in main and side dishes.

KOHLRABI

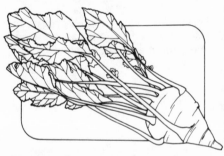

This odd-looking vegetable has turnip-like leaves and a bulbous stem. In German, its name means cabbage-turnip, and that's exactly how it tastes.

Though it looks like a root, the edible bulb grows above the ground. Eaten raw, its crisp texture and tangy flavor will remind you of radishes; cooked, it tastes more like turnips or mild cabbage. The leaves, when cooked, have the flavor of cabbage.

Kohlrabi is low in calories and high in vitamin C.

SEASONALITY: Available November through May.

SELECTION: Choose small or medium-size, thin-skinned bulbs 2 to 3″ in diameter. The tops should look fresh and not wilted. Avoid bulbs that are blemished or large.

STORAGE: Trim tops; refrigerate unwashed tops and leaves separately in plastic bags. Refrigerate tops 1 to 2 days; bulbs, 1 week.

Kohlrabi's tops and bulbs freeze well; just blanch and freeze.

PREPARATION: Rinse tops and bulbs under cold running water. Chop the tops. Peel bulbs.

Use bulbs sliced, cubed or chopped.

YIELD: For 1 serving, allow 1 medium kohlrabi.

COOKING: Both tops and bulbs can be boiled, blanched, steamed, braised, sautéed, stir-fried, baked or micro-waved.

To boil bulbs: In 2-qt. saucepan over high heat, bring 1″ salted water to a boil. Add 1 lb. bulbs, peeled and sliced, and let water return to a boil. Reduce heat to low. Cover and simmer 15 to 30 minutes or until tender-crisp. Drain.

To boil tops: In 2-qt. saucepan over high heat, bring 1″ salted water to a boil. Add 1 lb. tops, chopped, and let water return to a boil. Reduce heat to low. Cover and simmer 5 to 10 minutes or until tender. Drain.

SERVING: Use raw kohlrabi in appetizers and salads. Cooked kohlrabi can be used in soups, stews, main and side dishes or for pickles.

LEEKS

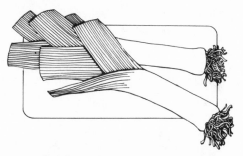

Known as the poor man's asparagus in France, leeks are the most subtle and sweet-tasting members of the onion family.

Leeks look like overgrown green onions with broad, flat leaves that shade to dark green at the tips. They range from 8 to 15″ long, with cylinder-shaped bases about an inch in diameter.

Soups, stews and quiches are all good ways to use leeks. If you object to the strong flavor that onion adds to your favorite recipes, experiment by substituting leeks.

SEASONALITY: Available year 'round; the peak season is October through June.

SELECTION: Choose small or medium-size leeks with tightly rolled bases and crisp green tops. Avoid ones that are soft, bruised or have yellowish tops.

STORAGE: Refrigerate, unwashed, in plastic bag 3 to 5 days. Leeks do not freeze well.

PREPARATION: Cut off roots and peel off tough outer leaves. Trim tops to the point where the dark green begins to turn pale. Rinse under cold running water.

As they grow, leeks tend to collect dirt and sand. To remove all the dirt from the inside, slit leeks lengthwise and halfway through, to within 1″ of root end. Gently spread leaves and base apart and rinse again.

Use whole, sliced or chopped.

YIELD: For 1 serving, allow 3 whole leeks. One lb. equals about 2 to 4 leeks, or ½ lb. trimmed, or 2 c. chopped.

COOKING: Boil, blanch, steam, braise, sauté, stir-fry, bake or microwave.

To boil: In 10″ skillet over high heat, bring 1″ salted water to a boil. Add 1 lb. whole leeks, trimmed, and let water return to a boil. Reduce heat to low. Cover and simmer 8 to 10 minutes or until tender. Drain. (Do not overcook or they will become mushy.)

SERVING: Use raw leeks in salads. Cooked leeks can be used just as you do onions, in soups, main and side dishes.

LETTUCE

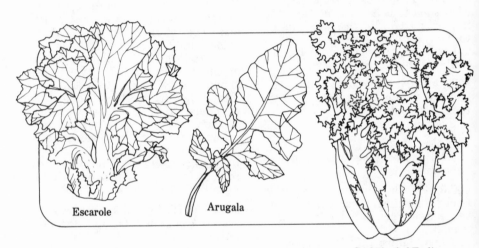

Escarole

Arugala

Curly-leafed Endive

As varied as the salads it's so often used to make, lettuce is a plant that's available in many forms.

Arugala, also known as *rucola, rocket and roquette,* resembles radish and turnip greens. Its young leaves have a pungent, biting flavor similar to horseradish. Use only a little to accent other salad greens.

Bibb and Boston lettuce are two of the more common types of butterhead lettuce. Their delicate leaves have a buttery flavor.

Curly-leafed endive, often called *chicory,* has a loose head with crisp, narrow white ribs and ragged-edged leaves. The center leaves form a yellow heart. Slightly bitter in flavor, it can be served raw or cooked.

Escarole, a variety of endive, is sometimes confused with curly-leafed endive. It grows in a flat head with broad, white-ribbed stems that have slightly curly green leaves.

Iceberg, or crisphead lettuce, has firm heads about 6″ in diameter with crisp, pale green leaves.

Loose-leaf, bunching or leaf lettuce has stems with tender leaves that may be curly or smooth-edged. The leaves don't form a head, and their color varies from light green to dark green with red tips.

Romaine or cos lettuce grows into long loaf-shaped heads with stiff, broad leaves that shade from yellow at the center to dark green at the tips. They taste rather sweet.

Watercress, although not a lettuce, is usually treated like one. A succulent, leafy, dark green plant of the mustard family, it grows wild alongside streams. Often used as a garnish, this peppery plant also can be used in salads and as a flavoring.

SEASONALITY: Available year 'round.

SELECTION: Choose well shaped heads with clean, crisp leaves. All the greens should look fresh and be free of excess dirt. Avoid dry or wilted leaves with large, coarse stems.

STORAGE: Refrigerate, unwashed, in plastic bag or crisper. Use crisphead lettuce in 3 to 5 days; use leafier kinds within 1 or 2 days. Lettuce does not freeze well.

PREPARATION: Remove cores and tough stems; trim bruised leaves. Rinse very well under cold running water to remove dirt and sand. Spin dry in salad spinner or pat dry with paper towels.

Tear, chop or shred leaves.

YIELD: For 3 to 4 servings, allow 1 head or bunch.

COOKING: Boil, steam, braise, sauté, stir-fry or microwave.

Generally lettuce is used raw in salads, but it can be cooked. To boil: in 12″ skillet over high heat, bring ¼″ salted water to a boil. Add 1 lb. tender lettuce (iceberg, loose-leaf or watercress), torn, and let water return to a boil. Reduce heat to low. Cover and simmer 1 to 3 minutes or until tender-crisp. Drain.

Cook 1 lb. hardier lettuce (curly-leafed endive, escarole or romaine), torn, 5 to 10 minutes.

SERVING: Use raw lettuce for garnishes or in salads and sandwiches. Cooked lettuce can be used in soups, main and side dishes.

MUSHROOMS

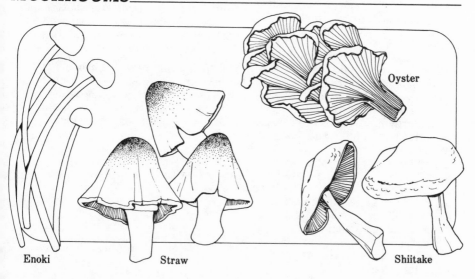

Enoki   Straw   Oyster   Shiitake

Proof that the simplest foods are often the best, mushrooms are one of the most botanically primitive plants, having neither leaves nor seeds.

Of course, they're fungi, not veg-

etables, but they can stand alone as a side dish or be used to enhance a wide range of other foods.

Thousands of mushroom species grow in the wild, but morels and many other edible species have poisonous look-alikes. When you pick mushrooms, you're literally taking your life in your hands, so get the help of an experienced mushroom hunter or an extensive field handbook.

Common, commercially grown mushrooms sold in supermarkets range in size from tiny ones called button mushrooms to ones that can weigh up to ⅓ lb. each. They have a delicate flavor and can be snow white, tan or brown in color.

Several luxury varieties of mushrooms are imported to the American market from the Orient: enoki, shiitake, tree oyster and straw. These intriguing varieties have fanciful shapes and stronger flavors.

Enoki mushrooms look a little like straight bean sprouts; they have long, slender stems, tiny heads and an ivory color. They have a crisp texture with a mild, slightly tangy taste, and are best eaten raw. Use them as you would sprouts in salads and sandwiches.

Shiitake or oak mushrooms, once available to Americans only in dried form, are dark brown to almost black in color. They have a rich, meaty flavor and can be used raw or cooked. Shiitake's stems and caps are both edible, and their intense flavor goes a long way.

Oyster mushrooms, or tree oysters, grow in clusters and have a ruffled crown. Pearl to grey in color, they are very tender and taste like oysters when cooked.

Straw mushrooms look like storybook toadstools. Their pointed crowns are dark brown at the tips and shade to taupe at the base. These mushrooms have a delicate texture and a distinct flavor.

Mushrooms are low in calories and a good source of potassium and other minerals.

SEASONALITY: Available year 'round; the peak season is October through June.

SELECTION: Common mushrooms should be firm, with white to brown-colored caps that are dry and closed around the stems. Avoid brown, shriveled or wilted mushrooms with wide-open caps.

STORAGE: Refrigerate, unwashed, in perforated plastic bag or crisper 1 to 2 days. Be sure to keep mushrooms dry. Mushrooms can be frozen; just blanch or sauté and freeze.

PREPARATION: Rinse under cold running water (do not soak), pat dry with paper towels and trim stem ends.

Stuff caps, or use caps and stems halved, sliced or chopped.

YIELD: For 4 servings, allow 1 lb.; 1 lb. yields about 6 c. sliced, or 4 c. chopped.

COOKING: Steam, sauté, stir-fry, bake, broil, deep-fry, microwave or grill.

To sauté: In 10″ skillet over medium heat, melt ¼ c. butter or regular margarine; add 1 lb. mushrooms, sliced. Cook, stirring occasionally, 10 minutes or until tender.

SERVING: Use raw mushrooms in appetizers, salads and sandwiches. Cooked mushrooms can be used in soups, sauces, baked goods, main and side dishes or for pickles.

OKRA

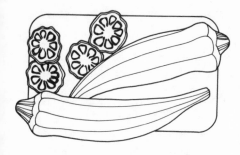

A favorite vegetable throughout the South, okra has a subtle flavor that goes well with corn, tomatoes, shellfish and smoked meats.

Okra is a main ingredient in gumbos and stews because of its natural ability to thicken liquids. Inside its tapering, fuzzy green pod is a soft tissue with a sticky quality. This stickiness is what makes okra a thickener; it's also why many people turn up their noses at the mere mention of okra. The trick to cooking okra is simply not to overcook it; prolonged cooking makes it gooey.

When cooked in utensils made of copper, brass, iron or tin, okra may discolor.

Okra is high in fiber.

SEASONALITY: Available year 'round; the peak season is June through September.

SELECTION: Choose bright green pods with a moderately firm texture; they should be 2½ to 3″ long, tender and easy to snap open. Avoid pods that are stiff, dry, flabby or blemished.

STORAGE: Refrigerate, unwashed, in perforated plastic bag or crisper 1 to 2 days.

Young, tender okra freezes well; just blanch and freeze.

PREPARATION: Scrub with stiff brush under cold running water to remove fuzz. Use small pods whole; trim stem and root ends of larger pods.

Use whole or sliced; okra larger than 3½″ should be sliced.

YIELD: For 3 to 4 servings, allow about 1 lb.; 1 lb. yields about 3 c. sliced.

COOKING: Boil, blanch, steam, braise, sauté, stir-fry, deep-fry or microwave.

To boil: In 2-qt. saucepan over high heat, bring ½″ salted water to a boil. Add 1 lb. small whole okra and let water return to a boil. Reduce heat to low. Cover and simmer 5 to 10 minutes or until tender-crisp. Drain.

Cook 1 lb. okra, sliced, 3 to 5 minutes.

SERVING: Cooked okra can be used in soups, stews, main and side dishes or for pickles.

ONIONS

An indispensable pantry staple, the onion is truly the most all-season vegetable of all. Folklore about the curative powers of this versatile vegetable is plentiful, including claims that you can soothe the pain of a toothache with a raw onion or stifle a cough with a sweetened brew of simmered onions.

All onions are members of the lily family, and the many varieities offer a wide range of shapes, sizes, colors and pungency. Once their bulbs have matured, they're called dry onions. For information about other onions, see Green Onions, Leeks and Shallots.

Bermuda and Spanish onions are the mildest. Their skins are light yellow, and they may measure 3½″ in diameter. They're at their best in the spring, and their sweet, delicate flavor can be enjoyed raw or cooked.

Red Italian, Creole or red-purple onions have a stronger flavor than Bermuda and Spanish onions, but they're still mild enough to be eaten raw. Their purplish color makes them a good addition to salads; chopped, they're a pretty garnish.

Small white onions and pearl onions have flaky white skins and are oval, with pointed ends. Pearl onions, the smallest of all onions, are used whole in soups and stews or simmered with other vegetables. The larger white onions, also called boiling onions, are used whole, too.

Yellow onions are the ones most often seen in supermarket bins. This all-purpose variety has a strong flavor and ranges in diameter from 1 to 3".

Onions are high in fiber and vitamin C.

SEASONALITY: Available year 'round.

SELECTION: Choose hard, well shaped onions with dry, blemish-free skins. Avoid soft onions with wet, soft necks or sprouted tops.

STORAGE: Store in a cool, dark, well ventilated place up to 3 months, or refrigerate in perforated plastic bag or crisper 1 month. Onions freeze well; just chop, blanch and freeze.

PREPARATION: Cut off stem and root ends; peel off dry outer skin.

Use whole, sliced, diced, chopped or minced.

YIELD: For 4 servings, allow 1 lb.; 1 lb. yellow onions (about 4 medium) yields 4 c. sliced or 2 c. chopped. One medium onion yields ½ c. chopped.

One lb. small white onions equals about 14 onions.

COOKING: Boil, steam, braise, sauté, stir-fry, bake, deep-fry, microwave, grill or pressure-cook.

To boil: In 3-qt. saucepan over high heat, bring 1" salted water to a boil. Add 1 lb. whole yellow or white onions and let water return to a boil. Reduce heat to low. Cover and simmer 15 to 20 minutes or until tender. Drain.

SERVING: Use raw onions in appetizers, salads and dressings. Cooked onions can be used in just about any dish, including baked goods, or for pickles and relishes.

PARSNIPS

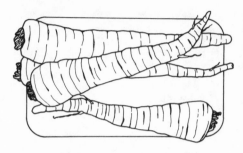

Often called a winter vegetable, this smooth, firm, carrot-like root must be exposed to cold temperatures for its flavor to sweeten. Some home gardeners leave their parsnips in the ground all winter; then, in the spring when the ground is soft, they harvest them and enjoy their sweet, nutty flavor.

Size is not an indication of quality. Some parsnips can be as long as 20" yet are tender and sweet.

Parsnips are high in fiber and a good source of vitamins and minerals.

SEASONALITY: Available year 'round; the peak season is January through April.

SELECTION: Choose well shaped, smooth-skinned parsnips, small to medium in size. Avoid blemished, discolored, soft and shriveled parsnips which look and feel woody.

STORAGE: Refrigerate, unwashed, in perforated plastic bag or crisper 1 to 2 weeks. Parsnips freeze well; just blanch and freeze.

PREPARATION: Rinse under cold running water. Cut off stem and root ends; peel as you would carrots.

Use whole, sliced, diced or chopped.

YIELD: For 2 to 3 servings, allow about 1 lb.; 1 lb. yields about 3 c. sliced.

COOKING: Boil, steam, braise, sauté, stir-fry, deep-fry, microwave or pressure-cook.

To boil: In 12" skillet over high

heat, bring 1" salted water to a boil. Add 1 lb. whole parsnips, peeled, and let water return to a boil. Reduce heat to low. Cover and simmer 20 to 30 minutes or until fork-tender. Drain.

Cook 1 lb. parsnips, peeled and sliced, 8 to 15 minutes.

SERVING: Cooked parsnips can be used in soups, stews, baked goods, main and side dishes.

PEAS

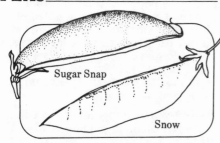

Sugar Snap

Snow

Truly a spring vegetable, English peas, like sweet corn, should be cooked right after they're picked. In a matter of hours, their sugar turns to starch and they lose flavor. It's well worth the time-consuming effort of shelling them to experience their delicate, sweet flavor—you'll wonder why you ever considered canned or frozen peas a substitute for fresh.

Sugar snap peas look just like traditional English peas. There's no need to shell them—the peas and the pods are both edible. These crisp, sweet-as-candy peas can be eaten out of hand or served raw with a dip. They're best if quickly sautéed or stir-fried for only about 2 minutes; the least overcooking destroys their crisp texture.

Snow peas, which are essential to Chinese cuisine, have firm, crisp, flat, bright green pods that taper at both ends. Like sugar snap peas, they have edible pods and should be cooked quickly.

Peas are a good source of vitamin A and minerals.

SEASONALITY: English and sugar snap peas are available March through June. Snow peas are available year 'round.

SELECTION: Rub a handful of pods in your hands; if they squeak, they're fresh!

For English and sugar snap peas, choose light green, well-filled, crisp pods. Avoid dark green, rubbery pods that are swollen with over-mature peas.

For snow peas, choose crisp, bright green, flat pods. Avoid light-colored, spotted pods, or pods with developed seeds.

STORAGE: Refrigerate all peas, unwashed, in perforated plastic bag 1 to 2 days. Use quickly for best flavor. All peas freeze well; just blanch and freeze.

PREPARATION: For English peas, press pods between thumb and forefinger to open. Run thumb through pod to remove peas. Discard pods. Rinse peas under cold running water.

For sugar snap and snow peas, cut off stem end, pulling string along outside edge of pod to remove. Rinse pods under cold running water; pat dry with paper towels. Use the whole pod.

YIELD: For 1 serving of English peas, allow about ¾ lb.; 1 lb. yields about 1 c. shelled peas.

For 3 to 4 servings of sugar snap or snow peas, allow 1 lb.

COOKING: All peas can be boiled, blanched, steamed, braised, sautéed, stir-fried or microwaved.

To boil English peas: In 2-qt. saucepan over high heat, bring 1" salted water to a boil. Add 1 lb. shelled peas and let water return to a boil. Reduce heat to low. Cover and simmer 5 minutes or until tender-crisp. Drain. (Do not overcook.)

To sauté snow or sugar snap peas: In 10" skillet over medium-high heat, melt ¼ c. butter or regular margarine. Add 1 lb. peas. Cook, stirring often, 2 to 3 minutes or until tender-crisp.

SERVING: Use raw snow and sugar snap peas in appetizers and salads. Any cooked peas can be used in soups, main and side dishes.

PEPPERS

Anyone who judges the spiciness of a pepper by its color is bound to be misled. Peppers and chilies vary in size and shape, and whether they're red, green or yellow offers no clue to their sweetness.

The hotness of a pepper is determined by a bitter substance called capsaicin that's located in the skins, seeds and in the interior ribbons of flesh. When the skins and seeds are removed, peppers are less spicy.

Bell, green or sweet peppers can be long and tapered or short, wide and heart-shaped. They're usually green, but they may be red or yellow.

Chilies are members of the pepper family. They're sold under many names, and they range in flavor from sweet to fiery hot. They're generally long and slender, tapering to a point, but they can be green, yellow, red or even blue-black.

Green serrano, jalapeno and pasilla chilies are hot.

Yellow-green California and poblano chilies are sweet.

Peppers and chilies are a good source of vitamins A and C.

SEASONALITY: Peppers and chilies are available year 'round; the peak season is May through September.

SELECTION: Choose peppers and chilies that are thick-fleshed, firm, glossy and heavy in relation to their size. Avoid cracked, shriveled, flabby peppers that have soft, watery skins.

STORAGE: Refrigerate, unwashed, in perforated plastic bag or crisper 1 week. Peppers and chilies freeze well; just chop and freeze.

PREPARATION: Cut around stem; remove core, seeds and white membrane.

Stuff whole peppers or chilies; or use halved, sliced, chopped or minced.

The juice, seeds and membranes of peppers and chilies are the hottest parts. Immediately after handling chilies, wash your hands. Be careful not to touch your eyes while handling peppers or chilies, because the residue will irritate them.

Some peppers and chilies have tough skins and should be peeled before using. To peel, cut out and discard stems. On foil-lined broiler pan place peppers; broil, 5″ from source of heat, 15 to 18 minutes or until skins turn dark brown, turning often with tongs. (Do not let peppers burn.) Remove from oven; place in paper bag. Close bag and let stand 5 minutes to let steam loosen skins. Then peel.

YIELD: For 1 serving, allow 1 medium pepper; 1 medium pepper yields about ⅔ c. chopped.

One chili yields about 2 tblsp. finely chopped.

COOKING: Boil, blanch, steam, braise, sauté, stir-fry, bake, broil, deep-fry, microwave or grill.

To boil: In 2-qt. saucepan over high heat, bring 1″ salted water to a boil. Add 1 whole, seeded pepper or chili and let water return to a boil. Cover and cook 3 to 5 minutes or until tender-crisp. Drain.

SERVING: Use raw peppers and chilies in appetizers and salads. Cooked peppers and chilies can be used in soups, sauces, relishes, main and side dishes or for pickles.

POTATOES

Highly versatile and low in cost, potatoes are the world's single most important vegetable.

They can be divided into five basic varieties, each of which has its own size, shape and starch content.

For more potato information, see Sweet Potatoes.

Long white potatoes are easy to peel because their thin, fawn-colored skins are virtually free of eyes. They're long and eliptical in shape, low in starch and are sometimes called California long whites.

New potatoes, just as their name suggests, are freshly harvested potatoes that haven't been stored. Light brown or red, they are likely to be smaller than other potatoes, and more thin-skinned.

Round red potatoes can be round to oblong in shape with smooth, dark red skins. They have a medium starch content.

Round white or Katahdin potatoes are round, with buff-colored, smooth skins. They have a medium starch content.

Russet potatoes, also known as *Idaho or baking potatoes,* are oblong, with thick skins. Because of their low starch content, they're especially well suited for baking or deep-frying.

Many cooks prefer the low-starch varieties for baking, salads or casseroles, because they tend to hold their shape when cooked. Potatoes higher in starch tend to be more mealy when cooked, and are often used for mashed potatoes. The longer the potato is stored, the higher its starch content.

Potatoes are moderately low in calories and high in vitamin C and iron.

SEASONALITY: Long white, round white, round red and russet potatoes are available year 'round. New potatoes are available March through August.

SELECTION: Choose potatoes that are firm, well shaped and free from blemishes or sprouts. Avoid soft, green, shriveled or blemished potatoes.

STORAGE: Store, unwashed, in a cool, dark, well ventilated place up to 2 months; new potatoes will keep up to 2 weeks. Potatoes stored at room temperature will keep about 1 week.

Do not refrigerate. Refrigeration causes the potatoes' starch to turn to sugar, and the potatoes will darken when cooked.

Long exposure to light causes potatoes to turn green and develop a bitter flavor. If greening occurs, cut off the affected area before using the potato.

Potatoes can be frozen, but their texture will change.

PREPARATION: Scrub with stiff brush under cold running water. To save nutrients, don't peel. If necessary, thinly peel skins.

To prevent peeled potatoes from darkening, place them in cold water if they will not be used immediately. If using shredded or grated potatoes, shred or grate just before using to prevent them from darkening.

Use unpeeled, whole, sliced, diced, chopped, shredded or grated.

YIELD: For 1 serving, allow 1 medium or 2 new potatoes; 1 lb. potatoes (about 3 medium) yields about 4 c. sliced or 1¾ c. mashed.

COOKING: Boil, steam, sauté, bake, deep-fry, microwave, grill or pressure-cook.

To boil: In 3-qt. saucepan over high heat, bring 1″ salted water to a boil. Add 1 lb. whole potatoes, peeled, and let water return to a boil. Reduce heat to low. Cover and simmer 25 to 30 minutes or until fork-tender. Drain.

Cook 1 lb. potatoes, peeled and sliced, or cut into 1″ pieces, 10 to 15 minutes.

Cook 1 lb. whole, unpeeled new potatoes 15 to 20 minutes.

To bake: Pierce skin several times with fork. (This allows steam to escape, preventing the potato from bursting during baking.) A medium potato will bake in about 45 minutes at 400°. Potatoes can be baked at temperatures as low as 325°, so you can bake them along with a roast or casserole.

SERVING: Cooked potatoes can be used in soups, stews, salads, baked goods, main and side dishes.

PUMPKIN

Many of us can remember hiking through a pumpkin patch as a child to pick out the perfect pumpkin for a jack-o'-lantern, but this vegetable has lots to offer adults, too.

Cousins of cucumbers and winter squash, pumpkins can range in size from less than a pound to more than 100 pounds. The smaller varieties, called sugar pumpkins, are generally best for cooking.

Pumpkin can be used in soups, stews and many baked goods in addition to pies, and may be substituted for winter squash.

High in fiber and vitamin A, pumpkins are a good source of minerals.

SEASONALITY: Available September through November.

SELECTION: Choose firm, deep orange pumpkins heavy in relation to their size, with stems intact. Avoid soft-skinned, cracked pumpkins and those that have no stems.

STORAGE: Store in a cool, dark, well ventilated place 1 month. Refrigerate cut-up pumpkin in perforated plastic bag 1 week. Pumpkin freezes well; just cook, mash and freeze.

PREPARATION: Rinse under cold running water.

For whole pumpkin: Cut out stem and part of top to make a lid. Scoop out seeds and stringy pulp. Don't throw away the seeds; they're edible (roasting directions follow).

For pumpkin pieces: Cut out stem end. Cut pumpkin in half from stem to blossom end. Scoop out seeds and

stringy flesh. Cut pumpkin into large 3 to 4″ cubes. Peel after boiling.

Stuff whole pumpkin, slice or cube.

YIELD: For 4 servings, allow 4 lb.; 4 lb. yields about 2 lb. cleaned flesh or about 2 c. pumpkin, cooked and mashed.

COOKING: Boil, steam, braise, bake, microwave or pressure-cook.

To boil pumpkin: In 4-qt. Dutch oven over high heat, bring 1″ salted water to a boil. Add 2 lb. pumpkin chunks and let water return to a boil. Reduce heat to low. Cover and simmer 25 to 30 minutes or until fork-tender. Drain and cool slightly; then peel.

To roast seeds: Separate seeds from pumpkin pulp (do not wash). Measure the amount of seeds. Then spread seeds in one layer on jelly-roll pan. For every 2 c. of seeds, sprinkle with 2 tblsp. vegetable oil and 1 tsp. salt. Bake in 250° oven about 1½ hours or until dry and crisp, but not brown. Cool completely. Store in tightly covered container. Crack shells to remove the seeds, and enjoy.

SERVING: Cooked pumpkin can be used in soups, baked goods, main and side dishes.

RADISHES

A beautiful garnish and a good brightener for any green salad, radishes have a crisp texture and fresh flavor that lets them stand alone as appetizers.

Their flavor can vary from mild to peppery, and you may see radishes that are white, pink, purple or even black as well as ruby red.

They're most often eaten just as they are, but they can be briefly steamed, too, and their flavor will be much like that of turnips. Some cooks also sauté their leafy green tops.

Daikon, the Oriental radish, is thick and about 6″ long, with a white skin.

Spanish radishes have black skins and a pungent flavor.

All radishes are excellent sources of potassium and other minerals.

SEASONALITY: Available year 'round; the peak season is March through May.

SELECTION: Choose medium-size, smooth, well formed radishes free from cuts or splits. Avoid spongy, soft, very large radishes with black spots or yellow tops.

STORAGE: Trim tops. Refrigerate, unwashed, in plastic bag 1 week. Radishes do not freeze well.

PREPARATION: Rinse under cold running water. Cut off stem and root ends.
Use whole, chopped or sliced.

YIELD: For 1 serving, allow about 4 medium radishes; 4 medium yield about ¼ c. chopped.

COOKING: Boil, steam, sauté, stir-fry or microwave.
To boil: In 2-qt. saucepan over high heat, bring 1″ salted water to a boil. Add 1 lb. whole radishes and let water return to a boil. Reduce heat to low. Cover and simmer 8 to 12 minutes or until tender-crisp. Drain.

SERVING: Use raw radishes in garnishes, appetizers and salads. Cooked radishes can be used in soups, main and side dishes.

RUTABAGAS

Though they're sometimes called Swedish turnips and often are sold as yellow turnips, rutabagas are not turnips; they're members of the cabbage family, while turnips are members of the mustard family.

Rutabagas are larger than turnips, and their big yellow bulbs have a sweeter, stronger flavor.

Their large, blue-green tops are usually trimmed before rutabagas are shipped to market, and their bulbs are waxed to prevent loss of moisture.

Rutabagas are a good source of vitamins A and C.

SEASONALITY: Available year 'round; the peak season is September through March.

SELECTION: Choose smooth-skinned, medium-size rutabagas, 3 to 4″ in diameter. They should be heavy in relation to their size. Avoid ones with cracked or bruised skins.

STORAGE: Store in a cool, dark, well ventilated place 1 to 2 weeks, or refrigerate, unwashed, in perforated plastic bag 2 to 3 weeks. Rutabagas can be frozen; just blanch and freeze.

PREPARATION: Cut off stem end. Peel off skin.
Use sliced, cut into chunks or diced.

YIELD: For 4 servings, allow about 1 lb.; 1 lb. yields about 4 c. chopped or 2 c. mashed.

COOKING: Boil, steam, braise, sauté, stir-fry, bake, deep-fry, microwave or pressure-cook.
To boil: In 2-qt. saucepan over high heat, bring 1″ salted water to a

boil. Add 1 lb. rutabagas, peeled and sliced, and let water return to a boil. Reduce heat to low. Cover and simmer 10 to 20 minutes or until fork-tender. Drain. (Do not overcook or they will become mushy.)

SERVING: Cooked rutabagas can be used in soups, stews, salads, main and side dishes.

SALSIFY

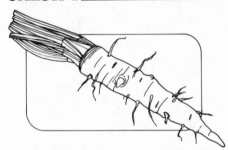

The mild oyster flavor of this root vegetable is something to look forward to in the fall.

Salsify, or oyster plant, is only available in October and November, and it makes wonderful soups and side dishes.

Generally imported to our markets from Belgium, it's also a popular vegetable grown in many home gardens.

It looks similar to parsnips, but the skin is darker.

Black salsify, or scorzonera, its cousin, has a brownish-black skin and a faint coconut flavor.

Salsify is high in fiber.

SEASONALITY: Available October through November.

SELECTION: Choose medium-size, well shaped, firm roots. Avoid soft or oversized roots that tend to be woody.

STORAGE: Refrigerate, unwashed, in perforated plastic bag 3 to 4 days. Salsify does not freeze well.

PREPARATION: Trim both ends; peel as you would carrots.

Salsify darkens when peeled and cut. To prevent darkening: In medium bowl stir together 3 c. water and 1 tblsp. vinegar. Peel salsify and immediately place in vinegar mixture until ready to use. Drain.

Use sliced, diced, cut into chunks or matchstick strips.

YIELD: For 3 servings, allow about 1 lb.; about 1 lb. salsify yields about 3 c. sliced.

COOKING: Boil, steam, braise, stir-fry or deep-fry.

To boil: In 2-qt. saucepan over high heat, bring 1″ salted water to a boil. Add 1 lb. salsify, peeled and sliced, and let water return to a boil. Reduce heat to low. Cover and simmer 15 to 20 minutes or until fork-tender. Drain.

SERVING: Cooked salsify can be used in soups, main and side dishes.

SHALLOTS

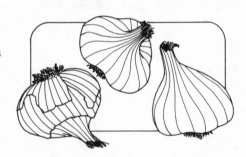

When you want just a hint of onion and garlic flavor, especially in sauces, use shallots. They not only have a mild flavor, but they're also tender, so they cook quickly.

Like garlic, shallots grow in bulbs. Beneath their papery brown skins are clusters of several purplish-skinned cloves. You may find them in the market separated into individual cloves.

In a pinch, you can use a mixture of a sweet, mild onion and garlic for shallots.

Shallots are a good source of minerals.

SEASONALITY: Available year 'round.

SELECTION: Choose dry, firm, rounded bulbs. Avoid shriveled bulbs and ones with sprouted tops.

STORAGE: Store in a cool, dark, well ventilated place 1 to 2 months.

PREPARATION: Trim top and root ends. Peel off dry outer skin.

Use peeled cloves whole, slivered, chopped or minced.

YIELD: One small clove yields about 1 tsp. chopped.

COOKING: Most often used as an ingredient, shallots may be boiled, steamed, sautéed, stir-fried or microwaved.

SERVING: Use raw shallots in appetizers, salads, sauces and dressings. Cooked shallots can be used just as you do onions, in soups, stews, sauces, main and side dishes.

SPINACH

The simplest and more nutritious way to serve spinach is raw. Its tender, crinkled leaves make excellent salad greens.

Spinach is very perishable and has a high water content, so the secret of cooking it is to cook it quickly in very little water.

Cooked spinach has a slightly acid aftertaste; many cooks enjoy this flavor, but if you're not one of them, try adding two pats of butter or a splash of milk or cream.

Spinach is high in iron and a good source of vitamins A and C.

SEASONALITY: Available year 'round; the peak season is January through May.

SELECTION: Choose fresh-looking, light to dark green bunches free of blemishes. Avoid wilted or yellow-colored bunches.

STORAGE: Refrigerate, unwashed, in perforated plastic bag 1 to 2 days. Spinach freezes well; just blanch and freeze.

PREPARATION: As they grow, these leaves trap sand and grit, so they must be thoroughly washed under cold running water.

Stem larger leaves by folding the leaf over lengthwise along the stem; then, holding leaf in the center, rip off stem. Small tender leaves needn't be stemmed.

Spin dry in salad spinner or pat dry with paper towels.

Use whole, torn or chopped.

YIELD: For 2 servings, allow 1 lb.; 1 lb. yields about 12 c. torn fresh leaves, enough for 3 to 4 main-dish salads, or 1 c. cooked.

COOKING: Boil, steam, braise, sauté, stir-fry, deep-fry or microwave.

To boil: In 4-qt. Dutch oven over high heat, bring 1/4" salted water to a boil. Add 1 lb. spinach, chopped, and let water return to a boil. Reduce heat to low. Cover and simmer 1 to 3 minutes or until wilted. Drain immediately. (Do not overcook, or it will become stringy and strong-flavored.)

Some cooks simply cook spinach with the water that clings to it. Use medium heat and steam it for 3 to 5 minutes or until wilted.

SERVING: Use raw spinach for garnishes or in appetizers and salads. Cooked spinach can be used in soups, baked goods, main and side dishes.

SPROUTS

Mung bean and alfalfa sprouts are the ones most often sold in supermarkets, but you can sprout most grains or legumes right in your own kitchen. Their crisp, crunchy texture makes them a great addition to salads and sandwiches, and you can use them fresh or cooked in a great many Oriental dishes.

The best beans to sprout are dried mung beans, dried lentils, dried whole peas, wheat berries and alfalfa seeds. The relative size of the legume or seed will give you a general idea of how large the sprouts will be: Lentil and mung bean sprouts will be smaller than garbanzo or lima bean sprouts.

Sprouts are a good source of vitamin C, protein, fiber and minerals.

SEASONALITY: Available year 'round.

SELECTION: Choose sprouts that are crisp and fresh-looking. Avoid ones that are dark with dry tips.

STORAGE: Refrigerate, unwashed, in perforated plastic bag 4 to 5 days. Sprouts do not freeze well.

PREPARATION: Rinse under cold running water; pat dry on paper towels.

To grow sprouts: Place ¼ c. dried lentils or mung beans or 2 tblsp. alfalfa seeds in 1-qt. glass jar. Cover with warm water. Secure a piece of cheesecloth over mouth of jar with rubber band. Soak overnight.

With cheesecloth in place, drain and rinse beans or seeds with warm water. Drain again.

Set jar at a 45° angle in a warm, dark place until sprouts emerge (2 to 3 days for lentils and mung beans, 4 to 5 days for seeds), rinsing sprouts twice a day and allowing them to drain at a 45° angle.

Place in indirect light and let sprouts develop until they're 1 to 2″ long, about 2 to 4 days. There will be about 3 c. sprouts. Use or store as directed.

YIELD: For 4 to 6 servings, allow about 1 lb.; 1 lb. yields about 5 c.

COOKING: Lentil or mung bean sprouts can be steamed, sautéed or stir-fried. Tender alfalfa sprouts are best not cooked.

To sauté: In 12″ skillet over medium heat, melt ¼ c. butter or regular margarine. Add 1 lb. lentil or mung bean sprouts. Cook, stirring frequently, 2 to 3 minutes or until barely wilted and tender-crisp.

SERVING: Use raw sprouts in appetizers, salads and sandwiches. Cooked sprouts can be used in main and side dishes.

SQUASH

There are as many different varieties of squash as there are shapes, but they're all edible gourds that grow on vines. Their blossoms are edible: just dip them in batter and deep-fry until golden.

We divided squash into two categories, summer and winter. Summer squash are fast-growing, thin-skinned and perishable. Winter squash have thick shell-like skins and they store well.

Squash are low in sodium and a good source of vitamin A and minerals.

SUMMER SQUASH

Quick-growing and usually small, summer squash have shiny, thin, tender skins and small seeds, both of which are edible.

Summer squash cook fast, so briefly cook them until tender-crisp. You'll find that crookneck, straightneck and zucchini can be interchanged for each other in many recipes.

Crookneck types range from 4 to 6″ long with long curved necks. They have bumpy, bright yellow skins and creamy yellow flesh.

Straightneck types have slightly bumpy, lemon-yellow skins. They're similar to crookneck squash, but their shapes are more club-like.

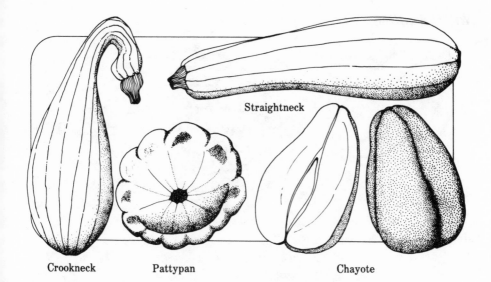

Straightneck

Crookneck   Pattypan   Chayote

Pattypan or scallop types are rather flat and disc-shaped, with prominent scalloped or fluted edges. They grow to about 4″ in diameter and their skins can be white, yellow or striped.

Zucchini has shiny, green and white striped or dark green skin with creamy yellow flesh. It ranges in size, best when 5 to 8″ long. Longer zucchini may have larger seeds which tend to be tough and may have to be removed before using.

Chayote, a tropical squash, is pear-shaped and about the same size as a small acorn squash. Its soft, pale green skin is smooth and ribbed. Its flesh looks and tastes like bland honeydew melon. Young, tender chayote need not be peeled; older ones are best peeled. Chayote has only one seed, and it's edible when cooked.

SEASONALITY: Available year 'round; the peak season is May through September.

SELECTION: Choose fresh, firm summer squash with tender skins. Size is an indication of quality: crooknecks, straightnecks and zucchini should be about 6″ long; pattypan should be less than 4″ in diameter. Avoid shriveled, soft ones or those with a dull, hard rind.

STORAGE: Refrigerate, unwashed, in perforated plastic bag 3 to 4 days. Summer squash freeze well; just blanch and freeze.

PREPARATION: Scrub gently with stiff brush under cold running water. Cut off stem and blossom ends.

Summer squash can be halved and stuffed, or sliced, chopped or shredded.

YIELD: For 2 to 3 servings, allow 1 lb.; 1 lb. yields about 3½ c. sliced or 4 c. shredded.

COOKING: Boil, blanch, steam, braise, sauté, stir-fry, bake, broil, deep-fry, microwave or grill.

To boil: In 2-qt. saucepan over high heat, bring 1″ salted water to a boil. Add 1 lb. summer squash, sliced, and let water return to a boil. Reduce heat to low. Cover and simmer 2 to 3 minutes or until tender-crisp. Drain. (Do not overcook summer squash or it will become mushy.)

SERVING: Use raw summer squash in appetizers, salads and sandwiches. Cooked summer squash can be used in soups, main and side dishes or for pickles.

WINTER SQUASH

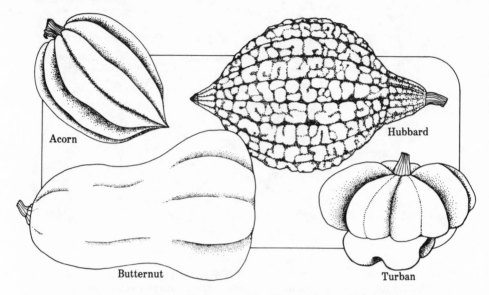

Acorn

Hubbard

Butternut

Turban

Longer growing and generally larger in size, winter squash have hard, shell-like skins with fully developed seeds. Most have orange-colored flesh and will keep for 1 to 3 months if stored properly.

Winter squash is enjoyed baked for its sweet and moist flesh. You'll find that once the flesh is cooked and mashed, most squash can be used interchangeably in recipes—custards, soufflés, baked goods and pies.

Acorn squash, named for their shape, are slightly oval, ribbed and pointed at one end. They grow up to about 2 lb. Their dark green skins will change to a mixture of orange and dull green during storage. The flesh is orange-colored and slightly dry. They have large seed cavities—perfect for stuffing—and they're best when baked.

Banana squash, weighing up to 30 lb., are long, cylindrical and pointed at both ends. They have thick, hard, pale olive skins and flesh that is creamy pink and dry.

Butternut squash have thick necks and bulbous bases and range from 9 to 12″ long. Their smooth, hard skins are tan, and their flesh is deep orange.

Green and golden delicious are 8 to 12″ long. They have dark green skins that are thin but hard, and they weigh about 5 to 7 lb. Their flesh ranges from yellowish orange to reddish orange and has a relatively dry texture.

Hubbards are round with tapered ends and range from dark green to blue-grey to orange-red. Weighing anywhere from 5 to 12 lb., these thick-skinned squash have thick flesh that is sweet and dry.

Spaghetti squash are round, with smooth, lemon-yellow skins. Weighing 2 to 4 lb., they have creamy yellow flesh that separates into spaghetti-like strands when cooked.

Turban squash, also called *buttercup,* are named because their blossom ends resemble a turban-like cap. Hard and thin-skinned, they are dark bluish green with dramatic reddish orange flecks and stripes. Weighing from 3 to 5 lb., these mild-flavored squash have a smooth, dry texture.

SEASONALITY: Available August through March; the peak season is October through January.

SELECTION: Choose hard winter squash with firm, deeply colored skins and ones that are heavy in relation to their size.

STORAGE: Store in dry, well ventilated place 1 month. Refrigerate, unwashed, 2 to 3 weeks. Winter squash freeze well; just cook, mash and freeze.

PREPARATION: Rinse under cold running water. Cut squash in half from stem to blossom end. Scoop out stringy flesh and seeds. Don't throw away the seeds; they're edible (for roasting information, see Pumpkins). Cut and peel squash. (If boiling winter squash, peel after cooking; it's much easier.)

Stuff whole or halved squash; or use whole, halved, sliced or cubed.

YIELD: For 2 to 3 servings, allow 1 lb.; 1 lb. yields about 2 c. mashed.

COOKING: Boil, steam, braise, sauté, stir-fry, bake, deep-fry, microwave or pressure-cook.

To boil: In 4-qt. Dutch oven or saucepot over high heat, bring 1" salted water to a boil. Add 1 lb. winter squash, cut into 3 to 4" pieces, and let water return to a boil. Reduce heat to low. Cover and simmer 10 to 15 minutes or until tender. Drain and cool slightly, then peel. Mash or purée squash.

To bake: On jelly-roll pan place 1 winter squash, halved, cut-side down. Bake in 325° to 375° oven 45 minutes to 1 hour and 30 minutes or until fork-tender.

SERVING: Cooked winter squash can be used in soups, baked goods, main and side dishes.

SWEET POTATOES_____

These native American vegetables are so nutritious that you could practically live on them—and in fact, during the Civil War, when food was scarce, many people did.

Whether you prefer varieties that are mealy or moist tends to depend upon where you live. Varieties with yellowish, fawn-colored skins are relatively dry and mealy, and these are most popular in the North. Sweeter, moister varieties with reddish skins and vivid orange flesh, as well as yams, are more common in the southern United States.

True yams are grown in the tropics, and their flesh may be yellow, red or even purple, but they're handled and cooked just like sweet potatoes. They may weigh as much as 12 lb., but the ones with the best flavor weigh less than a pound.

Both sweet potatoes and yams are excellent sources of vitamins A and C, iron and fiber.

SEASONALITY: Available year 'round; the peak season is October through March.

SELECTION: Choose well shaped, plump, firm sweet potatoes or yams with skins that are deep yellow to dark brown. Avoid ones that are soft or decayed.

STORAGE: Store in a cool, dry, well ventilated place 2 to 3 weeks. Do not refrigerate. Sweet potatoes and yams freeze well; just cook, mash and freeze.

PREPARATION: Scrub with stiff brush under cold running water. Trim off any woody or bruised spots.

Use whole and unpeeled, or peeled and halved, sliced or cubed.

YIELD: For 1 serving, allow 1 medium sweet potato or yam; 1 lb. equals about 2 to 3 sweet potatoes, or 1 to 2 yams.

COOKING: Boil, steam, braise, sauté, bake, deep-fry, microwave or pressure-cook.

To boil: In 4-qt. Dutch oven over

high heat, bring 1″ salted water to a boil. Add 1 lb. whole sweet potatoes or yams and let water return to a boil. Reduce heat to low. Cover and simmer 25 to 35 minutes or until fork-tender. Drain and peel.

To bake: Pierce sweet potatoes or yams several times with fork. (This allows steam to escape, preventing the potato or yam from bursting during baking.) A medium sweet potato or yam will bake in about 1 hour at 400°. Both can be baked at temperatures as low as 325°, so you can bake them along with a roast or casserole. Of course, the lower the oven temperature, the longer the baking time.

SERVING: Cooked sweet potatoes and yams can be used in soups, salads, baked goods, main and side dishes.

TOMATOES

There's nothing like a juicy, ripe, home-grown tomato. Because they're best when picked right from the vine, even people who aren't avid gardeners like to grow tomatoes.

Though most people would name them as their favorite vegetable, tomatoes are fruit. The most common shapes are the large, round varieties such as Jersey and beefsteak; the small, pear-shaped plum or Italian plum tomatoes, which make such good sauces; and the small, round cherry tomatoes.

Vine-ripened tomatoes taste the best. Ones that are sold in supermarkets may need a little help to finish ripening; keep them at room temperature, out of direct sunlight, until they fully ripen.

New varieties of tomatoes which taste less acid are being grown. However, taste can be deceiving, especially with pear-shaped and yellow tomatoes. You can't determine the acidity of a tomato by its taste.

The amount of acid a tomato has is critical to prevent spoilage when canning in a water bath. If you are in doubt of the acid content of your tomatoes, you may add 2 tsp. bottled lemon juice to each pt. of whole or quartered tomatoes, tomato juice or purée (4 tsp. per qt.). (For more information, ask your country extension agent or check *Farm Journal's Freezing & Canning Cookbook*.)

Tomatoes are a good source of vitamins A and C.

SEASONALITY: Available year 'round; the peak season is May through September.

SELECTION: Choose firm, smooth-skinned, even-colored tomatoes that are heavy in relation to their size. Avoid soft ones with blemished skins.

STORAGE: Refrigerate ripe tomatoes, unwashed, in perforated plastic bag or crisper 1 to 2 days. Tomatoes freeze well; just blanch and freeze whole.

PREPARATION: Rinse under cold running water. Cut out center core.

Stuff whole or halved tomatoes; or cut into wedges, slice or chop.

Tomatoes needn't be peeled unless specified in recipes.

To peel: Dip a tomato in boiling water 30 to 60 seconds. Then place under cold running water a few seconds to cool. Peel and core.

To seed: Cut tomato in half from stem to blossom end. Gently squeeze to remove seeds.

YIELD: For 1 serving, allow 1 medium tomato; 1 medium tomato yields about 1 c. chopped.

COOKING: Boil, blanch, steam, braise, sauté, stir-fry, bake, broil, microwave or grill.

To sauté: In 10″ skillet over medium heat, melt ¼ c. butter or regular margarine. Add 1 lb. tomatoes, sliced. Cook, stirring gently, 3 to 5 minutes or until heated through.

SERVING: Use raw tomatoes for garnishes or in appetizers or salads. Cooked tomatoes can be used in soups, sauces, main and side dishes or for pickles.

TURNIPS

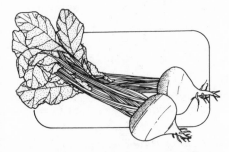

When it comes to cooking turnips, Southerners really know the secret: They simmer the tender, fuzzy green tops along with some sort of pork in a broth. The potlikker, the broth, is served with the mustard-flavored greens for a soup-like side dish.

Turnips have a sweet and tangy flavor similar to that of a mild radish, and they can be enjoyed either raw or cooked. They're most often cone-shaped, with purplish or greenish crowns.

Turnips often are confused with rutabagas. Although they taste similar and are interchangeable with rutabagas in recipes, turnips are smaller, more perishable, can be eaten raw, and are sold with their tops. Rutabagas tend to have larger, hardier roots and are only served cooked. (For more information, see Greens and Rutabagas.)

Both turnips and their greens are high in vitamins A and C.

SEASONALITY: Available year 'round; the peak season is October through March.

SELECTION: Choose turnips that are firm, smooth and heavy in relation to their size. Avoid large ones.

The greens should be crisp, young and tender. Avoid wilted yellow ones or greens with large mature leaves.

STORAGE: Cut off greens. Refrigerate turnips, unwashed, in plastic bag or crisper 5 to 7 days.

To store turnip greens: Cut tops 1 to 2″ from crowns and refrigerate,

unwashed, 1 to 2 days.

Turnips and tops freeze well; just blanch and freeze.

PREPARATION: Cut off tops and root ends. Scrub turnips with a soft brush under cold running water. Peel.

Use whole, sliced, cubed or shredded.

For greens: Rinse under cold running water to remove dirt and sand. Trim bruised leaves and tough stems. Cut tops and stems into 2″ pieces. Spin dry in salad spinner or pat dry with paper towels.

YIELD: For 1 serving, allow ½ lb. turnips; 1 lb. yields about 4 c. chopped.

For 2 to 3 servings, allow 1 lb. turnip greens; 1 lb. yields about 8 c. chopped.

COOKING: Both turnips and their greens can be boiled, steamed, braised, sautéed, stir-fried, baked or microwaved. Turnips also can be deep-fried and pressure-cooked.

To boil turnips: In 3-qt. saucepan over high heat, bring 1″ salted water to a boil. Add 1 lb. small turnips, peeled, and let water return to a boil. Reduce heat to medium. Cover and simmer 20 to 30 minutes or until fork-tender. Drain.

Cook 1 lb. turnips, cubed, 10 to 20 minutes.

To boil tops: In 3-qt. saucepan over high heat, bring ¼″ salted water to a boil. Add 1 lb. greens, chopped, and let water return to a boil. Reduce heat to low. Cover and simmer 5 to 10 minutes or until tender. Drain.

SERVING: Use raw turnips in salads. Cooked turnips and greens can be used in soups, main and side dishes.

MICROWAVE TIPS

The microwave oven is ideal for cooking vegetables because it can steam vegetables quickly preserving their fresh color and flavor. To make it even easier, we've added a chart. If you keep in mind these points, you'll be rewarded with flavorful, tender-crisp vegetables every time.

• All cooking times are for *fresh* vegetables.

• Each vegetable is cooked at either high setting (100% power) or medium setting (50% power). Because the power of microwave ovens does vary, use the minimum time listed and then check for doneness. These vegetables were tested in 600-watt and 675-watt ovens; your owner's manual tells the wattage of your own oven.

• Before cooking whole vegetables that have skins, such as squash, pierce the skin several times with a fork.

• Other basic information about preparation is contained in the chart, but if you want more information about how to prepare a certain vegetable for cooking, turn to the beginning of this chapter.

• The fresher the vegetable, the more quickly it will cook. Microwaves are attracted to moisture, so vegetables picked at the height of the season will cook faster than the same varieties picked later.

• Larger amounts cook more slowly. To double the amount of vegetables to be cooked, add half again as much water and increase the cooking time by half. Stir the vegetables more often, too.

• Starting temperatures for vegetables are normal storage temperatures: refrigerated for most vegetables, but room temperature for root vegetables such as potatoes and onions.

• Sliced and diced vegetables cook faster than whole vegetables because more surface area is exposed to absorb energy. The smaller and thinner the pieces, the faster they will cook.

• Arrange vegetables with the thicker portions to the outside of the dish or the oven, so that the entire vegetable cooks evenly. When cooking more than one whole vegetable arrange them at least 1" apart from each other.

• Cover when indicated with a lid or with a sheet of plastic wrap that is folded back (vented) to allow steam to escape.

• Turn over large vegetables halfway through cooking for even cooking.

• Stir when indicated to redistribute heat from the outside of the dish to the inside for even cooking.

• If you add salt, add it *after* cooking unless otherwise indicated.

• Standing time allows the centers of the vegetables to cook thoroughly, without overcooking or drying out the exteriors. Allow cooked vegetables to stand, covered, on a flat surface.

• Use only microwave-safe utensils in your oven—ones made of paper, heat-resistant glass and plastic, glass ceramic, and stoneware, porcelain and china without metallic trim.

MICROWAVING FRESH VEGETABLES

Vegetable	To Prepare	To Microwave
Anise *1 lb., trimmed*	In 12 x 8 x 2″ dish place ¼ c. water; add anise. Cover with vented plastic wrap.	Microwave at high setting 7 to 8 min., rearranging anise after 4 min. Let stand, covered, 3 min. Drain.
Artichokes *1 medium, trimmed*	In 10-oz. custard cup place 2 tblsp. water; add artichoke. Cover with vented plastic wrap.	Microwave at high setting 4 to 5 min., rotating cup one-quarter turn every 90 seconds. Drain.
4 medium, trimmed	In 8 x 8 x 2″ dish place ¼ c. water; add artichokes. Cover with vented plastic wrap.	Microwave at high setting 10 to 12 min., rotating dish one-quarter turn every 4 min. Drain.
Asparagus *1 lb. spears, trimmed*	In 12 x 8 x 2″ dish place ¼ c. water and 1 tsp. salt; add asparagus. Cover with vented plastic wrap.	Microwave at high setting 6 to 9½ min., rearranging outside spears to inside after 5 min. Drain.
1 lb. spears, cut into 1″ pieces	In 2-qt. casserole place ¼ c. water and ¼ tsp. salt; add asparagus. Cover with lid or vented plastic wrap.	Microwave at high setting 5 to 7 min., stirring after 4 min. Drain.
Beans: Green or Wax *1 lb. whole, trimmed*	In 2-qt. casserole place ½ c. water and ¼ tsp. salt; add beans. Cover with lid or vented plastic wrap.	Microwave at high setting 11 to 13 min., stirring after 6 min. Let stand, covered, 3 to 5 min. Drain.
1 lb. whole, cut into 1″ pieces	In 1½-qt. casserole place ⅓ c. water; add beans. Cover with lid or vented plastic wrap.	Microwave at high setting 9 to 11 min., stirring after 6 min. Let stand, covered, 3 to 5 min. Drain.
Beans: Lima *1 lb., shelled (about 2 c.)*	In 2-qt. casserole place 1 c. water; add lima beans. Cover with lid or waxed paper.	Microwave at high setting 5 min. Stir. Microwave at medium setting 25 to 30 min., stirring every 5 min. and adding more hot water if needed to cover beans. Let stand, covered, 5 min. Drain.
Beets *1 lb. small whole, trimmed*	In 1½-qt. casserole place ½ c. water and ½ tsp. salt; add beets. Cover with lid or vented plastic wrap.	Microwave at high setting 15 to 20 min., stirring every 5 min. Let stand, covered, 3 to 5 min. Drain.
1 lb. beet tops, trimmed and chopped	In 3-qt. casserole place ¼ c. water; add beet tops. Cover with lid or vented plastic wrap.	Microwave at high setting 7 to 8½ min., stirring after 4 min. Let stand, covered, 3 min. Drain.

Vegetable	To Prepare	To Microwave
Broccoli *1 to 1½ lb. spears, trimmed*	In 12 x 8 x 2″ dish place ½ c. water; add broccoli, placing flower ends toward center. Cover with vented plastic wrap.	Microwave at high setting 8 to 12 min., rotating dish one-half turn after 6½ min. Drain.
1 to 1½ lb., broken into flowerets	In 2-qt. casserole place ½ c. water; add broccoli. Cover with lid or vented plastic wrap.	Microwave at high setting 8 to 10 min., stirring after 4½ min. Drain.
Brussels Sprouts *1 lb., trimmed, with an X cut in the bottom of each stem*	In 1½-qt. casserole place ¼ c. water; add sprouts. Cover with lid or vented plastic wrap.	Microwave at high setting 4 to 8 min., stirring after 4 min. Let stand, covered, 3 min. Drain.
Cabbage *1 (1-lb.) head (red or green), cut into 4 wedges*	In 12 x 8 x 2″ dish place ¼ c. water; add cabbage. Cover with vented plastic wrap.	Microwave at high setting 12 to 15 min., rearranging wedges after 8 min. Let stand, covered, 2 min. Drain.
1 (1-lb.) head (red or green), shredded	In 1½-qt. casserole place ¼ c. water; add cabbage. Cover with lid or vented plastic wrap.	Microwave at high setting 7 to 13½ min., stirring after 6 min. Let stand, covered, 3 min. Drain.
1 (1-lb.) head (Savoy or Napa), shredded	In 3-qt. casserole place ¼ c. water; add cabbage. Cover with lid or vented plastic wrap.	Microwave at high setting 9 to 11 min., stirring after 6 min. Let stand, covered, 3 min. Drain.
Carrots *10 to 12 medium, cut into 2″ pieces*	In 1-qt. casserole place 2 tblsp. water; add carrots. Cover with lid or vented plastic wrap.	Microwave at high setting 6 to 8 min., stirring after 4 min. Let stand, covered, 3 min. Drain.
6 medium, sliced (2 c.)	In 1-qt. casserole place 2 tblsp. water; add carrots. Cover with lid or vented plastic wrap.	Microwave at high setting 4 to 7 min., stirring after 3½ min. Let stand, covered, 3½ min. Drain.
¾ lb. whole baby, trimmed	In 1-qt. casserole place 2 tblsp. water; add carrots. Cover with lid or vented plastic wrap.	Microwave at high setting 6 to 8 min., stirring after 4 min. Let stand, covered, 3 min. Drain.
Cauliflower *1 (1-lb.) head, trimmed*	Wrap head tightly in plastic wrap; place in 9″ pie plate or on paper plate.	Microwave at high setting 6 to 9 min., turning head over after 4 min. Let stand, covered, 3 min. Drain.
1 (1-lb.) head, broken into flowerets	In 1½-qt. casserole place ¼ c. water; add cauliflower. Cover with lid or vented plastic wrap.	Microwave at high setting 4 to 7 min., stirring after 3½ min. Let stand, covered, 3 min. Drain.

MICROWAVING FRESH VEGETABLES

Vegetable	To Prepare	To Microwave
Celery *6 to 8 medium ribs, sliced (about 2 c.)*	In 1½-qt. casserole place 2 tblsp. water; add celery. Cover with lid or vented plastic wrap.	Microwave at high setting 5 to 8 min., stirring after 4 min. Let stand, covered, 3 min. Drain.
Chinese Cabbage (Bok Choy) *2 lb. stalks, cut into ⅛" slices and leaves coarsely chopped*	In 3-qt. casserole place 1 c. water; add bok choy. Cover with lid or vented plastic wrap.	Microwave at high setting 4 to 5 min., stirring after 2 min. Drain.
Corn *1 medium ear*	Leave in husk; or remove husk and wrap ear in plastic wrap.	Microwave at high setting 3 to 5 min., turning ear over after 2½ min. Let stand, covered, 5 min.
2 medium ears	Leave in husks; or remove husks and wrap ears in plastic wrap.	Microwave at high setting 4 to 9 min., turning ears over after 3½ min. Let stand, covered, 5 min.
4 medium ears, husked	In 12 x 8 x 2" dish place ¼ c. water; add corn. Cover with vented plastic wrap.	Microwave at high setting 10 to 17 min., rearranging ears after 8½ min. Let stand, covered, 5 min. Drain.
3 medium ears, husked and scraped (1½ c.)	In 1½-qt. casserole place ¼ c. water; add corn. Cover with lid or vented plastic wrap.	Microwave at high setting 6 to 7 min., stirring after 3½ min. Drain.
Eggplant *1 lb., peeled and cut into ¾" cubes*	In 2-qt. casserole place 2 tblsp. butter; add eggplant. Cover with lid or vented plastic wrap.	Microwave at high setting 6 to 10 minutes, stirring every 3 min. Let stand, covered, 3 min.
Greens *2 lb. collard or turnip, coarsely chopped*	In 3-qt. casserole place 2 c. water; add greens. Cover with lid or vented plastic wrap.	Microwave at high setting 40 to 45 min., stirring every 10 min. Let stand, covered, 3 min. Drain.
1 lb. kale, coarsely chopped	In 3-qt. casserole place 1 c. water; add kale. Cover with lid or vented plastic wrap.	Microwave at high setting 14 to 21 min., stirring every 4 min. Let stand, covered, 3 min. Drain.
1 lb. mustard, coarsely chopped	In 3-qt. casserole place 2 c. water; add greens. Cover with lid or vented plastic wrap.	Microwave at high setting 25 to 35 min., stirring every 10 min. Let stand, covered, 3 min. Drain.
1 lb. Swiss chard, with stems and leaves cut into 1" pieces	In 2-qt. casserole place ¼ c. water; add chard. Cover with lid or vented plastic wrap.	Microwave at high setting 5 to 8 min., stirring after 3 min. Let stand, covered, 3 min.

MICROWAVING FRESH VEGETABLES

Vegetable	To Prepare	To Microwave
Jicama *1 lb., cut into ¼" pieces or ⅛" strips*	In 2-qt. casserole place ¼ c. water; add jicama. Cover with lid or vented plastic wrap.	Microwave at high setting 8 to 10 min., stirring after 5 min. Let stand, covered, 3 to 5 min. Drain.
Kohlrabi *4 to 5 medium, sliced*	In 2-qt. casserole place ¼ c. water; add kohlrabi. Cover with lid or vented plastic wrap.	Microwave at high setting 10 to 15 min., stirring every 4 min. Let stand, covered, 5 min. Drain.
Leeks *2 lb. whole, trimmed, with 2 slits cut in center of each*	In 8 x 8 x 2" dish place ¼ c. water; add leeks. Cover with vented plastic wrap.	Microwave at high setting 4 to 7 min., rearranging leeks after 3½ min. Drain.
Mushrooms *½ lb. whole, trimmed*	In 1-qt. casserole place 2 tblsp. butter; add mushrooms.	Microwave at high setting 3 to 4 min., stirring every 1½ min. Let stand, uncovered, 2 min.
1 lb. whole, trimmed	In 2-qt. casserole place 3 tblsp. butter; add mushrooms.	Microwave at high setting 3 to 6½ min., stirring every 2 min. Let stand, uncovered, 2 min.
½ lb., sliced	In 8 x 8 x 2" dish place 2 tblsp. butter; add mushrooms. Cover with vented plastic wrap.	Microwave at high setting 3 to 6 min., stirring after 1½ min.
Okra *1 lb., whole or sliced*	In 1-qt. casserole place ¼ c. water and ¼ tsp. salt; add okra. Cover with lid or vented plastic wrap.	Microwave at high setting 7 to 10 min., stirring after 5 min. Let stand, covered, 3 min. Drain.
Onions: Green *1 lb., trimmed*	In 12 x 8 x 2" dish place 2 tblsp. water; add green onions. Cover with vented plastic wrap.	Microwave at high setting 6 to 10 min., rearranging green onions after 3 min. Drain.
Onions: Small White, Spanish, Yellow *4 medium, whole, trimmed and peeled*	In 1½-qt. casserole place ½ c. water; add onions. Cover with lid or vented plastic wrap.	Microwave at high setting 7 to 8 min., turning onions over after 4 min. Drain.
1½ lb. small white, trimmed and peeled	In 2-qt. casserole place ½ c. water; add onions. Cover with lid or vented plastic wrap.	Microwave at high setting 6 to 10 min., stirring every 2 min. Drain.

MICROWAVING FRESH VEGETABLES

Vegetable	To Prepare	To Microwave
Parsnips *1 lb., sliced*	In 2-qt. casserole place ¼ c. water; add parsnips. Cover with lid or vented plastic wrap.	Microwave at high setting 5 to 7 min., stirring after 3 min. Let stand, covered, 3 min. Drain.
Peas: Green *2 lb., shelled*	In 1½-qt. casserole place ¼ c. water; add peas. Cover with lid or vented plastic wrap.	Microwave at high setting 5 to 7 min., stirring after 3½ min. Let stand, covered, 3 min. Drain.
Peas: Sugar Snap or Snow *¼ lb., trimmed*	In 9″ pie plate place 2 tblsp. water; add snow peas. Cover with vented plastic wrap.	Microwave at high setting 2 to 4 min., stirring after 1 min. Drain.
Peppers: *6 whole, stem ends* *and seeds* *removed*	In 12 x 8 x 2″ dish place 2 tblsp. water; add peppers, cut-side down. Cover with vented plastic wrap.	Microwave at high setting 10 to 12 min., rearranging peppers every 3 min. Let stand, covered, 5 min. Drain.
Potatoes: Baked *1 medium, pierced with* *fork*	Place potato on paper towel.	Microwave at high setting 3 to 5 min., turning potato over after 2 min. Wrap potato in foil. Let stand 5 to 10 min.
2 medium, pierced with *fork*	Place potatoes 1″ apart on paper towel.	Microwave at high setting 5 to 7 min., turning potatoes over after 3 min. Wrap potatoes in foil. Let stand 5 to 10 min.
4 medium, pierced with *fork*	Place potatoes 1″ apart on paper towel.	Microwave at high setting 10 to 12 min., turning potatoes over after 5 min. Wrap potatoes in foil. Let stand 5 to 10 min.
Potatoes: Boiled *4 medium, peeled and cut* *into quarters*	In 2-qt. casserole place ¼ c. water; add potatoes. Cover with lid or vented plastic wrap.	Microwave at high setting 7 to 9 min., stirring after 5 min. Let stand, covered, 3 min. Drain.
6 medium, peeled and cut *into quarters*	In 2-qt. casserole place ¼ c. water; add potatoes. Cover with lid or vented plastic wrap.	Microwave at high setting 9 to 11 min., stirring after 6 min. Let stand, covered, 3 min. Drain.
4 medium, peeled and cut *into ¼″ slices*	In 2-qt. casserole place ¼ c. water; add potatoes. Cover with lid or vented plastic wrap.	Microwave at high setting 8 to 10 min., stirring after 5 min. Let stand, covered, 3 min. Drain.

MICROWAVING FRESH VEGETABLES

Vegetable	To Prepare	To Microwave
Potatoes: Boiled (Continued)		
6 medium, peeled and cut into ¼" slices	In 2-qt. casserole place ¼ c. water; add potatoes. Cover with lid or vented plastic wrap.	Microwave at high setting 9 to 11 min., stirring after 6 min. Let stand, covered, 3 min. Drain.
4 medium, peeled and cut into 1" cubes	In 2-qt. casserole place ¼ c. water; add potatoes. Cover with lid or vented plastic wrap.	Microwave at high setting 7 to 8 min., stirring after 4 min. Let stand, covered, 3 min. Drain.
6 medium, peeled and cut into 1" cubes	In 2-qt. casserole place ¼ c. water; add potatoes. Cover with lid or vented plastic wrap.	Microwave at high setting 9 to 11 min., stirring after 6 min. Let stand, covered, 3 min. Drain.
Potatoes: New		
8 medium, pierced with fork	In 2-qt. casserole place 2 tblsp. water; add potatoes. Cover with lid or vented plastic wrap.	Microwave at high setting 5 to 8 min., stirring after 3 min. Let stand, covered, 3 min. Drain.
12 medium, pierced with fork	In 2-qt. casserole place 2 tblsp. water; add potatoes. Cover with lid or vented plastic wrap.	Microwave at high setting 8 to 10 min., stirring after 5 min. Let stand, covered, 3 min. Drain.
Potatoes: Sweet		
1 medium, pierced with fork	Place potato on paper towel.	Microwave at high setting 3 to 5 min., turning potato over after 2 min. Let stand 3 min.
2 medium, pierced with fork	Place potatoes 1" apart on paper towel.	Microwave at high setting 5 to 9 min., turning potatoes over after 3 min. Let stand 3 min.
4 medium, pierced with fork	Place potatoes 1" apart on paper towel.	Microwave at high setting 8 to 13 min., turning potatoes over after 5 min. Let stand 3 min.
Pumpkin		
1 (4-lb.) cut in half from stem to blossom end, and seeded	Wrap pumpkin half in plastic wrap.	Microwave, one-half at a time, at high setting 12 to 15 min. Let stand, covered, 5 to 10 min.
Rutabagas		
1½ lb., peeled and cut into ½" cubes	In 2-qt. casserole place ¼ c. water; add rutabagas. Cover with lid or vented plastic wrap.	Microwave at high setting 14 to 18 min., stirring every 4 min. Let stand, covered, 3 min. Drain.
Spinach		
1 lb., trimmed	In 3-qt. casserole place spinach. Cover with lid or vented plastic wrap.	Microwave at high setting 5 to 8 min., stirring after 3 min.

MICROWAVING FRESH VEGETABLES

Vegetable	To Prepare	To Microwave
Squash: Summer		
1 medium zucchini, cut into ¼" slices	In 2-qt. casserole place 2 tblsp. butter; add zucchini. Cover with lid or vented plastic wrap.	Microwave at high setting 2 to 6½ min., stirring after 2 min. Let stand, covered, 2 min.
1 medium yellow crook-neck or straightneck, cut into ¼" slices	In 2-qt. casserole place 2 tblsp. butter; add squash. Cover with lid or vented plastic wrap.	Microwave at high setting 4 to 7½ min., stirring after 3 min. Let stand, covered, 2 min.
1 medium pattypan, cut in half lengthwise and seeded	Wrap squash half in plastic wrap.	Microwave, one-half at a time, at high setting 2 to 4½ min. Let stand, covered, 3 min.
Squash: Winter		
1 medium acorn, pierced with fork	Place squash on paper towel.	Microwave at high setting 8 to 11½ min., turning squash over after 5 min. Let stand 5 to 10 min.
2 medium acorn, pierced with fork	Place squash on paper towel.	Microwave at high setting 13 to 16 min., turning squash over after 8 min. Let stand 5 to 10 min.
1 (1-lb.) butternut or Hubbard, cut in half from stem to blossom end and seeded	Wrap squash half in plastic wrap.	Microwave, one-half at a time, at high setting 3 to 4½ min. Let stand, covered, 5 min.
1 (2-lb.) butternut or Hubbard, cut in half from stem to blossom end and seeded	In 8 x 8 x 2" or 12 x 8 x 2" dish place squash. Cover with vented plastic wrap.	Microwave, one-half at a time, at high setting 5 to 12 min., rear-ranging squash after 4 min. Let stand, covered, 5 min.
1 (1-lb.) spaghetti, pierced with fork	Place whole squash on paper towel.	Microwave at high setting 4 to 6½ min., turning squash over after 3 min. Let stand 5 min. Cut in half; remove seeds. With fork separate flesh into spaghetti-like strands.
Turnips		
4 medium, cut into ¼" slices	In 1-qt. casserole place ¼ c. water; add turnips. Cover with lid or vented plastic wrap.	Microwave at high setting 9 to 11 min., stirring every 2 min. Let stand, covered, 3 min. Drain.
4 medium, cut into ½" cubes	In 1-qt. casserole place ¼ c. water; add turnips. Cover with lid or vented plastic wrap.	Microwave at high setting 12 to 14 min., stirring every 3 min. Let stand, covered, 3 min. Drain.

2

Incredible
Edibles

Even the simplest garnish gives food a lift—a sprig of parsley here, a
sprinkling of paprika there, are second nature to many of us. By using easy
but elegant garnishes made from vegetables, you can add a dash of color
and an element of surprise to just about any dish.

In this chapter you'll find directions for transforming thin slices of fresh
vegetables into eye-catching flowers and colorful doodads that can decorate
individual dinner plates or add the finishing touch to a big-batch slaw.
They're all easy, and you won't need utensils more specialized than a paring
knife to make most of them. Best of all, you can eat them.

Children will be fascinated with their box lunches if you toss in a few
Vegetable Jacks or Daisy Cutouts. They're so easy that a grade-schooler
could assemble them while you do the cutting. Zucchini and cucumber chains
make a good finishing touch for a big bowl of potato salad; just use them to
encircle the inner rim of the bowl.

Radishes, green onions and carrots can be cut into the shape of lilies, then
arranged on a platter as garnishes, or offered as appetizers with a bowl of
your favorite dip. To brighten a platter of cold meats, add an Onion Dahlia,
a mum made from a beet, or a trio of Radish Cup Flowers. Roasts, side
dishes and salads of all kinds can be dressed up with a scattering of Zucchini
Butterflies or Tomato Roses.

When you want to go all-out, create a centerpiece by assembling a mixed
bouquet of roses, black-eyed Susans, lilies and even jonquils made from cabbage, turnips, carrots, radishes, green onions and rutabagas; see the Garnish
Bouquet pictured facing page 87, with directions on page 57.

Most of these garnishes can be made a day or two in advance and then
refrigerated in a bowl of water until needed. Leftover portions of beets,
turnips or rutabagas also should be refrigerated in water until you're ready
to cook them.

These decorative vegetable shapes are bound to suggest other variations
to you, so let your imagination soar, and soon you'll be creating beautiful
garnishes of your own design.

VEGETABLE JACKS

Radishes, zucchini or peeled carrot

Slice radishes, zucchini or carrot into $1/8$"-thick slices.

Cut a slash from center to edge of each slice.

To make each jack: Hold 2 slices at right angles to each other with the slashed edges touching; then slide together.

VEGETABLE CHAIN

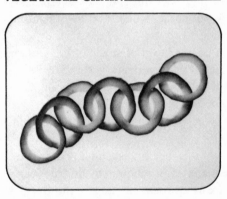

Radishes, cucumber or zucchini

Cut ends from radishes, cucumber or zucchini. Cut radishes into $1/8$"-thick slices; cut cucumber or zucchini into $1/4$"-thick slices.

Using a small round cookie cutter, cut centers from slices.

Cut through 1 side of half of the rings.

Link rings, alternating cut and uncut rings.

RED PEPPER POINSETTIA

1 large red pepper
1 parsley sprig

Cut pepper in half lengthwise and remove seeds.

Cut 8 pointed petal shapes from pepper halves.

Turn 4 petal shapes skin-side up and 4 skin-side down, and arrange them alternately to resemble a Poinsettia.

Place parsley sprig in center.

FLOWER CUTOUTS

1 zucchini
1 red pepper, turnip or rutabaga (or all 3)

Cut skin from zucchini in $1/4$"-thick slices. Cut stems and leaf shapes from zucchini skin. Reserve remaining zucchini for another use.

Cut pepper in half lengthwise and remove seeds; cut turnip or rutabaga into $1/4$"-thick slices.

With scalloped aspic cutters cut flower shapes from pepper halves, turnip slices or rutabaga slices.

Arrange stem, leaf and flower shapes to resemble flowers.

FLOWER CUTOUTS II
(see color photo facing page 87)

1 small zucchini
1 large carrot, peeled
1 small turnip, peeled
Toothpicks

Cut skin from zucchini in $1/8$"-thick slices. Reserve remaining zucchini for another use. Cut carrot and turnip into $1/8$"-thick slices.

With plain and scalloped aspic cutters in graduated small sizes, cut flower shapes from zucchini skin and from carrot and turnip slices.

To make each cutout, stack 3 or 4 flower shapes on a toothpick, starting with the largest size and alternating colors.

DAISY CUTOUTS
(see color photo facing page 87)

1 carrot, peeled
1 large rutabaga or turnip, peeled
Toothpicks

Cut carrot and rutabaga or turnip into $1/8$- to $1/4$"-thick slices.

With knife or round cookie cutter cut a $2 1/2$" circle from each slice of rutabaga or turnip.

With knife cut 8 pointed petal shapes evenly spaced around edge of each circle, being careful not to cut all the way to the center. With toothpick secure a carrot slice to center of each flower shape.

BEET FLOWERS_____
(see color photo facing page 87)

1 beet, peeled
1 small turnip, peeled
Iced water
Toothpicks

Slice beet very thinly. Then cut 3 wedges, evenly spaced, from each slice. Discard wedges.

Make narrow cuts in beet slices, from edges to within 1/4" of center. Soak slices in iced water 15 to 30 minutes to remove excess juice.

Cut turnip into 1/8"-thick slices. With 3/4" scalloped aspic cutter, cut scalloped circles from turnip slices.

With toothpick secure a scalloped turnip circle to center of each beet slice.

FLUTED MUSHROOMS_____

Large or medium mushrooms

Holding knife blade at an angle, cut thin curved wedges in a circular pattern in tops of mushrooms. Carefully remove wedges.

MUSHROOM CUPS_____

Large mushrooms
Parsley sprigs

Twist off mushroom stems and reserve for another use.

With knife cut scallops around edge of each mushroom cap.

Fill mushroom cups with parsley sprigs.

RADISH CUP FLOWERS_____
(see color photo facing page 87)

1 large radish
2 pimiento-stuffed olives
Toothpicks

Cut off root and stem ends of radish.

Hold radish at stem and root ends with thumb and middle finger. Cut around middle of radish in a sawtooth pattern, cutting to center of radish.

Using both hands, gently twist and pull radish apart.

To make each flower: With toothpick secure an olive in center of cut side of each radish cup. Makes 2 flowers.

RADISH FEATHERS

1 large elongated radish

Cut off root and stem ends of radish. Then cut radish lengthwise into quarters.

Cut a large, lengthwise wedge from the skin side of each radish quarter. Then cut a smaller wedge from the first wedge.

To make each radish feather, assemble wedges back into quarters and slide wedges apart. Makes 4 feathers.

TOMATO FLOWERS

4 cherry tomatoes
2 pitted ripe olives
Celery leaves

Remove stems from tomatoes.

Place tomatoes stem-end down on cutting board. With knife cut an X almost all the way through each tomato.

Gently spread tomatoes apart. Spoon out and discard pulp.

To make each tomato flower, place a tomato inside another, staggering petals. Place an olive in the center.

Arrange on celery leaves. Makes 2 flowers.

RADISH POMPONS
(see color photo facing page 87)

Large elongated radishes
Iced water

Cut off root ends of radishes. Place a radish on its side. Starting $\frac{1}{4}$" from stem end, cut lengthwise slices all the way to root end.

Roll radish over one-quarter turn. Holding cut ends together at tip, cut thin lengthwise slices through previous slices.

Repeat with remaining radishes.

Soak in iced water 30 minutes or until petals open; drain.

RADISH LILIES
(see color photo facing page 87)

Large elongated radishes
Iced water

Cut off root ends of radishes.
Starting at root end and cutting to
¼ " of the stem end, make 4 or 5
cuts evenly spaced around the side
of each radish, forming 4 or 5 petals.
Cut 4 or 5 slashes in each petal,
from top almost to bottom.
Soak in iced water 30 minutes or
until petals open; drain.

GREEN ONION LILY
(see color photo facing page 87)

1 green onion
Iced water

Cut off root end of green onion;
discard. Trim top so green onion
measures 4½ " long.
Cutting from top to ¾ " from root
end, cut green onion into as many
thin slivers as possible.
Soak in iced water 30 minutes or
until ends curl; drain.

WATER LILIES

1 zucchini or cucumber
Iced water
Parsley sprigs

Cut off and discard ends of zucchini. Cut zucchini into 1½ " chunks.
As a guide, make 5 marks on cut
side of one zucchini chunk to divide
it into fifths. Between each pair of
marks cut out a 1"-long V-shaped
wedge. Remove and discard wedges.
Cut down between outer skin and
pulp on each point to within ¼ " of
bottom. Scoop out seeds.
Repeat with remaining chunks of
zucchini.
Soak in iced water 30 minutes or
until petals open slightly.
Remove from iced water; drain.
Fill centers with parsley sprigs.

TURNIP CALLA LILY
(see color photo facing page 87)

1 carrot, peeled
1 large turnip (2½" in diameter), peeled
Toothpick
Iced water

Cut a 2¼ x ¼ x ¼" carrot stick.
Cut a very thin slice of turnip.
Roll turnip slice into a cone. Slide
carrot stick into the center of the
cone. Secure with toothpick.
Soak in iced water 30 minutes to
set shape; drain. Snip off ends of
toothpick to make them less visible.

Rutabaga Calla Lily: Use a very
thin slice of peeled rutabaga instead
of turnip and a 2¼"-long Green
Onion Lily (see facing page) instead
of carrot stick.

BEET AND TURNIP CALLA LILIES

1 beet, peeled
1 turnip, peeled
Iced water
Toothpicks

Slice beet and turnip very thinly.
Soak beet slices in iced water 15 to
30 minutes to remove excess juice.
To make each lily, loosely roll a
beet slice into a cone. Then roll a
turnip slice around beet cone, gently
folding back top edge of turnip slice.

Secure with toothpick. Snip off
ends of toothpick to make them
less visible.
Cut a turnip slice into ⅛"-wide
strips. Place 2 strips in center of
each blossom to resemble stamens.

CARROT LILY
(see color photo facing page 87)

1 thin carrot, peeled
Iced water

Cut a 3"-long piece from top of
carrot. Reserve remaining carrot for
another use.
Place 3" piece of carrot on its side.
Starting ½" from base, cut
lengthwise slices all the way to tip.
Roll carrot over one-quarter turn.
Holding cut ends of carrot together
at the tip, cut thin lengthwise slices
through previous slices.
Soak in iced water 30 minutes or
until petals open and curl slightly;
drain.

TURNIP OR BEET MUM

1 turnip or beet, peeled
Iced water

Cut off stem end of turnip or beet; place turnip or beet stem-end down.

Starting 1/8" from outside edge of turnip or beet, make a cut from top to within 1/2" from stem end. Continue cutting slices, 1/8" apart, all the way across turnip or beet.

Rotate turnip or beet one-quarter turn. Holding slices together, make another series of slices, 1/8" apart, all the way across turnip or beet to form a crisscross pattern.

Soak in iced water 2 hours or until petals open; drain.

SQUASH TULIP
(see color photo facing page 87)

1 medium yellow summer squash
1 leaf of red cabbage
Toothpick
Green onion tops

Cut a 2"-long piece from stem end of squash. Reserve remaining squash for another use. Holding the 2" piece cut end up, cut around the inside, 1/4" from the edge.

Spoon out and discard pulp, leaving a cup about 1/4" thick. (If squash is very narrow, use handle of teaspoon to scoop out pulp.)

Cut 3 evenly spaced scallops around side of squash cup.

Cut 2 (3x1/8") strips from cabbage leaf.

Push toothpick through center of cabbage strips and then down through center of squash cup to secure. Arrange green onion tops around squash tulip to form leaves.

BLACK-EYED SUSANS
(see color photo facing page 87)

1 large carrot, peeled
Pitted ripe olives, cut crosswise into halves
Iced water
Toothpicks

Cut several 1/4"-thick slices from carrot and set aside.

Cut remaining carrot diagonally into very thin slices. Soak diagonal slices in iced water 15 to 30 minutes or until slightly curled.

To make each flower, place a 1/4"-

thick slice of carrot on a toothpick; this will form a base to support carrot petals. Then secure 5 carrot slices, curled upward, on same toothpick. Push an olive half, cut-side down, on top of toothpick to form center of flower.

TURNIP OR RUTABAGA JONQUIL
(see color photo facing page 87)

1 turnip or rutabaga, peeled
1 carrot, peeled
Toothpick
Iced water

Cut 5 thin slices from turnip or rutabaga. Then cut a 1½"-long petal shape, pointed at one end, from each slice.

Soak slices in iced water 15 to 30 minutes or until slightly curled.

Cut a ¼"-thick slice of carrot and place on a toothpick; this will form a base to support petals. Then secure 5 petal slices, curled upward, on same toothpick.

Cut a slice of carrot about ¾" thick and secure on toothpick in center of petals.

CABBAGE ROSES
(see color photo facing page 87)

Red or green cabbage leaves, or
    1 cucumber
Toothpicks
Rubber bands
Iced water

With scissors cut a 1"-wide strip from the outer edge of each cabbage leaf, following the curve of the leaf; or with vegetable peeler cut long thin lengthwise strips from the cucumber, discarding first few strips, until you have white strips with green edges about 1" wide.

Start by making center of rose, rolling one end of a strip tightly to form a coil. Then gently fold back strip to reverse the direction of the roll, gathering at bottom and letting top flare out to form petals. Continue rolling and reversing where necessary until all of strip is rolled. For a larger rose, add another strip, rolling and reversing to add fullness.

Fasten bottom with 2 toothpicks. Then fasten a rubber band around base.

Soak in iced water 1 hour to set shape. Snip off ends of toothpicks to make them less visible.

TOMATO ROSE

1 medium tomato or cherry tomato

Starting at blossom end with knife, peel tomato in one continuous, circular strip. Reserve tomato for salad.

Coil tomato peel to form a rose.

ZUCCHINI BUTTERFLIES_____ ## TURNIP PEONY_____

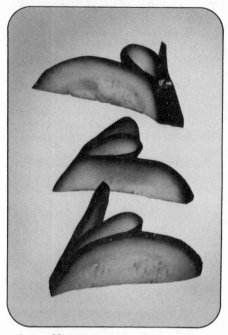

1 large turnip, peeled
Iced water
1 cherry tomato
Toothpick

Cut off stem end of turnip; place turnip stem-end down.

Starting halfway down the side of turnip, make a series of semicircular cuts all around the side, cutting to within ¼" of stem end.

Make a second circle of cuts just above the first circle, alternating so that each new cut is between 2 previous cuts.

Continue making concentric circles of cuts until a core about 1" in diameter remains at the top of the turnip. Cut and scoop out center, forming a cup in the middle.

Soak in iced water 2 hours or until petals open; drain.

Secure cherry tomato in center of cup with toothpick.

1 qt. cold water
1 tblsp. salt
1 medium zucchini

In bowl stir together water and salt until salt is dissolved; set aside.

Cut zucchini in half lengthwise. Refrigerate one half for another use.

Place remaining zucchini half cut-side down on cutting board. Cut off stem and blossom ends and discard; then diagonally cut zucchini half into ³/₈"-thick slices.

Cut 2 lengthwise slits from one end of each slice almost to the other end, to resemble a fan. Soak in salt water 10 minutes or until pliable.

Rinse and drain zucchini slices. For each butterfly, use one slice, tucking center strip between the other two strips.

ONION DAHLIA

1 medium onion
Iced water

Leaving root end intact, peel onion.

On cutting board place onion root end down. Cut a shallow X in top of onion.

Using the X as a guide, slice each quarter into very thin wedges, cutting to within ¼″ of root end, to form petals.

Soak in iced water 30 minutes or until petals open; drain.

ZUCCHINI SPRING

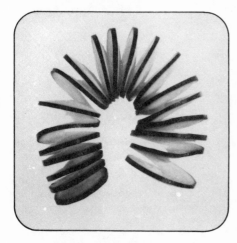

1 zucchini or summer squash
1 metal or wooden skewer

Cut ends from zucchini.

Insert skewer lengthwise through center of zucchini and place zucchini on its side.

Starting at one end, slice crosswise through the zucchini until knife rests on the skewer. Without removing the knife, slowly roll the zucchini so that knife continues to slice through the zucchini, creating a continuous spiral.

Remove skewer and gently pull and bend spring into desired shape.

GARNISH BOUQUET

(see color photo facing page 87)

7 Flower Cutouts II
6 Cabbage Roses, made with green
   cabbage
4 Green Onion Lilies
4 Squash Tulips
4 Radish Pompons
3 Beet Flowers
3 Radish Cup Flowers
2 Daisy Cutouts
2 Turnip Calla Lilies
2 Black-eyed Susans
2 Carrot Lilies
2 Radish Lilies
2 Turnip Jonquils
Wooden skewers
1 styrofoam block
1 small basket
Parsley sprigs
Carrot tops
Iced water

Assemble all vegetable flowers (see preceding pages for directions) and secure on wooden skewers.

Cut styrofoam block to fit securely in basket.

Arrange skewered vegetable flowers in basket by pushing skewers into styrofoam block. Tuck parsley sprigs and carrot tops into basket for added greenery. If not using immediately, spray with iced water. Place basket in large plastic bag and refrigerate up to 24 hours. Spray with iced water before placing on table.

3

Fresh Beginnings

For appetizing ideas for snacks, hors d'oeuvres and first courses, look to vegetables—sliced or diced, puréed or stuffed, and presented in a tantalizing array of dips, spreads and bite-size morsels.

First, think of all the ways you can use sliced vegetables in place of crackers. Spread slices of cucumber, zucchini or cooked new potatoes with chutney-flavored cream cheese and crown each one with a shrimp, slices of fresh radishes, with rolled anchovies, fresh dill or even caviar.

Then think of how to use vegetables as little containers. Crisp snow peas can cradle a stuffing of chicken or shrimp salad; cherry tomatoes and celery, cut imaginatively, can present herb cheese fillings in fresh-looking ways. For example, take a look at the sampling in the photograph facing page 86.

Vegetables make wonderful spreads and fillings. When eggplant is in good supply, set some aside for Eggplant Appetizer or Eggplant-Sesame Spread; both recipes can be either simmered or microwaved. Use cooked, chopped spinach for a cool, airy Spinach and Salmon Mousse, or spread sheets of phyllo pastry with smooth spinach and carrot purées and bake Spinach-Carrot Phyllo Roulades.

Present a chilled Antipasto Platter or a Marinated Vegetable Platter as an appetizer or instead of a salad. Both recipes are perfect for company because they can be made in advance, and each one yields up to 16 appetizer servings; for recipes, see page 63.

If you've never tasted Falafel, be adventurous and deep-fry a batch of these little round morsels of chick peas and sesame seed. The accompanying recipe for Sesame Yogurt Sauce also tastes good with Miniature Carrot Patties or as a low-cal dip for vegetables. An even simpler deep-fried appetizer is the recipe for Fried Potato Skins; sprinkle them with Parmesan cheese or serve them with a choice of toppings. Oven-fried Broccoli Flowerets can be readied in advance, then baked in just 20 minutes.

Once you get into the habit of looking into the vegetable bin, you'll start to discover lots more ideas for creating fresh beginnings for meals and get-togethers any time of day.

SOUR CREAM ONION DIP_____

Nothing could be simpler than this dip with a fresh onion flavor.

1 c. dairy sour cream
¼ c. finely chopped onion
1 tblsp. chopped fresh parsley
1 env. powdered beef bouillon

In bowl stir together all ingredients. Cover and refrigerate at least 2 hours to blend flavors. Makes 1 c.

CURRIED SOUR CREAM DIP_____

Mildly flavored, this goes well with flowerets of broccoli or cauliflower.

2 c. dairy sour cream
2 tblsp. chopped fresh parsley
1 tblsp. finely chopped green onion
½ tsp. celery salt
¼ tsp. curry powder

In bowl stir together all ingredients. Cover and refrigerate at least 2 hours to blend flavors. Makes 2 c.

CUCUMBER DIP_____

Surround a bowl of this dip with an assortment of raw vegetables.

1 (8-oz.) pkg. cream cheese, softened
¾ c. grated cucumber
2 tblsp. lemon juice
1 tblsp. finely chopped green pepper
1½ tsp. grated onion
¼ tsp. salt
⅛ tsp. pepper

In bowl stir together all ingredients. Cover and refrigerate at least 2 hours to blend flavors. Makes 1½ c.

CHILI-CHEESE DIP_____

Add a dollop of this to a hamburger, or roll it in a soft flour tortilla.

2 tblsp. butter or regular margarine
1 medium onion, finely chopped
1 (4-oz.) can green chilies, drained and chopped
1 c. chopped, peeled tomato (about 1 large tomato)
¼ tsp. salt
⅛ tsp. pepper
3 drops hot pepper sauce
2 (3-oz.) pkg. cream cheese, cut into ½" cubes
½ c. shredded Monterey Jack cheese (2 oz.)

In 2-qt. saucepan over medium-high heat, melt butter. Add onion and cook until tender.

Stir in chilies, tomato, salt, pepper and hot pepper sauce. Cover and cook 10 minutes.

Reduce heat to low. Slowly stir in cream cheese and Monterey Jack cheese. Cook, stirring constantly, until cheeses melt.

Serve hot. Makes 2½ c.

TO MICROWAVE: Use same ingredients.

In 1-qt. microwave-safe casserole place butter and onion. Cover with waxed paper. Microwave at high setting (100% power) 3 minutes.

Stir in chilies, tomato, salt, pepper and hot pepper sauce. Microwave at medium setting (50% power) 4 minutes, stirring after 2 minutes.

Stir in half of the cheeses. Cover again, and microwave at medium setting 2 minutes. Stir in remaining cheeses.

Cover again, and microwave at medium setting 3 minutes or until cheeses melt. Serve hot.

DILL DIP

Cottage cheese and parsley make this dip chunky and colorful.

1 (4-oz.) jar pimientos, drained and chopped
4 green onions, sliced
1 c. mayonnaise or salad dressing
1 c. small-curd creamed-style cottage
   cheese
1 c. dairy sour cream
¼ c. chopped fresh parsley
2 tblsp. chopped fresh dill or 2 tsp. dried
   dill weed
¼ tsp. seasoned salt
⅛ tsp. pepper
1 small clove garlic, minced

In bowl stir together all ingredients. Cover and refrigerate at least 4 hours to blend flavors. Makes 3 c.

CHICK PEA SPREAD

This Middle Eastern favorite tastes great with wedges of warm pita.

3 cloves garlic
2 tblsp. sesame seed, toasted
½ tsp. salt
⅛ tsp. pepper
½ c. vegetable oil
1 (20-oz.) can chick peas, rinsed and drained
2 tblsp. lemon juice
2 tblsp. chopped fresh parsley

In blender container place garlic, sesame seed, salt, pepper and ¼ c. oil; cover. Blend at high speed until smooth.

Add chick peas, lemon juice and remaining ¼ c. oil; cover. Blend until smooth and creamy, stopping several times to scrape down sides of blender. Spoon into bowl. Stir in parsley.

Cover and refrigerate at least 2 hours to blend flavors. Makes 2 c.

EGGPLANT-SESAME SPREAD

When eggplant is abundant, use it to make a creamy spread or dip.

2 medium eggplants (about 1 lb. each)
½ c. sesame seed, toasted
1 tsp. sesame or vegetable oil
¼ c. water
¼ c. lemon juice
1 tsp. salt
2 cloves garlic
2 tblsp. chopped fresh parsley

Place eggplants on foil-lined broiler pan; broil 5" from source of heat, turning occasionally, 25 minutes or until skins are charred and eggplants collapse. Cool eggplants; peel off skins. Set aside eggplants.

In blender container or food processor bowl with metal blade, place sesame seed and oil; cover.

Blending at high speed or with processor running, gradually pour water and lemon juice through center of blender cover or feed tube of processor and blend until smooth, stopping several times to scrape down sides.

Blend or process in salt and garlic until smooth. Add eggplant; cover.

Blend or process until mixture is smooth and creamy, stopping several times to scrape down sides. Spoon into bowl; stir in parsley.

Cover and refrigerate 2 hours to blend flavors. Makes 2¾ c.

TO MICROWAVE: Use same ingredients.

Prick skins of eggplants several times with fork.

Microwave at high setting (100% power) 8 to 10 minutes or until eggplants collapse. Cool; peel off skins.

Continue preparing spread as directed.

EGGPLANT APPETIZER

To wake up summertime appetites, try this lively blend of flavors.

¼ c. vegetable oil
2 medium onions, chopped
2 cloves garlic, minced
1 medium eggplant, cut into ¾" cubes
1 medium tomato, peeled and chopped
1 medium red or green sweet pepper, cut into strips
2 tblsp. lemon juice
1 tsp. salt
1 tsp. dried basil leaves
⅛ tsp. pepper
2 tblsp. chopped fresh parsley

In 12" skillet over medium-high heat, heat oil until hot. Add onions and garlic; cook until tender.

Add eggplant and remaining ingredients except parsley. Reduce heat to medium-low.

Cover and simmer, stirring occasionally, 15 minutes or until eggplant is tender. Spoon into bowl. Stir in parsley.

Cover and refrigerate at least 4 hours or until well chilled. Makes about 4 c.

TO MICROWAVE: Use same ingredients.

In 2-qt. microwave-safe casserole place oil, onions and garlic. Cover with lid or plastic wrap, turning back one section to vent steam.

Microwave at high setting (100% power) 3 to 4 minutes or until vegetables are tender, stirring after 2 minutes.

Stir in eggplant and remaining ingredients except parsley.

Microwave, uncovered, at high setting 10 to 12 minutes or until eggplant is tender, stirring every 3 minutes. Stir in parsley.

Cover, refrigerate and serve as directed.

ITALIAN ROASTED PEPPERS

Choose red or green sweet peppers; for twice the color, use both.

6 large red or green sweet peppers
⅓ c. vegetable oil
½ tsp. salt
½ tsp. dried oregano leaves
1 large clove garlic, minced

Cut out and discard stems from peppers. Place peppers on foil-lined broiler pan; broil, 5" from source of heat, 15 to 18 minutes or until pepper skins turn dark brown, turning often with tongs. (Do not let peppers burn.)

Remove peppers from oven; place in paper bag. Close bag and let stand 5 minutes to let steam loosen the skins.

Peel off skins. Cut peppers in half; remove seeds. Cut each half into 1"-wide strips and place in bowl. Add oil and remaining ingredients; toss to mix well.

Cover and refrigerate at least 2 hours to blend flavors. Makes 3 c.

MARINATED MUSHROOMS

For a good salad, toss these with sliced tomatoes and mixed greens.

⅓ c. vegetable oil
⅓ c. red wine vinegar
1 tblsp. packed brown sugar
1 tsp. prepared mustard
¼ tsp. salt
⅛ tsp. pepper
1 lb. small mushrooms
1 small onion, sliced
2 tblsp. chopped fresh parsley

In 3-qt. saucepan over medium heat, bring first 6 ingredients to a boil.

Add mushrooms and onion. Cover and cook 5 minutes. Pour into bowl. Stir in parsley.

Cover and refrigerate at least 24 hours to blend flavors. Makes about 3 c.

TO MICROWAVE: Use same ingredients.

In 3-qt. microwave-safe casserole place first 6 ingredients. Cover with lid or plastic wrap, turning back one section to vent steam.

Microwave at high setting (100% power) 3 to 5 minutes or until mixture boils, stirring after 2 minutes.

Stir in mushrooms and onion. Microwave, uncovered, at high setting, 1½ to 2 minutes, stirring after 1 minute. Stir in parsley.

Cover, refrigerate and serve as directed.

MARINATED VEGETABLE PLATTER

Perfect for company, because it's prepared in advance and serves 16.

2 c. Vinaigrette Dressing (see Index)
1 small head cauliflower, cut into flowerets with 1″ stems, cooked and drained
1 lb. whole green beans, trimmed, cooked and drained
1 lb. asparagus, trimmed, cooked and drained
1 (5¾-oz.) jar pimiento-stuffed olives, drained
3 large tomatoes, cut into wedges
2 bunches green onions, trimmed
1 large cucumber, peeled and sliced
¼ c. chopped fresh parsley

Prepare Vinaigrette Dressing.

Place cooked cauliflower, beans and asparagus in separate bowls; pour ⅔ c. dressing over each vegetable.

Cover and refrigerate overnight to blend flavors, stirring occasionally.

Drain marinated vegetables, reserving dressing for another use.

Arrange marinated vegetables, olives, tomatoes, onions and sliced cucumber on platter. Sprinkle with chopped parsley. Makes 16 servings.

CURRIED EGG AND ZUCCHINI ROUNDS

The topping also can be served as a salad or as a filling for a sandwich.

½ c. mayonnaise or salad dressing
½ tsp. curry powder
¼ tsp. dry mustard
¼ tsp. salt
¼ tsp. hot pepper sauce
4 hard-cooked eggs, finely chopped
½ c. finely chopped celery
2 tblsp. finely chopped onion
1 tblsp. chopped fresh parsley
30 zucchini or cucumber slices (¼″ thick)
Paprika

In bowl stir together first 5 ingredients. Stir in eggs, celery, onion and parsley.

Cover and refrigerate at least 2 hours to blend flavors.

To serve, spoon egg mixture on top of zucchini or cucumber slices and garnish with paprika. Makes 30 appetizers.

ANTIPASTO PLATTER

Makes enough for eight main-dish salads, or 14 to 16 appetizers.

Eggplant Appetizer (see facing page)
Marinated Mushrooms (see facing page)
Carrot Pickles (see Index)
Pickled Beets (see Index)
Italian Roasted Peppers (see facing page)
½ lb. sliced provolone cheese
½ lb. sliced pepperoni
1 pt. cherry tomatoes, stems removed
2 bunches green onions, trimmed
1 c. pitted ripe olives

Prepare first 5 recipes.

Cover and refrigerate at least 24 hours to blend flavors.

To serve, drain mushrooms, carrots, beets and peppers; arrange on large platter with Eggplant Appetizer, provolone cheese and remaining ingredients. Makes 14 to 16 servings.

ZUCCHINI-SHRIMP APPETIZERS

Start with crisp slices of zucchini or cucumber, then spread them with curried cheese and top with shrimp.

1 (8-oz.) pkg. cream cheese, softened
2 tblsp. chutney
1½ tsp. curry powder
⅛ tsp. salt
36 diagonally cut zucchini slices (¼" thick)
36 fresh small shrimp, cooked, cleaned and chilled

In small bowl using mixer at medium speed, beat cream cheese, chutney, curry powder and salt until well blended.

Spread some cheese mixture on one side of each zucchini slice; top each with a shrimp.

Cover and refrigerate until ready to serve. Makes 36 appetizers.

THREE-CHEESE STUFFED CELERY

This three-cheese blend can be used as a cracker spread, too.

½ (8-oz.) pkg. cream cheese, softened
1 oz. crumbled blue cheese (¼ c.)
½ c. shredded Cheddar cheese (2 oz.)
30 diagonally sliced celery pieces (2½" long)
Paprika

In small bowl using mixer at medium speed, beat together cream cheese, blue cheese and Cheddar cheese until smooth.

Spread cheese mixture into each celery piece (or use a pastry bag fitted with large star tube to pipe cheese mixture into pieces).

Arrange stuffed celery on platter; garnish with paprika.

Cover and refrigerate until ready to serve. Makes 30 appetizers.

SHRIMP-FILLED SNOW PEAS

(see photo facing page 86)

Crisp snow pea pods make wonderful containers for creamy fillings.

48 fresh snow peas (about ½ lb.)
2½ c. finely chopped cooked shrimp or chicken
1 c. finely chopped celery
½ c. mayonnaise or salad dressing
¼ c. finely chopped onion
¼ c. finely chopped fresh parsley
1 tblsp. lemon juice
¾ tsp. salt
½ tsp. sugar
⅛ tsp. pepper

String and split open each snow pea.

In 3-qt. saucepan over high heat, bring 1½ qt. water to a boil. Add snow peas; blanch 20 seconds. Immediately plunge snow peas into cold water. Drain and pat dry.

In medium bowl stir together shrimp and remaining ingredients.

Fill each snow pea with some shrimp mixture.

Cover and refrigerate until ready to serve. Makes 48 appetizers.

Herb-filled Snow Peas: Prepare and blanch snow peas as directed.

Prepare Herb Filling for Herb Tomato Stars (see page 67).

Spoon filling into pastry bag fitted with large star tube. Pipe filling into each snow pea.

Cover and refrigerate until ready to serve.

NEW POTATO CANAPÉS
(see photo facing page 86)

With slices of new potatoes in place of crackers, you can serve up a whole array of tantalizing tidbits.

1 lb. unpeeled new potatoes, cooked, drained and chilled
Salt
⅔ c. dairy sour cream
½ tsp. curry powder (optional)
Assorted garnishes: sliced ripe or pimiento-stuffed olives, sliced green onions, chutney, red or black caviar, fresh dill or parsley sprigs, sliced pimientos, sliced cheese, Radish Jacks (see Index), and/or rolled anchovy fillets

Cut each potato into ⅜"-thick slices. Sprinkle with salt.
In small bowl stir together sour cream and curry powder. Spread sour cream mixture on top of each potato slice; top with one or more assorted garnishes.
Serve immediately. Makes about 36 canapés.

CUCUMBER CANAPÉS

Open-faced tea sandwiches with a classic cucumber-cheese blend.

1 (8-oz.) pkg. cream cheese, softened
½ c. chopped, seeded, peeled cucumber
3 tblsp. snipped fresh chives or 1 tblsp. dried snipped chives
⅛ tsp. salt
24 (2"-round) slices pumpernickel or rye bread
12 radishes, thinly sliced

In small bowl using mixer at medium speed, beat together cream cheese, cucumber, chives and salt until well blended.
Cover and refrigerate at least 4 hours to blend flavors.
Spread cheese mixture on bread slices; top with sliced radishes. Makes 24 canapés.

TEX-MEX STUFFED BREAD

Rolled into a cheese ball, the spicy, colorful filling can stand alone.

3 (7"-long) Italian rolls
1 (8-oz.) pkg. cream cheese, softened
1 c. shredded Monterey Jack cheese
½ c. chopped pitted ripe olives
⅓ c. finely chopped celery
¼ c. finely chopped fresh parsley
¼ c. shredded carrot
3 tblsp. finely chopped green pepper
3 tblsp. finely chopped onion
1½ tsp. chili powder
Dash ground red pepper

Cut ½" slice from each end of rolls. Using serrated knife, hollow out center of each roll, leaving a ⅜"-thick shell; set aside shells. (Reserve inside of rolls to make crumbs for another use.)
In medium bowl using mixer at medium speed, beat together cream cheese and remaining ingredients until well blended.
Pack bread shells with cream cheese mixture. Wrap each in plastic wrap. Refrigerate at least 2 hours or until cheese mixture is firm.
To serve, cut each stuffed roll into 8 slices. Makes 24 appetizers.

Vegetable-Cheese Ball: Use same ingredients, but do not hollow out rolls.
Prepare cheese mixture as directed. Shape into ball; wrap with plastic wrap. Refrigerate at least 2 hours or until firm.
Roll cheese ball in an additional ⅓ c. chopped parsley.
Cut each roll into 8 slices and serve with Cheese Ball. Makes 1 cheese ball.

CELERY AND CHEESE ROSETTES

(see photo facing page 86)

So much prettier than ordinary stuffed celery—and not hard to do.

2 (8-oz.) pkg. cream cheese, softened
½ c. chopped walnuts
2 cloves garlic, minced
8 (9"-long) ribs celery
30 pitted large ripe olives, each cut into 4 slices

In medium bowl using mixer at high speed, beat together cream cheese, walnuts and garlic until well blended.

Divide mixture in half. Shape each half into 9"-long log. Press 4 celery ribs around each cheese log; wrap in plastic wrap.

Refrigerate at least 4 hours or until firm.

Cut each log into 20 slices. Top each slice with 3 olive slices. Arrange on platter; serve immediately. Makes 40 appetizers.

VEGETABLE PITAWICHES

There's lots of crunchiness in these lightly seasoned little sandwiches.

⅓ c. grated Parmesan cheese
¼ c. dairy sour cream
1 tsp. lemon juice
¾ tsp. garlic salt
⅛ tsp. pepper
Mayonnaise or salad dressing
1 c. chopped peeled tomato, drained
1 c. shredded carrots
½ c. chopped celery
½ c. sliced green onions
½ c. chopped seeded, peeled cucumber
⅓ c. chopped radishes
⅓ c. chopped green pepper
¼ c. chopped fresh parsley
8 small pita bread (about 4" in diameter), halved
1½ c. alfalfa sprouts

In medium bowl stir together first 5 ingredients and ⅓ c. mayonnaise. Add tomato and remaining ingredients except bread and sprouts; toss until well coated.

Gently spread each pita bread half apart, then spread the inside with some mayonnaise. Fill halves with vegetable mixture; top each with alfalfa sprouts. Serve immediately. Makes 16 mini-sandwiches.

SPINACH AND SALMON MOUSSE

A hollowed-out loaf of crusty bread holds the rich, dill-flavored mousse.

1 (1-lb.) round loaf of bread
1 (15½-oz.) can salmon, drained and flaked
1 (8-oz.) pkg. cream cheese, softened
1 lb. fresh spinach, cooked, drained, chopped and cooled
⅔ c. sliced green onions
2 tblsp. chopped fresh parsley
2 tblsp. chopped fresh dill or 2 tsp. dried dill weed
½ tsp. seasoned salt
⅛ tsp. pepper
1 c. heavy cream, whipped
Assorted crackers

Cut a thin slice from top of bread. Hollow out bread, leaving a 1"-thick shell; set aside. (Reserve inside of loaf to make bread crumbs for another use.)

In large bowl using mixer at medium speed, beat together salmon and remaining ingredients except whipped cream and crackers until well blended. Fold in whipped cream. Spoon salmon mixture into bread shell.

Cover and refrigerate at least 2 hours or until well chilled. Serve with crackers. Makes 4½ c. mousse.

HERB TOMATO STARS

(see photo facing page 86)

It's easy to stuff cherry tomatoes if you use this method to cut them.

2 pt. cherry tomatoes (about 60)
Herb Filling (recipe follows)

Remove stems from tomatoes. Place stem-end down on cutting board. With knife cut an X almost all the way through each tomato.

Gently spread tomato apart. With spoon scoop out and discard pulp.

Prepare Herb Filling.

Spoon filling into pastry bag fitted with large star tube. Pipe filling into center of each tomato.

Cover and refrigerate until ready to serve. Makes 60 appetizers.

Herb Filling: In medium bowl using mixer at medium speed, beat 2 (8-oz.) pkg. cream cheese, softened, ¼ c. finely chopped fresh parsley, 2 tblsp. grated onion, ¼ tsp. dried tarragon leaves and 2 small cloves garlic, minced, until light and fluffy.

OVEN-FRIED BROCCOLI FLOWERETS

(see photo facing page 86)

Serve these bite-size morsels of broccoli straight from the oven.

1½ c. dairy sour cream
1 tsp. Worcestershire sauce
½ tsp. garlic salt
1 bunch broccoli, cut into flowerets with 1″ stems
½ c. crushed cornflakes

In bowl stir together sour cream, Worcestershire sauce and garlic salt.

Dip broccoli flowerets into sour cream mixture, then roll in crushed cornflakes to coat. Place on greased baking sheet.

Bake in 400° oven 20 minutes or until tender-crisp. Serve warm. Makes about 48 appetizers.

FALAFEL

A spicy Middle Eastern snack that's served with a cool yogurt dressing.

2 (20-oz.) cans chick peas, drained and mashed
½ c. finely chopped celery
⅓ c. finely chopped onion
3 tblsp. sesame seed, toasted
1½ tsp. salt
½ tsp. ground turmeric
½ tsp. ground cumin
¼ tsp. ground red pepper
3 cloves garlic
2 eggs
Sesame Yogurt Sauce (recipe follows)
Flour
1 qt. vegetable oil

In large bowl stir together first 3 ingredients; set aside.

In blender container place sesame seed, salt, turmeric, cumin, red pepper, garlic and 1 egg; cover. Blend at high speed until smooth, stopping several times to scrape down sides of blender. Blend in remaining egg.

Pour egg mixture into chick pea mixture; stir until well blended. Cover and refrigerate 1 hour or until easy to handle. Meanwhile, prepare Sesame Yogurt Sauce.

With floured hands shape chilled chick pea mixture into 1″ balls. Roll balls in flour until well coated.

In 3-qt. saucepan over medium-high heat, heat oil to 365° on a deep-fat thermometer. Add 9 balls; fry about 3 minutes or until golden brown. Remove balls; drain on paper towels. Repeat with remaining balls.

Serve balls warm with sauce. Makes 54 appetizers.

Sesame Yogurt Sauce: In blender container place 2 tblsp. sesame seed, toasted, 2 tblsp. lemon juice and 2 tsp. water; cover. Blend at high speed until smooth, stopping several times to scrape down sides of blender.

Pour into small bowl; stir in ½ c. dairy sour cream, ½ c. plain yogurt, ¼ c. chopped green onions and 2 tblsp. chopped fresh parsley until well blended. Makes 1¼ c.

FRIED POTATO SKINS

These taste a lot like home fries, and you could serve them with many toppings; we've listed just three.

3 large baking potatoes, quartered
1 qt. vegetable oil
Salt; or Parmesan Topping, Mexican Topping or Pizza Topping (recipes follow)

Cut each potato quarter in half, lengthwise. Then cut potato from skins, leaving about 1/4" potato on skins; set aside skins. Place remaining potatoes in water; refrigerate for another use.

In 3-qt. saucepan over medium-high heat, heat oil to 365° on a deep-fat thermometer. With paper towels pat dry potato skins.

Add half of the skins to hot oil; cook about 4 minutes or until golden brown. Remove; drain on paper towels. Repeat with remaining skins.

Sprinkle with salt or top with desired toppings. Serve warm. Makes 24 appetizers.

Parmesan Topping: Sprinkle fried skins with 1/4 c. grated Parmesan cheese.

Mexican Topping: Place fried skins on large baking sheet, skin-side down. Top with 1/4 c. bottled taco sauce; sprinkle with 1 c. shredded Monterey Jack cheese. Then sprinkle with 1/4 c. chopped ripe olives or 1/4 c. chopped pickled hot peppers.

Bake in 350° oven 5 minutes, or just until cheese melts. Serve warm.

Pizza Topping: Place fried skins on large baking sheet, skin-side down. Top with 1/4 c. bottled pizza or spaghetti sauce; sprinkle with 1 c. shredded mozzarella cheese.

Bake in 350° oven 5 minutes, or just until cheese melts. Serve warm.

SPINACH-CARROT PHYLLO ROULADES

(see photo facing page 86)

Two smooth purées wrapped in flaky phyllo make this a special treat.

Carrot Purée (see Index)
Spinach Purée (see Index)
3 eggs
1 1/2 c. shredded Swiss cheese (6 oz.)
18 sheets phyllo
2/3 c. butter or regular margarine, melted

Prepare Carrot and Spinach Purées; place in separate bowls. Cover and refrigerate about 4 hours or until well chilled.

Stir 1 egg into Carrot Purée until well blended; then stir in cheese. Stir remaining 2 eggs into Spinach Purée until well blended; set aside.

For each roulade: Brush 6 sheets of phyllo with some of the melted butter. Stack sheets. Cover remaining phyllo with plastic wrap while making roulade.

Starting 2" from one long side, spread one-third of the carrot mixture in a 3"-wide strip to within 2" of the short sides. Spread one-third of the spinach mixture on top of the carrot mixture.

Fold each short side 2" over filling. Starting with the long side nearest the filling, roll up, jelly-roll fashion.

Repeat with remaining phyllo, melted butter, carrot and spinach mixtures, making 2 more roulades. Roulades can be wrapped and frozen at this point. (Thaw at room temperature 1 hour before baking.)

Place roulades, seam-side down, on greased baking sheets. Brush with remaining melted butter. Bake roulades in 375° oven 25 minutes (if thawed, 35 minutes) or until golden.

Cool 15 minutes. To serve, use serrated knife to cut each roulade into 12 slices. Makes 3 roulades or 36 slices.

MINIATURE CARROT PATTIES

You can make these in advance, then reheat in a 350° oven 10 minutes.

Creamy Cucumber-Dill Dressing
  (see Index)
3 c. soft bread crumbs
1½ c. shredded carrots
3 tblsp. finely chopped onion
¾ tsp. baking powder
½ tsp. salt
⅛ tsp. pepper
¼ c. milk
2 eggs, slightly beaten
4 tblsp. butter or regular margarine

Prepare Creamy Cucumber-Dill Dressing. Cover and refrigerate.

In large bowl stir bread crumbs, carrots, onion, baking powder, salt and pepper until well blended. Stir in milk and eggs.

With your hands, shape carrot mixture into 1¼" balls. Flatten each ball to form a small patty.

In 10" skillet over medium heat, melt 2 tblsp. butter. Add half of the patties; cook until golden brown on both sides. Remove; drain on paper towels. Repeat with remaining butter and patties.

Serve patties warm with dressing. Makes about 28 patties.

SPINACH PUFFS

Ricotta cheese gives the filling a melt-in-your-mouth creaminess.

1 lb. fresh spinach, cooked, well drained
  and chopped
1 c. ricotta cheese
½ c. grated Parmesan cheese
½ tsp. salt
¼ tsp. ground nutmeg
⅛ tsp. pepper
1 egg
16 sheets phyllo
2 tblsp. butter or regular margarine, melted

In medium bowl stir together all ingredients except phyllo and butter; set aside.

Cut each sheet of phyllo crosswise into 4 (3"-wide) strips. Cover strips with plastic wrap while making puffs.

For each puff: Stack 2 phyllo strips. Place a rounded teaspoonful of spinach mixture at one end of strip; fold over each long side of phyllo. Roll up jelly-roll fashion. Brush with melted butter.

Repeat with remaining phyllo strips, spinach mixture and melted butter. Puffs can be wrapped and frozen at this point.

Place fresh or frozen puffs, seam-side down, on greased baking sheets. Bake in 350° oven 25 minutes or until lightly browned. Serve immediately. Makes 32 puffs.

CRISPY SQUASH BALLS

Crunchy on the outside, these little tidbits have smooth, nutty centers.

1 (2½-lb.) butternut squash
¾ c. unsifted flour
¼ c. finely chopped onion
½ tsp. baking powder
½ tsp. salt
⅛ tsp. pepper
1 egg, slightly beaten
½ c. chopped peanuts
3 c. cornflakes, coarsely crushed
1 qt. vegetable oil

Cut squash into quarters; scoop out seeds. In 3-qt. saucepan over medium heat, bring 1" water to a boil. Add squash. Cover and cook until tender. Drain, peel and mash squash. (There should be 2 c. mashed squash.)

In large bowl stir together mashed squash, flour, onion, baking powder, salt, pepper and egg until smooth. Stir in peanuts.

Shape mixture into 1" balls; roll in crushed cornflakes until well coated.

In 3-qt. saucepan over medium-high heat, heat oil to 375° on a deep-fat thermometer. Cook squash balls, 4 at a time, in hot oil about 2 minutes or until golden brown. Remove; drain on paper towels. Serve immediately. Makes 28 balls.

4

Country Soups

Try to name a soup that's made without vegetables!

Without leeks and potatoes, beans and tomatoes, celery and squash and all the other vegetables, we'd have no vichyssoise to offer as a prelude to a midsummer supper, no chunky chowders to warm a winter's evening, and no delicate, creamy asparagus soup to celebrate the return of spring.

Soup is a perfect vehicle for vegetables. Some soups are so simple that they don't even need to be cooked; Chilled Cucumber Soup and Souper Gazpacho are both made in a food processor or blender. Simmered together, a mix of fresh produce can become such vegetarian delights as minestrone, Creamy Vegetable Soup, and a thick, satisfying Vegetable-Lentil Chowder.

Once you've tasted your own homemade Cream of Tomato Soup or Cream of Celery Soup, you'll think twice about using the canned variety. If you like the flavor of oysters, you'll probably enjoy Salsify Soup and eagerly look forward to salsify's arrival in the markets during October and November. The smoky flavor of bacon adds something special to Curried Broccoli Soup and to Dutch Potato Soup, a Michigan farm woman's recipe for a substantial soup that's rich and creamy.

Vegetables are good partners for meats and poultry, blending with their flavors to produce a rich and satisfying taste. Many stew-like soups and chowders in this chapter are good main dishes: Chicken Gumbo, Turkey Soup with Parslied Dumplings, and a chunky soup made with shin beef or beef shanks and topped with a pretty pastry cap. Chicken Jambalaya Soup is a knife-and-fork soup of cut-up chicken, tomatoes, zucchini, sweet peppers and fresh seasonings. Meatball and Pasta Soup (see photo following page 182) and Chunky Lentil Soup are both brimming with vegetables; serve either one with a crusty loaf of bread and a crisp salad, and you couldn't wish for a better meal on a cool autumn evening.

The trimmings from vegetables make a fine stock, so don't toss out the stems, skins, leaves and tops. Simmer them in an equal amount of water and soon you'll have a versatile vegetable stock to use as a base for soups, sauces or gravies; for the recipe, just turn the page.

VEGETABLE STOCK

*Use this flavorful, meatless stock
to make soups, sauces and gravies.*

2 qt. slightly packed cut-up vegetables
  and trimmings (stems, skins, leaves
  and tops)
2 qt. water
1 tblsp. salt

A stock can be made from any
combination of vegetables, and its
color and flavor will depend upon
your choice of ingredients. For a
mild, full-flavored stock, choose a
mix from among these: carrots,
potatoes, spinach, green beans, peas,
zucchini, summer squash, celery,
lettuce, mushrooms and onions.

Vegetables such as broccoli, cabbage, cauliflower and parsnips will
make a stronger-flavored stock.

In 4-qt. Dutch oven over high
heat, bring all ingredients to a boil.
Reduce heat to low.

Cover and simmer 20 minutes.
Remove from heat. Let stand,
covered, 20 minutes.

Ladle mixture into cheesecloth-
lined strainer. Pour stock into 1-c.
containers. Cover and refrigerate
up to 1 week, or freeze to use within
3 months. Makes 2½ qt.

CHILLED CUCUMBER SOUP

*Blend buttermilk, cucumbers and
fresh dill into a smooth refresher.*

3 medium cucumbers, peeled, seeded and
  chopped (3¼ c.)
1 medium onion, chopped
1 clove garlic, minced
3 c. buttermilk
¼ c. chopped walnuts
1 tblsp. chopped fresh dill or 1 tsp. dried
  dill weed
1 c. dairy sour cream
¼ tsp. salt
Dash white pepper
Fresh dill sprigs

In large bowl stir together first 6
ingredients.

In blender container or food processor bowl using metal blade place
half of the cucumber mixture; cover.
Blend at high speed or process until
smooth. Pour into another bowl.
Repeat with remaining cucumber
mixture.

Stir in sour cream, salt and pepper until well blended. Cover and
refrigerate at least 12 hours to blend
flavors.

To serve, ladle soup into bowls;
garnish with dill sprigs. Makes
6 (1-c.) servings.

CONTINENTAL BORSCHT

*If you're counting calories, skip the
sour cream—it's only a garnish.*

1 medium onion, chopped
2½ c. shredded fresh beets (about 3)
1 c. chopped carrots
3 c. water
1 tsp. salt
⅛ tsp. pepper
2 c. beef broth
1 c. shredded cabbage
1 tblsp. butter or regular margarine
1 tblsp. lemon juice
½ c. dairy sour cream

In 3-qt. saucepan over high heat
bring onion, beets, carrots, water,
salt and pepper to a boil. Reduce
heat to low. Cover and simmer 20
minutes or until vegetables are
tender.

Stir in beef broth and cabbage.
Cook, uncovered, 15 minutes. Stir in
butter and lemon juice.

To serve, ladle soup into bowls;
garnish with dollops of sour cream.
Or, to serve chilled, cover and
refrigerate at least 12 hours to blend
flavors. Makes 6 (1-c.) servings.

TO MICROWAVE: Use same ingredients, *changing amounts as indicated.*

In 3-qt. microwave-safe casserole, place onion, beets, carrots, cabbage and butter. Cover with lid or plastic wrap, turning back one section to vent steam. Microwave at high setting (100% power) 8 to 12 minutes or until vegetables are tender, stirring every 2 minutes.

Stir in *1¾ c. water,* salt, pepper and *1½ c. beef broth.* Cover again, and microwave at high setting 16 to 20 minutes or until vegetables are tender, stirring every 5 minutes. Stir in lemon juice. Let stand, covered, 5 minutes. Serve as directed.

SOUPER GAZPACHO

A no-cook soup that's a cool beginning for a summer meal.

1 (10¾-oz.) can condensed tomato soup
2 slices white bread, diced
3 c. tomato juice
1 c. water
1 c. chopped tomato
1 c. chopped green pepper
1 c. chopped peeled cucumber
½ c. chopped onion
¼ c. vinegar
2 tblsp. vegetable oil
4 drops hot pepper sauce
1 clove garlic, minced
Toasted Croutons (see Index)

In large bowl stir together all ingredients except croutons.

In blender container or food processor bowl using metal blade place half of the mixture; cover. Blend at high speed or process until smooth. Pour into another bowl. Repeat with remaining mixture.

Cover and refrigerate at least 3 hours to blend flavors.

To serve, ladle soup into bowls; garnish with croutons. Makes 7 (1-c.) servings.

TOMATO-DILL BISQUE

For full flavor, use the ripest, juiciest tomatoes you can find.

3 tblsp. butter or regular margarine
1 medium onion, chopped
1 clove garlic, minced
5 medium tomatoes, peeled, seeded and chopped (2 lb.)
1 c. chicken broth
2 tsp. chopped fresh dill or ¾ tsp. dried dill weed
½ tsp. sugar
¼ tsp. celery salt
⅛ tsp. pepper
½ c. milk
Fresh dill sprigs

In 3-qt. saucepan over medium-high heat, melt butter. Add onion and garlic; cook until onion is tender.

Stir in tomatoes and remaining ingredients except milk and dill sprigs; bring to a boil. Reduce heat to low. Cover and simmer 10 minutes. Cool slightly.

Cover and refrigerate at least 12 hours or until well chilled.

In blender container place half of the tomato mixture; cover. Blend at high speed until smooth. Pour into bowl. Repeat with remaining tomato mixture. Stir in milk.

To serve, ladle soup into bowls; garnish with dill sprigs. Makes 4 (1-c.) servings.

TO MICROWAVE: Use same ingredients.

In 2-qt. microwave-safe casserole place butter, onion and garlic. Cover with lid or plastic wrap, turning back one section to vent steam.

Microwave at high setting (100% power) 4 to 5 minutes or until onion is tender, stirring after 3 minutes. Stir in tomatoes and remaining ingredients except milk and dill sprigs.

Microwave, uncovered, at high setting 5 to 7 minutes or until tomatoes are soft, stirring after 3 minutes.

Chill, blend, add milk and serve as directed.

VICHYSSOISE

A classic cold soup of leeks and potatoes, enriched with cream.

3 tblsp. butter or regular margarine
4 medium leeks, finely chopped (2½ c.)
3 ribs celery, finely chopped
1 medium onion, finely chopped
2 medium potatoes, peeled and thinly sliced
4 c. chicken broth
2 tblsp. chopped fresh parsley
⅛ tsp. white pepper
⅛ tsp. ground nutmeg
3 drops Worcestershire sauce
1 c. heavy cream
Chopped chives

In 3-qt. saucepan over medium heat, melt butter. Add leeks, celery and onion; cook until vegetables are tender.

Stir in potatoes and remaining ingredients except cream and chives; bring to a boil.

Reduce heat to low. Cover and simmer 15 minutes or until potatoes are tender. Cool slightly.

In blender container place half of potato mixture; cover. Blend at high speed until smooth. Pour into bowl. Repeat with remaining potato mixture.

Stir in cream. Cover and refrigerate at least 12 hours to blend flavors.

To serve, ladle soup into bowls; garnish with chives. Makes 6 (1-c.) servings.

TO MICROWAVE: Use same ingredients, *reducing chicken broth as indicated.*

In 3-qt. microwave-safe casserole place butter. Microwave, uncovered, at high setting (100% power) 1 to 2 minutes or until melted.

Stir in leeks, celery, onion, potatoes and parsley. Cover with lid or plastic wrap, turning back one section to vent steam. Microwave at high setting 8 to 11 minutes or until vegetables are almost tender, stirring every 3 minutes.

Stir in *3 cups chicken broth,* pepper, nutmeg and Worcestershire sauce. Cover again, and microwave at high setting 8 to 12 minutes or

until potatoes are tender, stirring every 3 minutes. Cool slightly.

Blend, add cream, chill and serve as directed.

FRENCH ONION SOUP

Crusty bread and shredded Swiss cheese top the full-flavored broth.

¼ c. butter or regular margarine
6 medium onions, thinly sliced
1 tsp. sugar
1 tblsp. flour
1 c. dry white wine
4 c. beef broth
⅛ tsp. pepper
6 (½″) slices French bread, toasted
2 c. shredded Swiss cheese (8 oz.)
½ c. grated Parmesan cheese
Paprika

In 4-qt. Dutch oven over medium-high heat, melt butter. Add onions and sugar; cook, stirring occasionally, 30 minutes or until onions are tender and browned.

Stir in flour until well blended. Gradually stir in wine; cook, stirring constantly, until mixture boils and thickens.

Stir in beef broth and pepper; bring to a boil. Reduce heat to low. Cover and simmer 30 minutes.

Into 6 (1½-c. or 12-oz.) oven-proof crocks or bowls, ladle 1 c. soup. Top each with a bread slice; sprinkle with Swiss and Parmesan cheese. Sprinkle with paprika. Place crocks on jelly-roll pan.

Bake in 350° oven 25 to 30 minutes or until cheese melts and browns. Makes 6 (1-c.) servings.

TO MICROWAVE: Use same ingredients, *changing amounts as indicated.*

In 3-qt. microwave-safe casserole place butter. Microwave at high setting (100% power) 2 to 3 minutes or until melted.

Stir in onions and *2 tsp. sugar* until well blended. Cover with lid or plastic wrap, turning back one section to vent steam. Microwave at high setting 11 to 13 minutes or until onions are tender, stirring every 5 minutes.

Stir in 4½ tsp. *flour* until well blended. Stir in beef broth, pepper and ¾ *c. wine.*

Microwave, uncovered, at high setting 16 to 18 minutes or until mixture boils and thickens, stirring every 5 minutes.

Into 6 (1½-c. or 12-oz.) microwave-safe crocks or bowls, ladle 1 c. soup. Top each with a bread slice, then sprinkle with Swiss and Parmesan cheese. Sprinkle with paprika.

Place 3 crocks in a triangle in oven. Microwave at high setting 4 to 8 minutes or until cheese melts and soup is hot, rearranging crocks after 3 minutes. Repeat with remaining crocks.

CABBAGE PATCH SOUP

Thick with peas, carrots and cabbage — a tummy-warming soup.

5 slices bacon, diced
¼ c. chopped onion
¼ c. chopped celery
¼ c. flour
½ tsp. salt
⅛ tsp. pepper
3 c. chicken broth
2 c. shredded cabbage
1 c. chopped carrots
½ bay leaf
1 c. fresh or frozen peas, thawed
¾ c. dairy sour cream
2 tblsp. chopped fresh parsley

In 3-qt. saucepan over medium-high heat, cook bacon until browned. Drain bacon on paper towels. Pour off all but 2 tblsp. bacon drippings.

In bacon drippings over medium heat, cook onion and celery until tender. Gradually stir in flour, salt and pepper until well blended. Gradually stir in chicken broth until well blended.

Over high heat cook, stirring constantly, until mixture boils and thickens.

Stir in cabbage, carrots and bay leaf. Reduce heat to low. Cover and simmer 10 minutes or just until vegetables are tender.

Stir in peas; cook until tender. Remove bay leaf.

Remove saucepan from heat. In small bowl gradually stir some of the hot mixture into sour cream. Then stir sour cream mixture back into saucepan.

To serve, ladle soup into bowls; garnish with bacon and parsley. Makes 5 (1-c.) servings.

TO MICROWAVE: Use same ingredients.

In 3-qt. microwave-safe casserole place bacon. Cover with waxed paper. Microwave at high setting (100% power) 3 to 5 minutes or until crisp. Drain on paper towels. Pour off all but 2 tblsp. bacon drippings.

Add onion and celery to bacon drippings. Cover again, and microwave at high setting 2 to 3 minutes or until tender, stirring after 2 minutes.

Stir in flour, salt and pepper until well blended. Gradually stir in chicken broth until well blended. Cover again, and microwave at high setting 7 to 9 minutes or until mixture boils, stirring every 2 minutes.

Stir in cabbage, carrots and bay leaf. Cover again, and microwave at high setting 10 minutes or until vegetables are tender, stirring after 5 minutes.

Stir in peas. Cover again, and microwave at high setting 2 minutes. Remove bay leaf.

In small bowl gradually stir some of the hot mixture into sour cream. Then stir sour cream mixture back into casserole. Serve as directed.

VEGETABLE CHOWDER

This soup is a lot like minestrone, and it's good served hot or cold.

1 (28-oz.) can whole tomatoes
2 (13¾-oz.) cans beef broth
1 (15½-oz.) can kidney beans, drained
1½ c. diced zucchini
1½ c. coarsely chopped onions
1 c. sliced carrots
1 c. diagonally sliced, fresh green beans
  (1" pieces)
1 c. sliced celery
1 c. water
2 tsp. dried basil leaves
1 tsp. salt
¼ tsp. pepper
¾ c. elbow macaroni

In 4-qt. Dutch oven stir tomatoes until broken into small pieces. Stir in beef broth and remaining ingredients except macaroni. Over high heat bring to a boil.

Stir in macaroni; reduce heat to low. Cover and simmer 15 minutes or until vegetables and macaroni are tender. Makes 10 (1-c.) servings.

ZUCCHINI SOUP

A rich tomato sauce gives it color, and Parmesan cheese is the garnish.

1 lb. zucchini, cut into ⅛" slices
1 (8-oz.) can tomato sauce
1 medium onion, chopped
1½ c. beef broth
2 tblsp. chopped fresh parsley
¼ tsp. salt
¼ tsp. dried basil leaves
¼ tsp. dried oregano leaves
⅛ tsp. garlic powder
⅛ tsp. pepper
Grated Parmesan cheese

In 2-qt. saucepan over high heat, bring all ingredients except cheese to a boil. Reduce heat to medium. Cover and simmer, stirring occasionally, 10 minutes or until zucchini is tender.

To serve, ladle soup into bowls; garnish with cheese. Makes 4 (1-c.) servings.

TO MICROWAVE: Use same ingredients.

In 2-qt. microwave-safe casserole place all ingredients except cheese. Cover with lid or plastic wrap, turning back one section to vent steam.

Microwave at high setting (100% power) 10 minutes. Stir. Microwave 5 to 8 minutes more or until zucchini is tender, stirring every 2 minutes. Let stand, covered, 5 minutes. Serve as directed.

VALENCIA SOUP

This Spanish-style soup combines ham, potatoes, tomatoes and rice.

2 tblsp. vegetable oil
1 small onion, minced
2 c. diced peeled potatoes (¼" pieces)
2 c. shredded cabbage
1 tblsp. chopped fresh parsley
6 c. chicken broth
1 c. cut-up canned tomatoes
1 c. diced cooked ham (¼" pieces)
⅛ tsp. pepper
3 tblsp. uncooked long-grain rice
1 c. fresh or frozen peas

In 4-qt. Dutch oven over medium-high heat, heat oil until hot. Add onion, potatoes, cabbage and parsley; cook 10 minutes or until cabbage is wilted and potatoes are slightly soft.

Stir in chicken broth, tomatoes, ham and pepper; bring to a boil. Reduce heat to low. Cover and simmer 20 minutes.

Stir in rice. Cover and simmer 18 minutes. Stir in peas; simmer 2 minutes or until peas are tender. Makes 6 main-dish or 9 (1-c.) servings.

TO MICROWAVE: Use same ingredients, *changing amounts as indicated.*

In 3-qt. microwave-safe casserole place potatoes and *1 tblsp. oil.* Cover with lid or plastic wrap, turning back one section to vent steam. Microwave at high setting (100% power) 2 minutes.

Stir in onion, cabbage and parsley. Cover again, and microwave at high setting 3 to 4 minutes, stirring after 2 minutes.

Stir in tomatoes, ham, pepper and *5 c. chicken broth.* Cover again, and microwave at high setting 15 minutes, stirring every 5 minutes.

Microwave at medium setting (50% power) 10 to 12 minutes, or until vegetables are almost tender and soup is boiling, stirring after 6 minutes.

Stir in peas; *omit rice.* Cover again, and microwave at medium setting 3 to 4 minutes or until peas are tender. Let stand, covered, 5 minutes.

GARDEN ROW SOUP

A chunky, knife-and-fork soup that's brimful of fresh vegetables.

8 c. beef broth
½ tsp. dried oregano leaves
½ tsp. dried marjoram leaves
½ tsp. celery seed
⅛ tsp. ground cumin seed
6 whole peppercorns
1 clove garlic, minced
4 carrots, cut into ¼" slices
3 ears corn, cut into 3" pieces
1 large onion, chopped
¼ c. chopped parsley
¼ lb. green beans, cut into 1" pieces (1 c.)
2 large tomatoes, peeled and cut into 1" chunks
1 medium zucchini, cut into ½" slices
1 large sweet green pepper, cut into ¼" strips

In 4-qt. Dutch oven over high heat, bring first 7 ingredients to a boil. Reduce heat to low. Cover and simmer 30 minutes. Remove peppercorns.

Add carrots, corn, onion and parsley. Cover and simmer 20 minutes.

Add green beans. Cover and simmer 15 minutes. Stir in tomatoes, zucchini and green pepper. Cover and simmer 8 minutes or until vegetables are tender. Makes 12 (1-c.) servings.

ESCAROLE SOUP

Leafy kale tastes just as good in this chicken broth-and-rice soup.

8 c. chicken broth
3 c. tightly packed, chopped escarole (about 1 lb.)
¾ c. uncooked long-grain rice
2 tblsp. lemon juice
⅛ tsp. pepper
Grated Parmesan cheese

In 4-qt. Dutch oven over high heat, bring chicken broth to a boil. Stir in escarole, rice, lemon juice and pepper; bring to a boil.

Reduce heat to low. Cover and simmer 20 minutes or until rice is tender.

To serve, ladle soup into bowls; garnish with cheese. Makes 9 (1-c.) servings.

POTATO-LEEK SOUP

*This hot, bacon-flavored soup
tastes just as good served chilled.*

3 tblsp. butter or regular margarine
2 lb. leeks, sliced (4 c.)
1 lb. potatoes, peeled and diced
4 c. chicken broth
⅛ tsp. pepper
1 bay leaf
½ c. dairy sour cream
4 slices bacon, cooked, drained
    and crumbled

In 3-qt. saucepan over medium
heat, melt butter. Add leeks; cook
until tender.

Stir in potatoes, chicken broth,
pepper and bay leaf; bring to a boil.

Reduce heat to low. Cover and
simmer 20 minutes or until potatoes
are tender. Remove bay leaf. Cool
slightly.

In blender container place half of
the potato mixture; cover. Blend at
high speed until almost smooth.
Pour into bowl. Repeat with remaining potato mixture.

Pour blended mixture back into
saucepan. Gradually stir in sour
cream. Over low heat cook 3 minutes
or until heated through.

To serve, ladle soup into bowls;
garnish with bacon. Serve hot or
cold. Makes about 6 (1-c.) servings.

Watercress Soup: Use same ingredients, adding 1 bunch watercress,
finely chopped (1½ c.), to blended
potato mixture.

Pour watercress mixture back into
saucepan. Over low heat cook 3 minutes or until heated through. Serve
as directed. Makes 7 (1-c.) servings.

TO MICROWAVE: Use same ingredients,
reducing chicken broth as indicated.

In 3-qt. microwave-safe casserole
place butter, leeks and potatoes.
Cover with lid or plastic wrap, turning back one section to vent steam.

Microwave at high setting (100%
power) 6 to 8 minutes or until vegetables are tender, stirring every 2
minutes.

Stir in *3½ c. chicken broth,*
pepper and bay leaf. Cover again,
and microwave at high setting 8 to
12 minutes or until mixture boils,
stirring every 4 minutes. Remove
bay leaf. Cool slightly.

Blend, add sour cream and serve
as directed.

If preparing Watercress Soup, stir
chopped watercress into blended
potato mixture. Return watercress
mixture to casserole.

Cover again, and microwave at
medium setting (50% power) 2 to
3 minutes or until heated through.

DUTCH POTATO SOUP

*A Michigan farm woman's recipe
for a creamy, bacon-flavored soup.*

4 c. cubed peeled potatoes (½" cubes),
    about 10 medium potatoes
3 c. water
1½ tsp. salt
¼ tsp. dried thyme leaves
⅛ tsp. pepper
6 slices bacon, diced
1 medium onion, chopped
2 tblsp. flour
1 c. milk

In 3-qt. saucepan over high heat,
bring potatoes, water, salt, thyme
and pepper to a boil. Reduce heat to
low. Cover and simmer 15 minutes
or until potatoes are tender.

Meanwhile, in 10" skillet over
medium-high heat, cook bacon until
browned. Drain on paper towels.
Reserve 2 tblsp. bacon drippings

Drain potatoes, reserving broth.
Mash half of the potatoes. Set aside
broth, potatoes and mashed

potatoes. Wipe saucepan dry.

In same saucepan over medium heat, heat reserved bacon drippings until hot. Add onion; cook until tender. Stir in flour until well blended.

Gradually stir in reserved broth until smooth. Stir in mashed potatoes until smooth. Add bacon and cubed potatoes; cook, stirring constantly, until soup is slightly thickened. Stir in milk; cook until heated through. Makes 6 (1-c.) servings.

CREAMY VEGETABLE SOUP

Have-on-hand ingredients are the makings of this quick, easy soup.

3 c. water
2 c. shredded peeled potatoes (4 medium)
1 c. shredded carrot (1 large)
½ c. shredded onions (2 medium)
2 tblsp. chopped fresh parsley
1½ tsp. salt
⅛ tsp. white pepper
3 c. evaporated milk, warmed
1 tblsp. butter or regular margarine
1 tblsp. chopped fresh dill

In 3-qt. saucepan over high heat, bring all ingredients except milk, butter and dill to a boil. Reduce heat to low.

Cover and simmer 20 minutes. Remove from heat. Gradually stir in warm evaporated milk and butter until well blended.

To serve, ladle soup into bowls; garnish with dill. Makes 8 (1-c.) servings.

ORIENTAL VEGETABLE SOUP

Chicken, snow peas and cabbage simmer in a clear, gingery broth.

½ oz. dried mushrooms
2 c. boiling water
1 (8-oz.) can sliced bamboo shoots
1 cooked whole chicken breast, skinned, boned and cut into 2x⅛" strips
8 c. chicken broth
¼ c. dry sherry
1 tblsp. soy sauce
1 tsp. grated fresh ginger root
½ lb. bean curd (tofu), cut into ½" chunks
½ lb. snow peas, trimmed
4 c. shredded Chinese cabbage
2 tblsp. water
1 tblsp. cornstarch
¼ c. chopped green onions

In small bowl soak mushrooms in boiling water 30 minutes. Drain; remove stems and slice caps.

In 4-qt. Dutch oven over high heat bring mushrooms, bamboo shoots, chicken, chicken broth, sherry, soy sauce and ginger to a boil.

Reduce heat to low. Cover and simmer 5 minutes. Add bean curd, snow peas and cabbage. Over medium heat simmer 5 minutes.

In small bowl stir together water and cornstarch; stir into soup. Cook, stirring constantly, until soup boils and thickens.

To serve, ladle soup into bowls; garnish with green onions. Makes 8 main-dish or 12 (1-c.) servings.

CREAM OF TOMATO SOUP

Both the microwave and range-top methods take less than 20 minutes.

3 large ripe tomatoes, peeled and cut into 2" chunks
½ c. water
1 chicken bouillon cube
1½ tblsp. butter or regular margarine
1 tblsp. fresh or freeze-dried chopped chives
1 tsp. dried basil leaves
¼ tsp. seasoned salt
1 c. milk, warmed
Tomato slices
Chopped green onions

In 3-qt. saucepan over high heat, bring all ingredients except milk, tomato slices and green onions to a boil. Reduce heat to low. Cover and simmer 10 minutes. Remove from heat. Cool slightly.

In blender container place half of the tomato mixture; cover. Blend at high speed until smooth. Pour into bowl. Repeat with remaining tomato mixture.

Pour blended mixture back into saucepan. Gradually stir in warm milk. Over low heat, cook 3 minutes or until heated through.

To serve, ladle soup into bowls; garnish with tomato slices and green onions. Makes 4 (1-c.) servings.

TO MICROWAVE: Use same ingredients, *changing amounts as indicated.*

In 3-qt. microwave-safe casserole place butter. Microwave, uncovered, at high setting (100% power) 1½ to 2 minutes or until melted.

Dissolve bouillon cube in *2 tblsp. warm water.* Stir dissolved bouillon, tomatoes, chives, basil and seasoned salt into butter. (Do not add *½ c. water.*) Microwave at high setting 6 to 8 minutes or until tomatoes are soft, stirring after 4 minutes. Cool slightly.

In blender container place half of the tomato mixture; cover. Blend at high speed until smooth. Pour into bowl. Repeat with remaining tomato mixture. Pour blended mixture back

into casserole. Gradually stir in warm milk.

Microwave, uncovered, at high setting 2 to 4 minutes or until heated through, stirring after 1 minute. Serve as directed.

CURRIED BROCCOLI SOUP

The flavors of mushrooms, bacon, onion and broccoli in a savory blend.

6 slices bacon, diced
¼ lb. mushrooms, sliced
1 medium onion, chopped
3½ cups chopped fresh broccoli (1 large bunch)
2 c. chicken broth
½ tsp. curry powder
¼ tsp. salt
⅛ tsp. pepper
1 tblsp. cornstarch
2½ c. light cream or milk

In 4-qt. Dutch oven over medium-high heat, cook bacon until browned. Drain on paper towels. Pour off all but 2 tblsp. bacon drippings.

In bacon drippings over medium heat, cook mushrooms and onion until tender.

Stir bacon, broccoli, chicken broth, curry powder, salt and pepper into mushroom mixture; bring to a boil. Cover and simmer 8 minutes or until broccoli is just tender.

In small bowl, stir together cornstarch and milk.

Reduce heat to low. Gradually stir milk mixture into soup. Cook, stirring constantly, until mixture boils and thickens. Makes 6 (1-c.) servings.

CURRIED SQUASH BISQUE

A creamy, delicately flavored soup that's made with Cheddar cheese.

1 c. sliced carrots
1 c. water
½ c. chopped onion
¾ tsp. salt
1 chicken bouillon cube
2 medium yellow summer squash or
zucchini, halved lengthwise and sliced
2 c. milk
¼ c. flour
1 tsp. curry powder
1 (13-oz.) can evaporated milk
1 c. shredded Cheddar cheese (4 oz.)

In 3-qt. saucepan over high heat, bring first 5 ingredients to a boil. Reduce heat to low. Cover and simmer 5 minutes.

Stir in squash; simmer, covered, 5 minutes. In jar with tight-fitting lid shake together milk, flour and curry powder until blended. Stir milk mixture into squash mixture.

Over medium heat cook, stirring constantly, until mixture boils and thickens.

Remove from heat. Gradually stir in evaporated milk and cheese. Over low heat cook 3 minutes, stirring constantly, or until heated through. Makes 6 (1-c.) servings.

TO MICROWAVE: Use same ingredients.
In 3-qt. microwave-safe casserole place first 5 ingredients. Cover with lid or plastic wrap, turning back one section to vent steam.

Microwave at high setting (100% power) 8 to 10 minutes or until vegetables are tender, stirring after 5 minutes.

Add squash. Cover again, and microwave at high setting 6 to 8 minutes or until squash is tender, stirring after 4 minutes.

In jar with tight-fitting lid, shake together milk, flour and curry powder until well blended. Stir milk mixture into squash mixture.
Microwave, uncovered, at high setting 5 minutes. Stir. Microwave 5 to 7 minutes more or until mixture boils and thickens, stirring after each minute.

Gradually stir in evaporated milk and cheese. Microwave, uncovered, at medium setting (50% power) 2 minutes until cheese melts and soup is heated through, stirring after 1 minute.

CREAMY PARSNIP AND TOMATO SOUP

Simmer parsnips with onions in a tomato sauce for a full-bodied soup.

2 tblsp. butter or regular margarine
2 medium onions, sliced
1 lb. parsnips, peeled and chopped
3 tblsp. flour
½ tsp. salt
½ tsp. dried thyme leaves
⅛ tsp. pepper
4 c. chicken broth
1 (16-oz.) can whole tomatoes
½ c. milk
1 bay leaf
Tomato slices
Parsley sprigs

In 3-qt. saucepan over medium-high heat, melt butter. Add onions; cook until tender. Add parsnips; cook, stirring frequently, until parsnips begin to soften.

Stir in flour, salt, thyme and pepper until well blended. Gradually stir in chicken broth until well blended. Add tomatoes, milk and bay leaf, stirring to break up tomatoes.

Cook, stirring constantly, until mixture boils and thickens.

Reduce heat to low. Cover and simmer 40 minutes or until vegetables are tender. Remove bay leaf. Cool slightly.

In blender container, place half of the parsnip mixture; cover. Blend at high speed until smooth. Pour into bowl. Repeat with remaining parsnip mixture.

To serve, ladle soup into bowls; garnish with tomato slices and parsley. Makes 8 (1-c.) servings.

CREAMY CAULIFLOWER SOUP

If you prefer a smoother soup, cool slightly and blend before serving.

1 medium head cauliflower, broken into flowerets (2½ c.)
2 c. water
2 tblsp. butter or regular margarine
1 large onion, finely chopped
2 tblsp. flour
2 c. chicken broth
½ tsp. Worcestershire sauce
1 c. light cream
1 c. shredded Cheddar cheese (4 oz.)
Chopped chives
Paprika

In 3-qt. sauccpan over high heat bring cauliflower and water to a boil. Cover and simmer 4 minutes or until cauliflower is tender-crisp. Drain cauliflower, reserving 1 c. liquid.

In same saucepan over medium-high heat, melt butter. Add onion; cook until onion is tender.

Stir in flour until well blended. Gradually stir in chicken broth and Worcestershire sauce until well blended. Cook, stirring constantly, until mixture boils and thickens. Reduce heat to low.

Stir in cauliflower, reserved liquid, cream and cheese. Cook 3 minutes, stirring constantly, or until mixture is heated through.

To serve, ladle soup into bowls; garnish with chives and paprika. Makes 5 (1-c.) servings.

TO MICROWAVE: Use same ingredients, *changing amounts as indicated.*

In 3-qt. microwave-safe casserole place cauliflower and *2 tblsp. water.* Cover with lid or plastic wrap, turning back one section to vent steam.

Microwave at high setting (100% power) 5 to 7 minutes or until cauliflower is tender, stirring every 3 minutes. Drain cauliflower and set aside. *Do not reserve liquid.*

In same casserole place butter and onion. Cover again, and microwave at high setting 2 to 3 minutes or until onion is tender, stirring every 1½ minutes.

Stir in flour until well blended. Stir in chicken broth and Worcestershire sauce until well blended. Cover again, and microwave at high setting 5 to 8 minutes or until mixture begins to boil, stirring every 2 minutes.

Stir in cauliflower, cream and cheese. Microwave, uncovered, at medium setting (50% power) 3 to 5 minutes or until mixture is hot and cheese melts, stirring each minute. Serve as directed.

CARROT SOUP

This is good either hot or cold. Try adding 2 tblsp. chopped fresh dill.

2 tblsp. butter or regular margarine
2 medium onions, chopped
6 medium carrots, sliced
4 c. chicken broth
2 tblsp. uncooked long-grain rice
½ tsp. salt
¼ tsp. dried thyme leaves
⅛ tsp. pepper
½ c. light cream
Chopped fresh parsley

In 3-qt. saucepan over medium-high heat, melt butter. Add onions; cook until tender.

Add carrots and remaining ingredients except cream and parsley; bring to a boil. Reduce heat to low; simmer, uncovered, 30 minutes or until carrots are tender. Cool slightly.

In blender container, place half of the carrot mixture; cover. Blend at high speed until smooth. Pour into bowl. Repeat with remaining carrot mixture.

Pour blended mixture back into saucepan. Gradually stir in cream. Over low heat cook 3 minutes until heated through.

To serve, ladle soup into bowls; garnish with parsley. Serve hot or cold. Makes 5 (1-c.) servings.

TO MICROWAVE: Use same ingredients, *changing amounts and adding ingredients as indicated.*

In 3-qt. microwave-safe casserole place butter and onions. Cover with lid or plastic wrap, turning back one section to vent steam. Microwave at high setting (100% power) 3 to 4 minutes or until onions are tender, stirring every 2 minutes.

Add carrots, thyme and ¾ c. *chicken broth.* Cover again, and microwave at high setting 12 to 14 minutes or until carrots are tender, stirring every 3 minutes. Let stand, covered, 2 minutes. Cool slightly.

In blender container place half of the carrot mixture; cover. Blend at high speed until smooth. Pour into bowl. Repeat with remaining carrot mixture.

Pour blended mixture back into casserole. Stir in 4½ tsp. *flour* until smooth; *omit rice.* Stir in 2¾ c. *chicken broth,* salt and pepper.

Cover again, and microwave at high setting 2 to 3 minutes or until hot, stirring each minute. Microwave, uncovered, 5 to 7 minutes or until slightly thickened, stirring every 2 minutes.

Gradually stir in cream. Serve as directed.

CREAM OF CELERY SOUP_____

This pale green soup has a delicate celery flavor. Serve it hot or cold.

2 tblsp. vegetable oil
1 medium onion, chopped
1¾ c. chopped celery
2 tblsp. flour
4 c. water or Vegetable Stock (see Index)
2 medium potatoes, peeled and diced (¼" pieces)
¼ c. chopped fresh parsley
½ tsp. salt
¼ tsp. celery seed
¼ tsp. paprika
⅛ tsp. pepper
1 c. light cream
Celery leaves

In 3-qt. saucepan over medium-high heat, heat oil until hot. Add onion and celery; cook until vegetables are tender.

Stir in flour until well blended. Gradually stir in water until well blended. Stir in potatoes, parsley, salt, celery seed, paprika and pepper.

Cook, stirring constantly, until mixture boils and thickens. Reduce heat to low. Cover and simmer 15 minutes or until potatoes are tender. Cool slightly.

In blender container, place half of the celery mixture; cover. Blend at high speed until smooth. Pour into bowl. Repeat with remaining celery mixture.

Pour blended mixture back into saucepan. Gradually stir in cream. Over low heat cook, stirring constantly, 3 minutes or until heated through.

To serve, ladle soup into bowls; garnish with celery leaves. Serve hot or cold. Makes 8 (1-c.) servings.

CREAM OF ASPARAGUS SOUP

Save those ends of asparagus stalks for an elegant soup; just be sure to simmer the stalks until tender.

2 tblsp. butter or regular margarine
1 medium onion, finely chopped
3 tblsp. flour
4 c. chicken broth
¼ tsp. celery salt
¼ tsp. ground nutmeg
⅛ tsp. pepper
1 lb. asparagus, trimmed and chopped
1 c. light cream
1 hard-cooked egg, sliced

In 3-qt. saucepan over medium-high heat, melt butter. Add onion; cook until tender.

Stir in flour until well blended. Gradually stir in chicken broth, celery salt, nutmeg and pepper until well blended. Cook, stirring constantly, until mixture boils and thickens.

Stir in asparagus; reduce heat to low. Cover and simmer 20 minutes or until asparagus is tender. Cool slightly.

In blender container, place half of the asparagus mixture; cover. Blend at high speed until smooth. Pour into bowl. Repeat with remaining asparagus mixture.

Pour blended mixture back into saucepan. Gradually stir in cream. Over low heat cook 3 minutes or until heated through.

To serve, ladle soup into bowls; garnish with sliced egg. Makes 6 (1-c.) servings.

TO MICROWAVE: Use same ingredients, *changing amounts as indicated.*

In 3-qt. microwave-safe casserole place butter and onion. Cover with lid or plastic wrap, turning back one section to vent steam. Microwave at high setting (100% power) 2 to 3 minutes or until onion is tender, stirring each minute.

Add asparagus and ½ c. chicken broth. Cover again, and microwave at high setting 8 to 10 minutes or until asparagus is tender, stirring every 3 minutes. Let stand, covered, 3 minutes.

In blender container, place half of the asparagus mixture; cover. Blend at high speed until smooth. Pour into bowl. Repeat with remaining asparagus mixture. Pour blended mixture back into casserole.

Stir in flour, celery salt, nutmeg, pepper and *3 c. chicken broth* until smooth. Cover again, and microwave at high setting 2 to 3 minutes, stirring each minute.

Microwave, uncovered, 5 to 7 minutes or until hot and slightly thickened, stirring every 2 minutes.

Gradually stir in cream. Serve as directed.

CREAM OF MUSHROOM SOUP

For a richer soup, whisk in some shredded Cheddar cheese.

½ c. butter or regular margarine
1 lb. fresh mushrooms, sliced
¾ c. chopped onions
½ c. chopped celery
½ c. flour
2 c. milk
2 c. chicken broth
½ tsp. salt
½ tsp. Worcestershire sauce
⅛ tsp. paprika
⅛ tsp. ground nutmeg
Chopped fresh parsley

In 3-qt. saucepan over medium-high heat, melt butter. Add mushrooms, onions and celery; cook until vegetables are tender and lightly browned.

Stir in flour until well blended. Gradually stir in milk, then chicken broth, salt, Worcestershire sauce, paprika and nutmeg.

Reduce heat to medium. Cook 20 minutes or until soup is slightly thickened, stirring occasionally.

To serve, ladle soup into bowls; garnish with parsley. Makes 8 (1-c.) servings.

SALSIFY SOUP

The mild flavor of salsify makes this creamy soup an ideal appetizer.

1 tblsp. vinegar
Water
¾ lb. salsify
2 tblsp. butter or regular margarine
1 tblsp. chopped onion
2 tblsp. flour
½ tsp. salt
⅛ tsp. pepper
1 c. chicken broth
1 c. milk
2 tblsp. chopped fresh parsley
Paprika

In bowl stir together vinegar and 3 c. water. Peel and slice salsify and immediately place in vinegar mixture. (This prevents the salsify from darkening.)

Drain salsify. In 2-qt. saucepan place salsify and 2 c. water; over high heat bring to a boil. Reduce heat to low; cover and simmer 15 minutes or until tender. Remove from heat; *do not drain.*

Meanwhile, in 3-qt. saucepan over medium heat, melt butter. Add onion; cook until tender. Stir in flour, salt and pepper until smooth. Gradually stir in chicken broth and milk. Cook, stirring constantly, until mixture boils and thickens. Stir in salsify, cooking liquid and parsley

until well blended. Continue cooking until heated through.

To serve, ladle soup into bowls; garnish with paprika. Makes 4 (1-c.) servings.

TO MICROWAVE: Use same ingredients.

Peel and slice salsify as directed; drain.

In 1½-qt. microwave-safe casserole place salsify. Cover with lid or plastic wrap, turning back one section to vent steam.

Microwave at high setting (100% power) 6 minutes or until tender, stirring after 3 minutes. Let stand, covered.

In 2-qt. microwave-safe casserole place butter and onion. Cover with lid or plastic wrap, and microwave at high setting 2 minutes, stirring after 1 minute. Stir in flour, salt and pepper until smooth. Gradually stir in chicken broth and milk until well blended.

Cover again, and microwave at high setting 2 minutes. Stir. Microwave 7 minutes more or until mixture boils, stirring each minute. Stir in salsify, parsley and 2 c. hot water.

Cover again, and microwave 2 minutes or until heated through. Serve as directed.

PUMPKIN SOUP

*Served chilled, this is a good
first course for an autumn meal.*

2 tblsp. butter or regular margarine
2 medium onions, sliced
1 medium potato, peeled and chopped
1 rib celery, chopped
1 (8-oz.) can whole tomatoes
4 c. cubed, peeled pumpkin, cooked and
    mashed (1⅔ c.), or 1 (16-oz.) can solid-
    pack pumpkin
2 c. chicken broth
2 tblsp. lemon juice
2 tblsp. chopped fresh parsley
½ tsp. salt
¼ tsp. dried thyme leaves
⅛ tsp. pepper
1 bay leaf
1 c. milk, warmed
Toasted Croutons (see Index)

In 3-qt. saucepan over medium-high heat, melt butter. Add onions, potato and celery; cook until the vegetables are tender.

Stir in tomatoes and remaining ingredients except milk and croutons, stirring to break up tomatoes; bring to a boil. Reduce heat to low; cover and simmer 30 minutes or until vegetables are tender. Remove bay leaf. Cool slightly.

In blender container, place half of the pumpkin mixture; cover. Blend at high speed until smooth. Pour into bowl. Repeat with remaining pumpkin mixture. Gradually stir in warm milk.

To serve, ladle soup into bowls; garnish with croutons. Serve hot or cold. Makes 6 (1-c.) servings.

TO MICROWAVE: Use same ingredients, *changing amounts as indicated.*

In 3-qt. microwave-safe casserole place butter and onions. Cover with lid or plastic wrap, turning back one section to vent steam. Microwave at high setting (100% power) 3 to 4 minutes or until onions are tender, stirring after 2 minutes.

Stir in potato, celery, parsley and thyme. Cover again, and microwave at high setting 3 to 5 minutes or until potato is almost tender, stirring every 1½ minutes.

Stir in tomatoes, pumpkin, chicken broth, salt, pepper, bay leaf and *1 tblsp. lemon juice*, stirring to break up tomatoes. Cover again, and microwave at high setting 6 to 8 minutes or until mixture comes to a boil, stirring every 2 minutes. Remove bay leaf.

Blend, add milk and serve as directed.

VEGETABLE-LENTIL CHOWDER

*Lentils make this soup satisfying
and nutritious—inexpensive, too.*

¼ c. butter or regular margarine
1 large onion, chopped
1 large green pepper, chopped
1 carrot, chopped
1½ c. lentils, rinsed and drained
1 (28-oz.) can whole tomatoes
5 c. water
½ c. chopped pimientos
1 tsp. salt
¼ tsp. dried thyme leaves
⅛ tsp. pepper
1 bay leaf
Grated Parmesan cheese

In 4-qt. Dutch oven over medium-high heat, melt butter. Add onion, green pepper and carrot; cook until vegetables are tender.

Add lentils and remaining ingredients except cheese, stirring to break up tomatoes. Bring to a boil.

Reduce heat to low. Cover and simmer 1 hour or until lentils are

A festive beginning to any party—appetizers made with vegetables. Clockwise from top: Celery and Cheese Rosettes, page 66; Spinach-Carrot Phyllo Roulades, page 68; Shrimp-filled Snow Peas, page 64; New Potato Canapés, page 65; Oven-fried Broccoli Flowerets and Herb Tomato Stars, both on page 67.

Top: Simply elegant leeks and carrots, page 174, to serve hot or chilled.

Bottom: In Sautéed Tomatoes and Anise, page 172, the mild flavor of anise makes a good complement to the robust taste of garlic and tomatoes.

To make baked goods even more aromatic and taste-tempting, add some corn, garlic, onions or mushrooms to your usual bread makings. Clockwise from top: Raised Corn Muffins, page 234; Quick Garlic Loaves and Crunchy Onion Twists, both on page 235; and Brioche Mushroom Braid, page 236.

Even the humblest vegetables can become pretty garnishes, to be used singly
as an accent for a serving, or arranged in a big bouquet as a centerpiece. This
arrangement includes Turnip Calla Lilies, Cabbage Roses, Beet and Radish
Cup Flowers, Daisy Cutouts, Flower Cutouts II, Squash Tulips, Black-eyed
Susans, Radish Pompons, Turnip Jonquils, and Green Onion, Carrot and
Radish Lilies. To make this bouquet of garnishes, see page 57.

tender, stirring occasionally.
Remove bay leaf.

To serve, ladle soup into bowls; garnish with cheese. Makes about 6 main-dish or 10 (1-c.) servings.

PARSLIED CHICKEN CHOWDER

Just half an hour is all it takes to make this chicken-vegetable soup.

2 tblsp. butter or regular margarine
¼ c. chopped onion
2 c. water
1½ c. cubed cooked chicken (1" pieces)
1½ c. cubed peeled potatoes (½" pieces)
1½ c. diced carrots (¼" pieces)
1 tsp. salt
⅛ tsp. pepper
2 chicken bouillon cubes
3 tblsp. flour
2½ c. milk
Chopped fresh parsley

In 3-qt. saucepan over medium heat, melt butter. Add onion; cook until tender.

Stir in water, chicken, potatoes, carrots, salt, pepper and bouillon cubes. Over high heat bring to a boil.

Reduce heat to low. Cover and simmer 20 minutes or until vegetables are tender. Meanwhile, in jar with tight-fitting lid, place flour and ½ c. milk. Cover; shake until well blended.

Stir flour mixture and remaining 2 c. milk into chicken mixture. Over medium heat cook, stirring constantly, until mixture boils and thickens.

To serve, ladle soup into bowls; garnish with chopped parsley. Makes 5 main-dish or 7 (1-c.) servings.

MANHATTAN CLAM CHOWDER

Generously laced with minced clams; almost a meal in itself.

2 slices bacon, diced
2 medium onions, chopped
2 ribs celery, chopped
1 medium green pepper, finely chopped
1 (16-oz.) can whole tomatoes
2 medium potatoes, peeled and diced (¼" pieces)
1 carrot, diced (¼" pieces)
2 c. water
2 tblsp. tomato paste
¾ tsp. salt
½ tsp. dried thyme leaves
⅛ tsp. pepper
3 (6½-oz.) cans minced clams
1 tblsp. flour
Chopped fresh parsley

In 3-qt. saucepan over medium-high heat, cook bacon until browned. Drain on paper towels. Reserve bacon drippings.

In bacon drippings over medium heat, cook onions, celery and green pepper until tender. Stir in tomatoes, potatoes, carrot, water, tomato paste, salt, thyme and pepper, stirring to break up tomatoes. Bring to a boil.

Reduce heat to low. Cover and simmer 30 minutes.

Drain clams, reserving liquid. In small bowl, stir flour into reserved liquid until smooth. Add bacon and minced clams to soup; gradually stir in flour mixture. Increase heat to medium; cook until soup boils and thickens.

To serve, ladle soup into bowls; garnish with parsley. Makes 8 (about 1-c.) servings.

LIMA BEAN CHOWDER

A steaming cup of this chowder is a perfect winter warm-up.

2 tblsp. butter or regular margarine
2 large onions, chopped
1 medium green pepper, chopped
1 medium potato, peeled and diced
  (½" pieces)
3 c. water
2 c. fresh or frozen lima beans
2 tsp. salt
¼ tsp. pepper
2 c. fresh or frozen corn
1 c. shredded cabbage
1 (13-oz.) can evaporated milk
1 c. shredded Cheddar cheese (4 oz.)

In 3-qt. saucepan over medium heat, melt butter. Add onions and green pepper; cook until vegetables are tender. Stir in potato, water, lima beans, salt and pepper; bring to a boil.

Reduce heat to low. Cover and simmer 5 minutes. Stir in corn and cabbage; continue simmering 10 minutes or until vegetables are tender.

Gradually stir in milk and cheese. Cook, stirring constantly, 3 minutes or until heated through. Makes 7 (1-c.) servings.

FOR SLOW COOKER: Use same ingredients.

Cook onions and green pepper as directed.

In 3½-qt. slow cooker stir together cooked vegetables, potato, water, lima beans, salt and pepper. Cover and cook at low setting 6 hours.

Stir in corn and cabbage. Cover and cook at high setting 45 minutes.

Reduce heat to low; gradually stir in milk and cheese. Cook, stirring constantly, 3 minutes or until heated through.

CHEESY CORN CHOWDER

A rich and cheesy soup with lots of corn, onions and potatoes.

¼ lb. salt pork, cut into ¼" pieces
3 medium onions, finely chopped
3 medium potatoes, peeled and diced
  (¼" pieces)
½ c. water
4 c. fresh or frozen corn
3 tblsp. flour
3 c. milk
2 c. shredded Cheddar cheese (8 oz.)
½ tsp. salt
⅛ tsp. pepper
Ground nutmeg

In 3-qt. saucepan over medium-high heat, cook salt pork 5 minutes. Add onions; cook until onions are tender.

Stir in potatoes and water; bring to a boil. Reduce heat to medium. Cover and simmer 10 minutes, stirring occasionally.

Stir in corn. Cover and simmer 8 minutes, stirring occasionally.

Stir in flour until well blended. Gradually stir in milk, cheese, salt and pepper. Over low heat cook, stirring constantly, until soup thickens and cheese melts.

To serve, ladle soup into bowls; garnish with nutmeg. Makes 10 (1-c.) servings.

VEGETABLE BEEF SOUP WITH PASTRY CAP

For the finishing touch, this chunky soup is baked just long enough to brown the pretty pastry topping.

¼ c. flour
2 lb. shin beef with bone, or beef shanks, cross-cut into 1½" chunks; reserve marrow bones
2 tblsp. vegetable oil
½ lb. mushrooms, cut into ½" slices
2 medium cloves garlic, minced
6 c. beef broth
1½ tsp. salt
1 tsp. dried thyme leaves
¼ tsp. pepper
¼ lb. small white onions, peeled
2 ribs celery, cut into 1" pieces
1 medium turnip, peeled and cut into ½" pieces
1 c. sliced carrots
2 tblsp. chopped fresh parsley
1 (10-oz.) pkg. frozen patty shells

In plastic bag place flour. Add beef chunks, a few pieces at a time; shake until well coated.

In 4-qt. Dutch oven over medium-high heat, heat oil until hot. Cook beef until browned on all sides; remove and drain on paper towels.

To remaining oil in Dutch oven, add mushrooms, garlic and 2 tblsp. of the beef broth. Cook until mushrooms are tender, stirring frequently.

Stir in remaining beef broth, browned beef chunks, marrow bones, salt, thyme and pepper; bring to a boil.

Reduce heat to low. Cover and simmer 2 hours.

Add onions, celery, turnip, carrots and parsley. Simmer 40 minutes more; remove marrow bones.

Meanwhile, thaw patty shells about 30 minutes. On lightly floured surface with lightly floured rolling pin, roll each shell to a 7" circle.

Into 6 (2½-c. or 20-oz.) oven-safe crocks or bowls, ladle 1½ c. soup.

Dampen the edges of patty shells with water. Place one patty shell over each soup crock, keeping pastry taut. Press pastry firmly to sides of crock to seal. Brush tops of pastry with beaten egg. Place crocks on jelly-roll pan.

Bake in 400° oven 20 minutes or until pastry is puffed and golden brown. Makes 6 (1½-c.) main-dish servings.

CHICKEN GUMBO

Serve this hearty soup with bread and salad for Sunday supper.

2 tblsp. vegetable oil
1 (3- to 3½-lb.) broiler-fryer chicken, cut up
6 large tomatoes, peeled and chopped
1 medium onion, chopped
1 medium sweet green pepper, chopped
1 qt. water
1½ c. cubed cooked ham (½" cubes)
2 tblsp. chopped fresh parsley
1 tsp. salt
½ tsp. dried thyme leaves
¼ tsp. pepper
¼ tsp. crushed red pepper
1 bay leaf
½ lb. okra, cut into ⅛" slices (2 c.)
¼ c. uncooked long-grain rice

In 4-qt. Dutch oven over high heat, heat oil until hot. Cook chicken until browned on all sides.

Stir in tomatoes and remaining ingredients except okra and rice; bring to a boil.

Reduce heat to medium-low. Cover and simmer 20 minutes, stirring occasionally.

Add okra and rice. Cover; cook 20 minutes more, or until rice is cooked and chicken is fork-tender.

Remove chicken. Cut meat from bones and into bite-size pieces. Return meat to soup; stir to mix well. Remove bay leaf. Makes 8 main-dish or 14 (1-c.) servings.

CHICKEN JAMBALAYA SOUP

A meal in a dish—a hearty soup that you'll need a knife and fork to eat.

¼ c. flour
1 (3½-lb.) broiler-fryer, cut up
2 tblsp. olive or vegetable oil
½ lb. mushrooms, quartered
2 medium onions, sliced
2 cloves garlic, minced
4 large ripe tomatoes, peeled and chopped, or 1 (28-oz.) can whole tomatoes
4 c. chicken broth
2 tblsp. chopped fresh parsley
2 tsp. chopped fresh dill or ½ tsp. dried dill weed
1 tsp. salt
1 tsp. dried oregano leaves
½ tsp. dried basil leaves
¼ tsp. pepper
1 bay leaf
3 medium zucchini, cut into 1" chunks
2 medium green or red sweet peppers, cut into 1" chunks

In plastic bag place flour. Add chicken, a few pieces at a time; shake until well coated.

In 4-qt. Dutch oven over medium-high heat, heat oil until hot. Cook chicken until browned on all sides; remove and drain on paper towels.

To remaining oil in Dutch oven, add mushrooms, onions and garlic; cook until vegetables are tender.

Add tomatoes and remaining ingredients except zucchini and sweet peppers. (If using canned tomatoes, break up tomatoes.) Add chicken; bring to boil. Reduce heat to low. Cover and simmer 30 minutes.

Add zucchini and sweet peppers. Cover and cook 10 minutes more, or until vegetables and chicken are tender. Remove bay leaf. Makes 8 main-dish or 13 (1-c.) servings.

MEATBALL AND PASTA SOUP

(see photo following page 182)

Fresh spinach adds vibrant color to this hearty main-dish soup.

Meatballs (recipe follows)
2 tblsp. vegetable oil
1 medium onion, chopped
1 carrot, diced
1½ c. chopped celery
1 clove garlic, minced
1 (28-oz.) can Italian plum tomatoes
1 (6-oz.) can tomato paste
3 c. water
1 tsp. salt
1 tsp. dried basil leaves
1 tsp. dried oregano leaves
½ tsp. dried rosemary leaves
¼ tsp. pepper
2 bay leaves
½ c. corkscrew macaroni
1 c. chopped fresh spinach
Grated Parmesan cheese

Prepare meatballs. In 4-qt. Dutch oven over medium-high heat, heat oil until hot. Cook meatballs until browned on all sides. Remove meatballs and drain on paper towels.

In drippings in Dutch oven, cook onion, carrot, celery and garlic until vegetables are tender. Add tomatoes, tomato paste, water, salt, basil, oregano, rosemary, pepper and bay leaves, stirring to break up tomatoes. Add meatballs.

Over high heat bring to a boil. Reduce heat to low. Cover and simmer 30 minutes. Stir in macaroni; cook 10 minutes more. Stir in spinach; cook 5 minutes more or until spinach is tender. Remove bay leaves.

To serve, ladle soup into bowls; garnish with cheese. Makes 6 main-dish or 10 (1-c.) servings.

Meatballs: In large bowl mix together 1 lb. ground chuck, ½ c. soft whole-wheat bread crumbs, ¼ c. chopped onion, 2 tblsp. milk, 2 tblsp. chopped fresh parsley, ½ tsp. dried marjoram, ¼ tsp. salt, ⅛ tsp. pepper and 1 egg. Shape meat mixture into 18 (2") meatballs.

SPLIT PEA SOUP WITH MEATBALLS

Use either green or yellow peas; make the meatballs with pork.

4 slices bacon, diced
1 lb. yellow split peas, rinsed and drained
2 qt. water
1 c. chopped onions
¼ c. chopped fresh parsley
2 tsp. salt
½ tsp. dried marjoram leaves
¼ tsp. pepper
Pork Meatballs (recipe follows)
1 (8-oz.) can stewed tomatoes
1 c. thinly sliced celery
1 c. thinly sliced carrots
1 c. fresh or frozen cut green beans
　　(1″ pieces)

In 4-qt. Dutch oven over medium-high heat, cook bacon until browned. Stir in peas and next 6 ingredients; bring to a boil.

Reduce heat to low. Cover and simmer 1 hour. Meanwhile, prepare Pork Meatballs.

Stir Meatballs, stewed tomatoes and remaining ingredients into pea mixture. Cover and simmer 30 minutes or until peas are tender. Makes 8 main-dish or about 13 (1-c.) servings.

Pork Meatballs: In large bowl mix together 1 lb. ground pork, ½ c. soft bread crumbs, ¼ c. finely chopped onion, 2 tblsp. chopped fresh parsley, 2 tblsp. milk, ½ tsp. dried marjoram leaves, ¼ tsp. salt, ⅛ tsp. pepper and 1 egg.

Shape mixture into 36 meatballs.

In 10″ skillet over medium heat, heat 2 tblsp. vegetable oil until hot. Brown meatballs in oil, a few at a time. Remove meatballs and drain on paper towels.

TURKEY SOUP WITH PARSLIED DUMPLINGS

Try adding these light dumplings to any soup that has lots of broth.

3 lb. turkey thighs, skinned, boned, and cut into 1″ cubes (reserve bones)
6 c. chicken broth
¼ c. chopped fresh parsley
½ tsp. poultry seasoning
¼ tsp. browning sauce for gravy
⅛ tsp. pepper
Parslied Dumplings (recipe follows)
2 c. thinly sliced onions
1½ c. thinly sliced carrots
1½ c. fresh or frozen peas

In 4-qt. Dutch oven over high heat, bring diced turkey and bones, chicken broth, parsley, poultry seasoning, browning sauce for gravy and pepper to a boil.

Reduce heat to low. Cover and simmer 1 hour.

Meanwhile, prepare Parslied Dumplings.

Remove turkey bones from soup. Add onions, carrots and peas. Increase heat to medium so soup maintains a steady boil. Drop dumplings by tablespoonfuls onto simmering soup.

Simmer, uncovered, 10 minutes. Cover and simmer 10 minutes more or until dumplings are tender.

To serve, ladle soup and 2 dumplings into each bowl. Makes 6 main-dish or 10 (1-c.) servings.

Parslied Dumplings: In large bowl stir together 1½ c. sifted flour, 2 tblsp. chopped fresh parsley, 2 tsp. baking powder and ¾ tsp. salt.

Cut in 3 tblsp. shortening until mixture resembles coarse crumbs. Stir in ¾ c. milk until moistened.

SPLIT PEA VEGETABLE SOUP

*Save the bone from a ham
to give this soup extra flavor.*

1 lb. dried split peas, rinsed and drained
1 lb. meaty smoked pork hocks
2 qt. water
1 carrot, thinly sliced
1 c. chopped onions
½ c. sliced celery
2 tsp. salt
½ tsp. dried marjoram leaves
¼ tsp. pepper

In 5-qt. Dutch oven stir together
all ingredients; over high heat bring
to a boil.

Reduce heat to low. Cover and
simmer 1½ to 2 hours or until peas
are tender, stirring occasionally.

Remove pork hocks. Cut meat
from bones and into bite-size
pieces. Return meat to soup; stir to
mix well. Makes 8 main-dish or
12 (1-c.) servings.

TO MICROWAVE: Use same ingredients.

In 5-qt. microwave-safe casserole
stir together all ingredients. Cover
with lid or plastic wrap, turning
back one section to vent steam.

Microwave at high setting (100%
power) 50 minutes, stirring every
10 minutes. Remove pork hocks. Cut
meat from bones and into bite-size
pieces. Return meat to soup; stir to
mix well.

Cover again, and microwave at
high setting 20 to 30 minutes or until peas are tender, stirring every
15 minutes.

FOR SLOW COOKER: Use same ingredients.

In 3½-qt. slow cooker stir
together all ingredients. Cover and
cook at low setting 10 to 12 hours or
until peas are tender.

Remove pork hocks. Cut meat
from bones and into bite-size
pieces. Return meat to soup; stir to
mix well.

CHUNKY LENTIL SOUP

*To vary this soup, use ground pork
for beef and add a pinch of thyme.*

1 lb. ground chuck
1 (46-oz.) can tomato juice (5¾ c.)
4 c. water
1 c. dried lentils, rinsed and drained
1 c. diced carrots (¼″ pieces)
1 c. chopped celery
1 c. chopped cabbage
1 c. chopped onion
½ c. chopped green pepper
1 tsp. salt
½ tsp. pepper
2 beef bouillon cubes
1 bay leaf

In 6-qt. Dutch oven over medium-
high heat, cook ground chuck until
browned; pour off excess fat.

Stir in tomato juice and remaining
ingredients; bring to a boil.

Reduce heat to low. Simmer, uncovered, 1½ hours or until lentils
are tender. Remove bay leaf. Makes
8 main-dish or 12 (1-c.) servings.

FOR SLOW COOKER: Use same ingredients, *reducing water as indicated.*

In 10″ skillet over medium-high
heat, cook ground chuck until
browned; pour off excess fat.

In 3½-qt. slow cooker stir cooked
chuck, tomato juice, *2 c. water,* lentils and remaining ingredients until
well blended. Cover and cook at low
setting 8 to 10 hours or until lentils
are tender. Remove bay leaf.

FOR PRESSURE COOKER: Use same ingredients, *changing amounts and adding ingredients as indicated.*

In small bowl stir together lentils, *1 c. water, ¼ c. vegetable oil* and *1 tblsp. salt.* Let stand overnight to soak.

The next day, drain lentils. In 6-qt. pressure cooker over medium-high heat, cook ground chuck until browned; pour off excess fat. Stir in lentils, tomato juice, *2 c. water,* carrots and remaining ingredients; *omit salt.* (The pressure cooker should be *only* half full.)

Close cover securely and place cooker over high heat. Bring cooker to 15 lb. pressure, according to manufacturer's directions. When pressure is reached (control will begin to jiggle), reduce heat immediately to maintain a slow, steady rocking motion and cook 20 minutes. Remove from heat.

Let pressure drop of its own accord, about 30 minutes. Remove bay leaf.

VEGETARIAN MINESTRONE

To make this a meaty stew, add 1 lb. stew meat along with the beans.

8 c. water or Vegetable Stock (see Index)
1 c. dried red kidney beans, rinsed
    and drained
2 tblsp. olive or vegetable oil
1 medium onion, chopped
1½ c. coarsely chopped celery
½ c. chopped fresh parsley
1 clove garlic, minced
1 (28-oz.) can Italian plum tomatoes
1 (6-oz.) can tomato paste
1 tblsp. chopped fresh basil or 1 tsp. dried
    basil leaves
1 tsp. salt
1 tsp. dried oregano leaves
½ tsp. dried rosemary leaves
¼ tsp. pepper
2 bay leaves
½ lb. green beans, cut into 1" pieces
1 carrot, diced (¼" pieces)
1 c. sliced mushrooms
¼ c. tubettini or elbow macaroni

1 c. coarsely chopped spinach
Grated Parmesan cheese

In 4-qt. Dutch oven over high heat, bring water and beans to a boil; boil 2 minutes. Remove from heat. Cover and let stand 1 hour to soak.

In 12" skillet over medium-high heat, heat oil until hot. Add onion, celery, parsley and garlic; cook until vegetables are tender. Stir mixture into beans.

Stir tomatoes, tomato paste, basil, salt, oregano, rosemary, pepper and bay leaves into beans, stirring to break up tomatoes.

Over high heat bring to a boil. Reduce heat to low. Cover and simmer 1½ hours or until beans are tender.

Stir green beans, carrot and mushrooms into tomato mixture. Cover and cook 5 minutes.

Increase heat to medium; stir in tubettini. Cook 10 minutes or until pasta is tender. Stir in spinach; cook 5 minutes or until spinach is wilted. Remove bay leaves.

To serve, ladle soup into bowls; sprinkle with Parmesan cheese. Makes 8 main-dish or 14 (1-c.) servings.

PASTA AND BEAN SOUP_____

For a cold-weather supper, simmer beans with vegetables and spices.

1 lb. dried Great Northern beans, rinsed
  and drained
2 qt. water
2½ tsp. salt
6 slices bacon, diced
1 large carrot, thinly sliced
1 medium onion, chopped
½ c. chopped celery
1 small clove garlic, minced
1 (16-oz.) can stewed tomatoes
½ tsp. dried oregano leaves
¼ tsp. pepper
½ bay leaf
1 c. tubettini or small elbow macaroni,
  cooked and drained

In 6-qt. Dutch oven over high heat, bring beans, water and salt to a boil; boil 2 minutes. Remove from heat. Cover and let stand 1 hour to soak.

Meanwhile, in 10″ skillet over medium-high heat, cook bacon until browned. Drain bacon on paper towels. Pour off all but ¼ c. bacon drippings.

In bacon drippings over medium-high heat, cook carrot, onion, celery and garlic until vegetables are tender.

Stir cooked vegetables, stewed tomatoes, oregano, pepper and bay leaf into beans.

Over high heat bring beans to a boil. Cover and simmer 2 hours or until beans are tender, stirring occasionally. Remove bay leaf. Cool slightly.

In blender container, place half of the soup; cover. Blend at high speed until smooth. Pour blended mixture back into remaining soup with bacon and cooked pasta.

Over medium heat cook, stirring occasionally, until soup is hot. Makes 8 main-dish or 14 (1-c.) servings.

FOR SLOW COOKER: Use same ingredients, *reducing water as indicated.*

Cook and soak beans as directed, using only *5 c. water.*

Meanwhile, cook bacon and vegetables as directed.

In 3½-qt. slow cooker stir together beans and their liquid, cooked vegetables, stewed tomatoes, oregano, pepper and bay leaf.

Cover and cook at low setting 13½ hours or until beans are tender. Remove bay leaf. Cool slightly.

Blend half of soup as directed.

Stir blended mixture, bacon and cooked pasta into soup in slow cooker. Cover and cook at high setting 10 minutes or until heated through.

FOR PRESSURE COOKER: Use same ingredients, *adding ingredients as directed.*

In 6-qt. pressure cooker over high heat, bring beans, water, salt and *2 tblsp. vegetable oil* to a boil; boil 2 minutes. Remove from heat. Cover and let stand 1 hour.

Meanwhile, cook bacon and vegetables as directed.

Stir cooked vegetables, stewed tomatoes, oregano, pepper and bay leaf into beans. (The pressure cooker should be *only* half full.)

Close cover securely and place cooker over high heat. Bring cooker to 15 lb. pressure, according to manufacturer's directions. When pressure is reached (control will begin to jiggle), reduce heat immediately to maintain a slow, steady rocking motion and cook 30 minutes. Remove from heat.

Let pressure drop of its own accord, about 25 minutes. Remove bay leaf.

Blend, add bacon and pasta, and reheat as directed.

BLACK BEAN SOUP

A rich blend of black beans and vegetables with a squeeze of lemon.

1½ c. black beans, rinsed and drained
7 c. water
5 chicken bouillon cubes
Vegetable oil
2 ribs celery, chopped
1 carrot, finely chopped
1 medium potato, peeled and finely chopped
1 medium onion, finely chopped
1 clove garlic, minced
3 tblsp. lemon juice
½ tsp. dried oregano leaves
¼ tsp. dried savory leaves
1 bay leaf
Lemon slices

In 4-qt. Dutch oven over high heat, bring beans, water, bouillon cubes and 1 tblsp. oil to a boil. Reduce heat to low. Cover and simmer 1½ hours.

In 10″ skillet over medium-high heat, heat 1 tblsp. oil until hot. Add celery, carrot, potato, onion and garlic; cook until vegetables are tender.

Add vegetables, lemon juice and remaining ingredients except lemon slices to beans. Cover and simmer 1 hour more or until beans are tender. Remove bay leaf.

To serve, ladle soup into bowls; garnish with lemon slices. Makes 5 main-dish or 8 (1-c.) servings.

TO MICROWAVE: Use same ingredients, *changing amounts as indicated.*

In 4-qt. microwave-safe casserole place beans, water and bouillon cubes. Cover with lid or plastic wrap, turning back one section to vent steam.

Microwave at high setting (100% power) 10 to 15 minutes or until mixture boils. Stir.

Cover again, and microwave at medium setting (50% power) about 1 hour or until beans are almost tender, stirring every 15 minutes. Let stand, covered, 10 minutes.

Meanwhile, in 1½-qt. microwave-safe casserole place celery, carrot potato, onion, garlic, oregano, *1 tblsp. vegetable oil* and *½ tsp. savory.*

Cover with lid or plastic wrap. Microwave at high setting 3 to 4 minutes or until vegetables are tender-crisp, stirring after 2 minutes.

Stir vegetables and lemon juice into beans. Cover again, and microwave at medium setting 45 minutes to 1 hour or until beans are tender, stirring every 15 minutes. Remove bay leaf. Serve as directed.

5

Spectacular Salads

Until you've sampled the abundant variety of leafy greens and other vegetables—mixed, marinated and molded—you haven't tasted salads at their best. Even a simple green salad offers so many choices: Boston and bibb lettuce, romaine, escarole, leaf lettuce, spinach and watercress, not to mention arugala, curly-leafed and Belgian endives, Swiss chard, beet and mustard greens. All make fine ingredients for salads. You'll find more information about these types of greens and lettuce on pages 16 and 20; recipes for salad dressings begin on page 222.

Then consider adding a little something to that basic green salad. Mix romaine, escarole and leaf lettuce with sweet yellow pepper, green onions and celery. Drizzle hot bacon dressing over bite-size pieces of spinach, or toss cherry tomatoes and sliced hard-cooked eggs with tender young dandelion leaves. Even iceberg lettuce becomes interesting when you add bacon bits, croutons and ripe tomato wedges; top it all off with a creamy dressing and you have a B.L.T. Salad that's better than the sandwich.

Of course, you can make an infinite variety of salads without lettuce. In this chapter you'll find recipes for salads made with broccoli, jicama, snow peas, cucumbers, yams, spaghetti squash, Jerusalem artichokes and just about any other vegetable you can name.

For a piquant salad that can double as a burger topping, marinate sweet Spanish onions in a blue cheese dressing. Present thin slices of cucumbers in a rich sour cream sauce flavored with dill. Try Pasta and Vegetable Salad, a colorful mix of eight different vegetables plus corkscrew macaroni, for a summertime luncheon. Or grow your own bean sprouts (it's easy, and we tell how on page 32) to use in Oriental Salad.

For a shimmering salad made with gelatin, serve Molded Vegetable Ring, a tri-colored delight that combines fruits with vegetables. One of our favorite molded salads is Carrot Mousse, piled high in a soufflé dish.

Whether you serve salad as a first course, as an accompaniment to the main dish or as a cool refresher that follows, don't limit yourself to the same few salads—the four dozen choices in this chapter are just a sampling.

B.L.T. SALAD

All the makings of the classic
sandwich, served as a salad.

2 c. Toasted Croutons (see Index)
Creamy Garlic Dressing (see Index)
3 medium tomatoes, each cut into 6 wedges
1 lb. bacon, cut into 2" pieces, cooked
    and drained
1 medium head leaf lettuce, torn into
    bite-size pieces (8 c.)
1 small head iceberg lettuce, shredded
    (4 c.)

Prepare Toasted Croutons and
Creamy Garlic Dressing.
    In large bowl toss together
tomatoes, bacon, leaf lettuce, iceberg
lettuce and croutons. Pour dressing
over salad; toss until well coated.
Makes about 16 c. or 12 servings.

CAESAR SALAD

Using a blender makes the dressing
in this classic salad extra creamy.

2 c. Toasted Croutons (see Index)
1 medium head romaine, torn into bite-size
    pieces (6 c.)
½ c. grated Parmesan cheese
½ c. vegetable oil
¼ c. red wine vinegar
2 anchovy fillets
1 egg
¼ tsp. salt
⅛ tsp. pepper
1 clove garlic, minced

Prepare Toasted Croutons.
    In large bowl toss together
croutons, romaine and ¼ c. cheese.
    In blender container place oil and
remaining ingredients; cover. Blend
at high speed until smooth.
    Pour dressing over salad; toss un-
til well coated. Sprinkle with remaining ¼ c. cheese. Serve immediately.
Makes about 8 c. or 6 servings.

GREEK SALAD

Team this salad with broiled lamb
for dinner with a Greek theme.

⅓ c. olive or vegetable oil
¼ c. lemon juice
2 tblsp. red wine vinegar
¼ tsp. dry mustard
¼ tsp. ground cinnamon
⅛ tsp. pepper
1 to 2 cloves garlic, minced
1 (8-oz.) pkg. feta cheese, cut into 1" cubes
2 medium tomatoes, cut into 1½" chunks
1 medium head romaine, torn into bite-size
    pieces (6 c.)
1 medium cucumber, halved, seeded and
    cut into ¼" slices
1 medium green pepper, cut into ¼" strips
2 c. pitted ripe or Greek olives
⅓ c. sliced radishes

In jar with tight-fitting lid place
first 7 ingredients; cover. Shake until well blended.
    Refrigerate at least 2 hours to
blend flavors.
    In clear 3-qt. bowl alternately
layer feta cheese and remaining
ingredients.
    Pour dressing over salad; toss un-
til well coated. Serve immediately.
Makes about 12 c. or 8 servings.

HOT SPINACH SALAD

For a cold salad, substitute Sweet-
Sour Bacon Dressing (see Index).

1 lb. fresh spinach, stems removed and
    torn into bite-size pieces (2½ qt.)
3 green onions, chopped
2 hard-cooked eggs, chopped
Hot Bacon Dressing (see Index)

In large bowl toss together
spinach, green onions and eggs.
    Prepare Hot Bacon Dressing.
    Pour hot dressing over salad;
toss until well coated. Serve immediately. Makes about 8 c. or 6 to
8 servings.

TOSSED GREEN SALAD

Chopped yellow peppers give a
wonderful lift to this tossed salad.

Caraway Dressing (see Index)
1 medium head romaine, coarsely chopped
  (6 c.)
1 small head leaf lettuce, shredded (4 c.)
1 small head chicory, torn into bite-size
  pieces (2 c.)
1 large yellow or red sweet pepper,
  chopped
3 green onions, chopped
2 ribs celery, sliced

Prepare Caraway Dressing.
In large bowl toss together romaine and remaining ingredients. Pour dressing over salad; toss until well coated. Makes about 11 c. or 8 servings.

DANDELION SALAD

The younger the dandelion greens,
the sweeter your salad will be.

1/3 c. vegetable oil
2 tblsp. lemon juice
1 tsp. sugar
1/2 tsp. salt
1/8 tsp. garlic powder
1/8 tsp. pepper
10 cherry tomatoes, halved
3 hard-cooked eggs, chopped
2 slices bacon, cooked, drained
  and crumbled
1 lb. tender young dandelion greens,
  torn into 1/2" pieces (8 c.)

In large bowl using wire whisk, beat together first 6 ingredients.
Add tomatoes and remaining ingredients; toss until well coated. Makes about 10 c. or 6 to 8 servings.

ORIENTAL SALAD

Artfully arranged in the Oriental
manner with a spicy ginger dressing.

Ginger Dressing (see Index)
1 (10-oz.) pkg. fresh spinach, stems
  removed and torn into bite-size pieces
  (7 1/2 c.)
1/2 (10-oz.) pkg. fresh mung bean sprouts
3/4 c. unsalted sunflower seeds
1 large Bermuda onion, cut in half
  lengthwise and sliced
1 (11-oz.) can mandarin orange segments,
  drained

Prepare Ginger Dressing.
On 6 chilled salad plates, place about 1 c. spinach in center of each. Top each with 1/4 c. bean sprouts; then sprinkle with 2 tblsp. sunflower seeds.
Separate onion slices. Arrange 5 onion slices, overlapping slightly, on top of bean sprouts; then place 2 orange segments between each onion slice.
Pour dressing over each salad. Refrigerate at least 2 hours or until well chilled. Makes 6 servings.

WATERCRESS
AND NECTARINE SALAD

When nectarines are out of season,
substitute sliced, canned peaches.

Citrus Dressing (see Index)
1 medium head Boston lettuce, torn into
  bite-size pieces (4 c.)
1 bunch watercress, torn into bite-size
  pieces (2 c.)
2 nectarines, each cut into 8 wedges

Prepare Citrus Dressing.
In large bowl toss together lettuce, watercress and nectarines. Pour dressing over salad; toss until well coated. Makes about 7 c. or 6 servings.

BROCCOLI SALAD

Crunchy broccoli and chewy raisins provide a nice contrast of textures.

½ c. mayonnaise or salad dressing
1 tblsp. sugar
1 tblsp. cider vinegar
1 medium head broccoli, trimmed and coarsely chopped
1 small onion, chopped
½ c. raisins
10 slices bacon, cooked, drained and crumbled

In medium bowl using wire whisk, beat together mayonnaise, sugar and vinegar.

Add broccoli, onion and raisins; toss until well coated.

Cover and refrigerate at least 3 hours to blend flavors, stirring occasionally.

Garnish with bacon. Makes about 2½ c. or 5 servings.

BLUE DEVIL ONIONS

You also can use these cheesy onions as a burger topping.

1 (4-oz.) pkg. blue cheese, crumbled
½ c. vegetable oil
2 tblsp. lemon juice
½ tsp. sugar
¼ tsp. salt
⅛ tsp. pepper
2 large Spanish onions, sliced and separated into rings (1½ lb.)
1 tblsp. chopped fresh parsley

In blender container place first 6 ingredients; cover. Blend at high speed until smooth. Pour into medium bowl. Add onions; toss until well coated.

Cover and refrigerate at least 4 hours to blend flavors, stirring occasionally.

Garnish with parsley. Makes about 4 c. or 4 to 6 servings.

CAULIFLOWER SALAD

One Minnesota cook's favorite salad because it can be made ahead.

1 medium head cauliflower, thinly sliced (4 c.)
1 small green pepper, chopped
1 small onion, chopped
1 c. pitted ripe olives, each cut in half
2 tblsp. chopped pimiento
⅓ c. vegetable oil
¼ c. red wine vinegar
1 tsp. sugar
½ tsp. salt
⅛ tsp. pepper

In large bowl place first 5 ingredients.

In jar with tight-fitting lid place oil and remaining ingredients; cover. Shake until well blended.

Pour dressing over salad; toss until well coated.

Cover and refrigerate at least 12 hours to blend flavors, stirring occasionally. Makes about 6 c. or 6 servings.

CUCUMBER-SOUR CREAM SALAD

Dicing the cucumbers will make this salad into a sauce for poached fish.

1 c. dairy sour cream
3 tblsp. finely chopped onion
2 tblsp. chopped fresh dill or 2 tsp. dried dill weed
2 tblsp. vinegar
1 tblsp. sugar
1 tsp. salt
4 medium cucumbers, thinly sliced (5 c.)

In large bowl using wire whisk, beat together all ingredients except cucumbers.

Add cucumbers; toss until well coated.

Cover and refrigerate at least 2 hours to blend flavors, stirring occasionally. Makes about 5 c. or 6 servings.

GREEN BEAN AND PEANUT SALAD

For variety, use zucchini or carrot strips in place of green beans.

1 lb. green beans, trimmed and cut into
    2" pieces
⅓ c. chopped unsalted peanuts
1 c. Vinaigrette Dressing (see Index)
2 tblsp. finely chopped sweet red pepper
½ head leaf lettuce, torn into bite-
    size pieces
2 medium tomatoes, cut into 1½" chunks
2 hard-cooked eggs, chopped

In 2-qt. saucepan over high heat, bring 1" water to a boil; add beans. Reduce heat to medium. Cover and simmer 5 to 7 minutes or until tender-crisp; drain. Rinse under cold running water until cool. Drain well.

In medium bowl place beans and peanuts.

Prepare Vinaigrette Dressing. Stir together 1 c. dressing and add red pepper; pour over beans and toss until well coated.

Cover and refrigerate at least 30 minutes to blend flavors.

Drain beans, reserving dressing.

On 6 chilled salad plates, place lettuce. Arrange green beans and tomatoes on lettuce. Sprinkle with eggs. Spoon about 2 tblsp. dressing over each salad. Makes 6 servings.

BEET AND ORANGE SALAD

Any way you slice it, this colorful, tarragon-flavored salad will please.

Leaf lettuce
6 medium beets, cooked, peeled and sliced
3 medium navel oranges, peeled and sliced
1 c. Vinaigrette Dressing (see Index)
½ tsp. dried tarragon leaves

On large chilled platter, place leaf lettuce. Arrange beet slices in a circle, overlapping beets around the outside edge of platter.

Arrange orange slices in a circle, overlapping oranges, inside beets.

Prepare Vinaigrette Dressing. Stir together 1 c. dressing and tarragon; pour over salad.

Cover and refrigerate at least 2 hours to blend flavors. Makes 6 servings.

JICAMA SALAD

Serve this crunchy salad with tangy mustard dressing as the first course of a Mexican-style supper.

1 lb. jicama or celeriac, peeled and cut into
    matchstick strips
4 medium carrots, peeled and cut into
    matchstick strips
2 ribs celery, cut into matchstick strips
1 c. pitted ripe olives, sliced
½ c. vegetable oil
⅓ c. red wine vinegar
1 tblsp. water
2 tsp. prepared mustard
¼ tsp. salt
¼ tsp. ground cumin
⅛ tsp. pepper
⅛ tsp. paprika
1 clove garlic, minced

In large bowl place jicama, carrots, celery and olives.

In jar with tight-fitting lid place oil and remaining ingredients; cover. Shake until well blended. Pour dressing over salad.

Cover and refrigerate at least 2 hours to blend flavors, stirring occasionally.

Toss before serving. Makes about 6 c. or 6 servings.

FIVE-BEAN SALAD

The longer this big-batch recipe sits, the more fully the flavors develop.

1⅓ c. cider vinegar
1 c. vegetable oil
⅓ c. sugar
½ tsp. dry mustard
¼ tsp. hot pepper sauce
2 cloves garlic, minced
1 (20-oz.) can chick peas, drained
1 (20-oz.) can kidney beans, drained
1 lb. green beans, cut into 1" pieces, cooked and drained
1 lb. wax beans, cut into 1" pieces, cooked and drained
1 large red sweet pepper, chopped
2 c. lima beans, cooked and drained
1½ c. sliced celery
1 c. chopped onion

In large bowl using wire whisk, beat together first 6 ingredients.

Add chick peas and remaining ingredients; toss until well coated.

Cover and refrigerate at least 12 hours to blend flavors, stirring occasionally. Makes about 14 c. or 14 to 16 servings.

TOMATO-ONION SALAD

This simple salad is best made when tomatoes are at their peak.

6 medium tomatoes, peeled and sliced
1 c. sliced onions
¾ c. vegetable oil
¼ c. vinegar
½ tsp. salt
½ tsp. dry mustard
½ tsp. paprika
⅛ tsp. pepper
1 c. dairy sour cream
1 tblsp. chopped fresh parsley

In large bowl layer tomatoes and onions.

In jar with tight-fitting lid place oil and remaining ingredients except sour cream and parsley; cover. Shake until well blended.

Pour dressing over salad. Cover and refrigerate at least 12 hours to blend flavors, stirring occasionally.

In small bowl stir together sour cream and parsley. Place a dollop of sour cream dressing on each serving of salad. Makes about 5 c. or 6 servings.

SPROUT SALAD

This makes a good meatless stuffing for pita bread. You also could add 1 c. diced cooked turkey.

Caraway Dressing (see Index)
3 c. mung bean sprouts (see page 32)
3 c. lentil sprouts (see page 32)
2 c. alfalfa sprouts (see page 32)
½ c. shredded carrots
½ tsp. salt

Prepare Caraway Dressing.

In large bowl toss together mung bean sprouts and remaining ingredients. Pour dressing over salad; toss until well coated. Makes about 5½ c. or 6 servings.

ITALIAN-STYLE MARINATED TOMATOES

For lunch add feta or mozzarella cheese and serve on greens.

5 large tomatoes, sliced
¼ c. olive or vegetable oil
2 tblsp. red wine vinegar
½ tsp. salt
1 tblsp. chopped fresh basil or ½ tsp. dried basil leaves
½ tsp. dried oregano leaves
⅛ tsp. pepper
1 clove garlic, minced

In 12x8x2" baking dish place tomatoes.

In jar with tight-fitting lid place oil and remaining ingredients; cover. Shake until well blended. Pour dressing over tomatoes.

Cover and refrigerate at least 2 hours to blend flavors, stirring occasionally. Makes about 5 c. or 6 servings.

Greek-Style Marinated Tomatoes:
Use same ingredients. Prepare as directed, but omit salt and add ½ c. crumbled feta cheese and ½ c. sliced pitted ripe olives to tomato mixture. Makes about 6 c. or 6 servings.

CONFETTI CHEESE SALAD IN PEPPER CUPS

Calorie-counters will love this cool, crunchy and colorful salad for lunch.

3 medium green or red sweet peppers, each cut in half crosswise
1 (12-oz.) container small-curd cottage cheese (1½ c.)
½ c. plain yogurt
2 tblsp. chopped fresh dill or 2 tsp. dried dill weed
1 tsp. lemon juice
¾ tsp. garlic salt
⅛ tsp. pepper
½ c. shredded carrots
½ c. finely chopped celery
½ c. sliced green onions
½ c. chopped, seeded and peeled cucumber
2 tblsp. chopped radishes
Fresh dill sprigs

Remove seeds and white membrane of peppers; discard. If necessary, trim ends so peppers will have a level surface.

In 12" skillet with steamer rack, over high heat, bring 2 c. water to a boil. Place pepper halves cut-side down on rack. Reduce heat to medium. Cover and steam 3 minutes or until tender-crisp. Drain peppers on paper towels. Let cool until easy to handle, about 15 minutes.

In medium bowl using rubber spatula, stir cottage cheese, yogurt, dill, lemon juice, garlic salt and pepper until well blended.

Add carrots, celery, onions, cucumber and radishes to cheese mixture; stir gently until well coated.

Spoon about ½ c. vegetable mixture into each pepper half. Cover and refrigerate at least 30 minutes to blend flavors.

Garnish each pepper with fresh dill sprig. Makes 6 servings.

TANGY COLESLAW

This recipe serves 20, but it can be doubled or redoubled to serve more.

2 c. cider vinegar
2 c. sugar
1½ tsp. mustard seed
1½ tsp. celery seed
1 tsp. salt
½ tsp. ground turmeric
20 c. shredded cabbage (about 5 lb.)
3 c. chopped onions
2 (4-oz.) jars pimientos, drained and chopped

In 2-qt. saucepan over medium heat, cook vinegar, sugar, mustard seed, celery seed, salt and turmeric until mixture boils, stirring occasionally. Remove from heat. Cool to room temperature.

In very large bowl place cabbage, onions and pimientos. Pour dressing over salad; toss until well coated.

Cover and refrigerate at least 12 hours to blend flavors, stirring occasionally. Makes about 28 c. or 20 servings.

FARMHOUSE CABBAGE SLAW

Use the food processor to shred the cabbage for this Waldorf-type salad.

¾ c. mayonnaise or salad dressing
3 tblsp. lemon juice
1 tblsp. sugar
1 tblsp. milk
½ tsp. ground ginger
¼ tsp. salt
1 medium apple, diced
1 small onion, chopped
4 c. shredded cabbage (about 1 lb.)
¾ c. raisins
½ c. chopped celery
½ c. chopped walnuts

In large bowl using wire whisk, beat together first 6 ingredients.

Add apple, onion, cabbage, raisins and celery; toss until well coated.

Cover and refrigerate at least 2 hours to blend flavors, stirring occasionally.

Garnish with walnuts. Makes about 6 c. or 6 servings.

FRUITED CABBAGE SALAD

A crisp cabbage slaw, sweet with fruits and crunchy with walnuts.

1 (8-oz.) can crushed pineapple
½ c. mayonnaise or salad dressing
1 tblsp. sugar
1½ tsp. cider vinegar
⅛ tsp. salt
1 medium banana, sliced
4 c. shredded cabbage (about 1 lb.)
1 c. chopped celery
½ c. seedless green grapes
½ c. chopped walnuts

Drain pineapple, reserving 2 tblsp. juice. Set aside pineapple.

In large bowl using wire whisk, beat together reserved pineapple juice, mayonnaise, sugar, vinegar and salt.

Add pineapple, banana, cabbage, celery and grapes; toss gently until well coated.

Cover and refrigerate at least 2 hours to blend flavors, stirring occasionally.

Garnish with walnuts. Makes about 8 c. or 6 servings.

CONFETTI SALAD

Gelatin helps the dressing in this sweet slaw cling to the vegetables.

1 env. unflavored gelatin
¼ c. cold water
1 c. sugar
1 c. cider vinegar
1 tsp. salt
1 tsp. celery seed
¼ tsp. pepper
1 c. vegetable oil
1 medium green pepper, finely chopped
1 medium red pepper, finely chopped
1 medium onion, finely chopped
6 c. shredded cabbage (about 1½ lb.)
2 c. shredded carrots

In small bowl soak gelatin in ¼ c. cold water 5 minutes.

In 2-qt. saucepan over high heat, bring sugar, vinegar, salt, celery seed and pepper to a boil. Reduce heat to medium. Cook, uncovered, 3 minutes.

Stir in softened gelatin. Cook until gelatin and sugar are dissolved. Let cool to room temperature. Stir in oil until well blended.

In large bowl place green pepper and remaining ingredients. Pour cooled gelatin mixture over salad; toss until well coated.

Cover and refrigerate at least 12 hours to blend flavors, stirring occasionally. Makes about 9 c. or 8 to 10 servings.

CARROT-RAISIN SALAD

Chopped apple makes a fresh addition to this simple salad.

⅔ c. Honey-Orange Dressing
  (see Index)
2 medium apples, diced
3 c. shredded carrots
½ c. raisins

Prepare Honey-Orange Dressing; pour only ⅔ c. into large bowl. Add apples, carrots and raisins; toss until well coated.

Cover and refrigerate at least 2 hours to blend flavors, stirring occasionally. Makes about 5 c. or 6 servings.

JERUSALEM ARTICHOKE SLAW

Raw Jerusalem artichokes are mild and taste like water chestnuts.

3 c. water
1 tblsp. vinegar
1 lb. Jerusalem artichokes
Sweet-Sour Bacon Dressing (see Index)
3 ribs celery, diagonally sliced
2 medium carrots, each cut in half and
  sliced lengthwise
6 c. coarsely chopped cabbage (about
  1½ lb.)
⅔ c. pitted ripe olives, sliced

In medium bowl stir together water and vinegar.

Peel artichokes; slice ¼″ thick and immediately place in water mixture. (This prevents them from darkening.) Let soak until ready to use. Drain.

In large bowl prepare Sweet-Sour Bacon Dressing. Add artichokes, celery, carrots, cabbage and olives; toss until well coated.

Cover and refrigerate at least 3 hours to blend flavors, stirring occasionally. Makes about 11 c. or 8 servings.

BOK CHOY SALAD

The sweet Ginger Dressing gives this salad an Oriental flavor.

1 large bunch bok choy (about 1½ lb.),
   chopped (6 c.)
2 tsp. salt
Ginger Dressing (see Index)
½ c. coarsely chopped walnuts

In large bowl place bok choy; sprinkle with salt. Cover and refrigerate at least 2 hours.

Meanwhile, prepare Ginger Dressing. Cover and refrigerate.

Rinse bok choy under cold running water. Drain well and pat dry with paper towels.

In medium bowl place bok choy and walnuts. Pour dressing over salad; toss until well coated. Makes about 6 c. or 6 servings.

FAVORITE POTATO SALAD

When toting this to a picnic, put the dressing in a jar and refrigerate; toss with salad before serving.

½ c. mayonnaise or salad dressing
¼ c. vegetable oil
2 tblsp. cider vinegar
1 tsp. salt
⅛ tsp. pepper
3 hard-cooked eggs, diced
1 small onion, finely chopped
4 c. diced, warm, peeled, cooked potatoes
1 c. diced, peeled, seeded cucumber
1 c. sliced celery
¼ c. chopped green pepper
¼ c. chopped pimiento
Parsley sprigs
Tomato Rose (see Index)

In large bowl using wire whisk, beat together first 5 ingredients.

Add eggs and remaining ingredients except parsley and Tomato Rose; toss until well coated.

Garnish with parsley sprigs and Tomato Rose. Serve immediately.

To serve cold, cover and refrigerate at least 3 hours or until well chilled. Makes about 8 c. or 8 to 10 servings.

SOUR CREAM POTATO SALAD

Great for large get-togethers, this super-sized salad makes 24 servings.

¾ c. Italian Dressing (see Index)
2¼ c. mayonnaise or salad dressing
¾ c. dairy sour cream
1 tblsp. prepared mustard
1 tsp. salt
1 tsp. prepared horseradish
½ tsp. celery seed
¼ tsp. pepper
4 lb. new potatoes, cooked, peeled and sliced
6 hard-cooked eggs, chopped
1 c. thinly sliced celery
1 c. sliced green onions
1 c. chopped, peeled cucumber
2 tblsp. sliced green onion tops

Prepare Italian Dressing.

In large bowl stir mayonnaise, sour cream, prepared mustard, salt, prepared horseradish, celery seed and pepper until well blended. Stir in ¾ c. Italian Dressing.

Add potatoes, eggs, celery and green onions; toss until well coated.

Cover and refrigerate at least 3 hours to blend flavors, stirring occasionally.

Add cucumbers; toss until well coated. Garnish with green onion tops. Makes about 12 c. or 24 servings.

EGGCITING POTATO SALAD

An Iowa farm woman shared her adaptation of a Brazilian salad.

⅓ c. Italian Dressing (see Index)
1 c. mayonnaise or salad dressing
1 tsp. prepared mustard
¾ tsp. salt
⅛ tsp. pepper
⅛ tsp. Worcestershire sauce
6 c. cubed, peeled, cooked potatoes
¾ c. chopped celery
½ c. diced, cooked carrots
½ c. sliced radishes
¼ c. cooked peas
¼ c. chopped onion
1 medium tomato, peeled and diced
3 hard-cooked eggs, chopped
¼ c. chopped fresh parsley

Prepare Italian Dressing.

In large bowl place ⅓ c. Italian Dressing, mayonnaise, mustard, salt, pepper and Worcestershire sauce.

Add potatoes and remaining ingredients; toss lightly until well coated.

Cover and refrigerate at least 3 hours to blend flavors, stirring occasionally. Makes about 10 c. or 14 servings.

SKILLET POTATO SALAD

Bacon-studded potato salad has a wonderful sweet-sour flavor.

8 slices bacon, diced
1 medium onion, chopped
½ c. chopped celery
3 tblsp. sugar
1 tblsp. flour
1 tsp. salt
½ tsp. celery seed
¼ tsp. pepper
¾ c. water
6 tblsp. cider vinegar
2 lb. potatoes, cooked, peeled and cubed (½" pieces)

In 12" skillet over medium-high heat, cook bacon until browned. Drain bacon on paper towels. Pour off all but ¼ c. bacon drippings.

Add onion and celery to bacon drippings. Over medium-high heat cook until tender.

In small bowl stir together sugar, flour, salt, celery seed and pepper. Stir into skillet. Add water and vinegar. Cook, stirring constantly, until mixture boils and thickens.

Add bacon and potatoes. Cook, stirring occasionally, until potatoes are heated through. Serve warm or cold. Makes about 6 c. or 6 servings.

YAM FRUIT SALAD

Bananas are added last to this salad to keep them from turning dark.

⅔ c. mayonnaise or salad dressing
1 tblsp. lemon juice
1 tblsp. honey
2 medium apples, diced
1 lb. yams, cooked, peeled and cubed, or 1 (18-oz.) can yams or sweet potatoes, drained and cubed (½" pieces)
1 lb. seedless green grapes
2 medium bananas, sliced

In large bowl stir mayonnaise, lemon juice and honey until well blended.

Add apples, yams and grapes; toss gently until well coated.

Cover and refrigerate at least 2 hours to blend flavors, stirring occasionally.

Add bananas; toss gently until well coated. Makes about 8 c. or 12 servings.

PASTA AND SNOW PEA SALAD

To make this a main-dish salad, add 2 c. diced cooked chicken or pork.

Ginger Dressing (see Index)
1 tblsp. vegetable oil
1 (8-oz.) can sliced water chestnuts, drained
4 green onions, cut into 1" pieces
1 medium green pepper, cut into ¼" strips
½ lb. snow peas, trimmed
¼ lb. mushrooms, sliced
½ c. unsalted peanuts
½ lb. corkscrew or bow-tie macaroni, cooked and drained

Prepare Ginger Dressing. Pour into large bowl.

In 12" skillet over high heat, heat oil until hot. Add water chestnuts, onions, green pepper, snow peas, mushrooms and peanuts; cook until vegetables are tender-crisp.

Add vegetables and pasta to dressing; toss until well coated. Serve immediately.

To serve cold, cover and refrigerate at least 3 hours to blend flavors, stirring occasionally. Makes about 10 c. or 6 to 8 servings.

TO MICROWAVE: Use same ingredients.

Prepare Ginger Dressing as directed.

In 2-qt. microwave-safe casserole place oil and green onions. Cover with lid or plastic wrap, turning back one section to vent steam.

Microwave at high setting (100% power) 1 minute. Stir in water chestnuts, green pepper, snow peas, mushrooms and peanuts.

Cover again, and microwave at high setting 2 to 3 minutes or until tender-crisp, stirring each minute.

Toss vegetables and pasta with dressing. Serve as directed.

PASTA AND VEGETABLE SALAD

A perfect summer salad with a vinaigrette dressing.

2 tblsp. olive or vegetable oil
1 medium onion, chopped
1 c. sliced mushrooms
1 clove garlic, minced
1 medium carrot, thinly sliced
1 c. broccoli flowerets
1 c. thinly sliced zucchini
1 c. frozen peas
2 tblsp. chopped fresh basil or 2 tsp. dried basil leaves
2 tblsp. chopped fresh parsley
1 pt. cherry tomatoes, each cut in half
½ c. Vinaigrette Dressing (see Index)
½ lb. linguini or corkscrew macaroni, cooked and drained
½ c. grated Parmesan cheese
¼ c. pine nuts, toasted (optional)

In 12" skillet over medium-high heat, heat oil until hot. Add onion, mushrooms and garlic; cook until onion is tender.

Add carrot, broccoli, zucchini and peas; cook 2 minutes. Add basil and parsley; cover and cook 2 minutes. Stir in tomatoes. Remove from heat.

Prepare Vinaigrette Dressing; pour only ½ c. into large bowl.

Add vegetables and pasta to dressing; toss lightly until well coated. Serve chilled or at room temperature.

Garnish with cheese and pine nuts. Makes about 10 c. or 6 to 8 servings.

TO MICROWAVE: Use same ingredients, *reducing oil as indicated.*

In 2-qt. microwave-safe casserole place *1 tblsp. oil,* onion and garlic. Cover with lid or plastic wrap, turning back one section to vent steam.

Microwave at high setting (100% power) 3 to 4 minutes or until onion is tender, stirring after 2 minutes. Let stand, covered, 1 minute.

Add carrot and broccoli to casserole. Cover again, and microwave at high setting 2 minutes. Stir in mushrooms, zucchini and peas.

Cover again, and microwave at high setting 2 minutes.

Stir in basil and parsley. Cover again, and microwave at high setting 1 minute. Stir in tomatoes. Let stand, covered, 3 minutes.

Prepare Vinaigrette Dressing; pour ½ c. into large bowl.

Add vegetables and pasta to dressing; toss until well coated. Serve as directed.

BIG-BATCH MACARONI SALAD

Corkscrew macaroni, dotted with chopped vegetables, looks colorful.

2 c. mayonnaise or salad dressing
¾ c. milk
3 tblsp. lemon juice
4 tsp. sugar
2½ tsp. garlic salt
¼ tsp. pepper
1½ lb. corkscrew macaroni, cooked, rinsed and drained
1 medium red sweet pepper, finely chopped
1 medium green sweet pepper, finely chopped
1 c. shredded carrots
1 c. finely chopped celery
½ c. finely chopped onion
½ c. finely chopped radish
⅓ c. chopped fresh parsley

In large bowl stir first 6 ingredients until well blended.

Add macaroni and remaining ingredients; toss until well coated.

Cover and refrigerate at least 3 hours to blend flavors, stirring occasionally. Makes about 14 c. or 24 servings.

RICE SALAD

Brown rice is also good in this colorful vegetable-studded salad.

4½ c. cold cooked rice
1 c. thinly sliced celery
1 c. sliced radishes
¾ c. diced, pitted ripe olives (¼" pieces)
½ c. chopped red onion
¼ c. chopped fresh parsley
⅔ c. vegetable oil
¼ c. white wine vinegar
1 tblsp. water
1 tblsp. Vinaigrette Dressing Mix (see Index)
1 tsp. salt
8 oz. muenster cheese, cubed (½" cubes)
1 large red sweet pepper, chopped

In large bowl place rice, celery, radishes, olives, onion and parsley; set aside.

In jar with tight-fitting lid place oil, vinegar, water, Vinaigrette Dressing Mix and salt; cover. Shake until well blended.

Pour dressing over salad; toss until well coated.

Cover and refrigerate at least 12 hours to blend flavors, stirring occasionally.

Just before serving, stir in cheese and red pepper. Makes about 10 c. or 12 servings.

TABOULI WITH BEAN SPROUTS

Mint gives authentic flavor to this adaptation of a Middle Eastern dish.

1 c. cracked wheat (bulgur)
2 c. fresh mung bean sprouts or 1 (16-oz.) can bean sprouts, drained
2 medium tomatoes, peeled, seeded, and coarsely chopped
1 medium green pepper, chopped
½ c. shredded carrots
½ c. chopped fresh parsley
¼ c. finely chopped onion
¼ c. lemon juice
¼ c. vegetable oil
1 tsp. dried mint leaves
½ tsp. salt
⅛ tsp. pepper
1 clove garlic, minced

In large bowl place cracked wheat. Cover with warm water and soak 2 hours. Drain well.

In large bowl place cracked wheat, bean sprouts and remaining ingredients. Toss until well mixed.

Cover and refrigerate at least 2 hours to blend flavors, stirring occasionally. Makes about 5 c. or 6 to 8 servings.

DILLY CUCUMBER MOLD

The classic combination of dill and cucumbers in a creamy mold.

1 (3-oz.) pkg. lime-flavored gelatin
¾ c. boiling water
¼ c. cold water
2 tblsp. lemon juice
1½ c. finely chopped, peeled, seeded cucumbers
1 c. dairy sour cream
½ c. finely chopped celery
2 tblsp. minced green onion
1½ tsp. chopped fresh dill or ½ tsp. dried dill weed
Cucumber slices

In small bowl place gelatin. Add boiling water; stir until gelatin is completely dissolved. Stir in cold water and lemon juice.

Refrigerate, stirring occasionally, until uniformly thickened.

Fold in cucumbers, sour cream, celery, onion and dill. Spoon into 4-c. mold.

Cover and refrigerate until set, about 2 to 2½ hours.

Unmold gelatin and garnish with cucumber slices. Makes 6 servings.

MOLDED VEGETABLE RING

Both fruits and vegetables are folded into this tri-colored layered salad.

1 (6-oz.) pkg. lime-flavored gelatin
Boiling water
Cold water
1 (3-oz.) pkg. lemon-flavored gelatin
2 c. thinly sliced celery
2 c. shredded carrots
2 c. seedless green grapes, halved

In medium bowl place lime gelatin. Add 2 c. boiling water; stir until gelatin is completely dissolved. Stir in 1½ c. cold water; set aside.

In small bowl place lemon gelatin. Add 1 c. boiling water; stir until gelatin is completely dissolved. Stir in ¾ c. cold water; set aside.

Into another small bowl measure 2 c. lime gelatin mixture. Set remaining lime gelatin mixture aside. Place bowl in larger bowl of iced water. Stir gelatin until mixture is uniformly thickened.

Fold in celery. Spoon into 12-c. ring mold; refrigerate until set but not firm, about 20 minutes.

Stir lemon gelatin mixture over iced water until uniformly thickened. Fold in carrots. Spoon over celery; refrigerate until set but not firm, about 20 minutes.

Stir remaining 2 c. lime gelatin mixture over iced water until uniformly thickened. Fold in grapes. Spoon over carrots. Cover and refrigerate until firm.

Unmold onto platter. Makes 16 servings.

MIXED VEGETABLE SALAD

Chili sauce adds zip to the dressing for this crunchy, molded salad.

1 (6-oz.) pkg. lemon-flavored gelatin
1½ c. boiling water
1½ c. cold water
½ tsp. salt
8 ribs celery, chopped
3 medium onions, chopped
1 medium cucumber, chopped
1 medium red or green sweet pepper,
   chopped
1 c. mayonnaise or salad dressing
2 tblsp. chili sauce or ketchup
1 tsp. sugar
⅛ tsp. garlic powder

In medium bowl place gelatin. Add boiling water; stir until gelatin is completely dissolved. Stir in cold water and salt.

Refrigerate, stirring occasionally, until uniformly thickened.

Fold in chopped vegetables. Spoon into 13x9x2" (3-qt.) glass casserole.

Cover and refrigerate until firm, about 3 hours.

In small bowl stir together mayonnaise, chili sauce, sugar and garlic powder. Cover and refrigerate until ready to serve.

Top salad with dressing. Makes 12 servings.

INDIVIDUAL CARROT MOLDS

If you don't have individual molds, pour gelatin mixture into muffin-pan cups or into a 4-c. ring mold.

1 (3-oz.) pkg. lemon-flavored gelatin
1 c. boiling water
¾ c. cold water
¼ c. minced onion
2 tblsp. white wine vinegar
1 tblsp. lemon juice
½ tsp. salt
⅛ tsp. pepper
1½ c. shredded carrots
¼ c. minced green pepper
Lettuce leaves
Creamy French Dressing (see Index)

In medium bowl place lemon gelatin. Add boiling water; stir until gelatin is completely dissolved.

Stir in cold water, onion, vinegar, lemon juice, salt and pepper. Refrigerate, stirring occasionally, until uniformly thickened.

Fold in carrots and green pepper. Spoon into 6 (6-oz.) ramekins.

Cover and refrigerate until firm, about 2 hours.

Meanwhile, prepare Creamy French Dressing. Cover and refrigerate until ready to serve.

Unmold salads onto beds of lettuce. Top with dressing. Makes 6 servings.

CAULIFLOWER MOLD

Perfect for buffets; this will hold 45 minutes at room temperature.

1 (3-oz.) pkg. lemon-flavored gelatin
1 c. boiling water
¾ c. cold water
3 tblsp. lemon juice
3 tblsp. red wine vinegar
2 tblsp. sugar
½ tsp. salt
1 c. cauliflowerets
1 medium onion, finely chopped
½ c. shredded carrots
½ c. diced celery (¼" pieces)
½ c. diced cucumber (¼" pieces)
Lettuce leaves
½ c. mayonnaise or salad dressing
2 tblsp. sunflower seeds

In medium bowl place gelatin. Add boiling water; stir until gelatin is completely dissolved. Stir in cold water, lemon juice, vinegar, sugar and salt.

Refrigerate, stirring occasionally, until uniformly thickened.

Fold in cauliflowerets, onion, carrots, celery and cucumber. Spoon into 5-c. ring mold.

Cover and refrigerate at least 12 hours or until firm.

Unmold gelatin onto bed of lettuce. Spoon mayonnaise in center of ring; sprinkle with sunflower seeds. Makes 8 servings.

CARROT MOUSSE

Serve this for special occasions—it's rich, with just a whisper of curry.

3 env. unflavored gelatin
½ c. water
2 medium onions, chopped
4 c. sliced carrots
½ c. chopped celery
2 tblsp. chopped fresh parsley
2 cloves garlic, minced
2 c. mayonnaise or salad dressing
2 tblsp. lemon juice
½ tsp. salt
½ tsp. curry powder
1 c. heavy cream, whipped
¾ c. chopped celery leaves

In medium bowl place gelatin. Add ½ c. water; set aside to soften.

In 3-qt. saucepan over high heat, bring 1″ water to a boil; add onions, carrots, celery, parsley and garlic. Reduce heat to medium. Cover and simmer 25 to 30 minutes or until carrots are tender. Cool 15 minutes.

Drain vegetables reserving ¾ c. cooking liquid; add reserved liquid to softened gelatin. Stir until gelatin is completely dissolved. Stir in mayonnaise, lemon juice, salt and curry powder until well blended.

In blender container place half of the mayonnaise mixture and half of the vegetables; cover. Blend at high speed until smooth. Pour into 13x9x2″ baking pan. Repeat with remaining mayonnaise mixture and vegetables.

Freeze 30 minutes or until set 1″ from edges of pan, but still soft in center.

Meanwhile, cut a piece of aluminum foil 24x12″. Fold foil in half lengthwise. Wrap foil strip around outside of 1½-qt. soufflé dish so collar stands about 3″ above rim. Secure collar with tape.

In chilled large bowl using mixer at medium speed, beat frozen gelatin mixture until smooth.

Fold in whipped cream; spoon into prepared dish.

Cover and refrigerate until firm, about 4 hours.

Remove foil collar. Gently press celery leaves around edge of mousse. Makes 12 to 16 servings.

CHINESE CHICKEN NOODLE SALAD

Cooked chicken marinated in a spicy peanut butter sauce and arranged on a bed of pasta with vegetables.

Peanut-Pepper Sauce (see Index)
3 tblsp. dry sherry
5 c. cooked, shredded chicken
1 tblsp. vegetable oil
¾ lb. fresh snow peas, trimmed or 2 (6-oz.) pkg. frozen snow peas, thawed
1 clove garlic, minced
1 (8-oz.) pkg. very thin spaghetti or Chinese vermicelli, cooked and drained
2 tsp. sesame oil
4 green onions, sliced
1 (8-oz.) can sliced water chestnuts, drained

Prepare Peanut-Pepper Sauce, but increase soy sauce to 2 tblsp., and add dry sherry; pour into bowl.

Add chicken; toss until well coated. Cover and refrigerate at least 30 minutes to blend flavors, stirring occasionally.

Meanwhile, in 10″ skillet over medium-high heat, heat vegetable oil until hot. Add snow peas and garlic; cook, stirring constantly, 3 minutes or until tender-crisp; set aside.

In large bowl toss cooked spaghetti with sesame oil until well coated; set aside.

On 6 chilled salad plates place about ⅔ c. pasta in center. Top with about ¾ c. chicken. Place 4 snow peas in a spoke design on top of chicken. Sprinkle green onions between spokes.

Arrange remaining snow peas in a circle around pasta on each plate. Place a sliced water chestnut between each snow pea and at the center of the spoke design.

Serve at room temperature or chilled. Makes 10 c. or 6 main-dish servings.

MAIN-DISH POTATO SALAD_____

*A warm-weather entrée that
brings open-air freshness indoors.*

1 c. creamed-style small-curd cottage
   cheese
1 c. dairy sour cream
1 tblsp. prepared mustard
1 tblsp. sugar
1 tsp. salt
1/8 tsp. pepper
2 tblsp. chopped fresh parsley
2 lb. potatoes, cooked, peeled and diced
2 c. fully cooked, cubed ham
1/2 c. sliced green onions
1/2 c. finely chopped celery
2 hard-cooked eggs, chopped
Lettuce leaves
Paprika

In large bowl stir first 7 ingredients until well blended.

Add potatoes, ham, green onions,
celery and eggs; toss until well
coated.

Cover and refrigerate at least
3 hours to blend flavors, stirring
occasionally.

Arrange salad on bed of lettuce.
Sprinkle with paprika. Makes about
8 c. or 6 main-dish servings.

TUNA ARTICHOKE SALAD_____

*An overnight stay in the refriger-
ator allows the flavors to blend.*

1 (14-oz.) can artichoke hearts, drained and
   halved
1 (8-oz.) can tomato sauce
1 (7-oz.) can solid-pack white tuna, drained
   and chunked
1 (6-oz.) can pitted ripe olives, drained
1 1/2 c. sliced mushrooms
1 c. sliced celery
1 c. drained sweet mixed pickles
1/3 c. drained cocktail onions
1/4 c. wine vinegar
3 tblsp. vegetable oil
Lettuce leaves
Chopped fresh parsley
1 large tomato, cut into wedges

In large bowl place all ingredients
except lettuce leaves, parsley and tomato; toss gently until well mixed.

Cover and refrigerate at least
12 hours to blend flavors, stirring
occasionally.

Arrange salad on bed of lettuce.
Garnish with parsley and tomato
wedges. Makes about 8 c. or 4 main-
dish servings.

LAYERED SALMON SALAD_____

*Present this salad in a glass bowl
to let the colorful layers show.*

1/4 c. Italian Dressing (see Index)
1 1/2 c. mayonnaise or salad dressing
1 tblsp. finely chopped onion
2 tsp. chopped fresh dill or 1/2 tsp. dried
   dill weed
2 c. shredded lettuce
2 c. seashell macaroni, cooked and drained
1/2 c. sliced pimiento-stuffed olives
2 c. chopped tomatoes
2 c. sliced cucumbers
1 (15 1/2-oz.) can salmon, drained, boned and
   flaked
Paprika
Chopped fresh parsley

Prepare Italian Dressing; set
aside.

In large bowl stir together 1/4 c.
Italian Dresing, mayonnaise, onion
and dill. Cover and refrigerate at
least 2 hours to blend flavors.

Meanwhile, in large clear bowl,
layer lettuce, macaroni, olives, tomatoes, cucumbers and salmon.

Cover and refrigerate at least
2 hours or until well chilled.

Spoon mayonnaise mixture over
top of salad. Sprinkle with paprika
and chopped parsley. Makes about
10 c. or 6 main-dish servings.

Layered Tuna Salad: Use same ingredients and prepare as directed,
but substitute 2 (7-oz.) cans solid-
pack white tuna, drained and
flaked, for salmon.

TUNA-STUFFED SPAGHETTI SQUASH

One Oklahoma farm woman uses leftover spaghetti squash to make bar cookies, breads and salads.

1 spaghetti squash (about 4½ lb.)
1 (16-oz.) jar sweet pickles
½ c. mayonnaise or salad dressing
¼ c. vegetable oil
½ tsp. dry mustard
¼ tsp. celery seed
1 (7-oz.) can solid-pack white tuna, drained and flaked
2 hard-cooked eggs, chopped
1 c. chopped mushrooms
½ c. chopped green pepper
¼ c. chopped onion

In 6-qt. saucepot over high heat, bring 4 qt. water to a boil. Place whole spaghetti squash in boiling water. Reduce heat to medium. Cover and cook 20 minutes or until fork-tender. Remove squash from saucepot. Cool until easy to handle, about 15 minutes.

Drain juice from pickles and reserve. Chop enough pickles to make ½ c.; set aside.

In large bowl stir ¼ c. reserved pickle juice, mayonnaise, oil, mustard and celery seed until well blended; set aside.

Cut squash in half from stem to blossom end. Scoop out and discard seeds. Scrape the flesh, using a fork to separate the spaghetti-like strands.

Place squash in bowl with dressing; add pickles, tuna, eggs, mushrooms, green pepper and onion to bowl. Toss until well coated.

Cover and refrigerate at least 3 hours to blend flavors, stirring occasionally. Makes about 10 c. or 6 main-dish servings.

TO MICROWAVE: Use same ingredients, but omit water.

Pierce squash several times using a small, sharp knife. Place whole spaghetti squash on paper towel in center of microwave oven.

Microwave at high setting (100% power) 15 to 18 minutes or until flesh yields when pressed with finger, turning squash over after 8 minutes. Remove squash from oven. Cool as directed.

Continue recipe as directed.

SALAD NICOISE

Simple ingredients artfully arranged make a robust summer salad.

¾ c. Piquant French Dressing (see Index)
1 lb. potatoes, cooked, peeled and cubed (¾" pieces)
2 tblsp. chopped fresh parsley
Boston lettuce leaves
1 medium head Boston lettuce, torn into bite-size pieces (4 c.)
1 small head romaine, torn into bite-size pieces (4 c.)
1 (12-oz.) can solid-pack white tuna, drained and chunked
½ lb. whole green beans, cooked, drained and chilled
3 hard-cooked eggs, cut into wedges
2 medium tomatoes, cut into wedges
6 rolled anchovy fillets
½ c. pitted ripe olives

Prepare Piquant French Dressing.

In bowl toss potatoes and ¼ c. dressing until well coated. Cover and refrigerate at least 4 hours to blend flavors, stirring occasionally. Add parsley; toss until well mixed.

Line large platter with Boston lettuce leaves. Top with torn Boston lettuce and romaine. Arrange potatoes, tuna chunks, green beans, eggs, tomatoes, anchovies and olives on top of lettuce.

Serve with remaining dressing.

Makes about 14 c. or 6 main-dish servings.

PEA AND SHRIMP SALAD

Garden-fresh peas and delicate pink shrimp make a pretty luncheon dish.

3 lb. fresh peas, shelled (4 c.) or 2 (10-oz.)
   pkg. frozen peas
1 lb. cooked shrimp, shelled and cleaned
   (fresh or frozen and thawed)
4 hard-cooked eggs, coarsely chopped
2 green onions, chopped
1 c. diced celery
½ c. dairy sour cream
½ c. mayonnaise or salad dressing
2 tblsp. chopped fresh dill or 2 tsp. dried
   dill weed
1 tblsp. lemon juice
½ tsp. salt
Lettuce cups

In 3-qt. saucepan over high heat, bring 1″ water to a boil; add peas. Reduce heat to medium. Cover and simmer 5 to 7 minutes or until tender; drain and rinse under cold running water until cool. Drain well.

In large bowl place peas, shrimp, eggs, green onions and celery. Cover and refrigerate at least 2 hours or until well chilled.

In small bowl using wire whisk, beat together sour cream and remaining ingredients except lettuce cups. Cover and refrigerate at least 2 hours to blend flavors.

Pour dressing over salad; toss gently until well coated.

Spoon salad into lettuce cups. Serve immediately. Makes about 9 c. or 6 main-dish servings.

Tuna and Pea Salad: Use same ingredients and prepare as directed, but substitute 2 (7-oz.) cans solid-pack white tuna, drained and chunked, for shrimp.

Salmon and Pea Salad: Use same ingredients and prepare as directed, but substitute 2 (7¾-oz.) cans salmon, drained, boned and chunked, for shrimp.

CURRIED CHICKEN JULIENNE SALAD

Chicken, carrot and zucchini strips plus almonds in a curry dressing.

East Indies Dressing (see Index)
2 c. julienne carrot strips
3 c. julienne cooked chicken strips
2 c. julienne zucchini strips
½ c. slivered almonds, toasted
Lettuce leaves
¼ c. sliced green onions
Tomato wedges

Prepare East Indies Dressing.

In 2-qt. saucepan over high heat, bring 1″ water to a boil; add carrots. Cook 3 minutes or until tender-crisp; drain. Rinse under cold running water until cool. Refrigerate until chilled.

In large bowl place carrots, chicken, zucchini and almonds. Pour dressing over salad; toss until well coated.

Spoon salad onto bed of lettuce. Garnish with green onions and tomato wedges. Makes about 8 c. or 6 main-dish servings.

TOASTED CROUTONS

Make these crispy cubes with any type of bread—they're a great garnish for soups, too!

4 slices firm bread
2 tblsp. butter or regular margarine
¼ tsp. salt
¼ tsp. garlic powder
⅛ tsp. pepper

Cut crusts from bread.

Spread both sides of each slice with butter. Cut slices into ½″ cubes. Place in 13x9x2″ baking pan. Sprinkle with salt, garlic powder and pepper.

Bake in 400° oven 10 to 15 minutes or until golden brown. Cool completely. Makes 2 c.

6

Satisfying Main Dishes

With or without meat, you can use vegetables to create a truly amazing variety of main dishes—stews, stir-frys and quiches, deep-dish pies and crispy pancakes, airy soufflés, oriental hot pots, pizza and pasta dishes.

Entrées like Vegetable Balls with Pasta, Vegetarian Chili and Eggplant Parmesan make satisfying meatless meals when you round out the menu with hot rolls, a salad of mixed greens and a tall glass of milk.

The simplest dishes often are the most appealing to hearty appetites. Chicken and Lima Bean Stew is a no-fuss recipe made with four vegetables and chunks of chicken; simmered in a lightly seasoned gravy and topped with parsley-flecked Shortcut Dumplings, it's an easy one-pot meal. Two choices for a dinner in a dish are Moussaka and Deep-dish Chicken Liver Vegetable Pie, each one a savory casserole of vegetables and meat.

When you want something special for lunch, brunch or a light supper, try Spinach-Tomato Frittata, an omelet-like dish that requires little cooking time. Or serve Sunny Asparagus, spears of fresh asparagus on toast smothered with cream sauce and lavishly sprinkled with the sieved yolks of hard-cooked eggs. A mix of tender-crisp cooked vegetables tossed with linguini in a flavorful cheese sauce becomes Pasta Primavera; if you've never tried to make it yourself, you'll be surprised at how easy it can be.

Children will love both Potato Pizza and Zucchini Pizza; these pizzas are made with all the usual ingredients, but the crusts contain no flour. Vegetables also can take the place of noodles, as in Spaghetti Squash Lasagne and Turkey-Zucchini Lasagne.

We had such a hard time deciding between Saucy Cabbage Bundles and Creole Cabbage Rolls that we included them both, then added a recipe for a whole head of cabbage stuffed with chicken, spinach and rice. Vegetarian Stuffed Peppers is another favorite recipe we couldn't overlook.

For a real homemade treat, try your hand at making tender squares of carrot-flavored ravioli filled with cheese and spinach. Cook quickly, toss with melted butter and sprinkle generously with Parmesan cheese—then serve it proudly, and bask in the warmth of smiles all around the table.

POTATO-BACON OMELET

*You can feed six people with
this fluffy, potato-filled omelet.*

8 slices bacon, diced
1½ c. diced, peeled potatoes (¼" pieces)
3 tblsp. finely chopped onion
Salt
3 tblsp. chopped fresh parsley
2 tblsp. chopped pimientos
12 eggs, beaten
2 tblsp. water
¼ tsp. pepper
2 tblsp. vegetable oil

In 10" skillet over medium heat,
cook bacon until browned. Drain on
paper towels. Pour off all but
2 tblsp. drippings.

Add potatoes, onion and ½ tsp.
salt to drippings. Over medium heat
cook until potatoes are tender and
golden. Stir in bacon, parsley and
pimientos; set aside.

In medium bowl beat eggs, water,
pepper and 1 tsp. salt. Stir in vegetable mixture until well blended.

In 12" skillet over medium heat,
heat oil until hot. Pour egg mixture
into skillet. Cook, lifting cooked egg
portion around edge of pan with fork
so uncooked portion flows underneath. Slide pan back and forth to
prevent sticking. Continue cooking
until mixture is set, but top is
creamy. Fold in half and slide onto
serving platter. Makes 6 servings.

SPINACH-TOMATO FRITTATA

(see photo on front jacket)

*Cheddar cheese can replace the
muenster in this open-faced omelet.*

1 tblsp. vegetable oil
1 medium onion, chopped
1 clove garlic, minced
½ lb. spinach, coarsely chopped and
    drained on paper towels
1 medium tomato, chopped and
    drained on paper towels
6 eggs
½ c. shredded muenster cheese (2 oz.)
¼ c. grated Parmesan cheese
½ tsp. salt
½ tsp. dried basil leaves
½ tsp. dried thyme leaves
⅛ tsp. pepper

In 10" broiler-proof skillet over
medium-high heat, heat oil until hot.
Add onion and garlic; cook until
tender.

Add spinach and tomato. Cover
and cook until spinach wilts.

Meanwhile, in medium bowl beat
eggs and remaining ingredients until
well blended.

Pour egg mixture into skillet.
Reduce heat to medium-low. Cover
and cook 4 to 5 minutes or until eggs
are set around edge, but still runny
in the center.

Broil, 6" from the source of heat,
until top is lightly browned, about
2 minutes.

To serve, cut into wedges. Makes
4 to 6 servings.

TO MICROWAVE: Use same ingredients.
In 10" microwave-safe pie plate
place oil, onion and garlic. Cover
with waxed paper.

Microwave at high setting (100%
power) 2 to 3 minutes or until
tender, stirring after 1 minute.

Add spinach and tomato. Cover
again, and microwave at high setting
2 to 3 minutes or until spinach wilts,
stirring after 1 minute.

In medium bowl beat eggs and
remaining ingredients until well
blended.

Pour egg mixture into pie plate. Microwave, uncovered, at medium setting (50% power) 1 minute. Stir to break up cooked egg.

Microwave 2 to 3 minutes or until center top is moist but set below, lifting edge with spatula each minute, so uncooked portion spreads evenly underneath.

Broil as directed.

PORK EGG FOO YONG_____

An egg pancake that's chock-full of crispy vegetables—great for brunch!

Oriental Sauce (recipe follows)
3 to 4 tblsp. vegetable oil
1 c. shredded cabbage
½ c. sliced green onions
⅓ c. chopped green pepper
1 clove garlic, minced
6 eggs, beaten
1 c. diced, cooked pork
1 c. fresh mung bean sprouts
½ c. water chestnuts, chopped
1 tblsp. soy sauce
¼ tsp. grated fresh ginger root

Prepare Oriental Sauce; keep warm.

In 10″ skillet over medium heat, heat 1 tblsp. oil until hot. Add cabbage, green onions, green pepper and garlic; cook 2 minutes.

Spoon cabbage mixture into bowl; cool slightly. Stir in beaten eggs and remaining ingredients except remaining oil and Oriental Sauce.

In same skillet over medium-high heat, heat 1 tblsp. oil until hot. Pour ¼ c. egg mixture into skillet, spreading mixture to make a 5″ pancake. Cook, turning once, about 3 minutes or until golden brown on both sides. Repeat with remaining egg mixture, adding oil as needed, making 10 pancakes.

To serve, spoon sauce over pancakes. Makes 5 servings.

Oriental Sauce: In small saucepan stir together 1 tblsp. cornstarch and 1½ tsp. sugar until blended. Stir in 1 c. water, 2 tblsp. soy sauce and 1½ tsp. vinegar.

Over medium heat cook, stirring constantly, until mixture boils and thickens. Stir in 2 tblsp. sliced green onions. Makes about 1 c.

TO MICROWAVE: Use same ingredients, *reducing oil as indicated.*

Prepare Oriental Sauce; set aside.

In 2-qt. microwave-safe casserole place cabbage, green onions, green pepper, garlic and *1 tblsp. oil.* Cover with lid or plastic wrap, turning back one section to vent steam.

Microwave at high setting (100% power) 2 to 3 minutes or until tender, stirring after 1 minute. Cool slightly.

Stir beaten eggs and remaining ingredients except Oriental Sauce into vegetable mixture.

Pour half of mixture into 9″ microwave-safe pie plate. Cover with waxed paper. Microwave at medium setting (50% power) 1 minute; stir. Cover again, and microwave 2½ to 4 minutes or until center top is moist but set below, lifting edge with spatula each minute, so uncooked portion spreads evenly underneath. Let stand, covered, 1 minute. Repeat with remaining egg mixture. Cut into 5 wedges.

Reheat Oriental Sauce and spoon over pancakes.

TO MICROWAVE ORIENTAL SAUCE: Use same ingredients.

In 2 c. glass measure stir together cornstarch and sugar. Stir in water, soy sauce and vinegar.

Microwave at high setting (100% power) 1 to 3 minutes or until mixture boils and thickens, stirring each minute. Stir in green onions.

BROCCOLI SOUFFLÉ

This light and airy soufflé makes a great breakfast or luncheon dish.

6 tblsp. butter or regular margarine
⅓ c. flour
¾ tsp. salt
¼ tsp. ground nutmeg
⅛ tsp. pepper
1½ c. milk
1½ c. chopped fresh broccoli, cooked and
    drained, or 1 (10-oz.) pkg. frozen
    chopped broccoli, thawed and drained
6 eggs, separated
¼ tsp. cream of tartar
1 c. shredded Swiss cheese

Preheat oven to 400°.

In 2-qt. saucepan over medium-high heat, melt butter. Stir in flour, salt, nutmeg and pepper until smooth. Gradually stir in milk. Cook, stirring constantly, 5 minutes or until mixture boils and thickens. Remove from heat.

In small bowl beat egg yolks with fork. Stir some of the hot mixture into egg yolks, then stir egg yolk mixture back into hot mixture.

Over low heat, cook, stirring constantly, 1 minute. Remove from heat. Stir in broccoli.

In large bowl using mixer at high speed, beat egg whites and cream of tartar until stiff, but not dry peaks form. Fold egg yolk mixture and cheese into egg whites.

Pour into greased 2-qt. soufflé dish. Place on lowest rack of oven. Reduce oven temperature to 375° and bake 45 minutes or until top is puffy and browned. Serve immediately. Makes 6 servings.

Spinach Soufflé: Prepare as directed, but substitute 1 lb. fresh spinach, cooked, chopped and drained, or 1 (10-oz.) pkg. frozen chopped spinach, thawed and drained, for broccoli.

TO MICROWAVE: Use same ingredients, *changing amounts and substituting ingredients as indicated.*

In 1½-qt. microwave-safe casserole place ¼ *c. butter.* Microwave at high setting (100% power) 45 seconds to 1 minute or until melted. Stir in salt, nutmeg, pepper and ¼ *c. flour.* Using wire whisk stir in *1 (15-oz.) can evaporated milk; omit whole milk.*

Microwave at high setting 2 minutes; stir. Microwave 4 to 6 minutes or until sauce is thick and smooth, stirring after each minute. Stir in cheese until melted.

In small bowl beat egg yolks with fork. Stir some of the hot mixture into egg yolks, then stir egg yolk mixture back into hot mixture. Stir in broccoli or spinach; set aside.

Make waxed paper collar and tape around top of 2-qt. microwave-safe soufflé dish.

Beat egg whites and *1 tsp. cream of tartar* as directed. Fold egg yolk mixture into egg whites; pour into dish.

Microwave at low setting (30% power) 25 to 35 minutes or until center appears moist on top, but when touched with finger is dry underneath, rotating dish one-quarter turn every 6 minutes.

Place *1 tblsp. butter and ⅛ tsp. paprika* in microwave-safe custard dish. Microwave at high setting 1 minute or until melted. Brush on top of cooked soufflé before serving.

BLENDER SPINACH SOUFFLÉ

With the help of your blender, this soufflé is ready to bake in a flash.

2 c. creamed-style cottage cheese
½ c. shredded Cheddar cheese (2 oz.)
3 eggs
⅓ c. flour
¼ c. butter or regular margarine, melted
¾ tsp. salt
¼ tsp. ground nutmeg
¼ tsp. pepper
2 lb. fresh spinach, cooked, chopped and drained, or 2 (10-oz.) pkg. frozen chopped spinach, thawed and drained

In blender container place all ingredients except spinach; cover. Blend at high speed 1 minute or until smooth. Pour into bowl; stir in spinach.

Pour spinach mixture into greased 2-qt. soufflé dish. Set dish in pan of hot water.

Bake in 350° oven 1 hour or until set. Makes 8 servings.

BROCCOLI QUICHE

The chunks of cheese form a pretty pattern as this pie bakes.

1 unbaked 9" Pie Shell with fluted edge (see Index)
2 c. chopped fresh broccoli, cooked and drained, or 2 (10-oz.) pkg. frozen chopped broccoli, thawed and drained
1 whole chicken breast, cooked and cut into 1" pieces
6 oz. Swiss cheese, cut into ¼" cubes
3 eggs
1 c. heavy cream
2 tblsp. lemon juice
1 tsp. salt
⅛ tsp. pepper
Chopped chives

Prepare Pie Shell as directed. Refrigerate 30 minutes.

Sprinkle broccoli in bottom of shell. Top with chicken, then cheese.

In small bowl using wire whisk, beat eggs, cream, lemon juice, salt and pepper until blended, but not frothy. Pour over cheese mixture; sprinkle with chives.

Bake in 375° oven 35 to 40 minutes or until knife inserted in center comes out clean. Let stand 10 minutes before cutting. Makes 6 to 8 servings.

TO MICROWAVE: Use same ingredients, *but substitute Microwaved Pie Shell (see Index) for Pie Shell.*

Prepare *Microwaved Pie Shell.*
Sprinkle chicken in bottom of shell. Top with broccoli, then cheese.

In 1-qt. microwave-safe casserole using wire whisk, beat together eggs, cream, lemon juice, salt and pepper until blended, but not frothy.

Microwave at medium setting (50% power) 1 to 3 minutes or until warm and slightly thickened, stirring every 45 seconds. Pour over cheese mixture; sprinkle with chives.

Microwave at medium setting 13 to 16 minutes or until knife inserted 1" from center comes out clean, rotating plate one-quarter turn every 4 minutes. Let stand 10 minutes.

CORN QUICHE

Fresh sweet corn in a velvety custard flavored with Swiss cheese.

1 unbaked 9" Pie Shell with fluted edge (see Index)
5 slices bacon, cooked, drained and crumbled
2 c. fresh or frozen corn, cooked and drained
½ c. shredded Swiss cheese (2 oz.)
½ c. finely chopped onion
¼ c. chopped green onions
1 c. light cream
½ tsp. sugar
¼ tsp. seasoned salt
¼ tsp. ground nutmeg
⅛ tsp. pepper
4 eggs
Paprika

Prepare Pie Shell as directed. Refrigerate 30 minutes.

In medium bowl toss together bacon, corn, cheese, onion and green onions; sprinkle in bottom of shell.

In small bowl using wire whisk, beat together cream, sugar, seasoned salt, nutmeg, pepper and eggs. Pour over corn mixture; sprinkle with paprika.

Bake in 400° oven 25 minutes. Reduce heat to 325° and bake 20 minutes or until knife inserted in center comes out clean. Let stand 10 minutes before cutting. Makes 6 to 8 servings.

Zucchini Quiche: Prepare as directed, but substitute 2 c. shredded zucchini for corn.

To prepare zucchini: Place shredded zucchini in dish towel; wrap and twist to squeeze out as much liquid as possible.

TO MICROWAVE: Use same ingredients, *but substitute Microwaved Pie Shell (see Index) for Pie Shell.*

In 2-qt. microwave-safe bowl using wire whisk, beat together onion, green onions, cream, sugar, seasoned salt, nutmeg, pepper and eggs.

Microwave at medium setting (50% power) 4 to 6 minutes or until very hot and slightly thickened, stirring with wire whisk each minute. Stir in bacon, cheese, corn or zucchini.

Pour into baked pie shell. Sprinkle with paprika. Microwave at medium setting 11 to 13 minutes or until knife inserted 1" from center comes out clean, rotating plate one-quarter turn every 3 minutes. Let stand 10 minutes.

RICE AND GREENS IN SPICY PEANUT SAUCE

This East African main dish was given to a South Dakota farm woman by her college roommate, whose home was in Tanzania. It's also called Obe-epa.

3 tblsp. vegetable oil
2 medium onions, chopped
2 medium red or green sweet peppers, chopped
1 dried chili pepper, halved and seeded
1 tsp. dried rosemary leaves
½ tsp. salt
1 (16-oz.) can tomato sauce
¾ c. water
6 tblsp. peanut butter
6 c. lightly packed, chopped Swiss chard or spinach
Hot cooked rice
1 c. unsalted peanuts

In 12" skillet over medium-high heat, heat oil until hot. Add onions, sweet peppers, chili pepper, rosemary and salt; cook 5 minutes or until onions are tender.

Add tomato sauce, water and peanut butter. Cook, stirring constantly, until mixture is well blended and comes to a boil.

Stir in Swiss chard. Cover; cook 3 minutes or until Swiss chard is wilted. Remove chili pepper.

To serve, spoon mixture over rice; sprinkle with peanuts. Makes 4 main-dish or 12 (½-c.) servings.

SUNNY ASPARAGUS

For a spring luncheon, serve tender asparagus in a delicate cream sauce.

6 hard-cooked eggs
¼ c. butter or regular margarine
¼ c. flour
½ tsp. salt
¼ tsp. dry mustard
Dash of pepper
2¼ c. milk
¼ tsp. Worcestershire sauce
5 lb. fresh asparagus spears, trimmed,
  cooked and drained

Remove yolks from hard-cooked eggs. Press yolks through sieve; cover and set aside. Chop whites; set aside.

In 3-qt. saucepan over medium-high heat, melt butter. Stir in flour, salt, dry mustard and pepper until smooth. Gradually stir in milk and Worcestershire sauce until well blended.

Cook, stirring constantly, until mixture boils and thickens. Stir in egg whites.

To serve, spoon sauce over hot asparagus; sprinkle with egg yolks. Makes 12 servings.

Sunny Green Beans: Prepare as directed, but substitute 3 lb. trimmed green beans, cooked and drained, for asparagus.

TO MICROWAVE: Use same ingredients, *reducing milk as indicated.*

Sieve egg yolks and chop egg whites as directed.

In 4-c. glass measure place butter. Microwave at high setting (100% power) 1½ to 2 minutes or until melted. With wire whisk beat in flour, salt, dry mustard and pepper until smooth. Gradually beat in *2 c. milk* and Worcestershire sauce until well blended.

Microwave at high setting 1 minute; stir. Microwave at high setting 6 to 8 minutes or until sauce boils and thickens, stirring every 2 minutes. Stir in chopped egg whites.

Serve sauce with asparagus or green beans as directed.

VEGETABLE-FILLED DUTCH PANCAKE

(see photo following page 182)

This puffy pancake makes an ideal container for stir-fried vegetables.

½ c. flour
½ c. milk
2 eggs
Salt
1 tblsp. vegetable oil
3 tblsp. butter or regular margarine
1 lb. mushrooms, quartered
1 large green pepper, cut into 1" strips
2 c. sliced zucchini
2 c. sliced carrots, cooked and drained
1 c. sliced green onions
1 tsp. dried savory leaves
⅛ tsp. pepper
2 c. shredded Gouda cheese (8 oz.)

In 450° oven on lowest rack, preheat 10" casserole pan (or heavy oven-safe 10" skillet) 5 minutes.

In bowl using mixer at medium speed, beat flour, milk, eggs and ¼ tsp. salt 2 minutes or until well blended.

Add oil to hot pan, tilting to coat bottom and side. Pour batter into pan. Bake 10 minutes. Reduce heat to 350° and bake 10 minutes or until puffed and browned. (As the pancake bakes, it rises and looks like a popover. As it cools, it will shrink slightly.)

Meanwhile, in 12" skillet over medium-high heat, melt butter. Add mushrooms, green pepper and zucchini; cook 5 minutes. Stir in carrots, green onions, savory, pepper and ¾ tsp. salt; cook until liquid evaporates, about 5 minutes.

Reduce heat to low. Stir in 1½ c. cheese until melted.

Spoon vegetable-cheese mixture into pancake. Sprinkle with remaining ½ c. cheese.

Broil, 6" from source of heat, 1 to 2 minutes or until cheese melts.

Cut into wedges. Serve immediately. Makes 6 servings.

STIR-FRIED BEEF WITH VEGETABLES

Instead of rice, serve this ginger-flavored dish over cooked pasta.

4 tblsp. vegetable oil
1 lb. beef round steak, cut diagonally into 2x¼" strips
1 clove garlic, minced
⅛ tsp. pepper
4 small onions, quartered
2 beef bouillon cubes
¼ tsp. ground ginger
Water
1 medium green pepper, cut into ¼" strips
½ lb. fresh snow peas, trimmed, or 1 (6-oz.) pkg. frozen snow peas, thawed
2 medium tomatoes, each cut into 8 wedges
3 tblsp. soy sauce
2 tblsp. cornstarch
Hot cooked rice

In 12" skillet over medium-high heat, heat 2 tblsp. oil until hot.

Add beef, garlic and pepper; cook, stirring quickly and constantly, 3 minutes. Remove from skillet.

Add remaining 2 tblsp. oil to skillet; heat until hot. Add onions; cook, stirring quickly and constantly, until tender.

Stir in bouillon cubes, ginger and 1 c. water. Cover and simmer 4 minutes.

Add green pepper. Cover and simmer 3 minutes. Stir in beef, snow peas and tomatoes. Cook, stirring quickly and constantly, 2 minutes.

In small bowl stir together soy sauce, cornstarch and ½ c. water until well blended. Stir into beef mixture. Cook until mixture boils and thickens.

Serve over hot cooked rice. Makes 6 servings.

CHINESE PEPPER STEAK

Add more crushed red pepper for a hot 'n' spicy Szechuan flavor.

½ c. water or beef broth
½ c. soy sauce
½ c. dry sherry
2 tblsp. cornstarch
½ tsp. grated fresh ginger root
¼ tsp. crushed red pepper
3 tblsp. vegetable oil
1½ lb. beef top round or flank steak, cut diagonally into ⅛" strips
½ lb. mushrooms, sliced
4 green onions, cut into 1" pieces
3 medium green peppers, cut into ¼" strips
2 medium onions, coarsely chopped
1 clove garlic, minced
1 (8-oz.) can sliced water chestnuts, drained
1 pt. cherry tomatoes, each cut in half
Hot cooked rice

In small bowl stir first 6 ingredients until well blended; set aside.

In 12" skillet over high heat, heat 2 tblsp. oil until hot. Add half of the beef. Cook, stirring quickly and constantly, until beef loses its pink color. Remove beef to bowl. Repeat with remaining beef.

Add remaining 1 tblsp. oil; heat until hot. Add mushrooms, green onions, green peppers, onions and garlic; cook, stirring quickly and constantly, until vegetables are tender-crisp.

Stir in cornstarch mixture. Cook, stirring constantly, until mixture boils and thickens.

Add beef, water chestnuts and tomatoes. Cover and cook until mixture is heated through.

Serve over hot cooked rice. Makes 6 servings.

ORIENTAL HOT POT

Traditionally, each person cooks the vegetables, chicken and shrimp in chicken broth right at the table.

½ c. soy sauce
½ c. water
¼ c. dry sherry
2 tblsp. sugar
1 tblsp. vinegar
¼ tsp. ground ginger
2 green onions, minced
1 clove garlic, minced
1 medium carrot
1 (8-oz.) pkg. medium egg noodles, cooked and drained
½ lb. shrimp, fresh or frozen and thawed
¼ lb. fresh snow peas
¼ lb. mushrooms, cut into ¼" slices
2 leeks, cut into 1" pieces
1 whole chicken breast, skinned, boned and thinly sliced
1 small rutabaga, peeled, halved and thinly sliced
2 c. loosely packed fresh spinach
2 qt. chicken broth

In 1-qt. saucepan over medium heat, cook first 8 ingredients, stirring constantly, until sugar dissolves. Ladle sauce into 4 small bowls; set aside.

Using vegetable peeler cut carrot into long thin strips. Arrange carrot, noodles and remaining ingredients except chicken broth on large platter. Cover and refrigerate until ready to cook.

To cook on top of the range: In 6-qt. Dutch oven over high heat, bring chicken broth to a boil. Add one-quarter of the noodles, chicken, shrimp and vegetables. Cook until chicken and shrimp are tender and vegetables are tender-crisp. Remove with slotted spoon. Serve immediately with sauce. Repeat to cook remaining chicken, shrimp and vegetables.

To cook at the table: In electric wok at high setting, bring chicken broth to a boil. (An electric skillet can be used in place of the wok, but fill the skillet half-full with chicken broth.) Let each person cook noodles, chicken, shrimp and vegetables in boiling broth.

After all the cooking is done, ladle broth into bowls and serve as soup. Makes 4 servings.

CHINESE CHICKEN WITH VEGETABLES

For a festive stir-fry, cook ½ lb. shrimp with the chicken.

2 whole chicken breasts (about 12 oz. each), skinned and boned
3 tblsp. vegetable oil
1 lb. mushrooms, sliced
2 medium onions, sliced and separated into rings
1 c. diagonally sliced celery
2 cloves garlic, minced
¾ tsp. ground ginger
¼ c. soy sauce
Water
¾ lb. fresh snow peas, trimmed, or 2 (6-oz.) pkg. frozen snow peas, thawed
2 tblsp. cornstarch
Hot cooked rice
½ c. chopped walnuts

Freeze chicken 20 minutes to make cutting easier.

Cut chicken breasts crosswise into 2x¼" strips.

In 12" skillet over high heat, heat oil until hot. Cook, stirring quickly and constantly, until chicken is tender.

Add mushrooms, onions, celery, garlic, ginger, soy sauce and ½ c. water; cook until mixture boils.

Reduce heat to low. Cover and simmer 5 minutes. Increase heat to medium. Stir in snow peas and return to a boil. Cover and cook 3 minutes.

In small bowl stir together cornstarch and 2 tblsp. water; stir into chicken mixture. Cook, stirring constantly, until mixture boils and thickens.

Serve over hot cooked rice. Garnish with chopped walnuts. Makes 6 servings.

CHICKEN AND VEGETABLE TEMPURA

This versatile Tempura Batter can be used to coat most vegetables.

Tempura Batter (recipe follows)
Sweet-Sour Sauce
  (recipe follows)
Lemon Sauce (recipe follows)
2 qt. vegetable oil
1 small acorn squash
2 whole chicken breasts, skinned,
  boned and cut into ½" strips
2 c. fresh broccoli flowerets
1 c. diagonally sliced carrots
  (¼" thick)
Flour

Prepare Tempura Batter, Sweet-Sour and Lemon Sauces.

In 4-qt. Dutch oven over medium-high heat, heat oil to 360° on a deep-fat thermometer.

Meanwhile, cut acorn squash in half lengthwise. Refrigerate half for later use. Scoop out and discard seeds of remaining half; cut squash crosswise into ¼"-thick slices. Pat chicken and vegetables dry, then coat with flour; set aside on baking sheet.

Dip chicken and vegetables in Tempura Batter; set aside to dry.

Slide 8 chicken or vegetable pieces into hot oil. Cook 2 minutes or until golden brown on all sides. Remove with slotted spoon; drain on paper towels. Keep warm. Repeat with remaining chicken and vegetables. Serve with sauces. Makes 4 to 6 servings.

Tempura Batter: In bowl using a fork, mix together 2 eggs and 2 c. iced water. Add 2 c. sifted flour and ½ tsp. salt. Continue mixing just until combined.

Sweet-Sour Sauce: In small bowl mix together ¼ c. vegetable oil, ¼ c. soy sauce, 2 tblsp. ketchup, 1 tblsp. white vinegar, ¼ tsp. pepper and 2 cloves garlic, minced. Makes ⅔ c.

Lemon Sauce: In 1-qt. saucepan mix together ½ c. water and 2 tsp. corn-starch. Stir in ¼ c. lemon juice, ¼ c. honey, 2 tblsp. white vinegar, 2 tblsp. vegetable oil, 1 tblsp. ketchup and ½ tsp. garlic salt.

Over medium heat cook, stirring constantly, until mixture boils and thickens. Refrigerate until ready to serve. Makes 1 c.

VEGETARIAN STUFFED PEPPERS

Peppers are stuffed with a flavorful mix of rice, corn and cheese.

8 medium green peppers
1 tblsp. vegetable oil
½ c. finely chopped carrots
½ c. sliced green onions
¼ c. finely chopped celery
1 clove garlic, minced
½ c. spicy tomato juice
¾ tsp. chili powder
½ tsp. salt
⅛ tsp. pepper
½ lb. Monterey Jack cheese, cubed (2 c.)
2 c. cooked brown or white rice
1½ c. corn, fresh or frozen and thawed
1 large tomato, cut into 8 slices

Using sharp knife cut off tops of peppers. Remove seeds and membranes.

In 12" skillet place steamer rack and 2 c. water. Place peppers cut-side down on rack. Over high heat bring to a boil. Reduce heat to medium. Cover and steam peppers 5 minutes. Drain.

In 7" skillet over medium-high heat, heat oil until hot. Add carrots, onions, celery and garlic; cook until vegetables are tender-crisp.

Stir in tomato juice, chili powder, salt and pepper. Reduce heat to low. Cover and simmer 10 minutes or until vegetables are tender.

In large bowl stir together cheese, rice and corn. Stir in cooked vegetables.

Spoon about ½ c. vegetable-rice mixture into each pepper. In 13x9x2" baking dish place peppers. Top each with tomato slice.

Bake in 350° oven 20 minutes or until filling is hot and cheese melts. Makes 8 servings.

Stuffed Acorn Squash: Prepare as directed, but substitute 4 large acorn squash for green peppers, and omit tomato.

Cut squash in half crosswise; remove and discard seeds. Steam squash halves 10 minutes.

Continue recipe as directed.

Serve stuffed squash with Onion Sauce (see Index). Makes 8 servings.

TO MICROWAVE PEPPERS: Use same ingredients, *changing amounts as indicated.*

(Stuffed Acorn Squash is not recommended for this appliance.)

Prepare peppers as directed.

In 12x8x2" microwave-safe baking dish place ½ c. *water* and peppers, cut-side down. Cover with plastic wrap, turning back one section to vent steam.

Microwave at high setting (100% power) 10 to 12 minutes or until tender, rearranging peppers every 3 minutes. Let stand, covered, 5 minutes. Drain.

In 2-qt. microwave-safe casserole place oil, carrot, onions, celery and garlic. Cover with lid or plastic wrap.

Microwave at high setting 2 to 3 minutes or until vegetables are tender, stirring after 1 minute. Stir in tomato juice, salt, pepper and *1 tsp. chili powder.*

Microwave, uncovered, at high setting 2 to 3 minutes or until vegetables are tender and mixture is very hot, stirring after 1 minute.

In large bowl stir together cheese, rice, corn and cooked vegetables as directed.

Stuff peppers as directed.

In 12x8x2" microwave-safe baking dish place peppers. Top each with tomato slice. Cover with waxed paper.

Microwave at high setting 5 to 7 minutes or until cheese melts, rotating dish one-half turn every 2 minutes. Let stand, covered, 2 minutes.

MACARONI IN GREEN PEPPER CUPS

Serve these simple, cheese-filled peppers for a Saturday lunch.

6 large green peppers
2¼ c. shredded sharp Cheddar cheese (9 oz.)
1 (8-oz.) pkg. elbow macaroni, cooked and drained
1 c. dairy sour cream
2 tblsp. finely chopped onion
½ tsp. salt
¼ tsp. pepper
⅛ tsp. dry mustard
⅛ tsp. paprika

Using sharp knife cut off tops of peppers. Remove seeds and membrane.

In 12" skillet place steamer rack and 2 c. water. Place peppers cut-side down on rack. Over high heat bring to a boil. Reduce heat to medium. Cover and steam peppers 5 minutes. Drain; place in 3" muffin-pan cups.

In large bowl stir 2 c. cheese and remaining ingredients until well blended.

Spoon about 1 c. macaroni mixture into each pepper; sprinkle with remaining cheese.

Bake in 350° oven 10 to 15 minutes or until hot and cheese melts. Makes 6 servings.

TO MICROWAVE: Use same ingredients, *reducing water as indicated.*

In 12x8x2" microwave-safe dish place ½ c. *water* and peppers, cut-side down. Cover with plastic wrap, turning back one section to vent steam. Microwave at high setting (100% power) 10 to 12 minutes or until tender, rearranging peppers every 3 minutes. Let stand 5 minutes. Drain.

In large bowl stir 2 c. cheese and remaining ingredients until well blended.

Place green peppers in same dish. Spoon about 1 c. macaroni mixture into each pepper. Cover with waxed paper.

Microwave at high setting 8 to 10 minutes or until filling is hot, rotating dish one-half turn every 3 minutes. Sprinkle with remaining cheese.

Microwave, uncovered, 1 to 2 minutes more or until cheese melts.

SAUCY CABBAGE BUNDLES

A beer and herb sauce replaces the expected tomato sauce in this dish.

1 large head cabbage
1½ lb. ground pork
½ c. soft bread crumbs
½ c. milk
¼ c. chopped fresh parsley
2 eggs
¾ tsp. salt
¼ tsp. pepper
¼ tsp. ground nutmeg
1½ c. finely chopped onions
1½ tsp. dried thyme leaves
6 slices bacon, diced
1½ c. sliced carrots
2 cloves garlic, minced
1 (12-oz.) can beer
1 tblsp. cider vinegar
1 tsp. sugar
¼ tsp. dried rosemary leaves
1 chicken bouillon cube
⅓ c. water
3 tblsp. flour
¼ tsp. browning sauce for gravy

Core cabbage; carefully remove 16 large leaves. Cut coarse vein from each leaf. Place leaves in large bowl; cover with boiling water. Let stand 15 minutes or until leaves soften. Drain well.

In large bowl mix together ground pork, bread crumbs, milk, parsley, eggs, salt, pepper, nutmeg, ½ c. onions and 1 tsp. thyme.

In center of each cabbage leaf place about ¼ c. pork mixture. Roll up, folding in sides to form bundles.

In 4-qt. Dutch oven over medium-high heat, cook bacon until browned. Drain bacon on paper towels. Pour off all but 1 tblsp. bacon drippings.

Add carrots, garlic and remaining 1 c. onion to pan drippings. Over medium heat cook until onion is tender. Stir in beer, vinegar, sugar, rosemary, bouillon cube and remaining ½ tsp. thyme.

Arrange cabbage bundles in sauce. Bring to a boil. Reduce heat to medium-low. Cover and simmer 45 minutes or until tender.

Remove cabbage bundles with slotted spoon to serving dish.

In jar with tight-fitting lid, place water and flour; cover. Shake until blended. Stir flour mixture and browning sauce for gravy into Dutch oven.

Over medium-high heat cook, stirring constantly, until mixture boils and thickens.

To serve, spoon sauce over cabbage bundles. Sprinkle with bacon. Makes 6 to 8 servings.

STUFFED CABBAGE WITH CHEESE SAUCE

A whole cabbage, stuffed and bathed in a creamy cheese sauce.

1 (2½-lb.) cabbage
2 tblsp. butter or regular margarine
2 medium onions, chopped
1 clove garlic, minced
1½ c. diced cooked chicken
1 c. chopped cooked spinach
½ c. cooked rice
½ tsp. salt
½ tsp. dried thyme leaves
¼ tsp. pepper
⅛ tsp. ground allspice
2 eggs
½ c. chicken broth
Cheddar Sauce (see Index)

In 6-qt. saucepot over high heat, bring 2 qt. water to a boil.

Meanwhile, trim outer leaves and stem from cabbage.

Place cabbage in water. Cook, uncovered, 10 to 15 minutes or until cabbage is almost fork-tender. Drain well. Scoop out inside of cabbage, leaving a ½" shell. Chop cabbage; reserve ½ c. Use remaining cabbage for slaw or soup.

In 7″ skillet over medium-high heat, melt butter. Add onions and garlic; cook until tender.

In large bowl mix reserved chopped cabbage, onion mixture, chicken, spinach, rice, salt, thyme, pepper, allspice and eggs until well blended.

Spoon filling mixture into cabbage shell. Tie string around cabbage to secure filling.

Place cabbage, stuffed-side up, on rack set in 4-qt. Dutch oven. Pour in chicken broth. Cover and bake in 325° oven 30 minutes or until cabbage is tender.

Meanwhile, prepare Cheddar Sauce.

To serve, place cabbage, stuffed-side down, on serving platter. Discard string. Cut cabbage into 6 wedges. Ladle sauce over each wedge. Makes 6 servings.

TO MICROWAVE: Use same ingredients, *changing amounts as indicated.*

Trim cabbage as directed; *reserve 1 leaf.*

In 3-qt. microwave-safe casserole place cabbage and *½ c. water.* Cover with lid or plastic wrap, turning back one section to vent steam.

Microwave at high setting (100% power) 8 to 10 minutes or until cabbage yields when pressed with finger, turning cabbage over after 5 minutes. Drain well.

Scoop out cabbage as directed. Chop cabbage; reserve ½ c.

In 1-qt. microwave-safe casserole place butter, onions and garlic. Cover with lid or plastic wrap. Microwave at high setting 2 to 3 minutes or until tender, stirring after 1 minute.

Mix stuffing as directed. Stuff cabbage as directed. Place reserved leaf over stuffed cabbage to close opening; tie with string.

In 3-qt. microwave-safe casserole place cabbage, stuffed-side up. Pour in *¼ c. broth.* Cover with lid or plastic wrap.

Microwave at high setting 5 minutes. Turn cabbage over. Microwave 5 to 8 minutes or until cabbage

is tender. Let stand, covered, 3 minutes.

Prepare Cheddar Sauce.

To serve, place cabbage, stuffed-side down, on serving platter. Serve with sauce as directed.

CREOLE CABBAGE ROLLS

Using Chinese cabbage for the rolls makes the dish easy to prepare.

    2 c. Creole Sauce (see Index), or
        prepared tomato sauce
    1 (2¼-lb.) Chinese cabbage (Pe-tsai or
        Napa)
    1 lb. ground beef
    1 medium onion, minced
    1 c. cooked rice
    ¼ c. chopped fresh parsley
    1 tsp. salt
    ½ tsp. dried thyme leaves
    ¼ tsp. pepper
    1 egg

Prepare 2 c. Creole Sauce as directed.

Carefully remove 10 cabbage leaves. In 10″ skillet over high heat, bring 1″ water to a boil. Add 1 cabbage leaf; blanch for 30 seconds. Remove leaf with tongs. Drain; set aside. Repeat with remaining leaves.

In medium bowl mix ground beef and remaining ingredients until well blended.

Spoon ⅓ c. meat mixture onto cabbage leaf at the stem end. Roll up, folding in sides of leaf to secure filling. Repeat with remaining cabbage leaves and meat mixture.

In 12x8x2″ baking dish arrange cabbage rolls, seam-side down. Pour 1 c. of Creole Sauce over rolls. Cover dish tightly with aluminum foil.

Bake in 350° oven 1 hour or until cabbage is tender and sauce is bubbly. Remove cabbage rolls with slotted spoon to serving dish.

In 2-qt. saucepan place cooking liquid from rolls and remaining 1 c. Creole Sauce. Over high heat cook until heated through.

To serve, spoon sauce over rolls. Makes 5 servings.

STUFFED EGGPLANT

Scooped-out eggplants make perfect containers for this spicy dish from Louisiana's Cajun country.

2 medium eggplants (1 to 1¼ lb. each)
½ tsp. salt
3 tblsp. butter or regular margarine
⅔ c. chopped green onions
2 cloves garlic, minced
1½ tsp. dried thyme leaves
2 bay leaves
1½ c. soft bread crumbs
1 c. diced cooked ham (¼" cubes)
2 tblsp. chopped fresh parsley
⅛ tsp. pepper
1 egg, slightly beaten
3 tblsp. dry bread crumbs
1½ tblsp. grated Parmesan cheese
¼ tsp. paprika

Cut eggplants in half lengthwise from stem to blossom end. Sprinkle with salt. Place eggplants flesh-side down on paper towels 30 minutes to drain. Turn over, brush off salt and pat dry.

Loosen the pulp of each eggplant with knife by cutting all the way around inside of each half, ¼" from skin.

Bake in 350° oven 40 minutes or until skin yields when pressed with finger.

Carefully scoop out pulp so shells retain their shape. Chop pulp and set aside.

In 7" skillet over medium-high heat, melt 1½ tblsp. butter. Add green onions, garlic, thyme and bay leaves. Cook, stirring often, until onions are tender. Remove from heat. Remove bay leaves.

In large bowl toss together chopped eggplant, onion mixture, soft bread crumbs, ham, parsley and pepper. Add egg and toss until well coated.

Spoon about ½ c. eggplant mixture into each eggplant shell. Sprinkle each stuffed shell with dry bread crumbs, cheese and paprika. Dot with remaining butter.

Place stuffed shells on baking sheet. Bake in 350° oven 20 minutes or until cheese melts and filling is hot. Makes 4 servings.

TO MICROWAVE: Use same ingredients.

Cut and salt eggplant halves as directed.

Carefully scoop out pulp so shells retain their shape. Chop pulp and set aside.

In 2-qt. microwave-safe casserole place pulp, green onions, garlic, thyme, bay leaves, parsley, pepper and 1½ tblsp. butter. Cover with waxed paper. Microwave at high setting (100% power) 6 to 8 minutes or until vegetables are tender, stirring after 4 minutes. Remove bay leaves. Add soft bread crumbs, ham and egg; toss together until well coated. Stuff eggplant shells as directed.

Arrange stuffed shells in circle in 12" round glass pie plate or baking dish. Cover again, and microwave at high setting 6 to 8 minutes or until cheese melts and filling is hot, rotating dish one-half turn after 4 minutes.

EGGPLANT PARMESAN

No need to fry the eggplant; just brush with seasoned oil and broil.

2 medium eggplants (about 1½ lb. each)
⅓ c. olive or vegetable oil
¼ tsp. dried basil leaves
¼ tsp. dried oregano leaves
¼ tsp. dried marjoram leaves
1 clove garlic, minced
1 (15½-oz.) jar spaghetti sauce (1¾ c.)
1 (8-oz.) pkg. shredded mozzarella cheese
½ c. grated Parmesan cheese

Cut each eggplant crosswise into 9 slices about ½" thick.

In small bowl using wire whisk, beat oil, basil, oregano, marjoram and garlic until well blended.

On baking sheet place eggplant slices. Brush slices with half of the oil mixture. Broil, 6" from source of heat, 4 to 5 minutes or until lightly browned.

Turn slices over; brush with remaining oil mixture. Broil 4 to 5 minutes or until lightly browned and tender.

In greased 12x8x2″ glass baking dish spread ¼ c. spaghetti sauce. Layer one-third eggplant slices, top with one-third of the remaining spaghetti sauce and sprinkle with one-third of the mozzarella and Parmesan cheese. Repeat layers twice. Cover dish tightly with aluminum foil.

Bake in 400° oven 20 minutes. Remove foil; bake 10 minutes or until cheese is lightly browned and sauce is bubbly. Makes 6 servings.

GRILLED EGGPLANT AND CHEESE

A Georgia woman writes that eggplant was her family's least favorite vegetable until she served it this way.

2 c. soft bread crumbs
1 tsp. salt
1 tsp. dried oregano leaves
¼ tsp. pepper
¼ c. milk
1 egg, beaten
1 eggplant (1½ lb.), cut into 12 slices
Vegetable oil
¼ lb. piece sharp Cheddar cheese, cut into 12 slices
2 medium tomatoes, each cut into 6 slices
12 slices bacon

On a sheet of waxed paper mix together bread crumbs, salt, oregano and pepper.

In pie plate, beat milk and egg until well blended.

Dip eggplant slices into egg mixture, then in bread crumb mixture until well coated.

In 12″ skillet over medium-high heat, heat ¼ c. oil until hot. Add half of the eggplant slices. Cook until browned on both sides. Drain on paper towels. Continue frying remaining eggplant slices, adding more oil as needed.

Place half of the eggplant slices on broiler rack. Top each with a slice of cheese, tomato and bacon.

Broil, 6″ from source of heat, 5 minutes or until bacon is browned and cheese melts. Remove; drain on paper towels. Repeat with remaining eggplant, cheese, tomato and bacon slices. Makes 4 servings.

ZUCCHINI PIZZA

The "crust" for this rectangular pizza is made from zucchini and rice.

4 c. shredded zucchini
2 c. cooked rice
1½ c. shredded mozzarella cheese (6 oz.)
1½ c. grated Parmesan cheese
2 eggs
1 lb. ground beef
1 medium onion, finely chopped
1 clove garlic, minced
1 (15½-oz.) jar spaghetti sauce
¾ tsp. dried basil leaves
¾ tsp. dried oregano leaves

Place zucchini in dish towel; wrap and twist to squeeze out as much liquid as possible.

In large bowl stir zucchini, rice, 1 c. mozzarella cheese, 1 c. Parmesan cheese and eggs until well blended. Press mixture into greased 15½x10½x1″ jelly-roll pan.

Bake in 400° oven 15 minutes or until mixture is set and lightly browned.

Meanwhile, in 10″ skillet over high heat, cook ground beef 5 minutes. Add onion and garlic. Cook until beef is browned and onion is tender. Pour off fat.

Stir spaghetti sauce, basil and oregano into meat mixture until well blended.

Spoon meat mixture evenly over baked crust. Sprinkle remaining cheese over meat mixture.

Bake in 400° oven 15 minutes or until cheese melts. Let stand 5 minutes.

To serve, cut into 3½″ squares. Makes 6 servings.

POTATO PIZZA

If you have a food processor, use it to shred the potatoes for the crust.

2 lb. potatoes, peeled and coarsely shredded
¼ c. vegetable oil
⅔ c. grated Parmesan cheese
2 (8-oz.) pkg. mozzarella cheese slices
1 c. bottled pizza sauce or spaghetti sauce
½ lb. pork sausage, cooked, drained and crumbled
¼ lb. sliced hard salami, cut into quarters
½ tsp. dried oregano leaves

In large bowl mix together shredded potatoes, oil and ⅓ c. Parmesan cheese. Press mixture evenly into bottom of greased 15½x10½x1" jelly-roll pan.

Bake in 450° oven 40 minutes or until potatoes are lightly browned.

Arrange cheese slices over top of potatoes and spread with pizza sauce. Arrange sausage on top of sauce, then salami. Sprinkle with oregano and ⅓ c. Parmesan cheese.

Bake in 375° oven 15 minutes or until cheese melts and top is lightly browned.

To serve, cut into 3½" squares. Makes 6 to 8 servings.

PASTA PRIMAVERA

Steam fresh green vegetables and toss them with saucy linguini.

½ lb. green beans, trimmed and cut into 1" pieces (2 c.)
1 lb. asparagus, trimmed and cut into 1" pieces (2½ c.)
¾ lb. fresh peas, shelled (1 c.)
1 c. broccoli flowerets
2 tblsp. olive or vegetable oil
½ lb. mushrooms, sliced (2 c.)
1 small red sweet pepper, chopped
2 cloves garlic, minced
2 medium tomatoes, cut into 1" chunks
¼ c. butter or regular margarine
¼ c. flour
1 tsp. salt
1 tsp. dried basil leaves
1 tsp. dried oregano leaves
1 tsp. dried thyme leaves
⅛ tsp. pepper
2½ c. milk
¾ c. grated Parmesan cheese
¼ c. chopped fresh parsley
1 lb. linguini, cooked and drained

In 4-qt. Dutch oven place steamer rack and 3 c. water. Place beans on steamer rack. Over high heat, bring to a boil. Reduce heat to medium. Cover and steam 8 minutes or until beans are tender-crisp. Remove steamer rack and rinse beans under cold running water until cool; place in large bowl. Return rack to skillet.

Place asparagus on rack. Cover and steam 5 minutes or until tender-crisp. Rinse; add to beans.

Add more water to Dutch oven if necessary. Place peas and broccoli on rack. Cover and steam 3 minutes or until tender-crisp. Rinse; add to asparagus.

Meanwhile, in 12" skillet over medium-high heat, heat oil until hot. Add mushrooms, red pepper and garlic; cook until tender. Place in bowl with vegetables. Stir in tomatoes.

In same skillet over medium-high heat, melt butter. Stir in flour, salt, basil, oregano, thyme and pepper until smooth. Gradually stir in milk until well blended.

Cook, stirring constantly, until mixture boils and thickens. Remove from heat; stir in cheese and parsley. Add cooked linguini; toss until well coated.

Add linguini mixture to vegetables; toss until vegetables are well coated. Makes 6 to 8 servings.

TO MICROWAVE: Use same ingredients, *reducing water as indicated.*

In 2-qt. microwave-safe casserole place beans, asparagus and *½ c. water.* Cover with lid or plastic wrap, turning back one section to vent steam.

Microwave at high setting (100% power) 5 to 8 minutes or until tender-crisp, stirring every 2 minutes. Let stand, covered, 2 minutes. Drain and rinse; place in bowl.

In same casserole place peas and *½ c. water.* Cover again, and microwave at high setting 2 minutes. Stir in broccoli.

Cover again, and microwave 1 to 2 minutes or until tender-crisp, stirring each minute. Let stand, covered, 2 minutes. Drain and rinse; place in bowl with asparagus.

In same 2-qt. casserole place oil, mushrooms, red pepper and garlic. Cover again, and microwave at high setting 2 to 3 minutes or until tender, stirring after 1 minute. Place in bowl with other vegetables. Stir in tomatoes.

In same casserole place butter. Cover again, and microwave at high setting 2 to 3 minutes or until melted.

Using wire whisk, beat in flour, salt, basil, oregano, thyme and pepper until smooth. Gradually stir in milk until well blended.

Microwave, uncovered, at high setting 1 minute; stir. Microwave 5 to 7 minutes or until sauce boils and thickens, stirring every 2 minutes. Stir in cheese and parsley. Reheat vegetables if necessary.

Toss and serve as directed.

VEGETABLE BALLS WITH PASTA

Chopped nuts and rice add texture to this meatless main dish.

1 tblsp. vegetable oil
1 medium onion, chopped
1 clove garlic, minced
1 (20-oz.) can chick peas, drained
  (2 c. mashed)
2 tblsp. chopped fresh parsley
1 tsp. dried basil leaves
1 tsp. lemon juice
½ tsp. salt
½ tsp. dried oregano leaves
¼ tsp. ground cumin
⅛ tsp. pepper
1½ c. cooked brown or white rice
½ c. chopped cashews or walnuts
½ c. shredded Cheddar cheese (2 oz.)
2 eggs
Marinara Sauce (see Index) or 2 (15½-oz.)
  jars spaghetti sauce
1 lb. spaghetti, cooked and drained

In 7″ skillet over medium-high heat, heat oil until hot. Add onion and garlic; cook until tender.

In food processor bowl using metal blade, place cooked vegetables, chick peas, parsley, basil, lemon juice, salt, oregano, cumin and pepper; cover. Process until smooth.

In large bowl mix puréed chick pea mixture, rice, nuts, cheese and eggs until well blended. Shape mixture into 2″ balls. (Balls may be refrigerated at this point and cooked later.)

Place balls on greased baking sheet. Bake in 350° oven 25 minutes (if refrigerated, bake in 375° oven 15 to 20 minutes) or until golden brown.

Meanwhile, in 3-qt. saucepan over high heat, bring Marinara Sauce to a boil. Reduce heat to medium. Cook until heated through.

Stir in vegetable balls.

To serve, ladle over spaghetti; allow 3 vegetable balls per serving. Makes 6 servings.

RIGATONI WITH EGGPLANT SAUCE

This meatless tomato sauce is just bursting with garden-fresh flavor.

½ c. vegetable oil
½ lb. mushrooms, sliced (2 c.)
1 small eggplant (about 1 lb.), cut into 1" cubes
1 c. chopped onions
¼ c. chopped fresh parsley
1 clove garlic, minced
2 lb. tomatoes, peeled and cut into ½" chunks
2 (6-oz.) cans tomato paste
1 (8-oz.) can tomato sauce
1 c. water
1 tsp. salt
¾ tsp. dried oregano leaves
½ tsp. dried basil leaves
½ tsp. dried thyme leaves
¼ tsp. pepper
4 drops hot pepper sauce
1 bay leaf
1 lb. rigatoni, cooked and drained

In 4-qt. Dutch oven over medium heat, heat oil until hot. Add mushrooms, eggplant, onions, parsley and garlic; cook until vegetables are tender.

Meanwhile, in blender container place tomatoes; cover. Blend at high speed until smooth.

Stir blended tomatoes, tomato paste and remaining ingredients, except rigatoni, into eggplant mixture.

Over high heat, bring mixture to a boil.

Reduce heat to low. Cover and simmer 1 hour 15 minutes stirring occasionally. Remove bay leaf.

Serve over hot cooked rigatoni. Makes 8 servings.

FOR SLOW COOKER: Use same ingredients, *reducing water as indicated.*

In 12" skillet over medium heat, heat oil until hot. Add mushrooms, eggplant, onions, parsley and garlic; cook until vegetables are tender. Pour mixture into 3½-qt. slow cooker.

Meanwhile, blend tomatoes as directed.

Stir blended tomatoes, tomato paste, tomato sauce, ⅓ c. *water* and remaining ingredients except rigatoni into eggplant mixture; cover.

Cook at low setting 6 to 8 hours. Remove bay leaf.

Serve as directed.

FOR PRESSURE COOKER: Use same ingredients, *reducing water as indicated.*

In 6-qt. pressure cooker over medium heat, heat oil until hot. Add mushrooms, eggplant, onions, parsley and garlic; cook until vegetables are tender.

Blend tomatoes as directed.

Stir blended tomatoes, tomato paste, tomato sauce, ⅔ c. *water* and remaining ingredients except rigatoni into eggplant mixture.

Close cover securely and place over high heat. Bring to 15 lb. pressure, according to manufacturer's directions for pressure cooker. When pressure is reached (control will begin to jiggle), reduce heat immediately to maintain a slow, steady rocking motion and cook 25 minutes. Remove from heat. Reduce pressure instantly by placing pressure cooker under cold running water. Remove bay leaf.

Serve as directed.

CARROT RAVIOLI WITH SPINACH FILLING

(see photo following page 182)

Golden, puffy squares of pasta have a flavorful spinach-cheese filling.

1 lb. fresh chopped spinach, or 1 (10-oz.)
    pkg. frozen chopped spinach, cooked
1 c. shredded Gouda cheese (4 oz.)
1 c. ricotta cheese
1 egg
1 tsp. dried marjoram leaves
1/8 tsp. pepper
Salt
Carrot Pasta (see Index)
Water
1/2 c. butter or regular margarine, melted
2/3 c. grated Parmesan cheese

In sieve drain cooked spinach, pressing out as much liquid as possible.

In bowl mix together spinach, Gouda cheese, ricotta cheese, egg, marjoram, pepper and 1/2 tsp. salt. Cover and refrigerate until ready to use.

Prepare Carrot Pasta. On lightly floured surface roll half of dough as thinly as possible into a 20x16" rectangle. Dough may be gently pulled to stretch. Cover with plastic wrap to keep from drying out. Repeat with remaining half of dough.

Using a knife, lightly mark one rectangle into 80 (2") squares.

Place about 1 level teaspoonful of spinach mixture in the center of each square. Moisten edges of squares on marked lines with water. Place other dough rectangle on top. Press down firmly with side of hand to seal dough around each mound of spinach filling. Using pastry wheel or sharp knife, cut into squares on marked lines.

Ravioli may be frozen at this point and cooked later. To freeze: On baking sheets place ravioli in single layers and freeze until firm. Remove from baking sheets; place in plastic bags. Store in freezer up to 3 months.

In large saucepot over high heat, bring 4 qt. water and 1 tblsp. salt to a boil. Add ravioli; cook 6 to 8 minutes (if frozen, 8 to 10 minutes), or until tender. Remove with slotted spoon; plunge into cold water and drain on paper towels.

In large bowl toss ravioli with melted butter. On 15½x10½x1" jelly-roll pans, place ravioli in single layers. Sprinkle with Parmesan cheese.

Broil, 5" from source of heat, about 3 minutes or until lightly browned. Makes 8 servings.

Deep-Fried Ravioli: Prepare as directed, but do not boil ravioli and omit butter. In 3-qt. saucepan over medium heat, heat 1 qt. vegetable oil to 360° on deep fat thermometer.

Fry 8 ravioli 2 to 3 minutes or until golden brown, turning once. Drain on paper towels; sprinkle with Parmesan cheese. Keep warm. Repeat with remaining ravioli. Makes 8 servings.

TURKEY-ZUCCHINI LASAGNE

Here's a way to use leftover turkey in a completely different dish.

2 tblsp. butter or regular margarine
1 medium onion, chopped
1 clove garlic, minced
1 (8-oz.) can tomato sauce
1 (6-oz.) can tomato paste
2 c. cooked turkey, cut into
    bite-size pieces
¼ c. water
1½ tsp. Italian herb seasoning
½ tsp. salt
½ tsp. dried thyme leaves
¼ tsp. pepper
¾ c. ricotta cheese
¼ c. grated Parmesan cheese
1 tblsp. milk
1 egg
4 medium zucchini (1½ lb.)
¼ c. soft bread crumbs
1 (8-oz.) pkg. mozzarella cheese slices

In 10" skillet over medium-high heat, melt butter. Add onion and garlic; cook 5 minutes or until tender. Stir in tomato sauce, tomato paste, turkey, water, Italian herb seasoning, salt, thyme and pepper; bring to a boil. Reduce heat to low. Cover and simmer 5 minutes, stirring occasionally.

In small bowl, stir together ricotta cheese, Parmesan cheese, milk and egg; set aside.

Slice zucchini lengthwise into ¼" slices.

In bottom of 12x8x2" baking dish, layer half of the zucchini. Sprinkle with 2 tblsp. bread crumbs. Top with half of the cheese mixture, half of the turkey mixture and half of the mozzarella cheese slices. Repeat layers with remaining zucchini, bread crumbs, cheese mixture, turkey mixture and mozzarella.

Bake in 375° oven 40 minutes or until zucchini is fork-tender. Let stand 10 minutes for easier cutting. Makes 6 to 8 servings.

TO MICROWAVE: Use same ingredients.

Slice zucchini lengthwise into ¼" slices. Place in bottom of 12x8x2" microwave- safe baking dish. Cover with plastic wrap, turning back one section to vent steam.

Microwave at high setting (100% power) 8 to 10 minutes or until tender, rearranging slices from the outside to inside every 3 minutes. Let stand, covered, 2 minutes. Remove zucchini slices and drain.

In same baking dish place butter, onion and garlic. Cover with lid or plastic wrap. Microwave at high setting 2 to 3 minutes or until vegetables are tender, stirring after 1 minute. Stir in tomato sauce, tomato paste, turkey, water, Italian herb seasoning, salt, thyme and pepper.

Cover again, and microwave at high setting 2 minutes. Stir.

Reduce power to medium setting (50% power) and microwave 4 to 5 minutes or until heated through, stirring every 2 minutes.

Stir together cheeses, milk and egg as directed. Layer as directed, reserving last layer of mozzarella cheese. Cover with waxed paper. Microwave at medium setting 13 minutes, rotating dish one-quarter turn every 4 minutes.

Top with remaining mozzarella. Microwave at medium setting, uncovered, 2 to 3 minutes or until cheese melts. Let stand, covered, 5 minutes. Uncover and let stand 5 minutes more.

CREAMY LASAGNE BAKE

A cream sauce replaces tomato sauce in this elegant lasagne that you can make with your own pasta.

½ recipe Spinach Pasta Lasagne Noodles (see Index), or ¾ lb. to 1 lb. packaged spinach lasagne noodles
1½ lb. ground beef or ground pork
¾ c. finely chopped onions
¾ c. finely chopped carrots
¾ c. finely chopped celery
¼ c. chopped fresh parsley
2 cloves garlic, minced
1 (16-oz.) can stewed tomatoes
1 c. dry white wine
½ c. milk
1 tsp. salt
Cream Sauce (recipe follows)
2 c. shredded mozzarella cheese (8 oz.)
¼ c. grated Parmesan cheese

Prepare Spinach Pasta Lasagne Noodles. Do not cook.

In 4-qt. Dutch oven over medium-high heat, cook ground meat, onions, carrots, celery, parsley and garlic until meat is browned.

Add tomatoes and wine stirring to break up tomatoes. Over high heat cook, uncovered, stirring occasionally, until liquid is evaporated. Stir in milk and salt. Reduce heat to medium-low. Cover and cook 20 minutes.

Meanwhile, prepare Cream Sauce. Cook lasagne noodles as directed. Place one-fourth of the cooked lasagne noodles in single layer in bottom of lightly greased 13x9x2″ glass baking dish.

Layer one-third of the meat mixture, one-third of the mozzarella, then one-fourth of the Cream Sauce.

Repeat layers of lasagne noodles, meat mixture, mozzarella and Cream Sauce twice more, ending with a layer of lasagne. Top with remaining Cream Sauce and sprinkle with Parmesan cheese.

Bake in 450° oven 15 minutes or until top is golden brown.

Let stand 15 minutes for easier cutting. Makes 8 servings.

Cream Sauce: In 2-qt. saucepan over medium-high heat, melt ⅓ c. butter or regular magarine. Stir in ¼ c. flour and ½ tsp. salt until smooth. Gradually stir in 3 c. milk until well blended.

Cook, stirring constantly, until sauce boils and thickens. Remove from heat. Stir in ¾ c. grated Parmesan cheese until melted.

SPAGHETTI SQUASH LASAGNE

This low-calorie vegetable adds a crunchy texture—extra "al dente."

1 (3½-lb.) spaghetti squash
1 lb. ground beef
1 medium onion, chopped
1 (15½-oz.) jar spaghetti sauce
1 tsp. dried basil leaves
¼ tsp. dried oregano leaves
¼ tsp. dried thyme leaves
⅛ tsp. pepper
1 c. large-curd cottage cheese
1 c. shredded sharp Cheddar cheese (4 oz.)
1 c. shredded mozzarella cheese (4 oz.)

In 6-qt. Dutch oven over high heat, bring 4 qt. water to a boil. Add whole spaghetti squash. Cover and cook 20 to 30 minutes or until squash is fork-tender. Drain; cool until easy to handle.

Meanwhile, in 12″ skillet over high heat, cook ground beef 5 minutes. Add onion; cook until beef is browned and onion is tender. Stir in spaghetti sauce, basil, oregano, thyme and pepper. Reduce heat to low. Cover and simmer 15 minutes to blend flavors.

In medium bowl stir cottage cheese, Cheddar cheese and mozzarella cheese until well blended.

Cut squash in half from stem to blossom end. Scoop out seeds. Scrape the flesh with a fork to separate into spaghetti-like strands; place in bowl.

In bottom of 13x9x2″ baking dish, layer one-third of the squash. Top with one-third of the meat mixture, then one-third of the cheese mixture. Repeat layers of spaghetti squash, meat and cheese mixtures twice.

Bake, covered, in 400° oven 15 minutes. Uncover and bake 5 minutes more or until filling is bubbly and cheese melts.

Let stand 10 minutes for easier cutting. Makes 6 servings.

TO MICROWAVE: Use same ingredients. Microwave squash (see Index for Microwaving Fresh Vegetables).

In 2-qt. microwave-safe casserole, place onion. Cover with lid or plastic wrap, turning back one section to vent steam. Microwave at high setting (100% power) 1 minute.

Stir in ground beef, basil, oregano, thyme and pepper. Cover again, and microwave at high setting 4 to 6 minutes or until beef is browned, stirring every 2 minutes.

Stir in spaghetti sauce. Cover again, and microwave 3 minutes; stir. Microwave, uncovered, at medium setting (50% power) 5 to 7 minutes or until mixture is heated through and flavors are blended, stirring every 2 minutes.

Meanwhile, cut squash and remove flesh as directed. In large bowl stir together cheeses as directed; stir in beef mixture.

In 12x8x2" microwave-safe baking dish layer spaghetti squash, meat and cheese mixtures as directed. Cover with waxed paper.

Microwave at medium setting 10 to 12 minutes or until filling is bubbly and cheese melts, rotating dish one-half turn every 4 minutes. Let stand, covered, 5 minutes. Uncover and let stand 5 minutes more.

MOUSSAKA

To save time, the eggplant is baked rather than fried.

2 c. soft bread crumbs
1½ tsp. salt
½ tsp. pepper
2 medium eggplants, peeled and cut into
   ½" slices
½ c. mayonnaise or salad dressing
¾ lb. ground lamb
¾ lb. ground beef
¾ c. chopped onions
2 cloves garlic, minced
1 (16-oz.) can tomatoes
¼ c. chopped fresh parsley
1 tblsp. sugar
1 tblsp. Worcestershire sauce
1 tblsp. soy sauce
¾ tsp. dried oregano leaves
1 (15-oz.) container ricotta cheese
¾ c. shredded sharp Cheddar cheese
¾ c. shredded fontina cheese
1 c. light cream
3 egg yolks
3 egg whites, stiffly beaten

On sheet of waxed paper mix together bread crumbs, salt and ¼ tsp. pepper.

Thinly spread mayonnaise on both sides of each eggplant slice; coat with bread crumb mixture. Place on ungreased baking sheets.

Bake in 425° oven 15 minutes or until golden brown and tender.

Meanwhile, in 10" skillet over medium-high heat, cook lamb, beef, onions and garlic until browned. Pour off fat.

Add tomatoes, parsley, sugar, Worcestershire sauce, soy sauce, oregano and ¼ tsp. pepper, stirring to break up tomatoes. Bring to a boil.

Reduce heat to medium. Simmer, uncovered, until liquid evaporates, about 15 minutes. Remove from heat.

In 13x9x2" glass baking dish, layer half the eggplant slices. Spread meat mixture over eggplant. Layer remaining eggplant on top.

In bowl mix together ricotta cheese, Cheddar cheese, fontina cheese, cream and egg yolks. Stiffly beat egg whites and fold them into cheese mixture. Spread cheese mixture evenly over eggplant.

Bake in 400° oven 25 minutes or until puffy and well browned. Let stand 10 minutes for easier cutting. Makes 8 servings.

VEGETABLE-CHICKEN BAKE

You won't have to watch this one-dish meal if you bake it.

⅓ c. flour
Salt
Pepper
1 (3½-lb.) broiler-fryer, cut up
¼ c. butter or regular margarine
1 (4-oz.) jar chopped pimientos, drained
½ lb. mushrooms, sliced
3 medium onions, each cut in half lengthwise
1 medium eggplant, cut into ½" cubes
1¾ c. chicken broth
1 c. long-grain rice
1 clove garlic, minced

In plastic bag place flour, ½ tsp. salt and ¼ tsp. pepper; shake to mix well. Add chicken, a few pieces at a time; shake until well coated.

In 4-qt. Dutch oven over medium-high heat, melt butter. Add chicken pieces; cook until well browned on all sides. Remove chicken and pour off drippings.

Stir pimientos, remaining ingredients, ¾ tsp. salt and ⅛ tsp. pepper into Dutch oven. Place chicken pieces over vegetable mixture.

Cover and bake in 375° oven 50 minutes or until chicken is fork-tender. Makes 6 servings.

TO MICROWAVE: Use same ingredients, *changing amounts and adding browning sauce for gravy as indicated.*

In 12x8x2" microwave-safe baking dish, place chicken broth, rice, garlic, *¾ tsp. salt* and *⅛ tsp. pepper.* Cover with plastic wrap, turning back one section to vent steam.

Microwave at high setting (100% power) 5 minutes; stir. Cover again, and microwave at medium setting (50% power) 13 to 17 minutes or until rice is tender, stirring after 7 minutes. Stir and let stand, covered.

In 2-c. glass measure place butter. Microwave at high setting 1½ to 2 minutes or until melted. Stir in *1 tsp. browning sauce for gravy;* set aside.

Stir pimientos, mushrooms and eggplant into rice mixture. Arrange onion halves in a circle along the outside edge of dish. Place chicken pieces skin-side down on top of rice, with meatier portions facing the outside edges of dish.

Cover again, and microwave at high setting 10 minutes, rotating dish one-half turn after 5 minutes. Turn over chicken pieces. Brush with butter mixture.

Cover again, and microwave 8 to 12 minutes more or until chicken and eggplant are tender, rotating dish one-half turn after 5 minutes. Let stand, covered, 5 minutes.

HARVEST BEEF CASSEROLE

As easy as 1-2-3: Brown strips of steak, layer them with rice and vegetables, and bake.

2 tblsp. vegetable oil
1½ lb. round or flank steak, sliced
　　diagonally into ⅛" strips
1 (13¾-oz.) can beef broth (1⅔ c.)
2 tblsp. flour
1 tsp. salt
½ tsp. dried thyme leaves
½ tsp. dried marjoram leaves
¼ tsp. pepper
½ c. long-grain rice
2 carrots, sliced
1 medium green pepper, cut into
　　½" chunks
1½ c. sliced celery
4 medium tomatoes, cut into ½" slices
4 medium onions, cut into ¼" slices

In 12" skillet over high heat, heat oil until hot; Add steak strips; cook until browned on all sides, about 10 minutes.

Meanwhile, in small bowl stir together broth, flour, salt, thyme, marjoram and pepper until well blended.

Stir flour mixture into skillet; cook until mixture boils and thickens. Stir in rice.

In 12x8x2" baking dish place beef-rice mixture. Top with carrots, green pepper and celery. Arrange tomato and onion slices alternately, overlapping slightly, to completely cover vegetables.

Bake, covered, in 400° oven 40 minutes or until vegetables are tender. Makes 6 servings.

TO MICROWAVE: Use same ingredients, *changing amounts and substituting quick-cooking rice as indicated.*

In 12x8x2" microwave-safe baking dish place steak strips, carrots, celery and *1 tblsp. oil.* Cover with plastic wrap, turning back one section to vent steam.

Microwave at high setting (100% power) 5 to 7 minutes or until meat is browned.

In 4-c. glass measure stir together salt, pepper, *1 c. broth, 3 tblsp. flour, ¾ tsp. thyme* and *¾ tsp. marjoram.* Microwave, uncovered, 3 to 5 minutes or until mixture boils and thickens, stirring each minute. Stir in *½ c. quick-cooking rice.*

Stir broth-rice mixture into beef. Top with carrots, green pepper, celery and onions. Cover again.

Microwave at medium setting (50% power) 10 minutes, rotating dish one-half turn after 5 minutes. Arrange tomato slices around the outside edges of the dish, overlapping slightly.

Cover again, and microwave at medium setting 3 to 5 minutes or until tomatoes are soft, rotating dish one-half turn every 2 minutes. Let stand, covered, 5 minutes.

BEEF AND POTATO CASSEROLE

This recipe makes two casseroles— one to serve now, and one to freeze.

⅓ c. vegetable oil
1 (3-lb.) beef round steak, cut into
　　¼" strips
1 (6-oz.) can tomato paste
4 c. sliced onions (¼" slices)
2 c. coarsely chopped green peppers
½ c. vinegar
2 tblsp. packed brown sugar
2 tsp. salt
1 tsp. ground allspice
½ tsp. ground cloves
¼ tsp. pepper
4 beef bouillon cubes
3 cloves garlic, minced
1 bay leaf
1 (3") cinnamon stick
2¾ c. water
¾ lb. small mushrooms
½ c. flour
6 c. seasoned mashed potatoes
　　(about 3 lb. potatoes)
1 c. grated Parmesan cheese
Paprika

In 6-qt. Dutch oven over medium-high heat, heat oil until hot. Add beef strips; cook until browned on all sides.

Stir in tomato paste, next 12 ingredients and 2 c. water; bring to a boil.

Reduce heat to low. Cover and simmer 45 minutes. Stir in mushrooms; cook 30 minutes. Remove bay leaf and cinnamon stick.

In jar with tight-fitting lid, shake flour and remaining ¾ c. water until blended. Stir into beef mixture. Cook, stirring constantly, until mixture boils and thickens. Pour into 2 (2-qt.) cassseroles.

In bowl stir together hot mashed potatoes and Parmesan cheese. Spoon potato mixture around edge of each casserole. Sprinkle with paprika. (Casseroles may be frozen at this point and baked later.)

Bake in 375° oven 50 minutes or until heated through. (If frozen, bake, covered, in 400° oven 1 hour 20 minutes. Uncover and bake 30 minutes or until heated through.) Makes 2 casseroles, 6 servings each.

RANCH-STYLE LENTIL CASSEROLE

Chili-lovers will like this rich and spicy beef and bean dish.

2 c. lentils, rinsed and drained
4½ c. water
1 lb. ground beef
1 medium onion, chopped
1 c. ketchup
2 tblsp. sugar
2 tblsp. Worcestershire sauce
2 tblsp. cider vinegar
2 tsp. prepared mustard
½ tsp. salt
¼ tsp. chili powder
¼ tsp. pepper

In 3-qt. saucepan over high heat, bring lentils and 4 c. water to a boil. Reduce heat to medium-low. Cover and simmer 30 minutes.

Meanwhile, in 10″ skillet over high heat, cook ground beef and onion until beef is browned and onion is tender.

Stir beef mixture, ketchup, remaining ingredients and remaining ½ c. water into lentil mixture until well blended. Spoon mixture into 2½-qt. casserole.

Bake, covered, in 400° oven 30 minutes or until mixture is bubbly. Makes 8 servings.

TO MICROWAVE: Use same ingredients, *reducing water as indicated.*

In 3-qt. microwave-safe casserole place lentils and *3 c. water.* Cover with lid or plastic wrap, turning back one section to vent steam.

Microwave at high setting (100% power) 7 to 8 minutes or until mixture starts to boil; stir. Cover again, and microwave at medium setting (50% power) 8 to 10 minutes or until beans are tender but not soft. Set aside, covered.

Meanwhile, in 1-qt. microwave-safe casserole place ground beef and onion. Cover with lid or plastic wrap. Microwave at high setting 5 to 7 minutes or until beef is browned and onion is tender, stirring every 2 minutes to break up beef. Pour off fat.

Stir beef mixture, ketchup, remaining ingredients and remaining ½ c. water into lentil mixture.

Cover again, and microwave at high setting 25 to 30 minutes or until beans are soft, stirring every 10 minutes. Let stand, covered, 5 minutes.

LAYERED PEPPER-CHILI BAKE

To make this a meatless dish, just substitute Vegetarian Chili (see Index) for the beef mixture.

8 large sweet red peppers, each cut into 4 wedges
8 c. water
1½ lb. ground beef
1 medium onion, chopped
1 small green sweet pepper, chopped
1 c. finely chopped celery
1 (20-oz.) can red kidney beans, drained
1 (16-oz.) can tomato sauce
4 tsp. chili powder
1 tsp. salt
3 drops hot pepper sauce

In 4-qt. Dutch oven over high heat, bring red peppers and water to a boil. Cover and cook 3 minutes or until slightly softened. Drain.

In 12″ skillet over high heat, cook ground beef 5 minutes. Add onion, green pepper and celery; cook until beef is browned and vegetables are tender.

Stir in kidney beans and remaining ingredients. Cook 5 minutes or until mixture is heated through.

In 12x8x2″ baking dish layer half of the red pepper wedges, overlapping slightly. Spread beef mixture over peppers. Layer remaining pepper wedges over chili.

Bake in 350° oven 25 minutes or until bubbly. Makes 8 servings.

TO MICROWAVE: Use same ingredients, *changing amounts as indicated.*

In 12x8x2″ microwave-safe baking dish, place red peppers and ¼ c. *water.* Cover with plastic wrap, turning back one section to vent steam.

Microwave at high setting (100% power) 8 to 10 minutes or until peppers are tender, rearranging peppers every 4 minutes. Let stand, covered, 2 minutes. Drain.

In 3-qt. microwave-safe casserole place beef, onion, green pepper and celery. Cover with lid or plastic wrap.

Microwave at high setting 6 to 8 minutes or until beef is browned, stirring every 3 minutes to break up beef. Pour off fat.

Stir in kidney beans, tomato sauce, hot pepper sauce, *2 tsp. chili powder* and *1¼ tsp. salt.* Cover again, and microwave at high setting 3 minutes, stirring after 2 minutes.

Uncover and microwave at medium setting (50% power) 3 to 5 minutes or until mixture is heated through, stirring after 3 minutes.

In 12x8x2″ microwave-safe baking dish, layer pepper wedges and beef mixture as directed. Cover with waxed paper. Microwave at medium setting 5 to 7 minutes or until heated through, rotating dish one-half turn after 3 minutes. Let stand, covered, 3 minutes.

TEXAS-STYLE CHILI

The Texas ranchwoman who shared this spicy recipe says it's also great made with strips of venison or elk.

1 c. dried pinto beans, rinsed and drained
Water
4 slices bacon, diced
4 medium onions, chopped
3 cloves garlic, minced
2 tsp. chili powder
1 tsp. dried oregano leaves
2 tblsp. vegetable oil
3 lb. round steak, cut diagonally into ¼″ strips
2 medium green peppers, chopped
1 (4-oz.) can chopped green chilies, drained
4 large ripe tomatoes, chopped
1 tsp. ground peppercorns
1 tsp. seasoned salt
1 tsp. ground cumin
½ tsp. dried thyme leaves
½ tsp. dried basil leaves
2 bay leaves
Assorted toppings: chopped lettuce, chopped onion, shredded cheese

In 3-qt. saucepan over high heat, bring beans and 4 c. water to a boil; boil 2 minutes. Remove from heat. Cover and let stand 1 hour to soak. Drain. Wipe saucepan dry.

In same saucepan over medium heat, cook bacon until browned. Add half of the onions and garlic; cook until tender. Add beans, chili powder, oregano and 4 c. water; bring to a boil. Reduce heat to medium-low. Simmer, uncovered, 1 hour.

In 4-qt. Dutch oven over high heat, heat oil until hot. Add steak strips; cook until browned. Remove meat with slotted spoon.

Add green peppers and remaining onions and garlic to Dutch oven; cook until tender. Stir in browned beef, chilies and remaining ingredients except assorted toppings; bring to a boil.

Reduce heat to medium-low. Simmer, uncovered, 1 hour.

Add cooked bean mixture to Dutch oven. Simmer, uncovered, 1 hour or until beans are tender and liquid is reduced by one-fourth. Remove bay leaves.

To serve, ladle chili into bowls and garnish with assorted toppings. Makes 8 servings.

VEGETARIAN CHILI

A three-alarm chili! To make a meaty version, add 1 lb. browned ground beef to the tomato mixture when you add the kidney beans.

2 c. dried red kidney beans, rinsed and drained
4 c. water
6 c. Vegetable Stock (see Index) or water
3 tblsp. vegetable oil
2 medium green peppers, finely chopped
1 large onion, finely chopped
3 cloves garlic, minced
2 (16-oz.) cans tomato purée
1 (6-oz.) can tomato paste
4 ripe medium tomatoes, peeled, seeded and coarsely chopped
1 tblsp. chili powder
2 tsp. salt
¼ tsp. ground red pepper
¼ tsp. pepper
3 drops hot pepper sauce
1 bay leaf
1 c. shredded Cheddar cheese

In 3-qt. saucepan over high heat, bring beans and water to a boil; boil 2 minutes. Remove from heat. Cover and let stand 1 hour to soak. Drain.

In same saucepan over high heat, bring beans and Vegetable Stock to a boil. Reduce heat to medium-low. Cover and simmer until beans are almost tender, about 2 hours.

Meanwhile, in 4-qt. Dutch oven over medium-high heat, heat oil until hot. Add green peppers, onion and garlic; cook until tender.

Stir in tomato purée and remaining ingredients except cheese; bring to a boil. Reduce heat to low. Cover and simmer 20 minutes or until mixture is slightly thickened.

Drain beans again, reserving 2 c. cooking liquid (use remaining cooking liquid in another soup).

Add beans and reserved cooking liquid to tomato mixture; bring to a boil. Reduce heat to medium-low. Simmer, uncovered, 45 minutes or until beans are tender and mixture thickens. Remove bay leaf.

To serve, ladle chili into bowls; garnish with cheese. Makes 8 servings.

TO MICROWAVE: Use same ingredients, changing amounts as indicated, but omit water and Vegetable Stock, and substitute canned kidney beans for dried.

In 4-qt. microwave-safe casserole, place green peppers, onion, garlic and *2 tblsp. oil.* Cover with lid or plastic wrap, turning back one section to vent steam.

Microwave at high setting (100% power) 8 to 10 minutes or until tender, stirring every 3 minutes.

Stir in *2 (20-oz.) cans red kidney beans, drained.* Stir in tomato purée and remaining ingredients except cheese.

Cover again, and microwave 8 minutes, stirring every 3 minutes.

Cover again, and microwave at medium setting (50% power) 10 to 15 minutes or until heated through, stirring every 5 minutes. Let stand, covered, 5 minutes. Remove bay leaf. Serve as directed.

VEGETABLE STEW_____

This meatless stew cooks on top of the range in just an hour.

3 tblsp. vegetable oil
2 ribs celery with leaves, chopped
1 medium green pepper, cut into ¼" strips
3 cloves garlic, minced
Water
6 new potatoes
6 small white onions
3 ripe tomatoes, peeled and cut into 1" chunks
2 large carrots, sliced
1 small head cauliflower, broken into flowerets
1 medium yellow summer squash, diagonally cut into ¼" slices
2 c. tomato juice
2 tblsp. chopped fresh parsley
1 tblsp. Worcestershire sauce
1 tsp. salt
1 tsp. dried oregano leaves
1 tsp. dried thyme leaves
½ tsp. dried dill weed
⅛ tsp. pepper
2 bay leaves
1 c. fresh or frozen peas
1 c. fresh or frozen corn
4 tsp. cornstarch

In 4-qt. Dutch oven over medium-high heat, heat oil until hot. Add celery, green pepper and garlic; cook until tender.

Stir in 1 c. water, potatoes and remaining ingredients except peas, corn and cornstarch; bring to a boil. Reduce heat to low. Cover and simmer 50 minutes.

Stir in peas and corn. Cover and cook 5 minutes or until tender.

In small bowl stir together cornstarch and ¼ c. water until smooth. Stir into vegetable mixture. Cook, stirring constantly, until mixture boils and thickens. Remove bay leaves. Makes 8 servings.

TO MICROWAVE: Use same ingredients.

In 4-qt. microwave-safe casserole place oil, celery, and garlic. Cover with lid or plastic wrap, turning back one section to vent steam. Microwave at high setting (100% power) 2 minutes.

Stir in green pepper. Cover again, and microwave 3 to 4 minutes or until vegetables are tender.

Stir in onions, 1 c. water and remaining ingredients except potatoes, tomatoes, peas, corn and cornstarch. Arrange potatoes in a circle on top of vegetables. Cover again, and microwave at high setting 10 minutes.

Stir in tomatoes. Cover again, and microwave at high setting 25 to 30 minutes or until potatoes are tender, stirring every 10 minutes.

Stir in peas and corn. Cover again, and microwave 3 to 4 minutes or until tender. Spoon off ¼ c. liquid. In small bowl stir together cornstarch and liquid. Stir into vegetable mixture.

Cover again, and microwave at high setting 2 to 3 minutes or until sauce is slightly thickened, stirring after 1 minute. Let stand, covered, 5 minutes. Remove bay leaves.

CHICKEN AND LIMA BEAN STEW

Tummy-warming and comforting, and tastes even better reheated.

1 (3-lb.) broiler-fryer, cut up
2 tblsp. chopped fresh parsley
¾ tsp. poultry seasoning
¼ tsp. salt
4 chicken bouillon cubes
Water
Shortcut Dumplings (recipe follows)
¼ c. cornstarch
2 c. fresh or frozen corn
2 c. thinly sliced onions
1¾ c. fresh or frozen lima beans
1½ c. sliced carrots

In 4-qt. Dutch oven over high heat, bring first 5 ingredients and 4 c. water to a boil. Reduce heat to low.

Cover and simmer 1 hour or until chicken is fork-tender. Remove chicken from broth; cool until easy to handle. Remove chicken from bones and cut into large pieces.

Increase heat to medium so broth maintains a steady boil.

Meanwhile, prepare dumplings.

In small bowl stir together cornstarch and ¼ c. water until well blended; stir into simmering broth. Cook 1 minute.

Stir in chicken, corn, onions, lima beans and carrots.

Drop dumplings by rounded tablespoonfuls onto simmering stew.

Simmer, uncovered, 10 minutes. Cover and simmer 10 minutes or until dumplings are tender. Makes 8 servings.

Shortcut Dumplings: In large bowl stir together 2 c. buttermilk baking mix and 2 tblsp. chopped fresh parsley. Stir in ⅔ c. milk just until moistened.

NORTHERN PLAINS RABBIT

An Ohio teenager who likes to hunt on his family's farm shared this.

2 tsp. salt
¼ tsp. pepper
Flour
2 (3-lb.) rabbits or broiler-fryers, cut up
½ lb. bacon, diced
1 (28-oz.) can Italian plum tomatoes
1 large green pepper, cut into strips
1 c. chopped onions
1 c. chopped carrots
3 tblsp. dried basil leaves
1 tblsp. packed brown sugar
2 cloves garlic, minced
3 tblsp. water
Hot cooked noodles

In plastic bag place salt, pepper and ¾ c. flour; shake to mix well. Add rabbit, a few pieces at a time; shake until well coated.

In 8-qt. Dutch oven over medium-high heat, cook bacon until browned. Drain on paper towels. Pour off all but ¼ c. bacon drippings.

In drippings in Dutch oven over medium-high heat, cook rabbit, a few pieces at a time, until browned on all sides. Drain on paper towels.

Stir in tomatoes and remaining ingredients except water and noodles, stirring to break up tomatoes. Add bacon and rabbit; bring to a boil.

Reduce heat to low. Cover and simmer 1 hour and 30 minutes or until rabbit is tender. Remove rabbit to serving platter; keep warm.

In jar with tight-fitting lid, place water and 2 tblsp. flour; cover. Shake until well blended. Stir into vegetable mixture. Cook, stirring constantly, until mixture boils and thickens.

To serve, spoon sauce over rabbit. Serve with noodles. Makes 8 servings.

CHUNKY BEEF STEW

This stew simmers unattended and makes its own gravy.

2 lb. beef stew meat, cut into 1½" cubes
6 medium carrots, cut into ¼" cubes
4 medium potatoes, cut into ¼" cubes
4 ribs celery, chopped
2 medium onions, chopped
1 clove garlic, minced
1 (12-oz.) can spicy tomato juice
3 tblsp. quick-cooking tapioca
1 tsp. salt
½ tsp. dried basil leaves
½ tsp. dried thyme leaves
¼ tsp. seasoned salt

In 4-qt. Dutch oven stir together all ingredients. Cover.

Bake in 250° oven 5 hours or until meat and vegetables are tender. Makes 6 servings.

TO MICROWAVE: Use same ingredients, *changing amounts as indicated, but omit tapioca and add flour.*

In 4-qt. microwave-safe casserole place beef, onion and garlic. Cover with lid or plastic wrap, turning back one section to vent steam. Microwave at high setting (100% power) 3 minutes, stirring after 2 minutes.

Stir in salt, basil, thyme, seasoned salt and *⅓ c. flour.* Then stir in *2 c. spicy tomato juice.* Cover again, and microwave at medium setting (50% power) 25 minutes, stirring every 10 minutes.

Stir in carrots, potatoes and celery. Cover again, and microwave at medium setting 5 minutes. Stir.

Cover again, and microwave at medium setting 40 to 45 minutes or until meat and vegetables are tender, stirring every 10 minutes to cover meat with sauce. Let stand, covered, 10 minutes.

FOR SLOW COOKER: Use same ingredients.

In 3½-qt. slow cooker layer beef, vegetables, tomato juice, tapioca and spices. Cover and cook at low setting 9 to 10 hours or until beef and vegetables are tender.

FOR PRESSURE COOKER: Use same ingredients, *but increase salt to 2 tsp.*

In 6-qt. pressure cooker stir together all ingredients. (Fill cooker no more than two-thirds full.) Close cover securely and place cooker over high heat. Bring to 15 lb. pressure according to manufacturer's directions for pressure cooker.

When pressure is reached (control will begin to jiggle), reduce heat immediately to maintain a slow, steady rocking motion and cook 10 minutes. Remove from heat.

Let pressure drop of its own accord, about 20 minutes.

VENISON CURRY

Whenever her son-in-law bags a deer, one South Dakota ranchwoman makes this. Beef may be used, too.

3 lb. boneless venison or beef stew meat, cut into ¾" cubes
¼ c. lemon juice
¾ c. flour
2 to 4 tsp. curry powder
2 tsp. salt
1 tsp. dried thyme leaves
½ tsp. pepper
½ c. vegetable oil
6 medium onions, quartered
2 c. sliced celery
2 c. apple juice
1 tblsp. packed brown sugar
2 cloves garlic, minced
½ c. raisins
Hot cooked rice

In large bowl toss venison cubes with lemon juice until well coated.

In plastic bag place flour, curry powder, salt, thyme and pepper; shake to mix well. Add venison cubes a few pieces at a time; shake until well coated.

In 4-qt. Dutch oven over medium-high heat, heat oil until hot. Cook venison cubes, a few pieces at a time, until browned on all sides. Drain on paper towels. Pour off fat.

Return meat to Dutch oven; add onions, celery, apple juice, brown sugar and garlic.

Over high heat bring to a boil. Reduce heat to low. Cover and simmer 1 hour, stirring occasionally.

Stir in raisins. Cover and simmer 15 minutes or until meat is tender.

To serve, spoon curry over rice. Makes 6 to 8 servings.

TO MICROWAVE: Use same ingredients, *but decrease flour and omit oil as indicated.*

In large bowl toss venison cubes with lemon juice until well coated.

In plastic bag place curry powder, salt, thyme, pepper and ⅔ c. flour; shake to mix well. Add venison cubes, a few pieces at a time; shake until well coated.

In 4-qt. microwave-safe casserole place venison cubes. *Omit oil.* Cover with lid or plastic wrap, turning back one section to vent steam.

Microwave at high setting (100% power) 2 minutes, stirring after 1 minute. Stir in onions, celery and garlic.

Cover again, and microwave at high setting 3 to 4 minutes or until celery is tender-crisp, stirring after 2 minutes. Stir in apple juice.

Cover again, and microwave at medium setting (50% power) 25 to 30 minutes or until venison is tender, stirring every 8 minutes.

Stir in brown sugar and raisins. Cover again, and microwave at medium setting 10 to 15 minutes or until raisins are plump, stirring every 3 minutes. Serve as directed.

MEXICAN LIMA BEAN SKILLET

Spicy beef and vegetables topped with corn bread: a one-dish dinner.

1 lb. ground beef
1 large onion, chopped
1 medium green pepper, chopped
1 clove garlic, minced
1 (16-oz.) can whole tomatoes
1 (8-oz.) can tomato sauce
½ c. sliced ripe olives
¼ c. ketchup
4½ tsp. chili powder
½ tsp. salt
⅛ tsp. pepper
Dash ground red pepper
1¾ c. fresh lima beans, or 1 (10-oz.) pkg.
    frozen lima beans, thawed
Corn Bread Topping (recipe follows)

In oven-safe 12″ skillet over high heat, cook ground beef, onion, green pepper and garlic until beef is browned and vegetables are tender.

Add tomatoes, tomato sauce, olives, ketchup, chili powder, salt, pepper and ground red pepper, stirring to break up tomatoes. Reduce heat to medium. Cook 5 minutes.

Stir in lima beans. Reduce heat to low. Cover and simmer while preparing Corn Bread Topping.

Pour topping batter over ground beef mixture; using the back of a spoon, spread to cover.

Bake in 400° oven 30 minutes or until toothpick inserted in center of topping comes out clean. Makes 6 to 8 servings.

Corn Bread Topping: In medium bowl stir together ¾ c. yellow corn meal, ¾ c. sifted flour, 2 tblsp. sugar, 1 tsp. baking powder, 1 tsp. salt and 1 tsp. baking soda.

In small bowl beat together 1 c. buttermilk, 2 tblsp. vegetable oil and 1 beaten egg until well blended.

Stir milk mixture into flour mixture just until moistened.

LAMB PIE SUPREME

A biscuit crust crowns this savory dish of lamb and vegetables.

⅓ c. flour
½ tsp. ground sage
¼ tsp. pepper
Salt
2 lb. lamb shoulder, cut into 2″ cubes
2 tblsp. vegetable oil
2 medium onions, chopped
4 c. water
1½ c. sliced, peeled potatoes (¼″ slices)
1 c. sliced carrots
½ c. diced celery (¼″ pieces)
⅓ c. medium pearl barley
1 tsp. Worcestershire sauce
¾ tsp. dried rosemary leaves
1 clove garlic, minced
2 c. peas, fresh or frozen and thawed
Biscuit Topping (recipe follows)

In plastic bag place flour, sage, pepper and ½ tsp. salt; shake to mix well. Add lamb cubes, a few pieces at a time; shake until well coated.

In 4-qt. Dutch oven over medium-high heat, heat 1 tblsp. oil until hot. Cook half of the lamb cubes until browned on all sides. Remove lamb. Add remaining 1 tblsp. oil; heat until hot. Cook remaining lamb cubes until browned.

Add browned lamb, onions, water, potatoes, carrots, celery, barley, Worcestershire sauce, rosemary, garlic and 1 tblsp. salt. Over high heat, bring to a boil. Reduce heat to low. Cover and simmer 30 minutes. Stir in peas. Remove from heat.

Meanwhile, prepare Biscuit Topping.

Drop topping by tablespoonfuls onto lamb mixture; using the back of spoon, spread gently to cover.

Bake in 400° oven 30 minutes or until topping is golden brown. Makes 8 servings.

Biscuit Topping: In large bowl stir together 2 c. sifted flour, 2 tblsp. chopped fresh parsley, 2 tsp. baking powder and ½ tsp. salt.

In small bowl beat 1 c. milk, 3 tblsp. vegetable oil and 1 egg until well blended. Stir into flour mixture just until moistened.

SHEPHERD'S PIE

Ground beef or pork can be used in this potato-topped pie.

2 lb. potatoes, peeled
   and quartered
1½ lb. ground lamb
½ lb. mushrooms, sliced (2 c.)
2 medium carrots, diced (¼" pieces)
1 medium onion, chopped
½ c. chopped celery
1 clove garlic, minced
⅔ c. beef broth
2 tblsp. chopped fresh parsley
2 tsp. cornstarch
½ tsp. dried rosemary leaves
¼ tsp. dried marjoram leaves
¼ tsp. pepper
Salt
1 medium tomato, chopped
2 c. coarsely chopped fresh spinach
½ c. warm milk
2 tblsp. butter or regular margarine
1 egg, beaten
Paprika

In 3-qt. saucepan over high heat, bring 1" water to a boil; add potatoes. Reduce heat to medium-low. Cover and simmer 20 minutes or until tender.

Meanwhile, in 12" skillet over high heat, cook ground lamb until well browned, stirring occasionally.

Stir in mushrooms, carrots, onion, celery and garlic; cook until tender. Pour off excess fat.

In small bowl stir beef broth, parsley, cornstarch, rosemary, marjoram, pepper and ½ tsp. salt until well blended. Stir into lamb mixture.

Cook until mixture boils and thickens. Remove from heat. Stir in tomato and spinach. Pour into 2-qt. casserole.

Drain potatoes. Put through ricer or mash with fork until smooth. Beat in milk, butter, egg and ¾ tsp. salt until well blended.

Spoon potato mixture over lamb mixture; using back of spoon, spread to cover. Sprinkle with paprika.

Bake in 425° oven 15 minutes, or until potatoes are golden brown and filling is bubbly. Makes 6 to 8 servings.

TO MICROWAVE: Use same ingredients, *changing amounts as indicated.*

In 2-qt. microwave-safe casserole place potatoes and *½ c. water.* Cover with lid or plastic wrap, turning back one section to vent steam. Microwave at high setting (100% power) 12 to 14 minutes or until tender, stirring every 3 minutes. Let stand, covered, 3 minutes.

Drain and prepare potatoes as directed. Set aside.

In 3-qt. microwave-safe casserole place carrots, onion, celery and garlic. Cover with lid or plastic wrap. Microwave at high setting 3 to 5 minutes or until tender, stirring after 2 minutes.

Stir in ground lamb. Cover again, and microwave 8 to 10 minutes or until lamb is browned, stirring every 3 minutes to break up lamb. Pour off excess fat.

Stir in mushrooms, tomato and spinach. Microwave, uncovered, 3 to 4 minutes or until spinach wilts, stirring after 2 minutes.

In small bowl stir together parsley, rosemary, marjoram, pepper, *½ c. beef broth, 1 tblsp. cornstarch* and ½ tsp. salt until well blended. Stir into lamb mixture.

Microwave, uncovered, 3 to 5 minutes or until slightly thickened, stirring every 2 minutes.

Spread potatoes over lamb mixture as directed. Sprinkle with paprika.

Microwave, uncovered, 8 to 10 minutes or until potatoes are dry on top and filling is bubbly, rotating casserole one-quarter turn every 2 minutes. Let stand 5 minutes.

COUNTRY ASPARAGUS PIE_____

Celebrate spring with asparagus baked in a cheese sauce.

1 baked 9" Pie Shell with fluted edge
  (see Index)
1½ lb. asparagus, cut into 1" pieces (4 c.)
4 c. water
Salt
3 tblsp. butter or regular margarine
3 tblsp. flour
1 c. milk
1 chicken bouillon cube, crushed
1 tsp. instant minced onion
⅛ tsp. pepper
4 hard-cooked eggs
½ c. shredded Cheddar cheese (2 oz.)
Paprika

Prepare and bake Pie Shell as directed.

In 10" skillet place asparagus, water and ½ tsp. salt. Over high heat bring to a boil. Reduce heat to medium-low. Cover and simmer until asparagus is fork-tender. Drain.

In 3-qt. saucepan over medium heat, melt butter. Stir in flour until smooth. Gradually stir in milk until well blended.

Cook, stirring constantly, until mixture boils and thickens. Remove from heat. Stir in bouillon cube, onion, pepper and ¼ tsp. salt until bouillon is dissolved.

Chop 3 of the eggs. Stir asparagus and chopped eggs into milk mixture until well blended.

Pour into baked shell; sprinkle with cheese and paprika.

Bake in 350° oven 5 minutes or until cheese melts. Remove from oven.

Cut reserved egg into 6 wedges. Arrange wedges in petal design in center of pie. Makes 6 servings.

TO MICROWAVE: Use same ingredients, *but reduce water as indicated and substitute Microwaved Pie Shell (see Index) for Pie Shell.*

Prepare *Microwaved Pie Shell.*

In 12x8x2" microwave-safe baking dish place asparagus, ½ c. water and ½ tsp. salt. Cover with plastic wrap, turning back one section to vent steam.

Microwave at high setting (100% power) 3 minutes. Stir. Microwave 4 to 5 minutes or until asparagus is fork-tender. Drain.

In 2-qt. microwave-safe bowl place butter. Microwave at high setting 1 minute or until butter melts. Stir in flour and bouillon cube until smooth. Gradually stir in milk until well blended.

Microwave at high setting 4 minutes or until mixture boils and thickens, stirring each minute. Stir in onion, pepper and ¼ tsp. salt.

Chop 3 of the eggs. Stir asparagus and chopped eggs into milk mixture until well blended.

Pour into pie shell; sprinkle with cheese and paprika.

Microwave at medium setting (50% power) 3 minutes or until cheese melts, rotating dish one-quarter turn each minute.

Garnish as directed.

CHICKEN POT PIES

For chicken à la king, serve this chicken mixture over toast points.

2 (3-lb.) broiler-fryers with giblets, cut up
2 medium onions, quartered
2 ribs celery with leaves
2 medium carrots
3 c. hot water
8 sprigs fresh parsley
10 whole black peppercorns
2 tsp. dried thyme leaves
3 bay leaves
Salt
6 tblsp. butter or regular margarine
½ lb. mushrooms, sliced
2 medium onions, chopped
2 c. diced carrots (¼" pieces)
½ c. flour
1 tsp. poultry seasoning
¼ tsp. pepper
2 c. light cream
2 tblsp. lemon juice
3½ c. fresh or frozen peas
Sage Pastry (recipe follows)
Milk

In 8-qt. saucepot over high heat, bring first 9 ingredients and 1 tblsp. salt to a boil. Reduce heat to low. Cover and simmer 45 minutes or until chicken is fork-tender.

Remove chicken and giblets. Strain and reserve broth. Cool chicken until easy to handle. Remove skin; cut chicken from bones. Cut chicken and giblets into bite-size pieces; set aside.

In same saucepot over medium-high heat, melt butter. Add mushrooms, chopped onions and diced carrots; cook, stirring often, until vegetables are tender-crisp.

Stir in flour, poultry seasoning, pepper and 1 tsp. salt until smooth. Gradually stir in cream, lemon juice and 3 c. reserved broth. Cook, stirring constantly, until mixture boils and thickens.

Stir in chicken, giblets and peas until well blended.

Spoon hot chicken mixture into 12 (10-oz.) glass custard cups.

Prepare Sage Pastry. Divide pastry in half.

On lightly floured surface roll out half of pastry to ⅛" thickness. Using a 4½"-round floured cutter, cut out 6 circles, rerolling pastry as needed. Repeat with remaining dough.

Cut slits in pastry circles. Place one circle on top of filling in each custard cup. If you wish, reroll pastry scraps to make decorative cut-outs and place cut-outs on top of pies. (Pies may be frozen at this point and baked later.)

Brush crusts with milk. Bake in 425° oven 20 to 25 minutes (if frozen, 45 minutes) or until crusts are golden and chicken mixture is bubbly. Makes 12 servings.

Sage Pastry: In large bowl stir together 2⅔ c. sifted flour, 1 tsp. salt and 1 tsp. dried rubbed sage. Using pastry blender cut in 1 c. shortening until coarse crumbs form. Sprinkle 5 to 7 tblsp. iced water over crumb mixture a little at a time, tossing with fork until dough forms. Press dough firmly into a ball.

DEEP-DISH CHICKEN LIVER VEGETABLE PIE

A savory vegetable and liver pie that's nutritious and economical.

4 slices bacon, diced
2 lb. chicken livers
⅓ c. flour
2 tblsp. vegetable oil
1 (12-oz.) can beer
1 lb. small white onions, quartered
2 c. fresh or frozen lima beans
1 c. sliced carrots
1 c. fresh or frozen corn
2 tsp. salt
¼ tsp. pepper
2 cloves garlic, minced
Pastry for Pie Shell (see Index)
1 egg yolk
1 tblsp. water

In 4-qt. Dutch oven over medium-high heat, cook bacon until browned. Remove with slotted spoon; drain on paper towels.

Cut chicken livers in half. Pat dry on paper towels.

In plastic bag place flour. Add chicken livers, a few pieces at a time; shake until well coated.

In 4-qt. Dutch oven over medium heat, cook chicken livers, a few pieces at a time, in bacon drippings, until browned on all sides. Add more oil if needed. Drain on paper towels. Pour off excess fat.

In same Dutch oven mix together chicken livers, beer, onions, lima beans, carrots, corn, salt, pepper and garlic. Increase heat to high and bring mixture to a boil. Reduce heat to low. Cover and simmer 15 minutes. Spoon into 2-qt. baking dish.

On lightly floured surface roll out pastry to fit over top of dish, leaving 1″ border. Cut slits in pastry. Place over filling and fold under edge of crust and form a ridge. Flute ridge.

In small bowl mix together egg yolk and water. Brush crust with egg yolk mixture.

Bake in 400° oven 30 minutes or until top is golden brown.

Let stand 10 minutes before serving. Makes 6 to 8 servings.

SAVORY PORK SKILLET

Simmer pork chops with vegetables for an easy skillet supper.

1 tblsp. vegetable oil
6 center-cut pork chops, ¾″ thick
1 c. chicken broth
1½ tsp. dried savory leaves
1 tsp. salt
¼ tsp. pepper
2 ribs celery, chopped
2 tblsp. chopped fresh parsley
1 clove garlic, minced
1 bay leaf
2 medium zucchini, cut into ¼″ slices
2 medium tomatoes, chopped
1 medium onion, chopped
1 medium green pepper, chopped
1 c. fresh or frozen corn
3 tblsp. flour

In 12″ skillet over medium-high heat, heat oil until hot. Add pork chops; cook until browned on both sides.

Meanwhile, in small bowl stir together chicken broth, savory, salt and pepper.

Stir broth mixture, celery, parsley, garlic and bay leaf into skillet; bring to a boil. Reduce heat to medium-low. Cover and simmer 30 minutes.

Increase heat to medium. Stir in zucchini, tomatoes, onion, green pepper and corn. Cover and cook 15 minutes or until pork and vegetables are tender. Remove bay leaf. Remove pork chops and vegetables to serving platter.

In small bowl, stir together flour and 3 tblsp. of the pan juices until smooth. Stir flour mixture into liquid in skillet. Cook, stirring constantly, until mixture boils and thickens. Spoon sauce over pork chops and vegetables. Makes 6 servings.

RUSSIAN PIE

Layers of cheese, cabbage, ham and mushrooms encased in flaky pastry.

2 recipes for Pastry for 2-Crust Pie
2 (8-oz.) pkg. cream cheese, softened
2 tblsp. chopped fresh parsley
½ tsp. Worcestershire sauce
2 eggs
¼ c. butter or regular margarine
3 c. shredded cabbage
½ tsp. caraway seed
Salt
1 lb. mushrooms, sliced
2 medium onions, sliced
2 cloves garlic, minced
½ tsp. dried thyme leaves
1 egg yolk, slightly beaten
¾ lb. cooked ham, cut into 2x¼" strips

Prepare pastry as directed. Shape two thirds of the pastry into a large ball. Shape remaining pastry into another ball. Wrap each in plastic wrap and refrigerate until ready to use.

In small bowl using mixer at medium speed, beat cream cheese, parsley, Worcestershire sauce and eggs until smooth. Cover; set aside.

In 12" skillet over medium-high heat, melt 2 tblsp. butter. Add cabbage, caraway seed and ¼ tsp. salt. Cook, stirring constantly, until cabbage is tender-crisp. Spoon cabbage mixture into a bowl.

In same skillet over medium-high heat, melt remaining 2 tblsp. butter. Add mushrooms, onions, garlic, thyme and ¼ tsp. salt. Cook, stirring frequently, until vegetables are tender and all liquid has evaporated. Drain mushroom mixture in colander and set aside.

On lightly floured surface, with lightly floured rolling pin, roll large pastry ball into a 15x15" square, about ⅛" thick. With knife, cut out a 10" circle and two 14x3" strips, rerolling dough as necessary.

Carefully place circle in 9" springform pan. With fingers, lightly press pastry into bottom and slightly up the side of the pan. Carefully lift one strip, and with fingers lightly press pastry onto side and up to the rim of pan. Repeat with remaining strip.

Seal pastry strips together, using a small amount of water. Brush pastry with some beaten egg yolk.

Spoon cream cheese mixture into pastry-lined pan, spreading to make an even layer; top with cabbage mixture. Arrange ham strips evenly over cabbage. Spoon mushroom mixture over ham.

Fold edges of pastry over filling. Brush pastry with some beaten egg yolk.

Roll remaining pastry ball into a 9" circle. With knife, cut design in pastry. Place pastry circle over filling in pan, pressing lightly around edges to seal. Brush top of pastry with egg yolk. If you wish, decorate with pastry scraps; brush again.

Bake in 425° oven 20 minutes. Reduce heat to 350° and bake 45 minutes or until a knife inserted through slit in pastry comes out clean. Cool on rack 15 minutes.

To serve, carefully remove ring from springform pan. With a sharp knife, cut pie into wedges. Makes 8 servings.

STUFFED PORK ROAST

Corn bread and zucchini make a colorful stuffing for a pork roast.

Zucchini Corn Bread Stuffing (see Index)
1 (5-lb.) center loin pork roast
4 tblsp. flour
¼ tsp. salt
⅛ tsp. pepper
2 c. water
½ tsp. Worcestershire sauce

Prepare Zucchini Corn Bread Stuffing.

In meaty side of pork roast cut long and deep vertical pockets about 1″ apart. Generously fill pockets with stuffing.

Place roast on rack in shallow roasting pan. In center of roast insert meat thermometer into thickest part of meat, making sure it doesn't touch bone or fat.

Roast in 325° oven 2 hours and 30 minutes (30 to 35 minutes per pound) or until meat thermometer registers 170°.

Place roast on platter. Remove rack from pan.

Stir flour, salt and pepper into drippings in pan until smooth. Stir in water and Worcestershire sauce. Over medium-high heat cook, stirring constantly, until gravy boils and thickens.

To serve, cut roast into chops and serve with gravy. Makes 6 to 8 servings.

STUFFED TURKEY ROLL

No one will guess this company loaf is made with ground turkey—it has the texture of solid turkey meat.

Carrot-Celery Stuffing (see Index)
2 lb. ground turkey or pork
1 c. soft white bread crumbs
¼ c. milk
10 slices bacon
Sour Cream Mushroom Sauce (see Index)

Prepare Carrot-Celery Stuffing.

In large bowl mix ground turkey, bread crumbs and milk until well blended.

On 12″ sheet of waxed paper, pat turkey mixture to a 10″ square. Spread stuffing over turkey mixture to within 1″ from edges.

To roll: Lift narrow end of waxed paper and begin to roll up, jelly-roll fashion, pressing lightly with fingers to start roll. Peel paper back and continue rolling turkey and stuffing to form a roll. Place roll seam-side down on rack in shallow roasting pan.

Lay bacon slices crosswise on roll, overlapping slightly. Tuck ends under roll.

Bake in 375° oven 1 hour and 15 minutes or until browned. Remove and let stand 10 minutes for easier slicing.

Meanwhile, prepare Sour Cream Mushroom Sauce.

To serve, cut roll into 8 slices and serve with sauce. Makes 8 servings.

NEW ENGLAND BOILED DINNER

A traditional one-pot meal of corned beef, cabbage, potatoes and onions.

6 whole cloves
3 lb. corned beef brisket
3 qt. water
¼ tsp. whole black peppercorns
2 bay leaves
Creamy Horseradish Dressing (see Index)
6 medium potatoes, peeled
6 carrots, peeled and halved
3 medium onions, peeled and halved
3 parsnips, peeled and quartered
1 large head cabbage, cut into 6 wedges
Parsley sprigs

Insert cloves into brisket. In 6-qt. Dutch oven place brisket, water, peppercorns and bay leaves. Over high heat bring to a boil. Reduce heat to low. Cover and simmer 3 hours.

Meanwhile, prepare Creamy Horseradish Dressing. Cover and refrigerate.

Add potatoes, carrots, onions and parsnips to brisket. Cover and simmer 20 minutes. Add cabbage; cover and simmer 20 minutes or until meat and vegetables are tender.

Remove meat and vegetables to serving platter. (Cooking liquid may be saved for your favorite soup broth for another day.)

Remove cloves from brisket. Slice meat diagonally, across the grain. Garnish platter with parsley. Serve meat and vegetables with dressing. Makes 6 to 8 servings.

SALMON SQUASH PATTIES

Equally good if you substitute solid-pack white tuna for the salmon.

Sour Cream Dill Topping or East Indies Dressing (see Index)
1 medium zucchini, shredded
1 (7¾-oz.) can salmon, drained and finely flaked
1½ c. soft bread crumbs
2 tblsp. minced onion
1 tsp. lemon juice
½ tsp. salt
½ tsp. Worcestershire sauce
⅛ tsp. pepper
2 eggs, slightly beaten
¼ c. vegetable oil

Prepare topping or dressing. Cover and refrigerate.

Place zucchini in dish towel, wrap and twist to squeeze out as much liquid as possible.

In medium bowl mix together zucchini, salmon and remaining ingredients except oil and topping.

Shape mixture into 6 patties, about 3″ round and ½″ thick, using ⅓ c. mixture for each patty.

In 12″ skillet over medium-high heat, heat oil until hot. Add patties; cook, turning once, 8 to 10 minutes or until golden brown on both sides.

Serve patties with topping or dressing. Makes 3 servings.

FISH ROULADES
WITH ONION-LEMON SAUCE_____

Vegetables are rolled up in fillets and topped with an onion sauce.

3 medium carrots
3 ribs celery
1 medium zucchini
7 tblsp. butter or regular margarine
½ tsp. salt
4 tblsp. chopped fresh parsley
6 medium onions, chopped (3 c.)
1 clove garlic, minced
½ c. dry white wine
1 tsp. lemon juice
¼ tsp. grated lemon rind
10 lb. fresh flounder fillets (2 lb.)
Lemon slices

Cut carrots, celery, and zucchini in half lengthwise. Slice each into 2¼" matchstick strips.

In 12" skillet over medium-high heat, melt 3 tblsp. butter. Add carrot and celery strips; cook 5 minutes.

Add zucchini, salt and 1 tblsp. parsley; cook 5 minutes or until vegetables are tender-crisp. Remove from skillet and set aside.

In same skillet over medium heat, melt remaining 4 tblsp. butter. Add onions and garlic. Cover and cook 10 minutes or until tender.

Stir in wine, lemon juice and lemon rind. Cover and cook 5 minutes. Remove from heat and let cool 10 minutes.

Divide vegetables evenly among fish fillets. Roll up, jelly-roll fashion; secure ends with toothpicks. In 13x9x2" baking dish place fish rolls, seam-side down.

In blender container place onion mixture; cover. Blend at high speed until smooth. Pour sauce over fish rolls.

Bake in 375° oven 15 to 18 minutes or until fish flakes easily with fork.

To serve, arrange rolls on serving platter; spoon sauce over rolls. Sprinkle with remaining 3 tblsp. parsley. Garnish with lemon slices. Makes 5 servings.

TO MICROWAVE: Use same ingredients, *reducing amounts as indicated.*

Cut carrots, celery and zucchini as directed.

In 2-qt. microwave-safe casserole place 3 tblsp. butter. Microwave, uncovered, at high setting (100% power) 1 to 2 minutes or until melted. Stir in carrots and celery. Cover with lid or plastic wrap, turning back one section to vent steam.

Microwave at high setting 7 to 8 minutes or until tender-crisp, stirring every 2 minutes. Stir in zucchini, salt and 1 tblsp. parsley. Cover again, and microwave 3 to 4 minutes or until zucchini is tender, stirring each minute. Remove vegetables.

In same casserole place onions, garlic and *3 tblsp. butter.* Cover again, and microwave at high setting 6 to 7 minutes or until onion is tender, stirring every 2 minutes.

Stir in *2 tblsp. wine,* lemon juice and lemon rind. Microwave, uncovered, 3 minutes. Let cool 10 minutes.

Divide vegetables evenly among fish fillets; roll up and secure as directed.

In 10" microwave-safe pie plate place fish rolls, seam-side down, around outer rim of plate, leaving an open space in center.

Blend onion mixture as directed. Pour over fish rolls, spreading to cover outer edges of fish. Microwave, uncovered, at high setting 8 to 12 minutes or until fish flakes easily with fork, rotating dish one-quarter turn every 3 minutes. Let stand 3 minutes.

Serve as directed.

RED FLANNEL HASH

Beets give this New England-style hash its color and sweet flavor.

3 slices bacon, diced
1 medium onion, chopped
1 clove garlic, minced
Ketchup
1 (12-oz.) can corned beef, diced
2 c. coarsely chopped cooked beets (about 6 medium)
2 c. coarsely chopped cooked potatoes (about 6 medium)
½ tsp. dry mustard
¼ tsp. dried marjoram leaves
⅛ tsp. pepper
½ c. heavy cream
2 tblsp. vegetable oil
6 eggs

In 12" skillet over medium-high heat, cook bacon until browned. Remove and drain on paper towels.

In bacon drippings over medium-high heat, cook onion and garlic until tender.

In large bowl mix together bacon, onion mixture, 2 tblsp. ketchup and remaining ingredients except oil and eggs.

In same skillet over medium-high heat, heat oil until hot. Spread hash mixture over bottom of skillet. Cook, stirring occasionally, 5 minutes.

Using the back of a spoon, make 6 indentations in hash mixture. Break an egg into each indentation.

Reduce heat to medium-low. Cover and cook 20 to 25 minutes or until eggs are set and hash is browned on the bottom.

To serve, cut into wedges. Serve with ketchup, if you wish. Makes 6 servings.

POTATO FRANKS

Potato-wrapped franks are sure to be popular with children of all ages.

2 qt. vegetable oil
¾ c. sifted flour
½ c. milk
2 tblsp. butter or regular margarine, melted
1 tsp. baking powder
1 tsp. Dijon-style prepared mustard
½ tsp. salt
1 egg
6 frankfurters or 1¼ lb. Italian sweet sausage, cut into 5" links
2 c. cold seasoned mashed potatoes
1 c. cracker crumbs
Ketchup or Mustard

In 3-qt. saucepan pour in oil to a depth of 1". Over medium heat, heat oil to 350° on a deep-fat thermometer, about 20 minutes.

Meanwhile, in blender container place flour, milk, butter, baking powder, mustard, salt and egg; cover. Blend at high speed until smooth, stopping several times to scrape down sides of blender. Pour batter into a 9" pie plate. Set aside.

In 7" skillet over high heat, bring 1" water to a boil; add frankfurters. Reduce heat to medium. Cover and cook 5 minutes. (If using Italian sweet sausage, cook 10 minutes.) Drain.

With floured hands, pat ⅓ c. cold seasoned mashed potatoes around each frankfurter.

Spread cracker crumbs on waxed paper.

Using a fork roll each frankfurter in batter, then in crumbs.

Fry coated frankfurters, 2 at a time, in oil 6 minutes or until golden brown on all sides. Remove with slotted spoon and drain on paper towels.

Potato Franks can be refrigerated at this time and reheated later. To reheat: On baking sheet place franks; bake in 350° oven 25 to 30 minutes or until heated through.

Makes 6 servings.

7

Side by
Side

No matter what you're having for dinner, you'll find that it's easy to balance the colors, textures and flavors of the meal with a side dish of vegetables. The choices are so plentiful: single vegetables served with a simple sauce, airy purées, braised greens, light pancakes and crisp fritters, whipped squash, stuffed artichokes, and potatoes of almost every description.

If you have on hand a few carrots and some other common ingredients, you have the makings of all sorts of interesting dishes. Recipes in this chapter tell how to use your food processor to turn carrots into a creamy purée, and how to roll-cut them into chunks and simmer them in a lemony sauce. There's a simple recipe for braised leeks and carrots, and another for batter-dipped strips of carrots fried to a golden crisp. When blended with flour and eggs, mashed carrots make an unforgettable homemade pasta, and you can even combine shredded carrots with other vegetables into a stuffing for roast chicken or pork.

People who love potatoes will want to sample Gourmet Cheese Potatoes, a Pennsylvania cook's recipe for a rich casserole of shredded potatoes, muenster cheese and sour cream—it's hard on the waistline, but just as hard to resist. Try cooking sweet potatoes or yams New England-style, with a maple glaze, or stuffed and sprinkled with pecans. Can't decide between white potatoes and sweet? Cut several of each into matchstick strips, cook quickly, and serve as Two-Potato Sauté.

A lively mix of vegetables is always welcome at the table. Ratatouille has five different vegetables simmered with herbs, and it's good served either hot or cold. Basil Beans with Tomatoes is a fragrant skillet dish, and tomatoes also blend well with anise, cucumbers and okra. When you wash fresh beets, don't throw away the tops; steam them and serve them along with the beets, garnished with a dollop of sour cream. Or try braising young turnip or mustard greens with chopped red pepper.

Often there's a choice of cooking methods. Stir-fried Asparagus, Parmesan Jerusalem Artichokes, Sweet-Sour Red Cabbage and Sesame Green Beans can be cooked on top of the range or microwaved.

CITRUS ASPARAGUS

Orange flavors the buttery sauce for these tender-crisp asparagus.

¼ c. butter or regular margarine
½ c. orange juice
1 tsp. grated orange rind
¼ tsp. salt
2 lb. asparagus, trimmed
1 tblsp. flour
2 tblsp. water

In 12″ skillet over medium heat, melt butter. Stir in orange juice, grated rind and salt until well blended; add asparagus.

Cover and cook 8 to 10 minutes or until tender-crisp. With slotted spoon remove asparagus to serving platter.

In small bowl stir flour and water until smooth. Stir into juice mixture. Cook, stirring constantly, until mixture boils and thickens.

To serve, spoon sauce over asparagus. Makes 6 servings.

TO MICROWAVE: Use same ingredients.

In 12x8x2″ microwave-safe baking dish place butter. Microwave, uncovered, at high setting (100% power) 1½ to 2 minutes or until melted.

Stir in orange juice, grated rind and salt. Add asparagus, arranging thicker spears toward the outside of dish. Cover with plastic wrap, turning back one section to vent steam.

Microwave at high setting 9 to 12 minutes or until tender-crisp, rearranging spears after 4 minutes.

With slotted spoon remove asparagus to serving platter.

In small bowl stir flour and water until smooth; stir into juice mixture. Microwave, uncovered, at high setting 1 to 3 minutes or until mixture boils and thickens, stirring each minute. Serve as directed.

PARMESAN JERUSALEM ARTICHOKES

Firm-textured, these have a flavor as delicate as artichoke hearts.

1 lb. Jerusalem artichokes
½ tsp. salt
2 tblsp. butter or regular margarine
½ c. light cream
⅛ tsp. pepper
½ c. grated Parmesan cheese
2 tblsp. chopped fresh parsley

In 2-qt. saucepan over high heat, bring 1″ water to a boil; add Jerusalem artichokes and ¼ tsp. salt. Reduce heat to medium-low. Cover and simmer 15 minutes or until fork-tender. Drain; peel, cut into ¼″ slices and set aside.

In same saucepan over medium-high heat, melt butter. Add sliced Jerusalem artichokes, cream, pepper and remaining ¼ tsp. salt; cook 1 minute.

Stir in cheese; cook 1 minute or until cheese melts.

Garnish with parsley. Makes 4 to 6 servings.

TO MICROWAVE: Use same ingredients, *reducing water as indicated.*

In 2-qt. microwave-safe casserole place Jerusalem artichokes, ¼ c. *water* and ¼ tsp. salt. Cover with lid or plastic wrap, turning back one section to vent steam.

Microwave at high setting (100% power) 6 to 9 minutes or until fork-tender, stirring after 4 minutes. Let stand, covered, 3 minutes. Drain; peel, cut into ¼″ slices and set aside.

In same casserole place butter. Microwave, uncovered, at high setting 1 to 1½ minutes or until melted. Stir in Jerusalem artichokes, cream, pepper and remaining ¼ tsp. salt.

Cover again, and microwave at high setting 1 minute. Stir in cheese. Cover again, and microwave at medium setting (50% power) 2 to 3 minutes or until cheese melts.

Garnish with parsley.

SWEDISH RUTABAGAS

Slices of rutabagas in a brown-sugar glaze with ginger.

2¼ lb. rutabagas (2 large)
6 tblsp. butter or regular margarine
⅓ c. packed light brown sugar
1½ tsp. salt
1½ tsp. ground ginger
¼ tsp. pepper

Peel, quarter and cut rutabagas into ¼" slices.

In 3-qt. saucepan over high heat, bring 1" water to a boil; add rutabagas. Reduce heat to medium-low. Cover and cook 20 minutes or until fork-tender. Drain; set aside.

In same saucepan place butter and remaining ingredients. Over medium-high heat, cook until butter melts and sugar dissolves.

Stir in rutabagas. Cook and stir until well coated and heated through. Makes 6 servings.

Mashed Swedish Rutabagas:
Prepare rutabagas as directed. Drain and put through ricer. Prepare butter sauce as directed and stir in rutabagas. Makes 6 servings.

TO MICROWAVE: Use same ingredients, *reducing water as indicated.*

Prepare rutabagas as directed.

In 2-qt. microwave-safe casserole place rutabagas and ¼ c. water. Cover with lid or plastic wrap, turning back one section to vent steam.

Microwave at high setting (100% power) 10 to 12 minutes or until fork-tender, stirring every 4 minutes. Let stand, covered, 2 minutes. Drain; set aside.

In same casserole place butter and remaining ingredients. Microwave, uncovered, at high setting 1 to 2 minutes or until melted, stirring after 1 minute.

Stir in rutabagas until well coated.

CARROT PURÉE

To use this as a spread, add a little mayonnaise or soft cream cheese.

1 lb. carrots, peeled and cut into 1" pieces
1 small onion, chopped
2 tblsp. butter or regular margarine
½ tsp. salt
½ tsp. dried thyme leaves

In 2-qt. saucepan over high heat, bring 1" water to a boil; add carrots and onion. Reduce heat to medium. Cover and cook 25 minutes or until carrots are very tender. Drain.

In blender container or food processor bowl using metal blade, place carrot mixture; cover. Blend at high speed or process until smooth.

Return carrot mixture to saucepan. Over low heat cook, stirring frequently, 5 minutes or until dry.

Stir in butter, salt and thyme until well blended and butter melts. Makes 4 servings.

TO MICROWAVE: Use same ingredients, *reducing water as indicated.*

In 2-qt. microwave-safe casserole place carrots, onion and ½ c. water. Cover with lid or plastic wrap, turning back one section to vent steam.

Microwave at high setting (100% power) 16 to 19 minutes or until carrots are very tender, stirring every 3 minutes. Let stand, covered, 2 minutes. Drain.

In blender container or food processor bowl using metal blade, place carrot mixture, salt and thyme; cover. Blend at high speed or process until smooth.

Return carrot mixture to casserole. Microwave, uncovered, at high setting 2 minutes. Stir in butter until melted.

SPINACH PURÉE

For a gourmet main dish, serve poached fish on a bed of this purée.

1 lb. fresh spinach, washed and trimmed, or 1 (10-oz.) pkg. frozen spinach, thawed
1 c. light cream
2 tblsp. butter or regular margarine
1 small onion, finely chopped
2 tblsp. flour
¼ tsp. salt
¼ tsp. ground allspice

In 4-qt. Dutch oven over high heat, bring fresh spinach and ¼ c. water to a boil. Cover and cook 1 minute.

Drain; rinse under cold running water to cool.

Place cooked fresh spinach or thawed frozen spinach in sieve and press out excess liquid.

In blender container or food processor bowl using metal blade, place spinach and ¼ c. cream; cover. Blend at high speed or process until smooth; set aside.

In 2-qt. saucepan over medium heat, melt butter. Add onion; cook until tender. Stir in flour, salt and allspice until well blended.

Gradually stir in remaining ¾ c. cream until well blended. Cook, stirring constantly, until mixture boils and thickens.

Stir in puréed spinach until well blended. Cook until heated through. Makes 4 servings.

TO MICROWAVE: Use same ingredients, *changing amounts as indicated.*

In 3-qt. microwave-safe casserole place fresh spinach; *omit water.* Cover with lid or plastic wrap, turning back one section to vent steam.

Microwave at high setting (100% power) 1½ to 2 minutes or until wilted, stirring after 1 minute. Drain and rinse as directed.

Press out excess liquid and purée as directed.

In 1-qt. microwave-safe casserole place butter and onion. Cover with lid or plastic wrap.

Microwave at high setting 3 to 4 minutes or until onion is tender, stirring after 1 minute. Stir in 2½ tblsp. flour, salt and allspice until well blended.

Gradually stir in remaining ¾ c. cream until well blended. Microwave, uncovered, at high setting 3 to 4 minutes or until mixture boils and thickens, stirring each minute.

Stir in puréed spinach until well blended. Microwave, uncovered, at high setting 1 to 2 minutes or until heated, stirring after 1 minute.

HERBED CORN ON THE COB

Butter blended with parsley, chives and garlic brings out the flavor.

½ c. butter or regular margarine, softened
2 tblsp. chopped fresh parsley
2 tblsp. fresh or frozen chopped chives
¼ tsp. garlic salt
⅛ tsp. pepper
8 ears corn, husked

In small bowl stir all ingredients except corn until well blended.

Place each ear of corn on a 12"-long sheet of heavy-duty aluminum foil. Spread butter mixture evenly over each ear. Securely wrap each ear into a loose packet, crimping foil tightly to prevent leaking. Bake immediately or refrigerate.

To bake, place foil-wrapped packets directly on oven rack. Bake in 375° oven 25 to 30 minutes or until corn is tender. Makes 8 servings.

TO GRILL: Prepare and wrap corn as directed. Grill 4" from gray coals (medium heat) 20 to 30 minutes or until corn is tender.

BEST-EVER GREEN BEANS

*Tender-crisp beans in a piquant
sauce, sprinkled with diced bacon.*

1 lb. green beans, trimmed and cut into 1″
   pieces
1 tblsp. butter or regular margarine
1 small onion, finely chopped
1 tblsp. flour
1 tblsp. sugar
1 tblsp. chopped fresh parsley
¼ tsp. salt
½ c. milk
1 tblsp. cider vinegar
½ c. dairy sour cream
4 slices bacon, diced, cooked and drained

In 2-qt. saucepan over high heat,
bring 1″ water to a boil; add beans.
Reduce heat to medium-low. Cover
and simmer 7 to 9 minutes or until
beans are tender-crisp. Drain; set
aside.

In same saucepan over medium
heat, melt butter. Add onion; cook
until tender. Stir in flour, sugar,
parsley and salt until well blended.

Gradually stir in milk until well
blended. Cook, stirring constantly,
until mixture boils and thickens. Reduce heat to low. Stir in vinegar.

Stir some of the hot mixture into
sour cream; stir sour cream mixture
back into saucepan. Stir in green
beans. Cook over low heat until
heated through. (Do not boil.)

Garnish with bacon. Makes
6 servings.

TO MICROWAVE: Use same ingredients,
reducing water as indicated.

In 2-qt. microwave-safe casserole
place beans and ½ c. water. Cover
with lid or plastic wrap, turning
back one section to vent steam.

Microwave at high setting (100%
power) 8 minutes or until tender-
crisp, stirring every 3 minutes.
Drain and set aside.

In same casserole place butter and
onion. Cover again, and microwave
at high setting 2 to 3 minutes or until tender, stirring after 1 minute.

Stir in flour, sugar, parsley and
salt until well blended. Gradually
stir in milk until well blended.

Microwave, uncovered, at high
setting 2 minutes or until mixture
boils, stirring each minute. Stir in
vinegar.

Stir some of the hot mixture into
sour cream; stir sour cream mixture
back into casserole. Stir in green
beans.

Cover again, and microwave at
medium setting (50% power) 1
minute, or until heated through.

Garnish with bacon.

MARINATED GREEN BEANS

*Arrange on lettuce leaves with a
sprinkling of Parmesan cheese.*

1½ lb. green beans, trimmed
½ c. vegetable oil
⅓ c. red wine vinegar
1½ tsp. salt
1½ tsp. prepared mustard
⅛ tsp. pepper
1 small clove garlic, minced

In 3-qt. saucepan over high heat,
bring 1″ water to a boil; add beans.
Cover and cook 3 minutes. Drain, reserving 1 tblsp. water. Place beans
in 12x8x2″ baking dish.

In jar with tight-fitting lid, place
oil, vinegar, salt, mustard, pepper,
garlic and reserved 1 tblsp. water.
Cover; shake until well mixed. Pour
over beans; toss until well coated.

Cover and refrigerate at least 12
hours before serving, stirring twice.
Makes 8 servings.

TO MICROWAVE: Use same ingredients,
reducing water as indicated.

In 12x8x2″ microwave-safe baking
dish place beans and ½ c. water.
Cover with plastic wrap, turning
back one section to vent steam.

Microwave at high setting (100%
power) 5 to 7 minutes or until tender-crisp. Drain, reserving 1 tblsp.
water. Return beans to baking dish.

Continue with recipe as directed.

FESTIVE GREEN BEANS

Cut diagonally, beans are especially pretty and absorb more herb flavor.

2 tblsp. vegetable oil
1 lb. green beans, trimmed and diagonally
    cut into 1/8"-thick slices
1 tblsp. butter or regular margarine
3/4 c. minced onion
1/4 c. minced celery
1 clove garlic, minced
1/4 c. minced fresh parsley
1/4 tsp. salt
1/4 tsp. dried rosemary leaves
1/4 tsp. dried basil leaves

In 12" skillet over medium-high heat, heat oil until hot. Add green beans; cook, stirring often, until beans are tender-crisp. Remove from skillet; set aside.

In same skillet over medium heat, melt butter. Add onion, celery and garlic; cook until onion is tender.

Stir in parsley, salt, rosemary and basil. Cover and simmer 5 minutes.

Stir in green beans; cover and simmer 5 minutes more, or until beans are tender. Makes 6 servings.

TO MICROWAVE: Use same ingredients.

In 2-qt. microwave-safe casserole place oil and beans. Cover with lid or plastic wrap, turning back one section to vent steam.

Microwave at high setting (100% power) 8 minutes or until beans are tender-crisp, stirring every 3 minutes. Let stand, covered, 2 minutes. Remove from casserole; set aside.

In same casserole place butter, onion, celery and garlic. Cover again, and microwave at high setting 2 minutes.

Stir in parsley, salt, rosemary and basil. Cover again, and microwave at high setting 2 minutes.

Stir in green beans. Cover again, and microwave at high setting 4 minutes or until beans are tender, stirring after 2 minutes. Let stand, covered, 3 minutes.

TANGY BRUSSELS SPROUTS

Steamed in lemon juice, then served in a sour cream sauce.

2 pt. fresh Brussels sprouts, trimmed, or
    2 (10-oz.) pkg. frozen sprouts, thawed
2 tblsp. butter or regular margarine
2 tsp. lemon juice
3/4 c. dairy sour cream
1/4 c. chopped fresh parsley
1/2 tsp. salt
1/2 tsp. sugar
1/8 tsp. pepper

Cut an X in the stem end of each fresh Brussels sprout; set aside.

In 10" skillet over medium heat, melt butter. Add sprouts and lemon juice. Cover and cook, shaking skillet occasionally, 10 minutes or until sprouts are fork-tender. Remove from heat.

In small bowl stir together sour cream and remaining ingredients. Slowly stir sour cream mixture into skillet. Cook over low heat until heated through (but do not boil). Makes 8 servings.

TO MICROWAVE: Use same ingredients.

Prepare sprouts as directed.

In 2-qt. microwave-safe casserole place sprouts, butter and lemon juice. Cover with lid or plastic wrap, turning back one section to vent steam.

Microwave at high setting (100% power) 9 to 10 minutes or until sprouts are fork-tender, stirring every 3 minutes. Let stand, covered, 5 minutes. Meanwhile, prepare sour cream mixture as directed.

Stir sour cream mixture into casserole. Cover again, and microwave at medium setting (50% power) 1 1/2 to 2 minutes or until heated through.

HOT SPICED BEETS

*A variation of classic Harvard beets;
they're delicious either hot or cold.*

2 lb. beets, trimmed
3 tblsp. packed dark brown sugar
3 tblsp. cider vinegar
2 tblsp. butter or regular margarine
½ tsp. salt
½ tsp. ground cinnamon
¼ tsp. ground nutmeg
¼ tsp. ground cloves
1 tsp. cornstarch
¼ c. water

In 3-qt. saucepan over high heat,
bring 1" water to a boil; add beets.
Reduce heat to medium-low.

Cover and simmer 30 to 60 minutes or until beets are fork-tender.

Drain and rinse under cold water.
Peel and thinly slice.

In same saucepan place brown
sugar and remaining ingredients
except cornstarch and water. Over
medium heat cook, stirring constantly, until mixture boils.

In small bowl stir together cornstarch and water until smooth. Stir
into saucepan. Cook, stirring constantly, until mixture boils and
thickens.

Reduce heat to low. Stir in beets;
cook until heated through. Serve
warm or cold. Makes 6 to 8 servings.

Hot Spiced Carrots or Parsnips:

Prepare as directed, but substitute
8 medium carrots or parsnips, peeled
and sliced, for beets; and granulated
sugar for brown sugar.

Cook carrots 20 minutes until
tender-crisp; cook parsnips 20 to
30 minutes or until tender-crisp.

Continue recipe as directed.

TO MICROWAVE BEETS: Use same ingredients, *reducing water as indicated.*

In 2-qt. microwave-safe casserole
place beets and ½ c. water. Cover
with lid or plastic wrap, turning
back one section to vent steam.

Microwave at high setting (100%
power) 15 to 19 minutes or until
beets are fork-tender, stirring every
5 minutes. Let stand, covered,
5 minutes. Drain.

Peel and slice as directed.

In same casserole place brown
sugar and remaining ingredients
except cornstarch and water.

Microwave, uncovered, at high
setting 1 minute or until butter
melts.

In small bowl stir together cornstarch and water until smooth. Stir
into casserole. Microwave, uncovered, at high setting 1 minute or until mixture boils and thickens.

Stir in beets. Cover again, and
microwave at medium setting (50%
power) 1 to 2 minutes or until heated through. Serve as directed.

TO MICROWAVE CARROTS OR PARSNIPS:
Follow microwave directions for
beets, *changing ingredients and
amounts as indicated.*

For carrots, microwave at high
setting (100% power) *8 medium carrots, peeled and sliced, with ¼ c.
water* 7 to 11 minutes or until
tender-crisp, stirring every 4
minutes. Drain.

For parsnips, microwave at high
setting *8 medium parsnips, peeled
and sliced,* with ½ c. water 9 to
11 minutes or until tender-crisp, stirring every 4 minutes. Drain.

In same casserole place *3 tblsp.
granulated sugar* and remaining ingredients except cornstarch and
water; *omit brown sugar.*

Continue recipe as directed.

GOLDEN HARVEST ONIONS

A Kansas cook tells us the men in her house love these honeyed onions.

6 medium onions
2 tblsp. butter or regular margarine, melted
2 tblsp. chili sauce
2 tblsp. honey
1 tsp. paprika
½ tsp. salt
⅛ tsp. pepper

Peel onions and cut in half cross-wise. In greased 12x8x2" baking dish place onions, cut-side up.

In small bowl stir together butter and remaining ingredients. Brush over onion halves.

Bake, covered, in 350° oven 1 hour or until onions are fork-tender. Makes 6 servings.

TO MICROWAVE: Use same ingredients. Peel and cut onions as directed.

In ungreased 12x8x2" microwave-safe baking dish place onions, cut-side up.

In small bowl, stir together butter and remaining ingredients. Brush over onion halves. Cover with plastic wrap, turning back one section to vent steam.

Microwave at high setting (100% power) 10 to 12 minutes or until onions are fork-tender, rotating dish one-quarter turn every 3 minutes. Let stand, covered, 3 minutes.

SWEET-SOUR RED CABBAGE

Bacon gives this simple sweet-sour dish a lovely smoked flavor.

6 slices bacon, diced
1 medium head red cabbage, chopped
⅓ c. vinegar
¼ c. packed brown sugar
½ tsp. salt
¼ tsp. pepper

In 12" skillet over medium heat, cook bacon until crisp. Drain on paper towels.

Add cabbage to bacon drippings. Over medium heat cook, stirring often, 5 minutes. Reduce heat to medium-low. Cover and simmer 5 minutes.

Stir in bacon, vinegar, brown sugar, salt and pepper. Cover and simmer 10 minutes or until cabbage is tender. Makes 6 servings.

TO MICROWAVE: Use same ingredients.

In 3-qt. microwave-safe casserole place bacon. Cover with waxed paper. Microwave at high setting (100% power) 6 minutes or until crisp, stirring every 2 minutes. Drain bacon on paper towels.

Add cabbage to bacon drippings. Cover with lid or plastic wrap, turning back one section to vent steam.

Microwave at high setting 4 minutes, stirring after 2 minutes. Stir in bacon, vinegar, brown sugar, salt and pepper.

Cover again, and microwave at high setting 4 minutes or until cabbage is tender, stirring after 2 minutes.

CABBAGE AND APPLE SKILLET

Combine apples and cabbage for an easy skillet dish.

3 tblsp. butter or regular margarine
2 medium onions, finely chopped
2 medium apples, cored and cut into ⅛" slices
5 c. shredded cabbage
¼ c. water
3 tblsp. lemon juice
2 tblsp. packed brown sugar
½ tsp. salt

In 12" skillet over medium heat, melt butter. Add onions; cook until tender.

Add apples, cabbage and water. Reduce heat to medium-low. Cover and simmer 20 minutes, stirring occasionally.

Stir in lemon juice, brown sugar and salt. Cover again, and simmer 10 minutes or until cabbage is tender. Makes 6 servings.

GOLDEN CARROTS SUPREME

These glazed carrots, bathed in a sweet lemon sauce, go well with fish.

1 lb. carrots (6 medium)
Thinly sliced lemon peel from 1 small
    lemon
¼ c. butter or regular margarine
2 tsp. sugar
2 tsp. lemon juice
1 tsp. salt
⅛ tsp. pepper
Chopped fresh parsley

To roll-cut carrots: With knife make one diagonal cut through one end of carrot; roll carrot one-quarter turn. Cut 1″ from previous cut on a diagonal. Continue rolling and slicing, and repeat with remaining carrots.

In 3-qt. saucepan over high heat, bring carrots, lemon peel and remaining ingredients except parsley to a boil. Reduce heat to medium-low.

Cover and simmer 20 minutes, stirring occasionally, or until carrots are tender-crisp.

Garnish with parsley. Makes 6 servings.

Golden Parsnips Supreme: Prepare as directed, but substitute 1 lb. parsnips, peeled and sliced, for carrots.

Golden Rutabagas Supreme:
Prepare as directed, but substitute 2 medium rutabagas, trimmed, peeled, quartered and sliced, for carrots.

TO MICROWAVE CARROTS: Use same ingredients.

In 2-qt. microwave-safe casserole place butter. Microwave, uncovered, at high setting (100% power) 1½ to 2 minutes or until melted.

Stir in carrots, lemon peel and remaining ingredients except parsley. Cover with lid or plastic wrap, turning back one section to vent steam.

Microwave at high setting 12 to 14 minutes or until carrots are tender-crisp, stirring every 3 minutes. Let stand, covered, 2 minutes.

Garnish with parsley.

TO MICROWAVE PARSNIPS: Follow microwave directions for carrots, but microwave at high setting 7 to 11 minutes.

TO MICROWAVE RUTABAGAS: Follow microwave directions for carrots, but microwave at high setting 10 to 12 minutes.

SUCCOTASH

Classic combination of corn and lima beans in a light cream sauce.

2 c. fresh or frozen corn
2 c. fresh or frozen lima beans
1 c. light cream
2 tblsp. butter or regular margarine
1 tblsp. chopped fresh parsley
½ tsp. salt
¼ tsp. paprika

In 3-qt. saucepan over medium-high heat, bring all ingredients to a boil. Reduce heat to medium.

Cover and cook 10 to 12 minutes or until vegetables are tender. Makes 6 servings.

TO MICROWAVE: Use same ingredients, *changing ingredients as indicated.*

In 3-qt. microwave-safe casserole place corn, *1 (10-oz.) pkg. frozen lima beans,* thawed, cream and remaining ingredients. Cover with lid or plastic wrap, turning back one section to vent steam.

Microwave at high setting (100% power) 8 to 14 minutes or until vegetables are tender, stirring every 2 minutes. Let stand, covered, 2 minutes.

ROASTED POTATO FANS

Cut accordian-style, these potatoes fan out by themselves as they bake.

6 medium potatoes, peeled
6 tblsp. butter or regular margarine, melted
3 tblsp. ketchup or chili sauce
1½ tsp. paprika
1½ tsp. Worcestershire sauce

Slice potatoes crosswise almost through, making slices ¼ " apart. (Making the cuts uniform is easy if you place each potato in the bowl of a wooden spoon, then slice through until the blade touches the spoon.)

Place potatoes on 15½x10½x1" jelly-roll pan. Brush with some melted butter. Bake in 425° oven 30 minutes.

Meanwhile, stir ketchup, paprika and Worcestershire sauce into remaining melted butter.

Brush potatoes with some butter mixture. Bake 20 minutes or until potatoes are tender, brushing twice more with butter mixture. Makes 6 servings.

Roasted Potato Wedges: Prepare as directed, but do not peel potatoes. Cut each potato into 4 wedges. Slice each wedge crosswise as directed.

Place wedges skin-side down on 15½x10½x1" jelly-roll pan. Brush wedges with some melted butter. Bake in 425° oven 10 minutes.

Stir ketchup, paprika and Worcestershire sauce into remaining butter. Brush wedges with some butter mixture.

Bake wedges 20 minutes more or until tender, brushing twice more with remaining butter mixture.

Plain Roasted Potato Fans: Prepare as directed, but reduce butter to 2 tblsp. and omit ketchup or chili sauce and Worcestershire sauce.

Prepare potatoes for fans or wedges as directed. Place in jelly-roll pan. Brush with melted butter. Sprinkle with paprika.

Bake in 425° oven 50 minutes for fans or 30 minutes for wedges, or until tender.

POTATOES ANNA

Layers of wafer-thin potatoes—crusty on the outside, tender inside.

4 large potatoes, peeled and sliced ⅛" thick
Iced water
½ c. butter or regular margarine
¾ tsp. salt
¼ tsp. pepper

In large bowl place potatoes; cover with iced water. Soak 10 minutes. Drain well; pat potatoes dry with paper towels.

In 10" skillet with oven-safe handle and lid (or 4-qt. Dutch oven) over medium heat, melt butter. Spoon off 4 tblsp. melted butter; set aside. Tilt pan to coat bottom and side with remaining butter.

Keeping skillet over medium heat, layer some potato slices in a circular pattern, slightly overlapping slices. Drizzle with some melted butter; sprinkle with some salt and pepper. Repeat twice with remaining potatoes, butter and seasoning to make two more layers, shaking pan occasionally to make sure potatoes are not sticking.

Using saucepan or casserole dish that will fit inside skillet, press potatoes down to make them compact.

Cover skillet. Bake in 425° oven 25 minutes. Uncover and press potatoes down again.

Bake, uncovered, 25 minutes more, or until potatoes are golden brown on the edges and fork-tender. Let stand 5 minutes.

Using wide spatula, hold potatoes in place and carefully tilt pan to drain off excess butter.

Run a knife around the edges of pan. Gently shake pan to release potatoes. Invert potatoes onto plate. If any potatoes stick to pan, carefully lift out and replace.

To serve, cut into wedges. Makes 6 servings.

CREAMY MASHED POTATOES

For a large holiday get-together, double this make-ahead recipe.

2½ lb. potatoes, peeled and quartered
Salt
1 (3-oz.) pkg. cream cheese
1 tsp. fresh or frozen chopped chives
¼ tsp. garlic salt
⅛ tsp. pepper
3 tblsp. butter or regular margarine
1 c. heavy cream
Paprika

In 3-qt. saucepan over high heat, bring 1″ water to a boil; add potatoes and ½ tsp. salt. Reduce heat to medium-low. Cover and simmer 30 minutes or until fork-tender; drain.

In large bowl using potato masher, mash potatoes. Add cream cheese, chives, garlic salt, pepper, ½ tsp. salt and 2 tblsp. butter.

Using mixer at medium speed, beat until well blended. Gradually beat in cream until mixture is light and fluffy.

Pour mixture into 8″ square baking dish. (At this point mixture can be covered and refrigerated overnight.)

Dot with remaining 1 tblsp. butter and sprinkle with paprika. Bake in 350° oven 45 minutes or until heated through. (If potatoes have been refrigerated, let stand at room temperature 10 minutes and bake 45 to 50 minutes or until heated through.) Makes 6 servings.

Creamy Mashed Turnips: Use same ingredients, but substitute 2½ lb. turnips, peeled and quartered, for potatoes, and prepare as directed.

TO MICROWAVE: Use same ingredients, *changing amounts as indicated.*

In 3-qt. microwave-safe casserole place potatoes, ¼ c. *water* and ½ tsp. salt. Cover with lid or plastic wrap, turning back one section to vent steam.

Microwave at high setting (100% power) 13 to 16 minutes for potatoes (or 15 to 18 minutes for turnips) or until fork-tender, stirring every 4 minutes. Drain.

Mash and beat potatoes with other ingredients as directed. Pour into 2-qt. microwave-safe casserole. *Do not dot with butter.* (At this point mixture can be covered and refrigerated overnight.)

Cover with lid or plastic wrap, turning back one section to vent steam. Microwave at medium setting (50% power) 5 to 7 minutes or until heated through, stirring each minute. (If potatoes have been refrigerated, microwave 8 to 11 minutes or until heated through, stirring each minute.)

Sprinkle with paprika.

WHIPPED BUTTERNUT SQUASH

Nutmeg-scented squash—a holiday favorite of one Florida woman.

3 eggs, separated
6 c. puréed, cooked butternut squash (6½ lb.)
½ c. light cream
1 tsp. salt
¼ tsp. celery salt
¼ tsp. paprika
Freshly grated nutmeg

In large bowl using fork, beat egg yolks until well blended. Stir in squash and remaining ingredients except egg whites and nutmeg until well blended.

In small bowl using mixer at high speed, beat egg whites until stiff, but not dry, peaks form.

Fold egg whites into squash mixture. Pour mixture into greased 13x9x2″ baking dish. Sprinkle with nutmeg.

Bake in 350° oven 35 to 40 minutes or until center is set. Makes 12 servings.

CREAMED CORN

Use this rich cream sauce to cook either spinach or whole-kernel corn.

2 c. fresh or frozen corn
1 c. heavy cream
2 tblsp. butter or regular margarine
½ tsp. sugar
½ tsp. salt
⅛ tsp. pepper
⅛ tsp. paprika

In 2-qt. saucepan over medium-high heat, bring all ingredients to a boil. Reduce heat to medium.

Cook, uncovered, until corn is tender and liquid is reduced by half, about 12 minutes. Makes 6 servings.

Creamed Spinach: Use same ingredients, but substitute 2 lb. chopped fresh spinach, or 2 (10-oz.) pkg. frozen chopped spinach, thawed and well drained, for corn.

In 2-qt. saucepan over medium-high heat, bring all ingredients except spinach to a boil. Reduce heat to medium.

Simmer, uncovered, 5 minutes. Add spinach; simmer, stirring frequently, 6 minutes or until spinach is wilted and liquid is reduced by half. Makes 6 servings.

TO MICROWAVE CORN: Use same ingredients.

In 2-qt. microwave-safe casserole place all ingredients. Cover with lid or plastic wrap, turning back one section to vent steam.

Microwave at high setting (100% power) 7 to 9 minutes or until corn is tender, stirring every 2 minutes. Let stand, covered, 2 minutes.

TO MICROWAVE SPINACH: Use same ingredients.

In 2-qt. microwave-safe casserole place all ingredients except spinach. Cover with lid or plastic wrap, turning back one section to vent steam.

Microwave at high setting (100% power) 3 to 4 minutes or until mixture boils, stirring every minute.

Add spinach. Cover again, and microwave at high setting 3 to 4 minutes or until spinach is wilted, stirring every minute. Let stand, covered, 2 minutes.

CORN RAREBIT

For a light supper, serve this cheesy rarebit with soup and fresh fruit.

Cheddar Sauce (see Index)
1½ c. fresh or frozen corn, cooked and drained
6 slices white or whole-wheat bread, toasted and halved
2 large tomatoes, each cut into 6 slices
6 slices bacon, diced, cooked and drained

Prepare Cheddar Sauce, adding corn with the milk for the sauce.

Arrange 4 toast halves on each of 3 plates. Top each toast half with a tomato slice. Spoon Cheddar Sauce over tomatoes and toast. Sprinkle with bacon. Makes 3 servings.

STEWED TOMATOES

Once you taste these, you'll never want to eat canned tomatoes again.

¼ c. butter or regular margarine
1 medium green pepper, chopped
1 medium onion, chopped
1 clove garlic, minced
4 ripe tomatoes, peeled and cut into 1½" chunks
1 tblsp. packed light brown sugar
½ tsp. salt
½ tsp. dried basil leaves
2 tblsp. grated Parmesan cheese

In 10" skillet over medium-high heat, melt butter. Add green pepper, onion and garlic; cook until tender.

Stir in tomatoes, sugar, salt and basil until well blended. Reduce heat to medium-low. Cover and simmer 10 minutes to blend flavors. Stir in cheese. Makes 6 servings.

TO MICROWAVE: Use same ingredients, *reducing butter as indicated.*

In 2-qt. microwave-safe casserole place *2 tblsp. butter,* green pepper, onion and garlic. Cover with lid or plastic wrap, turning back one section to vent steam.

Microwave at high setting (100% power) 4 to 5 minutes or until vegetables are tender, stirring after 2 minutes.

Stir in tomatoes, sugar, salt and basil. Microwave, uncovered, at high setting 5 to 6 minutes or until flavors blend, stirring every 2 minutes.

Stir in cheese. Microwave at high setting 1 to 2 minutes or until cheese melts.

VEGETABLE KABOBS

Other herb butters also may be used in place of Dill Butter (see Index).

Dill Butter (see Index)
2 large ears corn, each cut into 6 pieces
2 medium zucchini, each cut into 6 pieces
1 large head cauliflower, broken into 12 flowerets

Prepare Dill Butter; set aside.

On each of 6 (12") metal skewers, loosely thread 2 pieces corn, 2 pieces zucchini and 2 cauliflowerets.

Place each skewer on a 13"-long sheet of heavy-duty aluminum foil. Spread kabobs with Dill Butter. Securely wrap each kabob into a loose packet, crimping foil tightly to prevent leakage. Bake immediately or refrigerate.

To bake, place foil-wrapped kabobs directly on oven rack. Bake in 375° oven 25 to 30 minutes or until vegetables are tender-crisp. Makes 6 servings.

TO MICROWAVE: Use same ingredients.

Prepare Dill Butter; set aside.

On 12" microwave-safe platter, arrange a ring of cauliflowerets, stem-side out, along the outer edge of the platter. Arrange corn in a ring inside the cauliflower. Arrange zucchini in the center.

Dot each vegetable with Dill Butter. Cover with plastic wrap, turning back one section to vent steam.

Microwave at high setting (100% power) 12 to 14 minutes or until all vegetables are tender-crisp, rotating platter one-quarter turn every 3 minutes. Let stand, covered, 3 to 5 minutes.

To serve, thread cooked vegetables on skewers as directed.

SESAME GREEN BEANS

Italian green beans are simmered in a cheesy tomato sauce.

Stewed Tomatoes (see facing page)
3 lb. Italian green beans, trimmed, or
   2 (10-oz.) pkg. frozen Italian green
   beans, thawed
⅓ c. grated Parmesan cheese
2 tblsp. sesame seed, toasted

In 12" skillet prepare Stewed Tomatoes as directed, but do not cook the last 10 minutes and do not add cheese.

Add beans to hot tomato mixture. Over high heat bring to a boil. Reduce heat to medium-low.

Simmer 5 minutes. Cover and simmer 5 minutes more or until beans are tender-crisp. Stir in Parmesan cheese.

Garnish with sesame seed. Makes 6 to 8 servings.

TO MICROWAVE: Use same ingredients.

In 3-qt. microwave-safe casserole prepare Stewed Tomatoes in microwave as directed, but do not add Parmesan cheese.

Add beans to hot tomato mixture. Cover with lid or plastic wrap, turning back one section to vent steam.

Microwave at high setting (100% power) 14 to 16 minutes or until beans are tender, stirring every 3 minutes.

Stir in cheese. Microwave at high setting 1 to 2 minutes or until cheese melts.

Garnish with sesame seed.

SAUTÉED TOMATOES AND ANISE

(see photo following page 86)

Also called fennel or finocchio, anise imparts a mild, licorice-like flavor.

2 lb. anise
¼ c. butter or regular margarine
2 cloves garlic, minced
2 large tomatoes, each cut into 6 wedges
½ tsp. salt

Wash anise. Trim about 1" from bulbs and cut off stems with leaves. Chop 1 tblsp. of the leaves; set aside. Cut anise bulbs crosswise into ¼" slices.

In 12" skillet over medium-high heat, melt butter. Add sliced anise and garlic; cook 10 minutes. Reduce heat to medium-low.

Add tomatoes and salt. Cover and simmer 10 minutes or until anise is tender-crisp.

Garnish with chopped anise leaves. Makes 6 servings.

TO MICROWAVE: Use same ingredients.
Wash and trim anise as directed.

In 2-qt. microwave-safe casserole place butter and garlic. Cover with lid or plastic wrap, turning back one section to vent steam.

Microwave at high setting (100% power) 2 to 3 minutes or until garlic is tender, stirring after 1 minute.

Add sliced anise. Cover again, and microwave at high setting 7 to 8 minutes or until anise is tender-crisp, stirring every 3 minutes.

Stir in tomatoes and salt. Microwave, uncovered, 2 to 3 minutes or until heated through, stirring after 1 minute.

Garnish with chopped anise leaves.

BASIL BEANS AND TOMATOES

If you have fresh basil leaves, use 2 tblsp., chopped.

¼ c. vegetable oil
2 lb. green beans, trimmed and cut diagonally into 1½" pieces
1 large onion, chopped
2 cloves garlic, minced
1 c. water
2 tsp. dried basil leaves
1 tsp. salt
¼ tsp. pepper
4 medium tomatoes, chopped

In 12" skillet over high heat, heat oil until hot. Add green beans, onion and garlic. Cook, stirring constantly, 4 minutes.

Stir in water, basil, salt and pepper. Reduce heat to low. Cover and simmer 20 minutes or until tender-crisp.

Stir in tomatoes. Increase heat to medium. Cook, stirring constantly, 2 minutes. Makes 8 servings.

TO MICROWAVE: Use same ingredients, *changing amounts as indicated.*

In 3-qt. microwave-safe casserole place oil, onion and garlic. Cover with lid or plastic wrap, turning back one section to vent steam.

Microwave at high setting (100% power) 2 to 3 minutes or until tender, stirring after 1 minute.

Stir in green beans, ¼ c. water, basil, pepper and 1½ tsp. salt. Cover again, and microwave at high setting 15 to 17 minutes or until beans are tender, stirring every 4 minutes.

Stir in tomatoes. Microwave, uncovered, at medium setting (50% power) 1 minute or until heated through. Stir before serving.

ZUCCHINI AND CARROT SAUTÉ

*Just shred the vegetables
and sauté them in a little butter.*

2 tblsp. butter or regular margarine
1 c. shredded carrots
½ c. sliced green onions
3 c. shredded zucchini
½ tsp. salt
Lemon juice

In 10″ skillet over medium heat,
melt butter. Add carrots and green
onions; cook, stirring frequently, until tender.

Stir in zucchini and salt. Cook
2 minutes or until zucchini is heated
through. Sprinkle with lemon juice.
Makes 4 servings.

BASIL TOMATO SAUTÉ

*Pick the plumpest, prettiest
tomatoes to make this herbed sauté.*

4 tblsp. butter or regular margarine
1 large green pepper, cut into ¼″ strips
1 clove garlic, minced
1 tsp. dried basil leaves
½ tsp. salt
5 green onions, cut into 1½″ pieces
4 medium tomatoes, peeled and cut into
    1″ chunks
1 c. fresh or frozen peas, snow peas or
    sugar snap peas

In 10″ skillet over medium heat,
melt butter. Add green pepper, garlic, basil and salt. Cook, stirring frequently, 3 minutes.

Add green onions; cook until vegetables are tender-crisp. Increase
heat to high. Stir in tomatoes and
peas; cook 5 minutes.

With slotted spoon remove vegetables to serving dish. Cook remaining
liquid in skillet until reduced by half.
Pour liquid over vegetables. Makes
4 to 6 servings.

CHERRY TOMATO SAUTÉ

*The buttery flavor of this sauté is
sparked by a dash of fennel seed.*

¼ c. butter or regular margarine
1 medium onion, chopped
1 pt. cherry tomatoes, halved, or 3 medium
    tomatoes, each cut into 8 wedges
½ tsp. salt
½ tsp. fennel seed
⅛ tsp. pepper

In 7″ skillet over medium-high
heat, melt butter. Add onion; cook
until tender.

Stir in tomatoes, salt, fennel and
pepper. Reduce heat to medium.
Cover and cook 3 to 5 minutes or
until tomatoes are soft (do not let
skins burst). Makes 6 servings.

Zucchini Sauté: Using 10″ skillet,
prepare as directed, except substitute 2 medium zucchini, sliced, for
cherry tomatoes.

TO MICROWAVE TOMATOES OR ZUCCHINI:

Use same ingredients, *reducing butter as indicated.*

In 2-qt. microwave-safe casserole
place *2 tblsp. butter* and onion. Cover with lid or plastic wrap, turning
back one section to vent steam.

Microwave at high setting (100%
power) 2 to 3 minutes or until onion
is tender, stirring after 1 minute.

Stir in tomatoes (or 2 medium zucchini, sliced), salt, fennel and pepper.

For tomatoes, microwave, uncovered, at high setting 2 to 4 minutes
or until tomatoes are soft, stirring
after 1 minute (do not let skins
burst).

For zucchini, cover with lid or
plastic wrap, turning back one section to vent steam. Microwave at
high setting 4 to 6 minutes or until
zucchini is tender, stirring every 2
minutes.

BRAISED LEEKS AND CARROTS

(see photo following page 86)

Matchstick-sliced vegetables are simply poached in chicken broth.

4 medium leeks
4 medium carrots
2 fresh mushrooms, sliced (optional)
½ c. chicken broth
1 tblsp. fresh or frozen chopped chives
2 tsp. lemon juice
½ tsp. salt
Leaf lettuce

Trim root and 1″ above white portion of leeks. Cut in half lengthwise and rinse well under cool water. Cut into 3″ julienne strips.

Cut carrots into 3″ julienne strips.

In 10″ skillet over high heat, bring leeks, carrots, mushrooms, chicken broth, chives, lemon juice and salt to a boil. Reduce heat to low. Cover and simmer 20 minutes or until vegetables are tender. Remove mushrooms.

To serve warm: On lettuce-lined platter arrange leeks and carrots in 4 alternating strips as shown in photo. Spoon cooking liquid over vegetables. Garnish with reserved mushrooms.

To serve cold: Cover and refrigerate vegetables at least 4 hours or until well chilled. On lettuce-lined platter arrange leeks and carrots as shown in photo. Spoon cooking liquid over vegetables. Garnish with mushrooms.

Makes 4 servings.

TO MICROWAVE: Use same ingredients.

Prepare leeks and carrots as directed.

In 2-qt. microwave-safe casserole place chicken broth, chives, lemon juice and salt. Cover with lid or plastic wrap, turning back one section to vent steam.

Microwave at high setting (100% power) 1½ to 2 minutes or until steaming.

Stir in carrots. Cover again, and microwave at high setting 4 to 5 minutes or until carrots are tender-crisp, stirring every 2 minutes.

Stir in leeks and mushrooms. Cover again, and microwave at high setting 1 to 2 minutes or until vegetables are tender, stirring each minute. Serve as directed.

TWO-POTATO SAUTÉ

A simple, colorful combination of yams and white potatoes.

6 tblsp. butter or regular margarine
2 medium onions, chopped
2 cloves garlic, minced
1 lb. potatoes, peeled and cut into 2x¼x¼″ strips
1 lb. sweet potatoes or yams, peeled and cut into 2x¼x¼″ strips
¾ tsp. salt
⅛ tsp. pepper
2 tblsp. chopped fresh parsley

In 12″ skillet over medium heat, melt butter. Add onions and garlic; cook until tender.

Stir in potatoes, yams, salt and pepper. Reduce heat to medium-low. Cover and cook 15 minutes or until potatoes are tender, stirring gently after 8 minutes.

Garnish with parsley. Makes 6 servings.

BRAISED GREENS WITH RED PEPPER

Young, tender greens will produce a more mildly flavored dish.

1 bunch young, tender greens (turnip, mustard, collard, escarole or kale)
¼ c. butter or regular margarine
1 medium red sweet pepper, cut into ½" pieces
3 cloves garlic, minced
½ tsp. salt
⅛ tsp. pepper

Wash greens well and drain. Trim tough stems. Coarsely chop greens.

In 10" skillet over high heat, bring ¼" water to a boil. Add greens. Cover and cook 1 minute or until greens are wilted. Drain; set aside.

In same skillet over medium-high heat, melt butter. Add red pepper and garlic; cook until tender.

Stir in greens, salt and pepper. Cover and cook 3 to 5 minutes or until greens are tender. Makes 6 servings.

TO MICROWAVE: Use same ingredients, *reducing water as indicated.*

Wash, drain, trim and chop greens as directed.

In 3-qt. microwave-safe casserole place greens and ¼ c. water. Cover with lid or plastic wrap, turning back one section to vent steam. Microwave at high setting (100% power) 2 minutes or until wilted, stirring after 1 minute. Drain; set aside.

In same casserole place butter. Microwave, uncovered, at high setting 1½ to 2 minutes or until melted. Stir in red pepper and garlic. Cover again, and microwave at high setting 3 to 4 minutes or until tender, stirring after 1 minute.

Stir in greens, salt and pepper. Cover again, and microwave 3 to 4 minutes or until greens are tender, stirring after 2 minutes.

HOT LETTUCE AND PEAS

Romaine or leaf lettuce also can be used in this thyme-flavored dish.

¼ c. butter or regular margarine
1 medium onion, chopped
1 c. shredded carrots
1 clove garlic, minced
1 tsp. dried thyme leaves
½ tsp. salt
1 bay leaf
1 medium head iceberg lettuce, chopped (4 c.)
2 lb. fresh peas, shelled (2½ c.) or 2 (10-oz.) pkg. frozen peas, thawed
2 tblsp. chopped fresh parsley

In 4-qt. Dutch oven over medium heat, melt butter. Add onion, carrots, garlic, thyme, salt and bay leaf. Cook until tender.

Stir in lettuce and peas. Cover and cook 8 minutes or until peas are tender. Remove bay leaf.

Garnish with parsley. Makes 6 servings.

TO MICROWAVE: Use same ingredients, *increasing salt as indicated.*

In 4-qt. microwave-safe casserole place butter. Microwave, uncovered, at high setting (100% power) 1½ to 2 minutes or until melted.

Stir in onion, carrots, garlic, thyme, ¾ tsp. salt and bay leaf. Cover with lid or plastic wrap, turning back one section to vent steam. Microwave at high setting 4 to 5 minutes or until vegetables are tender, stirring every 2 minutes.

Stir in peas. Cover again, and microwave at high setting 4 to 5 minutes or until peas are almost tender, stirring after 2 minutes.

Stir in lettuce. Cover again, and microwave at high setting 4 to 5 minutes or until lettuce and peas are almost tender, stirring each minute. Remove bay leaf.

Garnish with parsley.

FRIED TOMATOES WITH SOUR CREAM SAUCE

Good and simple! Fried tomatoes make a fine garnish for meat, too.

Sour Cream Sauce (recipe follows)
½ c. cornstarch
½ c. water
2 tsp. onion salt
2 tsp. dried marjoram leaves
2 eggs
Flour
2 c. vegetable oil
4 medium tomatoes, cut into ½" slices

Prepare Sour Cream Sauce as directed.

In medium bowl beat cornstarch, water, onion salt, marjoram, eggs and ½ c. unsifted flour until smooth.

In 10" skillet over medium-high heat, heat oil until hot.

Meanwhile, coat tomato slices with flour; dip into batter.

Fry tomato slices, 4 at a time, until golden brown on both sides. Drain on paper towels.

Serve warm with sauce. Makes 4 servings.

Sour Cream Sauce: In small bowl stir 1 c. dairy sour cream, 2 tblsp. sliced green onions, 2 tblsp. finely chopped green pepper, 2 tblsp. chopped pimientos and ½ tsp. onion salt until well blended.

Cover and refrigerate until ready to use.

BEETS AND GREENS

Smoky bacon and cool sour cream add contrasting flavors.

1 lb. beets with tops
4 slices bacon, diced
1 medium onion, finely chopped
2 cloves garlic, minced
1 tblsp. prepared horseradish
¼ tsp. salt
¼ c. dairy sour cream

Trim tops from beets. Wash tops and set aside.

In 3-qt. saucepan over high heat, bring 1" water to a boil; add whole beets. Reduce heat to medium-low. Cover and cook 30 minutes or until beets are fork-tender. Drain and peel. Cut beets into ½" cubes.

Pat greens dry and coarsely chop.

In 10" skillet over medium heat, cook bacon until browned. Drain bacon on paper towels.

Add onion and garlic to bacon drippings; over medium heat cook until tender. Add beet greens; cover and cook 2 to 3 minutes or until wilted.

Stir in beets, bacon, horseradish and salt. Cook 1 minute more.

Garnish with sour cream. Makes 6 servings.

TO MICROWAVE: Use same ingredients, *reducing water as indicated.*

Trim beets as directed.

In 1½-qt. microwave-safe casserole place whole beets and ¼ c. *water.* Cover with lid or plastic wrap, turning back one section to vent steam.

Microwave at high setting (100% power) 10 to 15 minutes or until beets are fork-tender, stirring after 4 minutes. Drain, peel and cut as directed.

Meanwhile, prepare beet tops as directed.

In same casserole place bacon. Cover with waxed paper. Microwave at high setting 2½ to 3 minutes or until crisp, stirring after 1 minute. Drain bacon on paper towels.

Add onion and garlic to bacon drippings. Cover with lid or plastic

wrap. Microwave at high setting 3 to
4 minutes or until onion is tender,
stirring after 2 minutes.

Add beet greens. Cover again,
and microwave at high setting 5 to
7 minutes or until stems are tender,
stirring after 3 minutes.

Stir in beets, bacon, horseradish
and salt. Microwave, uncovered,
1 minute more.

Garnish with sour cream.

FRIED GREEN TOMATOES AND OKRA

*Use this chili-flavored combination
as a filling for an omelet.*

8 slices bacon, diced
¼ c. yellow corn meal
1 tsp. chili powder
¾ tsp. salt
⅛ tsp. pepper
1 lb. okra, trimmed and cut into ¼″ slices
(2½ c.)
1 medium onion, chopped
3 green or red tomatoes, peeled and
coarsely chopped

In 12″ skillet over medium heat,
cook bacon until browned. Drain
bacon on paper towels.

Meanwhile, in plastic bag place
corn meal, chili powder, salt and
pepper; shake until well blended.
Add okra; shake until well coated.

Add onion to bacon drippings;
over medium heat cook until tender.
Add okra and tomatoes. Cook 3 to
5 minutes or until okra is tender-
crisp, stirring frequently. (Do not
overcook okra.)

Garnish with bacon. Makes 6
servings.

SAVORY BASIL BEANS

*Quickly steamed in very little liquid,
basil-flavored beans stay crunchy.*

1 tblsp. vegetable oil
1 tblsp. minced onion
1 clove garlic, minced
1 lb. green beans, trimmed and cut in half
crosswise
2 tblsp. water
1 tsp. dried basil leaves
½ tsp. salt
½ tsp. sugar
⅛ tsp. pepper

In 12″ skillet over medium heat,
heat oil until hot. Add onion and
garlic; cook until tender.

Stir in beans and remaining ingredients. Cover and cook 12 to 15 minutes, stirring occasionally, until
beans are tender-crisp. Makes
6 servings.

TO MICROWAVE: Use same ingredients.

In 2-qt. microwave-safe casserole
place oil, onion and garlic. Cover
with lid or plastic wrap, turning
back one section to vent steam.
Microwave at high setting (100%
power) 1 to 2 minutes or until onion
is tender.

Stir in beans and remaining ingredients. Cover again, and microwave
at high setting 12 to 15 minutes or
until beans are tender-crisp, stirring
every 4 minutes. Let stand, covered,
3 minutes.

CUCUMBER AND TOMATO SKILLET

*Serve this vegetable dish as
a hot salad on a cold, blustery day.*

3 slices bacon, diced
2 medium cucumbers, peeled and cut into
　½" slices
1 large green pepper, chopped
1 medium onion, chopped
1 tsp. salt
¾ tsp. dried oregano leaves
⅛ tsp. pepper
4 ripe tomatoes, each peeled and cut into 8
　wedges
¼ c. soft bread crumbs

In 10″ skillet over medium heat,
cook bacon until browned. Drain
bacon on paper towels.
Stir cucumbers and next 5 ingredients into bacon drippings; over
medium heat cook until tender.
Add bacon and tomatoes. Cover
and cook 5 minutes or until heated
through. Stir in bread crumbs.
Makes 6 servings.

TO MICROWAVE: Use same ingredients.
In 2-qt. microwave-safe casserole
place bacon. Cover with waxed
paper. Microwave at high setting
(100% power) 3 to 4 minutes or until
browned, stirring after 2 minutes.
Drain bacon on paper towels.
Stir cucumbers and next 5 ingredients into bacon drippings. Cover
with lid or plastic wrap, turning
back one section to vent steam.
Microwave at high setting 6 to
7 minutes or until vegetables are
tender, stirring after 3 minutes.
Add bacon and tomatoes. Microwave, uncovered, 2 minutes or until
heated through. Stir in bread
crumbs.

TOMATO, OKRA AND RICE SKILLET

*There's a strong Creole influence
in this spicy skillet dish.*

3 slices bacon, diced
1 medium onion, chopped
1 c. sliced okra (¼"-thick slices)
2 ripe tomatoes, peeled and cut into
　1½" chunks
1 c. uncooked long-grain rice
¾ c. hot water
1¼ tsp. salt
½ tsp. dried basil leaves
⅛ tsp. pepper
3 drops hot pepper sauce

In 10″ skillet over medium heat,
cook bacon until browned. Drain
bacon on paper towels.
Add onion and okra to bacon
drippings. Over medium heat cook,
stirring occasionally, until okra
is tender.
Stir in bacon, tomatoes and
remaining ingredients; bring to a
boil. Reduce heat to low. Cover and
simmer 20 minutes or until rice is
tender. Makes 6 servings.

TO MICROWAVE: Use same ingredients.
In 2-qt. microwave-safe casserole
place bacon. Cover with waxed
paper. Microwave at high setting
(100% power) 2½ to 3 minutes or
until browned, stirring after 1 minute. Drain bacon on paper towels.
Add onion, okra and tomatoes
to bacon drippings. Cover with lid
or plastic wrap, turning back one
section to vent steam. Microwave
at high setting 8 to 10 minutes or
until okra is tender.
Stir in bacon, rice and remaining
ingredients. Cover again, and
microwave 4 to 6 minutes or
until mixture boils; stir.
Cover again, and microwave at
medium setting (50% power) 8 to
10 minutes or just until rice swells
and is tender. Let stand, covered,
5 minutes.

ZUCCHINI SKILLET MEDLEY

Team up assorted vegetables to accompany a simple meat dish.

¼ c. vegetable oil
¾ c. sliced celery
½ c. sliced onion
1 clove garlic, minced
1 lb. zucchini, cut into ¼" slices (about 4 c.)
2 tomatoes, each cut into 8 wedges
½ c. green pepper strips (¼" thick)
½ c. shredded carrot
1 (8-oz.) can tomato sauce
2 tsp. prepared mustard
¾ tsp. salt
¼ tsp. dried basil leaves
⅛ tsp. pepper

In 12" skillet over medium heat, heat oil until hot. Add celery, onion and garlic; cook until tender.

Stir in zucchini, tomatoes, green pepper and carrot. Cook, stirring frequently, until tender.

Stir in tomato sauce and remaining ingredients until well blended. Reduce heat to medium-low. Simmer, uncovered, stirring occasionally, until vegetables are tender and heated through.

Serve hot or cold. Makes 6 servings.

BUTTERY ONIONS AND TURNIPS

Spicy turnips that look like home-fried potatoes are the recipe of one Texas vegetable lover.

1 lb. turnips (about 5 medium), peeled and cut into ½" cubes
2 tblsp. butter or regular margarine
1 medium onion, chopped
¾ tsp. dried marjoram leaves
½ tsp. salt
⅛ tsp. pepper

In 3-qt. saucepan over high heat, bring 1" water to a boil; add turnips.

Reduce heat to medium-low. Cover and cook 15 to 20 minutes or until fork-tender; drain.

In same saucepan over medium heat, melt butter. Add onion; cook until tender. Stir in turnips, marjoram, salt and pepper until well blended.

Cook, stirring often, 5 minutes or until turnips are golden brown. Makes 6 servings.

TO MICROWAVE: Use same ingredients, *reducing water as indicated.*

In 1½-qt. microwave-safe casserole place turnips and ¼ c. water. Cover with lid or plastic wrap, turning back one section to vent steam.

Microwave at high setting (100% power) 9 to 11 minutes or until fork-tender, stirring after 4 minutes. Drain.

In same casserole, place butter and onion. Cover again, and microwave at high setting 3 to 4 minutes or until onion is tender, stirring after 2 minutes.

Stir in turnips, marjoram, salt and pepper until well blended. Cover again, and microwave at high setting 2 minutes or until heated through; stir. Let stand, covered, 2 minutes.

SAUCY ARTICHOKES

Sautéed vegetables cook down into a savory dipping sauce.

½ c. vegetable oil
2 c. chopped onion
1 c. chopped carrot
1 c. chopped celery with leaves
½ c. chopped fresh parsley
6 cloves garlic, minced
½ tsp. dried rosemary leaves
1⅔ c. water
½ c. white wine vinegar
2 tsp. salt
6 artichokes

In deep 12″ skillet with dome lid or large saucepot over medium-high heat, heat oil until hot. Add onion, carrot, celery, parsley, garlic and rosemary; cook until vegetables are tender. Stir in water, vinegar and salt.

Wash artichokes. Cut off stems and cut 1″ from top of each artichoke. Remove any loose leaves from the bottom of each artichoke and snip off points of remaining leaves.

Add artichokes to vegetable mixture; bring to a boil. Reduce heat to medium. Cover and simmer 50 minutes or until artichokes are tender and a leaf may be easily removed.

To serve, place each artichoke in bowl. Serve with vegetable sauce for dipping. Makes 6 servings.

SWEET-SOUR GREEN BEANS

Leftover marinade from this dish can be used as a salad dressing.

3 lb. green beans, trimmed
3 onions, thinly sliced and separated into rings
1⅓ c. sugar
1 c. cider vinegar
⅓ c. water
3 tblsp. vegetable oil
1½ tsp. salt
½ tsp. pepper

In 4-qt. Dutch oven over high heat, bring 1″ water to a boil; add beans. Reduce heat to medium-low. Cover and simmer 10 to 15 minutes or until tender-crisp. Drain.

In large bowl place beans and onions.

In small bowl using wire whisk, beat sugar, vinegar, water, oil, salt and pepper until well blended.

Pour vinegar mixture over beans.

Cover and refrigerate at least 24 hours, stirring occasionally. Makes 10 to 12 servings.

EGGPLANT WITH TOMATOES____

Serve this bacon-flavored medley of vegetables hot or cold.

¼ c. unsifted flour
2 medium tomatoes, diced
1 medium eggplant (about 1½ lb.), peeled and cut into ½" cubes
12 slices bacon, diced
¾ c. coarsely chopped onion
¼ c. water
1 tsp. salt
⅛ tsp. pepper

In plastic bag place flour. Add tomatoes and eggplant; shake until well coated. Set aside.

In 4-qt. Dutch oven over medium heat, cook bacon until browned. Drain bacon on paper towels. Pour off all but ¼ c. bacon drippings.

Add onion to bacon drippings; over medium-high heat cook until tender. Stir in tomatoes, eggplant, bacon, water, salt and pepper.

Cover and cook, stirring occasionally, 35 minutes or until eggplant is tender. Makes 4 servings.

BARBECUED LIMA BEANS_____

No pre-soaking or long hours of cooking are needed for these beans.

3 lb. fresh lima beans, shelled, or 2 (10-oz.)pkg. frozen lima beans, cooked and drained
4 slices bacon, diced
2 ribs celery, chopped
1 medium onion, sliced
1 medium green pepper, chopped
1 clove garlic, minced
2 c. tomato juice
¼ c. packed light brown sugar
¼ c. cider vinegar
1 tblsp. prepared mustard
2 tsp. Worcestershire sauce
1 tsp. chili powder
½ tsp. salt

In 4-qt. Dutch oven over high heat, bring 1" water to a boil; add beans. Reduce heat to medium. Cover and simmer 20 minutes or until beans are tender-crisp. Drain well.

In same Dutch oven over medium heat, cook bacon until browned. Drain on paper towels.

To bacon drippings add celery, onion, green pepper and garlic; over medium heat cook until tender. Stir in bacon, beans and remaining ingredients.

Cover and bake in 300° oven 1 hour or until mixture is bubbly. Makes 6 servings.

TO MICROWAVE: Use same ingredients, *changing amounts as indicated.*

In 3-qt. microwave-safe casserole place lima beans and *½ c. water.* Cover with lid or plastic wrap, turning back one section to vent steam.

Microwave at high setting (100% power) 6 to 8 minutes or until tender, stirring every 3 minutes. Drain.

In same casserole place bacon. Cover with waxed paper. Microwave at high setting 3 to 5 minutes or until bacon is browned, stirring after 2 minutes. Drain bacon on paper towels.

To bacon drippings add celery, onion, green pepper and garlic. Cover with lid or plastic wrap, turning back one section to vent steam. Microwave at high setting 6 to 8 minutes or until vegetables are tender, stirring every 2 minutes.

Stir in bacon, beans, brown sugar, vinegar, mustard, Worcestershire sauce, *1¼ c. tomato juice,* salt and *1½ tsp. chili powder.* Cover again, and microwave at high setting 10 minutes, stirring every 3 minutes.

Microwave, uncovered, 12 to 15 minutes or until flavors are blended, stirring every 3 minutes.

RATATOUILLE

Tuck some of this spicy vegetable medley inside a pita bread pocket.

¼ c. olive or vegetable oil
2 medium onions, sliced
3 cloves garlic, minced
3 medium tomatoes, peeled and cut into 1½" chunks
2 small zucchini, cut into ½" slices
1 medium eggplant, cut into 1" cubes
1 large green pepper, cut into ¼" strips
2 tblsp. chopped fresh parsley
1 tsp. salt
¾ tsp. dried basil leaves
¾ tsp. dried oregano leaves
⅛ tsp. pepper
¼ c. grated Parmesan cheese

In 12" skillet over medium-high heat, heat oil until hot. Add onions and garlic; cook until tender.

Stir in tomatoes and remaining ingredients except cheese; bring to a boil. Reduce heat to medium. Cover and cook, stirring occasionally, 15 minutes or until vegetables are tender.

Stir in cheese. Cook, uncovered, 5 minutes or until cheese melts and sauce is slightly thickened. Makes 8 servings.

TO MICROWAVE: Use same ingredients.
In 3-qt. microwave-safe casserole place oil, onions and garlic. Cover with lid or plastic wrap, turning back one section to vent steam.

Microwave at high setting (100% power) 3 to 4 minutes or until tender, stirring after 1 minute.

Stir in zucchini, eggplant and green pepper. Cover again, and microwave at high setting 7 to 8 minutes or until tender, stirring every 3 minutes.

Stir in parsley and remaining ingredients. Microwave, uncovered, at medium setting (50% power) 2 to 4 minutes or until tomatoes are heated through and cheese melts, stirring after 1 minute.

ORIENTAL SNOW PEAS

To make this into a main dish, stir in leftover cooked chicken or pork.

2 tblsp. white wine or rice vinegar
2 tblsp. soy sauce
1 tsp. sugar
1 tsp. sesame oil
¼ tsp. crushed red pepper
3 tblsp. vegetable oil
½ lb. mushrooms, sliced
1 tsp. grated fresh ginger root
1 clove garlic, minced
1 lb. fresh or 3 (6-oz.) pkg. frozen snow peas, thawed
4 green onions, sliced
1 (8-oz.) can bamboo shoots, drained
1 (8-oz.) can sliced water chestnuts, drained

In small bowl stir together first 5 ingredients; set aside.

In 12" skillet over medium-high heat, heat vegetable oil until hot. Add mushrooms, ginger and garlic; cook until mushrooms are tender.

Add snow peas and green onions; cook until tender-crisp. Stir in soy mixture, bamboo shoots and water chestnuts. Cook until mixture boils. Makes 6 servings.

TO MICROWAVE: Use same ingredients.
In small bowl stir together first 5 ingredients.

In 3-qt. microwave-safe casserole place vegetable oil, ginger root, garlic and green onions. Cover with lid or plastic wrap, turning back one section to vent steam.

Microwave at high setting (100% power) 1 to 2 minutes or until onions are tender, stirring after 30 seconds.

Stir in mushrooms and snow peas. Cover again, and microwave at high setting 3 to 5 minutes or until tender-crisp, stirring each minute.

Stir in soy mixture, bamboo shoots and water chestnuts. Cover again, and microwave 2 to 4 minutes or until heated through, stirring each minute.

Top: Creamy Cucumber-Dill Dressing, page 229, completes a simple salad.

Center: Pesto Butter, page 219 — delicious over corn as well as pasta.

Bottom: Blender Hollandaise Sauce, page 216, to top most any vegetable.

Top: Vegetable-filled Dutch Pancake, page 123, yields six bountiful main-dish servings. This pancake bakes in the oven like a popover.

Bottom: Carrot Ravioli with Spinach Filling, page 135.

Meatball and Pasta Soup, page 90, is a meal in a bowl. Simmer onion, carrots and celery in tomato sauce along with meatballs and corkscrew macaroni. To give this soup its color, add some chopped fresh spinach and a generous sprinkling of freshly grated Parmesan cheese.

Summer's bounty of beans, cucumbers, peppers and squash can yield an abundance of easy accompaniments to enjoy year 'round. From front to back: Three-Bean Salad, page 259; Tomato-Apple Chutney, page 260; Cucumber Refrigerator Pickles, page 256; and Summer Squash Relish, page 260.

STIR-FRIED ASPARAGUS

*Roll-cutting the asparagus makes it
look pretty and helps it cook evenly.*

1 lb. asparagus, trimmed
⅓ c. chicken broth
2 tblsp. soy sauce
2 tsp. cornstarch
1 tsp. sugar
1 tsp. grated fresh ginger root
3 tblsp. vegetable oil
½ lb. mushrooms, cut in matchstick strips
2 medium carrots, cut in matchstick strips
1 clove garlic, minced
2 tblsp. sesame seed, toasted

To roll cut asparagus: With knife
make one diagonal cut through one
end of asparagus; roll asparagus one-
quarter turn. Cut ½" from previous
cut on a diagonal. Continue rolling
and slicing, and repeat with remaining asparagus.

In small bowl stir together chicken
broth, soy sauce, cornstarch, sugar
and ginger root until well blended.

In 12" skillet over high heat, heat
oil until hot. Add asparagus, mushrooms, carrots and garlic. Cook, stirring mixture quickly and constantly,
until vegetables are tender, about 5
minutes.

Stir in soy mixture. Cook, stirring
constantly, until mixture boils and
thickens.

To serve, spoon mixture onto
serving dish. Sprinkle with sesame
seed. Makes 6 servings.

TO MICROWAVE: Use same ingredients,
reducing oil as indicated.

Cut asparagus as directed.

In 1-c. glass measure stir
together chicken broth, soy sauce,
cornstarch, sugar and ginger root
until well blended.

In 2-qt. microwave-safe casserole
place *1 tblsp. oil* and carrots. Cover
with lid or plastic wrap, turning
back one section to vent steam.

Microwave at high setting (100%
power) 1 minute. Stir in asparagus
and garlic. Cover again, and microwave 4 to 5 minutes more or until
vegetables are tender, stirring every
2 minutes.

Stir in mushrooms. Microwave,
uncovered, at high setting 2 to 3
minutes or until tender, stirring
each minute.

Microwave soy mixture, uncovered, at high setting, 1 to 3 minutes
or until mixture boils and thickens,
stirring each minute.

Stir soy mixture into casserole.
Cover again, and microwave at high
setting 1½ to 2 minutes or until
heated through, stirring after 1 minute. Serve as directed.

CHOW MEIN CABBAGE

*Sweet pepper adds color to this
crunchy stir-fry dish.*

2 tblsp. butter or regular margarine
2 medium onions, chopped
2 ribs celery, cut diagonally into ¼" slices
1 small red or green sweet pepper,
  chopped
3 c. shredded cabbage
2 tblsp. soy sauce

In 12" skillet over medium heat,
melt butter. Add onions, celery,
pepper and cabbage. Cook, stirring
frequently, 5 minutes. Reduce heat
to medium-low.

Stir in soy sauce. Cover and simmer 2 minutes or until vegetables
are tender-crisp. Makes 6 servings.

TO MICROWAVE: Use same ingredients.

In 2-qt. microwave-safe casserole
place butter. Microwave, uncovered,
at high setting (100% power) 30 seconds to 1 minute or until melted.

Add celery. Cover with lid or
plastic wrap, turning back one section to vent steam. Microwave at
high setting 2 minutes.

Stir in cabbage. Cover again and
microwave at high setting 2 minutes.
Stir in onions and pepper. Cover
again, and microwave 3 to 4
minutes.

Stir in soy sauce. Cover again, and
microwave at high setting 1 minute
or until vegetables are tender-crisp.
Let stand, covered, 2 minutes.

ORIENTAL GREEN BEANS

Mildly flavored with ginger, this stir-fry cooks in 10 minutes.

3 tblsp. vegetable oil
1 lb. green beans, trimmed and cut diagonally into 1" slices
2 ribs celery, cut diagonally into ¼" slices
¼ lb. mushrooms, sliced
½ c. beef broth
2 tblsp. soy sauce
1 tblsp. cornstarch
¼ tsp. ground ginger

In 12" skillet over medium-high heat, heat oil until hot. Add green beans. Cook, stirring frequently, 5 minutes.

Add celery; cook 2 minutes. Add mushrooms; cook 3 minutes or until beans and celery are tender-crisp.

In small bowl stir beef broth, soy sauce, cornstarch and ginger until well blended. Stir into skillet; cook, stirring constantly, until mixture boils and thickens. Makes 6 servings.

TO MICROWAVE: Use same ingredients, *changing amounts as indicated.*

In 2-qt. microwave-safe casserole place *2 tblsp. vegetable oil* and beans. Cover with lid or plastic wrap, turning back one section to vent steam.

Microwave at high setting (100% power) 8 minutes, stirring after 4 minutes. Add celery; cover again, and microwave at high setting 3 minutes.

Stir in mushrooms. Cover again, and microwave at high setting 3 to 4 minutes or until beans and celery are tender-crisp, stirring after 2 minutes. Let stand, covered, 3 minutes.

Stir together beef broth, soy sauce, *4 tsp. cornstarch* and ginger. Stir into casserole. Microwave, uncovered, at high setting 2 minutes or until mixture boils and thickens, stirring each minute.

STIR-FRIED VEGETABLES

In the spring, use sweet sugar snap peas instead of snow peas.

1 large bunch fresh broccoli (1½ lb.)
¼ c. vegetable oil
1 clove garlic, minced
½ tsp. salt
1 c. chicken broth
½ (10-oz.) pkg. fresh or ½ (16-oz.) can bean sprouts, drained
1 (8-oz.) can sliced water chestnuts, drained
½ lb. fresh or 1 (6-oz.) pkg. frozen snow peas
¼ lb. mushrooms, sliced
1 tblsp. soy sauce
2 tsp. cornstarch
1 tsp. sugar
¼ tsp. grated fresh ginger root
1 tblsp. sesame seed, toasted

Remove flowerets from broccoli and cut in half. Cut stalks into 2x¼" strips.

In 12" skillet over medium heat, heat oil until hot. Add broccoli; cook, stirring quickly and constantly (stir-frying), 1 minute.

Stir in garlic, salt and ½ c. chicken broth. Cover and cook 3 minutes. Uncover; stir-fry 3 minutes.

Add sprouts, water chestnuts, snow peas and mushrooms; stir-fry 2 minutes.

In small bowl stir soy sauce, cornstarch, sugar, ginger root and remaining ½ c. chicken broth until well blended.

Stir cornstarch mixture into skillet. Cook, stirring constantly, until mixture boils and thickens.

Garnish with sesame seed. Makes 6 servings.

CANTONESE VEGETABLES_____

A saucy medley of vegetables that complements meat, fish or poultry.

¼ c. vegetable oil
1 (8-oz.) can sliced water chestnuts, drained
½ lb. mushrooms, sliced
1 medium green pepper, cut into ¼" strips
2 c. fresh or frozen French-cut green beans
1 c. diagonally-sliced celery
¾ tsp. salt
½ tsp. garlic salt
¼ tsp. pepper
1½ c. chicken broth
2 tblsp. cornstarch
1 (4-oz.) jar pimientos, drained and diced
⅓ c. slivered almonds, toasted

In 12" skillet over medium-high heat, heat oil until hot. Add water chestnuts, mushrooms, green pepper, green beans, celery, salt, garlic salt and pepper.

Cook, stirring frequently, until vegetables are tender-crisp.

In small bowl stir chicken broth and cornstarch until well blended. Stir into skillet; cook, stirring constantly, until mixture boils and thickens.

Stir in pimientos. Garnish with almonds. Makes 6 servings.

TO MICROWAVE: Use same ingredients, *changing amounts as indicated.*

In 3-qt. microwave-safe casserole place *2 tblsp. oil,* green beans and celery. Cover with lid or plastic wrap, turning back one section to vent steam.

Microwave at high setting (100% power) 3 to 5 minutes or until vegetables are tender-crisp, stirring after 2 minutes.

Stir in water chestnuts, green pepper, salt, garlic salt and pepper. Cover again, and microwave at high setting 3 to 4 minutes or until green pepper is tender-crisp, stirring after 2 minutes.

Stir in mushrooms. Microwave, uncovered, at high setting 2 minutes; stir. Set aside.

In 2-c. glass measure stir cornstarch and *1 c. broth* until well blended. Microwave, uncovered, at high setting 2 to 3 minutes or until slightly thickened, stirring after 1 minute.

Stir into vegetables. Microwave, uncovered, at high setting 2 minutes. Stir in pimientos. Microwave 1 to 3 minutes more or until vegetables are tender.

Garnish with almonds.

SCALLOPED POTATOES_____

To cut calories, replace milk with skim milk and chicken broth.

2 tblsp. flour
1 tsp. salt
⅛ tsp. pepper
2 lb. potatoes, peeled and thinly sliced
2 c. milk, scalded
Paprika

In small bowl stir together flour, salt and pepper.

In lightly greased 2-qt. casserole arrange one-third of the potato slices. Sprinkle with one-third of the flour mixture. Repeat layers of potatoes and flour mixture twice.

Pour hot, scalded milk over potatoes. Sprinkle with paprika and cover.

Bake in 375° oven 1 hour. Uncover and bake 30 minutes or until potatoes are fork-tender. Makes 6 to 8 servings.

TO MICROWAVE: Use same ingredients, *increasing flour as indicated.*

In small bowl stir together salt, pepper and *3 tblsp. flour.*

In *ungreased* 2-qt. microwave-safe casserole arrange potatoes and flour mixture as directed.

Pour hot, scalded milk over potatoes. Cover with lid or plastic wrap, turning back one section to vent steam.

Microwave at high setting (100% power) 18 to 24 minutes or until potatoes are fork-tender, stirring every 5 minutes.

Sprinkle with paprika. Let stand, covered, 5 to 8 minutes.

GOURMET CHEESE POTATOES

A sensational dish enriched with muenster cheese and sour cream.

6 medium potatoes (about 1½ lb.)
2 c. shredded muenster cheese (8 oz.)
1 c. dairy sour cream
⅓ c. butter or regular margarine, melted
⅓ c. minced onion
½ tsp. salt
¼ tsp. pepper
Paprika

In 3-qt. saucepan over high heat, bring 1" water to a boil; add potatoes. Reduce heat to medium. Cover and cook 20 minutes or until potatoes are fork-tender. Drain and cool slightly, about 15 minutes. Peel and shred into bowl.

In medium bowl stir together cheese, sour cream, melted butter, onion, salt and pepper. Fold in potatoes.

Pour mixture into lightly greased 2-qt. casserole. Sprinkle with paprika.

Bake in 350° oven 30 minutes or until top is golden brown. Makes 6 to 8 servings.

TO MICROWAVE: Use same ingredients, *but do not melt butter.*

Wash and pierce potatoes with fork. Place potatoes on a paper towel on bottom of oven.

Microwave at high setting (100% power) 16 to 18 minutes, or until potatoes give slightly when pressed with finger, turning potatoes after 8 minutes. Let stand 15 minutes. Peel and shred into bowl.

In 2-qt. microwave-safe casserole place *unmelted butter* and onion. Cover with lid or plastic wrap, turning back one section to vent steam.

Microwave at high setting 2 to 3 minutes or until onion is tender, stirring after 1 minute.

Stir in cheese, sour cream, salt and pepper. Fold in potatoes.

Using a spatula smooth mixture into an even layer. Sprinkle with paprika. Cover with waxed paper. Microwave at medium setting

(50% power) 15 to 17 minutes, or until top is golden brown, rotating dish one-quarter turn every 4 minutes. Let stand, covered, 2 minutes.

AU GRATIN POTATOES

This slice-and-bake variation of a classic recipe makes its own sauce.

1 c. shredded Cheddar cheese (4 oz.)
2 tblsp. flour
¾ tsp. salt
⅛ tsp. pepper
2 lb. potatoes, peeled and thinly sliced
2 c. milk, scalded
⅓ c. soft bread crumbs
Paprika
3 tblsp. butter or regular margarine

In small bowl toss together cheese, flour, salt and pepper.

In lightly greased 2-qt. casserole arrange one-third of the potato slices. Sprinkle with one-third of the cheese mixture. Repeat layers of potatoes and cheese mixture twice.

Pour hot, scalded milk over potatoes.

Sprinkle with bread crumbs and paprika. Dot with butter and cover.

Bake in 375° oven 1 hour. Uncover and bake 30 minutes or until potatoes are fork-tender. Makes 6 to 8 servings.

TO MICROWAVE: Use same ingredients, *changing amounts and substituting ingredients as indicated.*

In small bowl toss together cheese, *3 tblsp. flour,* salt and pepper.

In *ungreased* 2-qt. microwave-safe casserole arrange potatoes and cheese mixture as directed.

Pour hot, scalded milk over potatoes. Cover with lid or plastic wrap, turning back one section to vent steam.

Microwave at high setting (100% power) 25 to 28 minutes or until potatoes are fork-tender, stirring every 5 minutes. Let stand, covered, 5 minutes.

Sprinkle with *⅓ c. toasted, buttered bread crumbs* and paprika.

CREAMED KALE AND ONIONS

A nutritious dish, because kale is rich in both iron and vitamin A.

2 lb. small white onions, peeled
Salt
1½ lb. kale, washed, trimmed and coarsely
    chopped
2 tblsp. butter or regular margarine
2 tblsp. flour
¾ tsp. dried rosemary leaves
⅛ tsp. pepper
1 c. milk
¾ tsp. Worcestershire sauce

In 4-qt. Dutch oven over high heat, bring 1″ water to a boil, add onions and 1 tsp. salt. Reduce heat to medium-low. Cover and simmer 10 minutes.

Add kale. Cover; cook 5 minutes or until onions are tender and kale is wilted. Drain.

Meanwhile, in 2-qt. saucepan over medium heat, melt butter. Stir in flour, rosemary, pepper and ½ tsp. salt until smooth. Gradually stir in milk and Worcestershire sauce until well blended. Cook, stirring constantly, until mixture boils and thickens.

To serve, place kale and onions on serving platter; spoon sauce over vegetables. Makes 6 servings.

TO MICROWAVE: Use same ingredients, *reducing water as indicated.*

In 4-qt. microwave-safe casserole place onions, 1 tsp. salt and ¼ c. *water.* Cover with lid or plastic wrap, turning back one section to vent steam.

Microwave at high setting (100% power) 14 to 16 minutes or until tender, stirring every 4 minutes.

Stir in kale. Cover again, and microwave at high setting 2 to 4 minutes or until kale is wilted, stirring after 1 minute. Drain.

In same casserole place butter. Microwave, uncovered, at high setting 1 to 1½ minutes or until melted.

Stir in flour, rosemary, pepper and ½ tsp. salt until smooth. Gradu-

ally stir in milk and Worcestershire sauce until well blended. Microwave, uncovered, at high setting 1 minute; stir.

Microwave 3 to 4 minutes or until mixture boils and thickens, stirring every 2 minutes.

Serve as directed.

CABBAGE CASSEROLE

Cabbage baked in a cream sauce is a good partner for baked ham.

1 (2½-lb.) large head cabbage, chopped
2 c. water
2 tsp. salt
4 tblsp. butter or regular margarine
2 tblsp. flour
1¼ c. milk
1 c. light cream
1 c. buttered bread crumbs

In 6-qt. saucepot over high heat, bring cabbage, water and salt to a boil. Reduce heat to medium. Cook, stirring occasionally, 12 to 15 minutes or until cabbage is tender. Drain.

Meanwhile, in 2-qt. saucepan over medium heat, melt butter. Stir in flour until smooth. Gradually stir in milk and cream until smooth. Cook, stirring constantly, until mixture boils and thickens.

In 3-qt. casserole place cabbage. Pour sauce over cabbage. Sprinkle with bread crumbs.

Bake in 350° oven 30 minutes or until bubbly. Makes 6 servings.

TO MICROWAVE: Use same ingredients, *reducing amounts and adding ingredients as indicated.*

In 3-qt. microwave-safe casserole place cabbage, salt and ½ c. *water.* Cover with lid or plastic wrap, turning back one section to vent steam.

Microwave at high setting (100% power) 8 to 10 minutes or until cabbage is tender, stirring every 4 minutes. Let stand, covered, 2 minutes. Drain.

In 1-qt. microwave-safe bowl place

butter. Microwave, uncovered, at high setting 30 seconds to 1 minute or until melted.

Stir in flour until smooth. Gradually stir in ¾ c. milk and cream until smooth. Microwave at high setting 5 minutes or until mixture boils and thickens, stirring each minute.

Pour sauce over cabbage. Microwave, uncovered, at high setting 2 minutes or until heated through. Sprinkle with *1 c. toasted, buttered bread crumbs.*

SPICY BAKED CORN

Ears of corn are painted with sauce, foil-wrapped, then grilled or baked.

¾ c. ketchup or chili sauce
¼ c. butter or regular margarine
2 tblsp. wine vinegar
1 tblsp. packed brown sugar
1 tblsp. molasses
2 tsp. dry mustard
1 tsp. Worcestershire sauce
½ tsp. onion salt
¼ tsp. hot pepper sauce
6 ears corn, husked

In 1-qt. saucepan stir all ingredients except corn until well blended.

Over high heat bring to a boil. Reduce heat to low. Simmer, uncovered, 5 minutes. Remove from heat and set aside.

Place each ear of corn on a 12"-long sheet of heavy-duty aluminum foil. Spoon the sauce equally over each ear. Securely wrap each ear into a loose packet, crimping foil tightly to prevent leaking. Bake immediately or refrigerate.

To bake, place foil-wrapped packets directly on oven rack. Bake in 375° oven 25 to 30 minutes or until corn is tender. Makes 6 servings.

TO GRILL: Prepare and wrap corn as directed. Grill corn 4" from gray coals (medium heat) 20 to 30 minutes or until corn is tender.

NEW ENGLAND-STYLE SWEET POTATOES

Maple-glazed potatoes cook on top of the range or in the pressure cooker.

1 c. maple-flavored syrup
3 tblsp. butter or regular margarine, melted
1 tsp. salt
6 sweet potatoes or yams, each peeled and cut into 4 wedges

In 12" skillet stir together syrup, butter and salt; add potatoes.

Over high heat bring to a boil. Reduce heat to medium-low. Cover and simmer 25 minutes or until potatoes are fork-tender, turning twice to coat evenly. Makes 6 servings.

FOR PRESSURE COOKER: Use same ingredients.

In 4-qt. pressure cooker stir together syrup, butter and salt; add potatoes. (Fill cooker no more than half full.)

Close cover securely and place cooker over high heat. Bring cooker to 15 lb. pressure, according to manufacturer's directions. When pressure is reached (control will begin to jiggle), reduce heat immediately to maintain slow, steady rocking motion and cook 6 minutes.

Remove cooker from heat. Reduce pressure instantly by placing cooker under cold running water. Remove potatoes with slotted spoon to serving dish.

Over high heat cook liquid in pressure cooker, uncovered, until liquid is reduced by half. Pour over potatoes.

BRUSSELS SPROUTS CHEESE BAKE

Water chestnuts and almonds add crunch to sprouts in a velvety sauce.

2 pt. fresh Brussels sprouts, trimmed, or
   2 (10-oz.) pkg. frozen Brussels sprouts,
   thawed
1 (8-oz.) can sliced water chestnuts, drained
3 tblsp. butter or regular margarine
1/4 lb. mushrooms, sliced
1 tblsp. flour
1/8 tsp. pepper
1 c. milk
1 c. shredded sharp pasteurized process
   American cheese
1/2 c. sliced or slivered almonds, toasted

Using a small, sharp knife, cut an X in the stem of each sprout. (Cut any large sprouts in half lengthwise.)

In 3-qt. saucepan over high heat bring 1″ water to a boil; add sprouts. Reduce heat to medium-low. Cover and simmer 10 minutes or until fork-tender; drain.

In 1½-qt. baking dish place sprouts. Top with water chestnuts.

In same saucepan over medium heat, melt butter. Add mushrooms; cook until tender. Stir in flour and pepper until well blended.

Gradually stir in milk until well blended. Cook, stirring constantly, until mixture boils and thickens. Remove from heat; stir in cheese until melted.

Pour over sprouts in baking dish. Sprinkle with almonds.

Bake in 350° oven 20 minutes or until bubbly. Makes 6 servings.

TO MICROWAVE: Use same ingredients, *reducing water as indicated.*

Prepare Brussels sprouts as directed.

In 1½-qt. microwave-safe casserole place brussels sprouts and *½ c. water.* Cover with plastic wrap, turning back one section to vent steam.

Microwave at high setting (100% power) 10 minutes or until fork-tender, stirring after 5 minutes. Let stand, covered, 5 minutes. Drain. Return sprouts to casserole and top with water chestnuts.

In 1-qt. microwave-safe casserole place butter and mushrooms. Cover with lid or plastic wrap, turning back one section to vent steam.

Microwave at high setting 2 to 3 minutes or until mushrooms are tender, stirring after 1 minute.

Stir in flour and pepper until well blended. Gradually stir in milk until well blended. Microwave, uncovered, at high setting 5 minutes or until mixture boils and thickens, stirring each minute.

Stir in cheese until melted. Pour over sprouts in casserole. Sprinkle with almonds.

Microwave, uncovered, at high setting 5 minutes or until bubbly, rotating casserole one-quarter turn every 2 minutes.

SWISS CHARD IN MORNAY SAUCE

Tender chard baked in a cheesy sauce has a golden crumb topping.

2 lb. Swiss chard
Salt
5 tblsp. butter or regular margarine
3 tblsp. flour
2 c. milk
1/4 c. shredded Swiss cheese (1 oz.)
1/4 c. grated Parmesan cheese
1/4 c. soft bread crumbs

Wash chard well; drain. Cut off stalks and cut into 1″ pieces. Coarsely chop leaves.

In 4-qt. Dutch oven over high heat, bring 1″ water to boil; add chard stalks and ½ tsp. salt. Reduce heat to medium. Cover and cook 5 minutes. Stir in chopped chard leaves. Cover and cook 3 to 5 minutes or until leaves are wilted and stalks are tender. Drain well.

In 2-qt. saucepan over medium heat, melt 3 tblsp. butter. Stir in flour and ½ tsp. salt until smooth. Gradually stir in milk until smooth. Cook, stirring constantly, until mixture boils and thickens. Remove from heat.

Stir in chard, Swiss and Parmesan cheese. Turn into greased 2-qt. casserole. Top with bread crumbs; dot with remaining 2 tblsp. butter.

Bake in 425° oven 15 to 20 minutes or until mixture is bubbly. Makes 6 servings.

TO MICROWAVE: Use same ingredients, *changing amounts and substituting ingredients as indicated.*

Wash, drain and chop chard as directed.

In 4-qt. microwave-safe casserole place chard stalks, *½ c. water* and ½ tsp. salt. Cover with lid or plastic wrap, turning back one section to vent steam.

Microwave at high setting (100% power) 10 minutes, stirring every 3 minutes. Stir in chopped chard leaves. Cover again, and microwave 5 minutes or until leaves are wilted and stalks are tender. Drain well.

In same casserole place 3 tblsp. butter. Microwave, uncovered, at high setting 1 to 1½ minutes or until melted. Stir in flour and ½ tsp. salt until smooth. Gradually stir in milk until smooth.

Microwave, uncovered, at high setting 1 minute; stir. Microwave 4 to 6 minutes or until mixture boils and thickens, stirring every 2 minutes. Stir in chard, Swiss and Parmesan cheese.

In glass custard cup place remaining 2 tblsp. butter. Microwave, uncovered, 1 minute or until melted. Stir in ¼ *c. toasted bread crumbs.*

Sprinkle buttered crumbs over chard mixture. Microwave, uncovered, at high setting 4 to 6 minutes or until mixture is bubbly.

BROCCOLI-CHEESE SQUARES____

Buttery squares of phyllo dough baked with a broccoli-cheese filling.

1½ c. chopped fresh broccoli, cooked, or 1 (10-oz.) pkg. frozen chopped broccoli, thawed
11 tblsp. butter or regular margarine
1 small onion, finely chopped
1 clove garlic, minced
3 tblsp. flour
¼ tsp. dried basil leaves
¼ tsp. salt
⅛ tsp. pepper
1 c. milk
2 eggs, beaten
1 c. ricotta cheese
½ c. shredded muenster cheese (2 oz.)
12 sheets phyllo dough

Wrap broccoli in dish towel. Twist to squeeze out as much liquid as possible; set aside.

In 2-qt. saucepan over medium-high heat, melt butter. Spoon off ½ c. melted butter; set aside.

To butter in saucepan add onion and garlic; cook until tender. Stir in flour, basil, salt and pepper until well blended. Gradually stir in milk until well blended.

Cook, stirring constantly, until mixture boils and thickens. Remove from heat.

Stir some of the hot mixture into beaten eggs. Then stir egg mixture back into saucepan. Stir in broccoli, ricotta and muenster cheese until well blended.

Unroll phyllo dough; cover with plastic wrap. Remove 1 sheet of phyllo and ease into bottom and up sides of greased 8″ square baking pan. Brush with melted butter. Repeat with 5 more sheets of phyllo, brushing each sheet with butter. Trim phyllo level with top of pan.

Spead broccoli mixture over phyllo in pan. Repeat 6 layers of phyllo as directed. Again, trim phyllo level with top of pan. Using sharp knife, cut about halfway through phyllo to make 9 squares.

Bake in 375° oven 35 minutes or until golden brown. Let stand 10 minutes. Makes 9 servings.

SALSIFY AU GRATIN

Delicately flavored salsify lends itself to a Cheddar cheese sauce.

1 tblsp. vinegar
Water
1½ lb. salsify, trimmed
1 egg, beaten
5 tblsp. butter or regular margarine
⅔ c. soft bread crumbs
3 tblsp. flour
½ tsp. salt
¼ tsp. celery salt
¼ tsp. dry mustard
Dash pepper
1½ c. milk
½ tsp. Worcestershire sauce
1 c. shredded Cheddar cheese (4 oz.)
Paprika
6 rolled anchovies with capers (optional)

In medium bowl stir together vinegar and 3 c. water. Peel salsify; cut into 1″ pieces and immediately place into vinegar mixture. (This prevents the salsify from darkening.) Drain.

In 2-qt. saucepan over high heat, bring 1″ water to a boil; add salsify. Reduce heat to medium-low. Cover and cook 20 minutes or until fork-tender; drain.

In large bowl place drained salsify. Mash with potato masher. (Mixture will be chunky.) Stir in beaten egg.

In same 2-qt. saucepan over medium heat, melt butter. Spoon off 2 tblsp. butter; toss with bread crumbs until well coated.

To remaining butter in saucepan, stir in flour, salt, celery salt, mustard and pepper until smooth. Gradually stir in milk and Worcestershire sauce until well blended. Over medium heat, cook, stirring constantly, until mixture boils and thickens. Add cheese; stir until melted. Remove from heat.

Stir in salsify mixture. Spoon into 6 greased (6-oz.) broiler-safe casseroles or large scallop shells. Sprinkle with buttered bread crumbs and paprika. Place an anchovy on top of each casserole. On baking sheet, place casseroles. Broil, 7″ from the source of heat 2 to 3 minutes or until golden brown. Turn off broiler. Place on lowest rack in oven and let stand 7 minutes before serving. Makes 6 servings.

TO MICROWAVE: Use same ingredients. Prepare salsify as directed.

In 2-qt. microwave-safe casserole place salsify; *omit water.* Cover with lid or plastic wrap, turning back one section to vent steam.

Microwave at high setting (100% power) 12 to 14 minutes or until tender, stirring after 4 minutes.

Drain, mash and add egg as directed.

In 1½-qt. microwave-safe casserole place butter. Microwave, uncovered, at high setting 1 minute or until melted.

Spoon off 2 tblsp. butter; toss with bread crumbs until well coated.

To remaining butter in casserole, stir in flour, salt, celery salt, mustard and pepper until smooth.

Gradually stir in milk and Worcestershire sauce until well blended. Microwave, uncovered, at high setting 2 minutes; stir. Microwave 3 minutes or until mixture boils and thickens, stirring each minute. Add cheese; stir until melted.

Stir in salsify mixture. Spoon into 6 greased (6-oz.) microwave-safe casseroles. Sprinkle with buttered bread crumbs and paprika. Place an anchovy on top of each casserole.

Arrange 3 casseroles in a ring in microwave oven. Microwave, uncovered, at high setting 3 minutes or until bubbly. Repeat with remaining casseroles.

ZUCCHINI PUDDING

So easy to prepare—just blend all the ingredients, pour and bake.

2 c. shredded zucchini
½ c. heavy cream
¼ c. finely chopped onion
½ tsp. salt
¼ tsp. pepper
¼ tsp. dry mustard
6 eggs
1 (8-oz.) and 1 (3-oz.) pkg. cream cheese, cubed
1 c. shredded Cheddar cheese (4 oz.)

Wrap zucchini in dish towel. Twist to squeeze out as much liquid as possible; set aside.

In blender container place cream, onion, salt, pepper, mustard and eggs; cover. Blend at high speed until smooth.

Remove center of cover on blender. Blending at high speed, gradually add cream cheese and Cheddar cheese. Continue blending until smooth.

In greased 2-qt. soufflé dish place zucchini and cheese mixture. Gently stir until well blended. Dish can be covered and refrigerated 2 hours at this point.

Bake in 375° oven 50 minutes to 1 hour (if refrigerated, 60 to 70 minutes) or until center is set. Serve immediately. Makes 6 to 8 servings.

Yam Pudding: Use same ingredients, but substitute 1 c. cooked, mashed yams for zucchini, ½ tsp. ground ginger for dry mustard, and omit Cheddar cheese.

In blender container place yams and ¼ c. cream; cover. Blend at high speed until smooth. Pour into large bowl.

In same blender container place remaining ¼ c. cream, onion, salt, pepper, eggs and ½ tsp. ground ginger; cover. Blend at high speed until smooth.

Remove center of cover on blender. Blending at high speed, gradually add cream cheese. Continue blending until smooth, stopping several times to scrape down sides of blender. Stir into yam mixture.

Pour yam mixture into greased 2-qt. soufflé dish. Bake or refrigerate as directed. Makes 6 to 8 servings.

TO MICROWAVE: Use same ingredients.

Prepare zucchini or yam pudding mixture as directed. Pour into 2-qt. microwave-safe soufflé dish.

Microwave, uncovered, at low setting (30% power) 15 minutes or until thickened, stirring after 10 minutes.

Pour into blender container; cover. Blend at high speed until smooth. Pour mixture back into dish. Cover with waxed paper.

Microwave at low setting 15 to 18 minutes more or until center is set, rotating dish one-quarter turn every 3 minutes.

Let stand, covered, 5 minutes.

OLD-FASHIONED BAKED BEANS

Slow-simmered, moist and flavored with molasses and brown sugar.

2 lb. dried navy beans, rinsed and drained
Water
2 medium onions, chopped
12 slices bacon, diced
⅓ c. packed dark brown sugar
⅓ c. molasses
⅓ c. ketchup
3 tsp. salt
1 tsp. dry mustard

In 4-qt. Dutch oven over high heat, bring beans and 2 qt. water to a boil. Boil 2 minutes. Remove from heat. Let stand, covered, 1 hour. Drain.

In same Dutch oven over high heat bring beans and 10 c. fresh water to a boil. Reduce heat to low. Cover and simmer 20 minutes.

Into 4-qt. glass casserole or bean pot pour beans with liquid. Stir in onions and remaining ingredients; cover.

Bake in 300° oven 5½ hours, adding some hot water during the last 2 hours if needed to keep beans moist.

Uncover and bake 30 minutes or until beans are tender. Makes 12 servings.

SWEET-AND-SOUR BAKED BEANS

Tote these to a picnic right in your slow-cooker and they'll stay warm.

1 lb. dried navy beans, rinsed and drained
6 c. water
8 slices bacon, cut into 1" pieces
1 c. chopped onions
1 c. chopped celery
1 clove garlic, minced
1 (15-oz.) can tomato sauce
½ c. chili sauce
¼ c. packed brown sugar
¼ c. molasses
1 tsp. salt
¼ tsp. pepper
3 drops hot pepper sauce
2 (8-oz.) cans pineapple chunks, drained and cut into halves
½ c. chopped sweet pickles
¼ c. sliced pimiento-stuffed olives

In 3½-qt. slow cooker place beans and water. Let soak at least 12 hours.

Cover and cook at low setting 3 hours or until tender. Drain and set aside.

In 10" skillet over medium heat, cook bacon until browned. Drain bacon on paper towels.

In bacon drippings over medium heat, cook onions, celery and garlic until tender. Stir in tomato sauce, chili sauce, brown sugar, molasses, salt, pepper and hot pepper sauce until well blended.

Over high heat, bring mixture to a boil. Remove from heat.

In slow cooker stir together beans, bacon, tomato sauce mixture, pineapple, pickles and olives until well blended.

Cover and cook at high setting 3½ to 4½ hours. Makes 6 servings.

SUPER BAKED BEANS

First simmered, then baked in a savory tomato-molasses sauce.

1 lb. dried navy beans, rinsed and drained
Water
1 (28-oz.) can tomatoes
1 (12-oz.) can lemon-lime-flavored soda
6 slices bacon, cut into 1" pieces
1 tsp. salt
½ tsp. pepper
1 (8-oz.) can tomato sauce
¾ c. chopped onion
¾ c. chopped celery
½ c. chopped green pepper
½ c. molasses
½ c. ketchup
⅓ c. packed brown sugar
1 tblsp. prepared mustard
1 tblsp. Worcestershire sauce
2 tsp. cider vinegar

In 4-qt. Dutch oven over high heat, bring beans and 1 qt. water to a boil. Boil 2 minutes. Remove from heat. Cover and let stand 1 hour; drain.

Into same Dutch oven add beans, tomatoes, soda, bacon, salt, pepper and ¼ c. water, stirring to break up tomatoes. Over high heat bring to a boil.

Reduce heat to low. Cover and simmer 1 hour, stirring occasionally.

Stir in tomato sauce and remaining ingredients. Cover and simmer 1 hour, stirring occasionally.

Into 3-qt. casserole pour hot bean mixture. Cover and bake in 250° oven 4 hours.

Uncover and bake 30 minutes or until beans are tender. Makes 8 servings.

TWICE-BAKED POTATOES

Scooped-out potato shells piled high with a cheesy onion filling.

6 large baking potatoes
Cheddar-Onion Topping (see Index)
Paprika

Wash and scrub potatoes. Bake in 400° oven 1 hour or until fork-tender. Remove from oven and cool until easy to handle, about 10 minutes.

Meanwhile, prepare Cheddar-Onion Topping.

Cut a ¼"-thick slice, lengthwise, off top of each potato. (Reserve tops for eating or discard.) Scoop out potatoes, leaving skins intact. Put potatoes through ricer or mash with fork.

In medium bowl stir together mashed potatoes and topping until well blended.

Spoon potato mixture back into skins, piling mixture about ½" above the tops of the skins. Sprinkle with paprika.

On baking sheet place stuffed potatoes.

Bake in 400° oven 10 minutes or until heated through. Makes 6 servings.

TO MICROWAVE: Use same ingredients.

Wash, scrub and prick potatoes with a fork. Place potatoes on paper towels in microwave oven. Microwave at high setting (100% power) 16 to 18 minutes or until potatoes give slightly when pressed with finger, turning over and rearranging every 5 minutes.

Wrap in foil and let stand 5 minutes.

Meanwhile, prepare Cheddar-Onion Topping.

Prepare and stuff potatoes as directed.

Arrange stuffed potatoes in a ring on microwave-safe serving plate or paper towels. Microwave at high setting 4 to 6 minutes or until hot, rotating plate one-half turn or rearranging potatoes every 2 minutes.

STUFFED SWEET POTATOES

Festive-looking potatoes, fragrant with pineapple and orange juice.

6 medium sweet potatoes or yams
1 (8-oz.) can crushed pineapple, drained
1/2 c. orange juice
1/4 c. butter or regular margarine, melted
3/4 tsp. salt
1/4 c. chopped pecans

Wash and scrub potatoes. Bake in 400° oven 45 minutes to 1 hour or until fork-tender. Remove from oven and cool until easy to handle, about 10 minutes.

Cut a 1/4"-thick slice, lengthwise, off top of each potato. (Reserve tops for eating or discard.) Scoop out potatoes, leaving skins intact. Put potatoes through ricer or mash with fork.

In large bowl place mashed potatoes, pineapple, orange juice, butter and salt. Using mixer at medium speed beat until well blended.

Spoon potato-pineapple mixture back into potato skins, piling mixture about 1/2" above the tops of the skins. Sprinkle with pecans.

On baking sheet place stuffed potatoes.

Bake in 400° oven 10 minutes or until heated through. Makes 6 servings.

TO MICROWAVE: Use same ingredients.

Wash, scrub and prick potatoes with a fork. Place on paper towels in microwave oven. Microwave at high setting (100% power) 13 to 15 minutes or until potatoes give slightly when pressed with finger, turning over and rearranging every 5 minutes.

Wrap in foil and let stand 5 minutes.

Prepare and stuff potatoes as directed.

Arrange stuffed potatoes in a ring on microwave-safe serving plate or paper towels. Microwave at high setting 5 to 7 minutes or until heated through, rotating plate one-half turn or rearranging potatoes every 2 minutes.

STUFFED ARTICHOKES

Steaming cuts cooking time and makes it easier to remove the choke.

4 artichokes
Water
1/2 c. butter or regular margarine
1 1/2 c. chopped onions
1 1/2 c. shredded carrots
1/3 c. chopped fresh parsley
2 1/4 tsp. dried basil leaves
3 cloves garlic, minced
3 c. soft bread crumbs
1 1/2 tsp. salt
1/8 tsp. pepper

Wash artichokes and cut off stems. With serrated knife cut 1" from top of each artichoke. Remove any loose leaves from bottom of each artichoke and use scissors to snip thorny tips from remaining leaves.

In 4-qt. Dutch oven over high heat, bring artichokes and 1 qt. water to a boil. Reduce heat to medium. Cover and cook 30 minutes. Drain artichokes, top-side down, on paper towels. Cool until easy to handle, about 15 minutes.

Gently pull out purple-tipped, prickly leaves in center of each cooked artichoke to expose the fuzzy choke. Using a small spoon, carefully scrape out fuzzy choke; discard.

In 10" skillet over medium heat, melt butter. Add onions, carrots, parsley, basil and garlic; cook until tender. Remove from heat. Stir in bread crumbs, salt, pepper and 3 tblsp. water.

Gently spread leaves apart and spoon vegetable mixture between leaves and inside center of each artichoke.

Pour 1 c. boiling water into 8" square glass baking dish. Place stuffed artichokes in dish. Cover dish tightly with aluminum foil.

Bake in 400° oven 20 to 30 minutes or until artichokes are tender and a leaf may be easily removed.

To serve, cut each artichoke in half from blossom to stem end. Makes 8 servings.

PECAN-SWEET POTATO BALLS

Studded with nuts, orange-flavored potato balls hold a sweet surprise.

4 c. mashed, cooked sweet potatoes or yams
¼ c. butter or regular margarine, melted
½ tsp. salt
¼ tsp. pepper
6 marshmallows, cut into halves
2 c. chopped pecans, walnuts or peanuts

In medium bowl stir potatoes, butter, salt and pepper until well blended. Divide mixture into 12 portions.

Shape each portion around 1 marshmallow half; roll in pecans. Place 2" apart on greased baking sheet. Potato balls may be individually wrapped and frozen up to 1 month at this point.

Bake in 350° oven 20 minutes (if frozen, 35 minutes) or until heated through. Makes 6 servings.

STUFFED TURBAN SQUASH

Not "just decorative," turban squash makes good eating, too.

1 large turban squash (about 5 lb.)
2 tblsp. butter or regular margarine
2 tblsp. packed brown sugar
2 tblsp. orange juice
1 tsp. grated orange rind
¼ tsp. salt
⅛ tsp. pepper

Wash squash and pierce top and body deeply 8 to 10 times, using a large carving fork or ice pick.

Place squash directly on oven rack. Bake in 400° oven 60 to 75 minutes, or until flesh yields when pressed with finger. Remove and cool until easy to handle, about 10 minutes.

Using small, sharp knife, slice off blossom end, cutting around the line dividing bottom from top.

Scoop out seeds and pulp. Put pulp through food mill. Discard seeds or reserve for roasting.

In medium bowl place puréed squash. With wire whisk or fork, beat in butter and remaining ingredients until well blended.

Spoon squash mixture back into larger half of shell; top with remaining half. Bake in 400° oven 10 minutes or until heated through. Makes 6 servings.

TO MICROWAVE: Use same ingredients.

Pierce squash as directed.

On paper towel place squash. Microwave at high setting (100% power) 12 to 15 minutes or until squash yields when pressed with finger, rotating squash one-quarter turn every 4 minutes.

Cut, purée and mix squash mixture as directed.

Spoon squash mixture back into larger half of shell; top with remaining half.

Microwave at medium setting (50% power) 3 to 5 minutes or until heated through.

OVEN-FRIED EGGPLANT SLICES

No messy frying — brush with herbed mayonnaise, dip in crumbs and bake.

1/3 c. grated Parmesan cheese
1/3 c. mayonnaise or salad dressing
1 tsp. dried basil leaves
1 tsp. dried oregano leaves
3/4 tsp. onion salt
1 large eggplant (1½ lb.), peeled and cut into ½" slices
1 c. soft bread crumbs

In small bowl stir together cheese, mayonnaise, basil, oregano and onion salt.

Thinly spread mayonnaise mixture on both sides of eggplant slices.

On sheet of waxed paper place bread crumbs. Dip each eggplant slice into crumbs until well coated on both sides.

On ungreased baking sheet place eggplant slices. Bake in 425° oven 15 minutes or until golden brown and fork-tender. Makes 6 servings.

CRISPY VEGETABLES

To vary the seasoning, add ½ tsp. thyme or oregano to the crumbs.

Vegetables: 1½ lb. asparagus spears, trimmed; or 4 medium carrots, each cut into 4x½" strips; or 2 medium zucchini, each cut into 4x½" strips
1 c. unsifted flour
2 eggs
2 c. soft bread crumbs
1 tsp. salt
1/4 c. vegetable oil

If using asparagus or carrots:
In 12" skillet over high heat, bring 1" water to a boil; add asparagus or carrots. Reduce heat to medium. Cover and cook 4 to 6 minutes or until tender-crisp.

Drain and pat dry with paper towels. Wipe skillet.

On sheet of waxed paper place flour.

In 9" pie plate beat eggs with fork until well blended.

On another sheet of waxed paper mix together bread crumbs and salt.

Dip vegetables in flour, then egg and finally roll in bread crumbs until well coated.

In 12" skillet over medium heat, heat oil until hot. Add half of the vegetable pieces. Cook, turning vegetables to brown evenly, 5 minutes or until golden brown.

Drain on paper towels. Repeat with remaining vegetables. Serve warm. Makes 4 to 6 servings.

DEEP-FRIED VEGETABLES

Eggplant and onions take especially well to this light batter.

Vegetables: 1 medium eggplant; or 2
   bunches broccoli, broken into flowerets;
   or 4 medium onions, sliced; or 3 medium
   zucchini, each cut into 4x½" strips
4 c. water
1 tsp. salt
8¼ c. vegetable oil
1 c. self-rising flour
2 tsp. curry powder
1 tsp. dried rubbed sage
1 tsp. dried marjoram leaves
1 tsp. ground turmeric
1 c. milk
1 egg

If using eggplant: slice into 4x½" strips. In large bowl place water and salt. Add eggplant; soak 20 minutes. Drain well and pat dry with paper towels.

In 4-qt. Dutch oven over medium heat, heat 8 c. oil to 375° on deep-fat thermometer, about 20 minutes.

In medium bowl stir together flour, curry powder, sage, marjoram and turmeric until well blended.

In small bowl beat together milk, egg and remaining ¼ c. oil until well blended. Stir into flour mixture just until moistened.

Dip vegetables into batter until well coated. Slide 6 pieces into hot oil. Fry 2 minutes or until golden brown.

Remove with slotted spoon. Drain on paper towels. Repeat with remaining vegetables and batter. Makes 12 to 14 servings.

Beer Batter: Prepare batter as directed, but omit spices and substitute 1 c. flat beer for the milk.

FRENCH-FRIED POTATO BALLS

These golden brown nuggets can be made in advance, then reheated.

1 qt. vegetable oil
2 c. warm, unseasoned mashed potatoes
¼ c. finely chopped onion
3 tblsp. finely chopped fresh parsley
¾ tsp. salt
2 eggs, beaten
1¼ c. soft bread crumbs

In 3-qt. saucepan over medium heat, heat oil to 365° on deep-fat thermometer, about 20 minutes.

Meanwhile, in medium bowl mix together potatoes, onion, parsley, salt, eggs and ¼ c. bread crumbs just until combined.

Lightly shape potato mixture into 28 balls. Roll balls in remaining 1 c. bread crumbs until well coated.

Fry 9 or 10 balls until golden brown, about 1 minute. Remove with slotted spoon. Drain on paper towels. Repeat with remaining balls.

Serve immediately; or cover and refrigerate.

To reheat, place balls on baking sheet; bake in 350° oven 10 to 15 minutes or until heated through.

Makes 4 to 6 servings.

Duchess-style Potatoes: Use same ingredients, but omit parsley and add 2 tblsp. butter or regular margarine, melted. Prepare potato mixture as directed.

Drop potato mixture by rounded tblsp. onto greased baking sheet. Drizzle with melted butter. Bake in 500° oven 10 minutes or until golden brown.

To pipe potatoes: Fill a pastry bag with potato mixture. Using large star tube #9, pipe potato mixture into 6 rosettes on greased baking sheet, or pipe rosettes around the rim of broiler-safe platter.

Drizzle with melted butter. Broil, 6" from source of heat, 5 to 6 minutes or until golden brown.

SWISS POTATO PANCAKE

*One big pancake makes 4 servings
—each one a crisp wedge of
potatoes, Swiss cheese and onion.*

4 medium potatoes
1 small onion, finely chopped
1 c. shredded Swiss cheese (4 oz.)
¼ tsp. salt
⅛ tsp. pepper
4 tblsp. butter or regular margarine

In 2-qt. saucepan over high heat,
bring 1″ water to a boil; add potatoes. Reduce heat to medium. Cover
and cook 15 minutes or until potatoes are almost fork-tender.

Drain. Cool until easy to handle,
about 15 minutes. Peel and shred
into medium bowl.

Stir in onion, cheese, salt and
pepper until well blended.

In 12″ skillet over medium heat,
melt butter. Add potato mixture,
spreading to within 1½″ from edge
of skillet. Lightly press down and
smooth the top with spatula to form
a compact pancake.

Cover and cook 8 to 10 minutes or
until cheese melts and pancake is
golden brown on the bottom.

Cut cake into 4 wedges. With
metal spatula, lift out each wedge
and invert onto serving platter.
Makes 4 servings.

OKRA FRITTERS

*Corn, carrots or zucchini can easily
be substituted for the okra.*

1 qt. vegetable oil
1½ c. sliced okra (¼″ slices), about ½ lb.
½ c. water
1½ c. sifted flour
2 tsp. baking powder
¾ tsp. salt
½ tsp. chili powder
1 c. milk
1 egg, beaten

In 3-qt. saucepan over medium
heat, heat oil to 360° on deep-fat
thermometer, about 20 minutes.

In 1-qt. saucepan over high heat,
bring okra and water to a boil. Reduce heat to medium. Cover and
cook 2 minutes. Drain well; set aside
on paper towels.

Meanwhile, into large bowl sift
together flour, baking powder, salt
and chili powder.

In small bowl beat milk and egg
until well blended. Stir milk mixture
into flour mixture just until combined. Stir in okra.

Drop 5 tblsp. batter into hot oil.
Fry 2 to 3 minutes or until golden
brown. Remove fritters with slotted
spoon and drain on paper towels.
Repeat with remaining okra mixture. Makes 6 servings.

Corn Fritters: Prepare as directed,
but substitute 1½ c. fresh or frozen
corn for the okra.

Carrot Fritters: Prepare as directed,
but substitute 1 c. shredded carrots
for the okra; do not cook carrots;
and substitute ¼ tsp. dried thyme
leaves for the chili powder.

Zucchini Fritters: Prepare as directed, but substitute 1 c. shredded and
well drained zucchini for the okra;
do not cook zucchini; and substitute
¼ tsp. curry powder for the chili
powder.

ZUCCHINI PANCAKES

Use any summer squash in place of zucchini for these curried pancakes.

4 c. shredded zucchini
⅓ c. finely chopped onion
3 tblsp. chopped fresh parsley
1 tsp. salt
½ tsp. curry powder
¼ tsp. pepper
2 eggs, slightly beaten
¼ c. unsifted flour
1 to 2 tblsp. vegetable oil
Dairy sour cream (optional)

Wrap zucchini in dish towel; twist to squeeze out as much liquid as possible.

In medium bowl stir together zucchini, onion, parsley, salt, curry powder, pepper and eggs until well blended. Stir in flour just until moistened.

In 10″ skillet over medium-high heat, heat 1 tblsp. oil until hot. Drop 4 rounded tblsp. zucchini mixture into skillet, pressing each one down gently to form a 3″ pancake. Cook, turning once, 4 to 5 minutes or until golden brown on both sides. Repeat with remaining zucchini mixture, adding oil as needed.

Serve warm with sour cream, if desired. Makes 6 servings.

POTATO PANCAKES

Serve these crisp pancakes with either sour cream or applesauce.

4 medium potatoes, peeled and grated
1 medium onion, grated
2 tblsp. chopped fresh parsley
2 tblsp. flour
½ tsp. salt
½ tsp. baking powder
¼ tsp. ground nutmeg
⅛ tsp. pepper
1 egg, beaten
⅓ c. butter or regular margarine
Applesauce (optional)

In medium bowl stir all ingredients except butter and applesauce until well blended.

In 12″ skillet over medium-high heat, melt butter. Drop 8 rounded tblsp. potato mixture into skillet, pressing each one down gently to form a 3″ pancake. Cook, turning once, 4 to 5 minutes or until golden brown on both sides. Remove and keep warm. Repeat with remaining potato mixture.

Serve warm, with applesauce if desired. Makes 16 pancakes or 4 servings.

SALSIFY PANCAKES

Substitute carrots for half of the salsify for two-toned pancakes.

3 c. water
1 tblsp. vinegar
¾ lb. salsify, trimmed
3 eggs
1 small onion, grated
½ tsp. salt
Dash pepper
Butter or regular margarine
Vegetable oil
Dairy sour cream (optional)

In medium bowl stir together water and vinegar. Peel salsify and immediately place in vinegar mixture. (This prevents salsify from darkening.)

In another medium bowl beat eggs with fork until well blended. Add onion, salt and pepper; stir until well blended.

Drain salsify. Grate directly into egg mixture; stir until well blended. In 10″ skillet over medium heat, heat 1 tblsp. each butter and oil until hot.

Drop 4 rounded tblsp. salsify mixture into skillet, pressing each one down gently to form a 3″ pancake. Cook, turning once, 6 to 8 minutes or until golden brown on both sides. Repeat with remaining salsify mixture, adding butter and oil as needed.

Serve warm, with sour cream if desired. Makes 6 servings.

POTATO KNISHES

This slice-and-bake version is faster than the old method of wrapping each knish individually.

3 lb. potatoes, peeled and cut into
  ½″ cubes
2 tblsp. butter or regular margarine
2 medium onions, finely chopped
1 clove garlic, minced
⅛ tsp. pepper
2 tsp. salt
2 c. sifted flour
¾ c. shortening
4 to 5 tblsp. iced water
1 egg yolk, beaten

In 4-qt. Dutch oven over high heat, bring 1″ water to a boil. Add potatoes. Reduce heat to medium-low. Cover and cook 20 minutes or until tender. Drain. Put through ricer and set aside.

Meanwhile, in 10″ skillet over medium heat, melt butter. Add onions and garlic; cover and cook 10 minutes or until very tender. Stir into riced potatoes with pepper and 1½ tsp. salt.

In large bowl stir together flour and remaining ½ tsp. salt. Using a pastry blender, cut in shortening until coarse crumbs form. Sprinkle iced water over crumb mixture, a little at a time, tossing with fork until dough forms. Press mixture into a ball. Divide in half.

On heavily floured surface with heavily floured rolling pin, roll half of the dough to a 12″ square about ⅛″ thick. Spoon half of the potato mixture along one edge to form a 3″-wide log. Roll pastry around potato mixture, jelly-roll fashion. Cut pastry roll crosswise into 1″ slices. Place slices 2″ apart on greased baking sheet. Brush with some of the beaten egg yolk.

Repeat with remaining pastry, potato mixture and egg yolk.

Bake in 450° oven 15 minutes or until golden brown. Makes 12 servings.

EGGPLANT PATTIES

*A corn meal coating lets these
patties fry up extra-crisp.*

1 medium eggplant (1 lb.), peeled and cut
    into ¼" slices
1 small onion, chopped
1 c. water
Salt
⅛ tsp. pepper
1 c. cracker crumbs
½ c. yellow corn meal
½ c. vegetable oil
Aioli Sauce (optional; see Index)

In 3-qt. saucepan over high heat,
bring eggplant, onion, 1 c. water and
½ tsp. salt to a boil. Reduce heat to
medium. Cover and simmer until
tender; drain well and set aside to
cool.

In medium bowl place eggplant
mixture, pepper and ½ tsp. salt.
With fork mash eggplant and mix
until well blended. Stir in cracker
crumbs.

On sheet of waxed paper place
corn meal. Drop eggplant mixture
by rounded tblsp. onto corn meal.
Roll in corn meal until well coated.
Pat each into a 3" patty.

In 10" skillet over medium-high
heat, heat 2 tblsp. oil until hot. Cook
4 patties, turning once, 4 to 5 minutes or until golden brown on both
sides. Repeat with remaining patties, adding oil as needed.

Serve warm with Aioli Sauce, if
desired. Makes 8 servings.

EGGPLANT SANDWICHES

*Eggplant replaces bread in these
fried, knife-and-fork sandwiches.*

1 medium eggplant (about 1 lb.)
1 c. shredded Cheddar cheese (4 oz.)
¼ c. finely chopped green onions
¼ tsp. dried marjoram leaves
2 eggs
1 tblsp. water
1 c. soft bread crumbs
¼ tsp. salt
¼ c. vegetable oil

Peel eggplant and cut into 12
slices, ¼" thick.

In medium bowl stir cheese, green
onions, marjoram and one egg until
well blended.

Top 6 eggplant slices with cheese
mixture, spreading mixture almost
to edge of each slice. Top with remaining eggplant slices to make
sandwiches, pressing down slightly.

In pie plate using fork, beat remaining egg and water until well
blended.

On sheet of waxed paper mix
bread crumbs and salt.

Dip each eggplant sandwich in egg
mixture, then in bread crumb mixture, until well coated on both sides.

In 12" skillet over medium-high
heat, heat oil until hot. Cook eggplant sandwiches, carefully turning
once, 6 to 8 minutes or until golden
brown on both sides. Makes 6
servings.

VEGETABLE LOAF_____

This nutty vegetable mixture also can be shaped into patties and fried.

2 tblsp. vegetable oil
1 c. chopped onions
1 c. shredded carrots
1 c. sliced mushrooms
½ c. chopped celery
½ c. cut green beans (1″ pieces)
½ c. fresh or frozen peas
1 clove garlic, minced
2 c. soft bread crumbs
½ c. chopped unsalted peanuts
½ tsp. salt
¼ tsp. dried basil leaves
¼ tsp. dried thyme leaves
⅛ tsp. pepper
2 eggs
2 tblsp. toasted wheat germ
4 Tomato Sauce Cubes (see Index), or 1 c.
  prepared spaghetti sauce
½ c. water

In 10″ skillet over medium-high heat, heat oil until hot. Add onions, carrots, mushrooms, celery, green beans, peas and garlic; cook until tender.

In large bowl stir together vegetable mixture, bread crumbs and remaining ingredients except wheat germ, Tomato Cubes, and water until well blended.

Lightly grease 8½x4½x2⅝″ loaf pan. Sprinkle with wheat germ. Spoon vegetable mixture into prepared pan, spreading and lightly packing to form an even, compact loaf.

Bake in 400° oven 20 minutes or until lightly browned. Cool on rack 10 minutes.

Meanwhile, in 1-qt. saucepan place Tomato Sauce Cubes and water. Over low heat cook, stirring constantly, until mixture boils and thickens. (Or, heat prepared spaghetti sauce.)

Remove from pan. Slice loaf and serve with sauce. Makes 6 servings.

Vegetable Cutlets: Prepare vegetable mixture as directed, but do not bake.

Prepare Tomato Sauce Cubes as directed; keep warm.

Shape ½ c. vegetable mixture into 3″-round cutlet, about ½″ thick; repeat to make 5 more.

In 12″ skillet over medium heat, heat 2 tblsp. oil until hot. Cook cutlets, turning once, 6 to 8 minutes or until golden brown on both sides.

Serve cutlets with sauce. Makes 6 servings.

TO MICROWAVE VEGETABLE LOAF: Use same ingredients, *changing amounts as indicated.*

In 2-qt. microwave-safe casserole place *1 tblsp. oil,* onions, carrots, celery, green beans, peas, garlic, basil and thyme. Cover with lid or plastic wrap, turning back one section to vent steam.

Microwave at high setting (100% power) 6 to 7 minutes or until tender-crisp, stirring every 2 minutes.

Stir in mushrooms. Microwave, uncovered, at high setting 1 minute. Stir in bread crumbs, peanuts, salt, pepper and eggs until well blended.

Line 8½x4½x2⅝″ microwave-safe loaf dish with waxed paper. Sprinkle bottom of dish with wheat germ. Spoon vegetable mixture into pan, spreading and lightly packing to form an even, compact loaf.

Cover with waxed paper. Microwave at medium setting (50% power) 10 to 12 minutes or until set, rotating dish one-quarter turn every 3 minutes. Cover any brown spots that appear with small flat pieces of aluminum foil. (Check use-and-care manual for your oven before using foil.) Let stand, covered, 5 minutes.

Meanwhile, in 1-qt. microwave-safe casserole place Tomato Sauce Cubes. (Or, heat prepared spaghetti sauce.) Cover with lid or plastic wrap, turning back one section to vent steam.

Microwave at high setting 2 to 2½ minutes or until cubes are melted, stirring each minute. Stir in water.

Cover again, and microwave at high setting 2 to 4 minutes or until mixture boils and thickens.

Remove loaf from pan; peel away waxed paper. Slice loaf and serve with sauce.

CARROT PASTA

(see photo following page 182)

Homemade pasta made with carrots—colorful and flavorful.

2 c. sliced carrots, cooked and drained
4 eggs
1 tsp. salt
3¼ c. unsifted flour

In medium bowl using potato masher, coarsely mash carrots. In sieve drain carrots, pressing out as much liquid as possible.

In blender container place carrots, eggs and salt; cover. Blend at high speed until smooth, about 1 minute.

Place flour in mound on pastry cloth. Make a deep well in center of mound. Pour carrot mixture in center of well. Stir with fork, gradually mixing flour into carrot mixture, until dough starts to form. Using your hands, mix and knead in more flour until a stiff dough forms. Knead 8 minutes or until smooth, adding flour as needed. Cover with plastic wrap. Let rest 15 minutes.

Form noodles with pasta machine or by hand.

If rolling by hand, work with half of the dough at a time, keeping remaining half covered with plastic wrap. On lightly floured surface roll and gently stretch dough as thin as possible, into 18″ square. Let dry 10 minutes before cutting. Repeat with remaining half of dough.

Cut dough into desired shape and cook as directed (see below). Makes about 1½ lb.

Lasagne Noodles: Cut dough into 4½″-wide strips.

In large saucepot over high heat, bring 4 qt. water and 1 tblsp. salt to a boil. Add 4 pasta strips. When water returns to a boil, cook 4 minutes. Remove with slotted spoon; plunge into cold water and drain on paper towels. Repeat with remaining pasta. Use immediately.

Fettucini Noodles: Loosely roll a dough square around rolling pin; slip out rolling pin. Cut dough into ⅛″-wide strips. Gently shake out noodles. Repeat with remaining dough square. Noodles may be placed in plastic bag at this point and frozen up to one month.

In large saucepot over high heat, bring 6 qt. water and 1 tblsp. salt to a boil. Add noodles. When water returns to a boil, cook 4 to 6 minutes (if frozen, 8 to 12 minutes) or until tender.

Drain in colander. Serve immediately.

SPINACH PASTA

Depending on how you cut the dough, this recipe will yield either lasagne noodles or fettucini.

1 lb. fresh spinach, cooked, or
1 (10-oz.) pkg. frozen spinach, cooked
4 eggs
1 tsp. salt
3 c. unsifted flour

In sieve drain spinach, pressing out as much liquid as possible. Chop spinach.

In blender container place spinach, eggs and salt; cover. Blend at high speed until smooth, about 1 minute.

Place flour in mound on pastry cloth. Make a deep well in center of mound. Pour spinach mixture in center of well. Stir with fork, gradually mixing flour into spinach mixture, until dough starts to form. Using your hands, mix and knead in more flour until a stiff dough forms. Knead 8 minutes or until smooth, adding flour as needed. Cover with plastic wrap. Let rest 15 minutes.

Form noodles with pasta machine or by hand.

If rolling by hand, work with half of the dough at a time, keeping remaining half covered with plastic wrap. On lightly floured surface roll and gently stretch dough as thin as possible, into 18″ square. Let dry 10 minutes before cutting. Repeat with remaining half of dough.

Cut dough into desired shape and cook as directed (see preceding recipes for Lasagne Noodles and Fettucini Noodles). Makes about 1½ lb.

POTATO GNOCCHI

Serve these with tomato sauce, Salsa Verde or Pesto (see Index).

2 large potatoes
Water
Salt
⅛ tsp. pepper
⅛ tsp. paprika
7 tblsp. butter
Flour
1 egg
2 tblsp. grated Parmesan cheese

Wash and scrub potatoes. Bake in 400° oven 1 hour or until fork-tender. Cool until easy to handle, about 10 minutes. Peel and put through ricer.

In 4-qt. Dutch oven over high heat, bring 3 qt. water and 2 tsp. salt to a boil. Reduce heat so water maintains a steady boil.

In 2-qt. saucepan over high heat, bring ½ c. water, pepper, paprika, ½ tsp. salt and 3 tblsp. butter to a boil. Cook until butter melts. Remove from heat.

Stir in ½ c. flour all at once. Return saucepan to range top; over low heat cook, stirring constantly, until dough forms a ball. Beat in egg until well blended. Stir in riced potatoes until well blended. Remove from heat.

Gnocchi may be shaped by hand or piped with a pastry bag.

To shape by hand: Roll potato mixture in flour until well coated. With floured hands shape mixture into 1″ balls. Drop 11 balls into simmering water. Simmer, uncovered, 10 to 12 minutes or until gnocchi rise to the top and are slightly firm. Remove with slotted spoon and drain on paper towels. Repeat with remaining balls.

To pipe: Spoon half of the potato mixture into a pastry bag. Over simmering water, squeeze dough and cut at 1″ intervals, letting all the dough drop into water. Simmer, uncovered, 3 to 5 minutes or until gnocchi rise to the top and are slightly firm. Remove with slotted spoon. Drain on paper towels. Repeat with remaining potato mixture.

Melt remaining 4 tblsp. butter. Roll cooked gnocchi in butter. Place on greased jelly-roll pan.

Bake in 425° oven 10 to 15 minutes or until lightly browned. Sprinkle with Parmesan cheese. Serve warm. Makes 6 to 8 servings.

SPINACH-FRIED RICE

Cilantro, an herb, adds a lemon-parsley flavor to this dish.

3 tblsp. vegetable oil
¼ lb. mushrooms, finely chopped
4 green onions, cut into 1″ pieces
1 c. shredded carrot
1 lb. fresh spinach, washed,
   trimmed and coarsely chopped, or
   1 (10-oz.) pkg. frozen chopped spinach,
   thawed and well drained
3 eggs, beaten
3 c. cooked rice
¼ c. chopped fresh cilantro (optional)
3 tblsp. soy sauce

In 12″ skillet over high heat, heat oil until hot. Add mushrooms, green onions and carrot; cook, stirring often, until tender.

Add spinach. Cover and cook 1 minute. Reduce heat to medium. Uncover and add eggs. Cook, stirring constantly, 2 minutes or until eggs are cooked and spinach is wilted.

Stir in rice, cilantro and soy sauce until well blended. Cook until mixture is heated through. Makes 6 to 8 servings.

CRACKED WHEAT PILAF

This Middle Eastern rice dish has a crunchy texture and nutty flavor. If you prefer brown rice, soak it for 4 hours and drain before using.

2 tblsp. butter or regular margarine
4 large mushrooms, chopped
1 medium rib celery, chopped
1 medium carrot, chopped
½ medium green pepper, chopped
¼ c. raisins
1 bay leaf
1¾ c. chicken or vegetable broth
1 c. cracked wheat (bulgur)
¼ tsp. salt
¼ tsp. dried rubbed sage
¼ tsp. dried savory leaves
¼ c. chopped almonds, toasted
1 tblsp. chopped fresh parsley

In 2-qt. saucepan over medium-high heat, melt butter. Add mushrooms, celery, carrot, green pepper, raisins and bay leaf. Cook until vegetables are tender-crisp.

Stir in chicken broth, cracked wheat, salt, sage and savory. Over high heat bring to a boil. Reduce heat to low. Cover and simmer 20 minutes or until most of the liquid is absorbed. Remove from heat.

Let stand, covered, 5 minutes. Remove bay leaf. With fork fluff pilaf. Garnish with almonds and parsley. Makes 6 servings.

TO MICROWAVE: Use same ingredients, *reducing broth as indicated.*

In 2-qt. microwave-safe casserole place butter, celery, carrot, green pepper, raisins and bay leaf. Cover with lid or plastic wrap, turning back one section to vent steam.

Microwave at high setting (100% power) 3 minutes. Stir in mushrooms. Microwave, uncovered, at high setting 2 to 3 minutes, or until vegetables are tender-crisp.

Stir in *1½ c. hot chicken broth,* cracked wheat, salt, sage and savory. Cover again, and microwave at medium setting (50% power) 15 minutes or until most of the liquid is absorbed, stirring every 5 minutes.

Let stand, covered, 5 minutes. Remove bay leaf. Fluff and garnish as directed.

ZUCCHINI CORN BREAD STUFFING

Use this moist, flavorful dressing to stuff a pork roast or a chicken.

¼ c. butter or regular margarine
2 c. chopped zucchini
1 c. chopped onions
2 tblsp. chopped fresh parsley
1 clove garlic, minced
1 tsp. salt
1 tsp. dried marjoram
⅛ tsp. pepper
2 eggs
3 c. coarsely crumbled corn bread

In 10″ skillet over medium heat, melt butter. Add zucchini and remaining ingredients except eggs and corn bread; cook until tender. Remove from heat.

In medium bowl beat eggs with fork until well blended. Stir in vegetable mixture and corn bread just until combined.

Turn into greased 1½-qt. casserole. Bake in 350° oven 30 minutes or until golden brown. Makes 6 servings.

CARROT-CELERY STUFFING

You won't find bread in this stuffing —just vegetables, herbs and cheese.

½ c. butter or regular margarine
1½ c. shredded carrots
1½ c. finely chopped celery
1 c. finely chopped onions
¼ c. chopped fresh parsley
1 tsp. dried marjoram leaves
1 tsp. Worcestershire sauce
½ tsp. dried rubbed sage
½ tsp. poultry seasoning
¼ tsp. salt
⅛ tsp. pepper
1 c. shredded Swiss cheese (4 oz.)

In 12" skillet over medium heat, melt butter. Stir in remaining ingredients except cheese. Cook, stirring occasionally, until vegetables are tender.

Remove from heat. Stir in cheese until melted. Makes 4 c. or enough stuffing for a 6-lb. chicken.

SPINACH STUFFING

A North Carolina woman's recipe for a quick and moist herb stuffing.

2 lb. fresh spinach, trimmed and cooked, or 2 (10-oz.) pkg. frozen leaf spinach, thawed
½ c. butter or regular margarine
1⅔ c. finely chopped onions
4 c. herb-flavored stuffing mix
½ c. grated Parmesan cheese
½ c. milk
1½ tsp. dried thyme leaves
1 tsp. garlic salt
⅛ tsp. pepper
2 eggs, beaten

Drain spinach well and chop.

In 10" skillet over medium heat, melt butter. Add onions; cook until tender.

In large bowl mix spinach, onion mixture, stuffing mix and remaining ingredients until well blended. Turn into greased 2-qt. casserole.

Bake in 350° oven 20 minutes or until golden brown and heated through. Makes 6 to 8 servings.

RISOTTO

For classic risotto, replace some of the broth with dry white wine.

3 tblsp. butter or regular margarine
½ c. sliced green onions
½ c. shredded carrots
1 clove garlic, minced
1¼ c. uncooked long-grain rice
2¼ c. chicken broth or stock
¼ tsp. salt
⅛ tsp. dried thyme leaves
1 bay leaf
¼ c. chopped fresh parsley

In 3-qt. saucepan over medium heat, melt butter. Add green onions, carrots and garlic. Cook, stirring often, until tender.

Add rice; cook, stirring often, until rice is opaque and most of the butter is absorbed, about 10 minutes.

Stir in chicken broth, salt, thyme and bay leaf. Over high heat bring to a boil. Reduce heat to low. Cover and simmer until most of the liquid is absorbed, about 15 minutes. Remove from heat.

Let stand, covered, 5 minutes. Remove bay leaf. With fork fluff rice. Stir in parsley. Makes 6 servings.

TO MICROWAVE: Use same ingredients, *changing amounts as indicated.*

In 3-qt. microwave-safe casserole place *2 tblsp. butter,* green onions, carrots and garlic. Cover with lid or plastic wrap, turning back one section to vent steam.

Microwave at high setting (100% power) 5 to 7 minutes or until tender, stirring after 3 minutes.

Stir in rice. Cover again, and microwave at high setting 5 minutes or until most of the butter is absorbed, stirring after 3 minutes.

Stir in *2½ c. hot chicken broth,* salt, thyme and bay leaf. Cover again, and microwave at high setting 18 to 20 minutes or until most of the liquid is absorbed, stirring after 10 minutes.

Let stand, covered, 5 minutes. Remove bay leaf. With fork fluff rice. Stir in parsley.

8

Seasonings, Sauces and Salad Dressings

It's so simple to spark the natural flavors of foods with delicate seasonings, velvety sauces and tangy dressings. Often it's just a question of adding a dash of an herb or a spice. Some of the choices are summed up in the chart on the next four pages, showing which herbs and spices best complement the flavors of certain vegetables. In this chapter you'll also find more than 50 recipes for sauces and salad dressings.

Some sauces are full-bodied enough to serve over cooked rice, noodles, meats or poultry. Sour Cream Mushroom Sauce will add flair to baked chicken, and for asparagus and red meat there's buttery Béarnaise Sauce. If you hesitate to make this sauce because you're afraid it will curdle, use our blender recipe; it can't fail.

When you treat yourself to the luxury of a simple butter topping for baby carrots or fresh broccoli, take a few extra minutes to prepare one of our four herb butter recipes. Or try Pesto Butter, made by adding a few spoonfuls of a thick paste of fresh basil, parsley, cheese and nuts to softened butter. Each one can be made in advance and kept in the refrigerator, ready whenever you want to add a special touch to vegetables.

Lighter sauces include Cucumber-Yogurt Sauce, a tangy, one-step sauce that you can use as a salad dressing, a sandwich topping or even a dip. Spicy sauces such as Creole Sauce, Salsa and Marinara Sauce are made with tomatoes, onions and garlic. Once you've tasted the lively flavor of Aioli, you'll think of lots of ways to serve this garlic mayonnaise.

Cheddar-Onion and Blue Cheese toppings are good partners for baked and boiled potatoes, but try them over cauliflower or green beans, too.

Salad dressings offer a multitude of easy ways to vary a simple green salad. Many can be made in a blender, including Italian and Green Goddess dressings. The diet-conscious will savor the piquant flavors of salads dressed with Low-Calorie Creamy French Dressing or Low-Calorie Vinaigrette.

The best-tasting salad dressings usually have been allowed to stand in the refrigerator at least several hours so their flavors can marry. But if you're short of time, by all means enjoy the dressing as soon as you've mixed it.

SEASONINGS FOR VEGETABLES

Vegetable	Herbs		Spices		Blends and Seeds
Anise	Parsley		Paprika		
Artichokes	Bay Leaf Parsley	Tarragon Thyme			Fennel Seed Sesame Seed
Asparagus	Basil Bay Leaf Chives Marjoram	Parsley Savory Tarragon	Paprika		Caraway Seed Fennel Seed Sesame Seed
Beans: Green, Lima and Wax	Basil Chives Cilantro Dill Marjoram Mint	Oregano Parsley Rosemary Savory Tarragon Thyme	Cloves Ginger Nutmeg Paprika Red Pepper		Celery Seed Chili Powder Curry Powder Fennel Seed Mustard Seed Sesame Seed
Beets	Bay Leaf Dill Tarragon		Allspice Cinnamon Cloves	Ginger Nutmeg	Caraway Seed Mustard Seed
Broccoli	Chives Marjoram Oregano	Tarragon Thyme	Mace Nutmeg	Paprika Red Pepper	Mustard Seed Sesame Seed
Brussels Sprouts	Marjoram Sage Savory		Mace Nutmeg		Sesame Seed
Cabbage	Dill Oregano Parsley	Sage Savory Tarragon	Allspice Cloves Mace	Paprika Red Pepper	Caraway Seed Curry Powder Sesame Seed
Carrots	Basil Bay Leaf Chervil Chives Cilantro Dill	Marjoram Mint Oregano Parsley Thyme	Allspice Cinnamon Cloves Ginger Mace Nutmeg		Celery Seed Chili Powder Curry Powder Mustard Seed Sesame Seed
Cauliflower	Basil Chives Dill Parsley	Rosemary Savory Tarragon	Ginger Mace Nutmeg	Paprika Red Pepper	Caraway Seed Celery Seed Curry Powder Sesame Seed

SEASONINGS FOR VEGETABLES

Vegetable	Herbs		Spices	Blends and Seeds
Celeriac	Basil Chives	Dill Parsley	Red Pepper	Curry Powder Mustard Seed Sesame Seed
Celery	Basil Chives Cilantro Marjoram	Oregano Parsley Tarragon Thyme	Paprika Red Pepper	Chili Powder Curry Powder Mustard Seed Sesame Seed
Chinese Cabbage	Chives		Ginger Red Pepper	Sesame Seed
Corn	Basil Chives Parsley Thyme		Mace Nutmeg Paprika Turmeric	Chili Powder Coriander Curry Powder Mustard Seed
Cucumbers	Chives Dill	Mint Parsley	Red Pepper	Curry Powder Mustard Seed
Eggplant	Basil Bay Leaf Chives Cilantro Marjoram Oregano	Parsley Rosemary Sage Savory Thyme	Paprika Red Pepper Turmeric	Celery Seed Chili Powder Curry Powder Sesame Seed
Greens	Marjoram Rosemary	Savory Tarragon	Nutmeg Red Pepper	Curry Powder Mustard Seed Sesame Seed
Jerusalem Artichokes	Oregano Parsley			Curry Powder Mustard Seed Sesame Seed
Jicama	Parsley		Ginger	Cumin Seed Curry Powder
Kohlrabi	Parsley		Ginger Paprika Red Pepper	Celery Seed Mustard Seed Sesame Seed
Leeks	Chives Oregano	Parsley	Red Pepper	Mustard Seed

SEASONINGS FOR VEGETABLES

Vegetable	Herbs		Spices		Blends and Seeds
Mushrooms	Basil Chives Marjoram Oregano	Parsley Tarragon Thyme	Nutmeg Paprika Red Pepper		Caraway Seed Chili Powder Cumin Seed
Okra	Dill Oregano Parsley Thyme		Paprika Red Pepper Turmeric		Celery Seed Chili Powder Cumin Seed Curry Powder
Onions	Basil Marjoram Oregano	Parsley Sage Thyme	Cinnamon Cloves Ginger	Paprika Red Pepper Turmeric	Caraway Seed Chili Powder Cumin Seed Curry Powder
Parsnips	Parsley		Allspice Cinnamon		Chili Powder Sesame Seed
Peas	Basil Bay Leaf Chervil Dill Marjoram	Mint Oregano Savory Tarragon Thyme	Cinnamon		Chili Powder
Peppers	Basil Chives Marjoram	Oregano Parsley Thyme	Red Pepper		Caraway Seed Celery Seed
Potatoes: Sweet	Parsley		Allspice Cinnamon Cloves	Mace Nutmeg	
Potatoes: White	Basil Chives Dill Mint	Parsley Rosemary Thyme	Paprika		Sesame Seed
Pumpkin and Rutabagas	Chives		Allspice Cinnamon Cloves	Ginger Mace Nutmeg	
Salsify	Chives Parsley		Paprika		Celery Seed

SEASONINGS FOR VEGETABLES

Vegetable	Herbs		Spices		Blends and Seeds
Spinach	Basil Chervil Chives Dill Marjoram	Mint Oregano Rosemary Tarragon Thyme	Allspice Cinnamon Mace Nutmeg Red Pepper		Chili Powder Cumin Seed Curry Powder Fennel Seed Sesame Seed
Squash: Summer	Basil Chives Marjoram Oregano	Parsley Sage Savory Thyme	Paprika Red Pepper Turmeric		Mustard Seed Sesame Seed
Squash: Winter	Parsley		Allspice Cinnamon Ginger	Mace Nutmeg Paprika	
Tomatoes	Basil Bay Leaf Chives Cilantro Dill Marjoram	Oregano Parsley Sage Savory Tarragon Thyme	Allspice Cinnamon Cloves Red Pepper Turmeric		Celery Seed Chili Powder Curry Powder Fennel Seed Mustard Seed Sesame Seed
Turnips	Basil Chives Dill Marjoram	Parsley Rosemary Sage	Allspice Cinnamon Paprika Red Pepper		

MEDIUM WHITE SAUCE

To vary this sauce, add 1 tblsp.
chopped fresh dill or parsley.

¼ c. butter or regular margarine
3 tblsp. flour
¼ tsp. salt
⅛ tsp. white pepper
2 c. milk or light cream

In 2-qt. saucepan over medium
heat, melt butter. Using wooden
spoon stir in flour, salt and pepper
until smooth; cook 2 minutes (do not
brown). Gradually stir in milk.
   Cook, stirring constantly, until
mixture boils and thickens. Makes
2 c.

TO MICROWAVE: Use same ingredients,
changing amounts as indicated.
   Place butter in 4-c. glass measure.
Microwave at high setting (100%
power) 1½ to 2 minutes or until
melted. Using wire whisk beat in
4 tblsp. flour, salt and pepper until
smooth. Gradually beat in *1¾ c.*
milk until well blended.
   Microwave at high setting 1 minute; stir. Microwave 4 to 6 minutes
or until mixture boils and thickens,
stirring every 2 minutes.

ONION SAUCE

Use this sauce to enhance a mix
of asparagus and carrots.

2 tblsp. butter or regular margarine
1 small onion, finely chopped
1 tblsp. flour
¼ tsp. salt
⅛ tsp. pepper
1 c. milk

In 1-qt. saucepan over medium
heat, melt butter. Add onion; cook
until tender. Using wooden spoon
stir in flour, salt and pepper until
well blended; cook 2 minutes (do not
brown). Gradually stir in milk.
   Cook, stirring constantly, until
mixture boils and thickens.
Makes 1 c.

TO MICROWAVE: Use same ingredients,
increasing flour as indicated.
   Place butter and onion in 1-qt.
microwave-safe casserole. Microwave
at high setting (100% power) 2 to
3 minutes, or until onion is tender,
stirring after 1 minute.
   Using wire whisk beat in *2 tblsp.*
flour, salt and pepper until well
blended. Gradually beat in milk.
   Microwave at high setting 4 to
6 minutes, or until mixture boils and
thickens, stirring each minute.

CHEDDAR SAUCE

Gruyère or processed cheese
may be substituted for Cheddar.

¼ c. butter or regular margarine
3 tblsp. flour
¼ tsp. salt
⅛ tsp. white pepper
2 c. milk
2 c. shredded sharp Cheddar cheese (8 oz.)
¼ tsp. Worcestershire sauce

In 2-qt. saucepan over medium
heat, melt butter. Using wooden
spoon stir in flour, salt and pepper
until smooth; cook 2 minutes (do not
brown). Gradually stir in milk.
   Cook, stirring constantly, until
mixture boils and thickens. Stir in
cheese and Worcestershire sauce;
continue cooking until cheese melts
(do not boil). Makes 2⅔ c.

TO MICROWAVE: Use same ingredients,
reducing amounts as indicated.
   Place *3 tblsp. butter* in 4-c. glass
measure. Microwave at high setting
(100% power) 1½ to 2 minutes or
until melted. Using wire whisk beat
in flour, salt and pepper until
smooth. Gradually beat in *1½ c.*
milk and Worcestershire sauce until
well blended.
   Microwave at high setting 1 minute; stir. Microwave 5 to 7 minutes
or until mixture boils and thickens,
stirring every 2 minutes.

Stir in cheese and microwave 30 seconds, or until cheese melts. Stir before serving.

SOUR CREAM MUSHROOM SAUCE

A full-bodied sauce, good spooned over rice, noodles or cooked meats.

2 tblsp. butter or regular margarine
¼ lb. mushrooms, sliced (1 c.)
1 tblsp. flour
¼ tsp. salt
⅛ tsp. white pepper
1 c. milk
½ c. dairy sour cream

In 2-qt. saucepan over medium heat, melt butter. Add mushrooms; cook until tender. Using wooden spoon stir in flour, salt and pepper until well blended. Gradually stir in milk.

Cook, stirring constantly, until mixture boils and thickens. Remove from heat.

Stir some of the hot sauce into sour cream. Then stir sour cream mixture back into remaining sauce. Over low heat cook 2 minutes or until heated through. Makes 1½ c.

TO MICROWAVE: Use same ingredients, *increasing flour as indicated.*

Place butter and mushrooms in 1½-qt. microwave-safe casserole. Microwave at high setting (100% power) 2 to 3 minutes, or until mushrooms are tender, stirring each minute.

Using wooden spoon stir in *2 tblsp. flour,* salt and pepper until well blended. Gradually stir in milk.

Microwave at high setting 1 minute; stir. Microwave 3 to 5 minutes or until mixture boils and thickens, stirring every 2 minutes.

Stir some of the hot sauce into sour cream. Then stir sour cream mixture back into remaining sauce. Microwave at medium setting (50% power) 1 minute, until sauce is hot; stir.

BÉARNAISE SAUCE

Wonderful for vegetables or meats, this sauce doesn't skimp on butter.

¼ c. white wine
2 tblsp. tarragon vinegar
1 tblsp. finely chopped onion
1 tsp. chopped fresh parsley
¼ tsp. dried tarragon leaves
Dash pepper
3 egg yolks
¾ c. butter or regular margarine, cut into tblsp.

In 1-qt. saucepan over medium-high heat, cook wine, vinegar, onion, parsley, tarragon and pepper until mixture is reduced by half, about 3 minutes. Remove from heat; strain, reserving wine mixture.

In double-boiler top using wire whisk, beat egg yolks. Rapidly beat in wine mixture.

Place double-boiler top over hot, not boiling, water. Cook, stirring constantly, until egg yolk mixture thickens slightly. Beat in butter, 1 tblsp. at a time, until melted. Continue cooking, stirring constantly, until sauce is light and fluffy.

Serve immediately. Makes 1 c.

TO MICROWAVE: Use same ingredients, *reducing wine as indicated.*

In 1-c. glass measure place *3 tblsp. wine,* vinegar, parsley, tarragon and pepper. Microwave, uncovered, at high setting (100% power) 3 to 5 minutes or until liquid is reduced by half. Strain, reserving wine mixture.

Place ½ c. butter and onion in 1-qt. microwave-safe casserole. Microwave at high setting 2 to 3 minutes or until onion is tender, stirring after 1 minute.

Add wine mixture and egg yolks to butter mixture. Using wire whisk, beat until well blended.

Microwave at medium setting (50% power) 30 to 90 seconds or until thickened, beating with whisk every 30 seconds. Serve as directed.

BLENDER BÉARNAISE SAUCE___

A shortcut version of the classic recipe—you needn't beat by hand.

½ c. butter or regular margarine
1 tblsp. white vinegar
2 egg yolks
1 tblsp. chopped onion
1 tsp. dried tarragon leaves
⅛ tsp. salt
2 drops hot pepper sauce

In 1-qt. saucepan over medium heat, melt butter and heat vinegar until hot. Remove from heat.

In blender container place egg yolks and remaining ingredients; cover. Blend at high speed until smooth.

With blender at high speed, gradually pour butter mixture in steady stream through center of cover into egg yolk mixture. Continue blending until sauce is light and fluffy, stopping several times to scrape down sides of blender.

Serve immediately. Makes 1 c.

HOLLANDAISE SAUCE___
(see photo facing page 182)

Spoon this light, fluffy lemon sauce over vegetables, or serve as a dip.

2 egg yolks
½ c. butter or regular margarine, cut into tblsp.
4½ tsp. lemon juice
⅛ tsp. salt
⅛ tsp. white pepper

In 1-qt. heavy saucepan place all ingredients. Over very low heat cook, stirring constantly with wire whisk, until butter melts and sauce thickens (do not boil). Remove from heat and continue beating 1 minute.

Serve immediately or pour sauce into insulated container to keep until ready to serve. Makes 1 c.

TO MICROWAVE: Use same ingredients, *changing amounts and adding water as indicated.*

In 1-qt. microwave-safe casserole place butter. Microwave at high setting (100% power) 2 to 3 minutes or just until melted.

In small bowl using wire whisk, beat together egg yolks, *4 tsp. lemon juice, 1 tblsp. water,* salt and pepper. Pour egg yolk mixture into melted butter; using wire whisk beat until well blended.

Microwave at medium setting (50% power) 30 to 90 seconds or until thickened, beating with whisk every 30 seconds. Serve as directed.

Blender Hollandaise Sauce: Use same ingredients as basic recipe.

In 1-qt. saucepan over low heat, melt butter. Remove from heat.

In blender container place egg yolks and remaining ingredients; cover. Blend at high speed until smooth.

With blender at high speed, gradually pour butter in steady stream through center of cover into egg yolk mixture. Continue blending until sauce is light and fluffy, stopping several times to scrape down sides of blender.

Serve immediately. Makes ¾ c.

CUCUMBER-YOGURT SAUCE___

A cool contrast for pancakes or burgers; a low-cal dressing, too.

1 (8-oz.) container plain yogurt (1 c.)
½ c. chopped, seeded cucumber
1 tblsp. minced onion
1 tblsp. minced fresh parsley
1 tsp. lemon juice
⅛ tsp. garlic salt

In small bowl stir together all ingredients until well blended. Cover and refrigerate at least 2 hours to blend flavors.

Keeps up to 2 weeks in refrigerator. Makes 1½ c.

CREOLE SAUCE

It's good over pasta, or mixed with shrimp for a southern creole.

2 tblsp. butter or regular margarine
1/4 lb. mushrooms, sliced
1 medium onion, chopped
1 small green pepper, chopped
1 clove garlic, minced
1 (28-oz.) can tomatoes
2/3 c. water
1/4 c. chopped fresh parsley
1/4 c. diced cooked ham
1/4 c. chili sauce
2 tblsp. chopped pimiento-stuffed olives
1 tsp. sugar
1/2 tsp. salt
1/4 tsp. dried thyme leaves
1 bay leaf

In 3-qt. saucepan over medium-high heat, melt butter. Add mushrooms, onion, green pepper and garlic; cook until vegetables are tender.

Add tomatoes and remaining ingredients, stirring to break up tomatoes; cook until mixture comes to a boil. Reduce heat to low. Cover and simmer 45 minutes or until sauce is thickened, stirring occasionally. Remove bay leaf; discard. Makes 4 1/2 c.

TO MICROWAVE: Use same ingredients, *but omit water.*

Place butter, onion, green pepper and garlic in 3-qt. microwave-safe casserole. Cover with lid or plastic wrap, turning back one section to vent steam. Microwave at high setting (100% power) 4 to 5 minutes or until vegetables are tender, stirring every 2 minutes.

Stir in mushrooms. Microwave, uncovered, at high setting 1 1/2 to 2 minutes or until tender, stirring after 1 minute.

Add tomatoes and remaining ingredients; *omit water.* Stir to break up tomatoes. Microwave, uncovered, 17 to 20 minutes, or until sauce is thick, stirring every 5 minutes. Remove bay leaf; discard.

TOMATO SALSA

This hot, spicy Mexican sauce is a good dip for vegetables and chips.

1 (4-oz.) can chopped green chilies, drained
1 large onion, finely chopped
2 cloves garlic, minced
2 c. peeled, seeded, diced tomatoes
3 tblsp. cider vinegar
2 tblsp. vegetable oil
1/2 tsp. salt
1/2 tsp. dried oregano leaves
1/4 tsp. sugar
1/4 tsp. crushed red pepper

In 2-qt. saucepan over high heat, bring all ingredients to a boil. Reduce heat to low; simmer, uncovered, 15 minutes.

Serve warm or cold. Keeps up to 2 weeks in refrigerator. Makes 3 c.

PEANUT-PEPPER SAUCE

Served hot, this is a good sauce for green beans or fried chicken; chilled, it's a flavorful dip.

3/4 c. chicken broth
1/2 c. creamy peanut butter
2 tblsp. finely chopped red or green sweet pepper
1/2 tsp. soy sauce
1/4 tsp. dried thyme leaves
1 clove garlic, crushed

In 1-qt. saucepan over low heat, cook all ingredients until sauce is smooth and heated through, stirring constantly.

Serve hot or cold. Makes 1 1/3 c.

TO MICROWAVE: Use same ingredients.

In 1-qt. microwave-safe casserole place green pepper and garlic. Microwave at high setting (100% power) 30 to 60 seconds or until tender.

Stir in chicken broth and remaining ingredients. Microwave at high setting 2 to 3 minutes or until smooth and heated through, stirring every minute.

Serve as directed.

MARINARA SAUCE

A versatile sauce that complements vegetables, pasta, meat or fish.

2 tblsp. olive or vegetable oil
1 c. finely chopped onions
1 clove garlic, minced
10 medium Italian plum tomatoes, peeled and chopped, or 1 (28-oz.) can Italian plum tomatoes, undrained
1 c. water
⅓ c. grated Parmesan cheese
¼ c. chopped fresh parsley
1 tsp. sugar
1 tsp. dried oregano leaves
1 tsp. dried basil leaves
½ tsp. salt
6 anchovy fillets
1 bay leaf

In 3-qt. saucepan over medium-high heat, heat oil until hot. Add onions and garlic; cook until tender. Stir in tomatoes and remaining ingredients. (If using canned tomatoes, do not add 1 c. water.)

Partially cover and cook 30 minutes, stirring occasionally. Remove bay leaf. Cool sauce slightly.

Pour half of sauce into blender container or food processor bowl using metal blade. Blend or process at high speed until smooth. Repeat with remaining sauce.

Serve hot. Keeps in refrigerator up to 1 week or freezer up to 1 year. Makes 1 qt.

TO MICROWAVE: Use same ingredients, *reducing water as indicated.*

In 3-qt. microwave-safe casserole place oil, onions and garlic. Cover with lid or plastic wrap, turning back one section to vent steam. Microwave at high setting (100% power) 3 to 4 minutes or until vegetables are tender, stirring after 2 minutes.

Add tomatoes, ¾ c. *water,* parsley, sugar, oregano, basil, salt, anchovies, and bay leaf. (If using canned tomatoes, do not add water and use only ¾ c. tomato liquid.)

Microwave, uncovered, at high setting 10 minutes, stirring every 3 minutes. Remove bay leaf. Stir in cheese. Cool slightly.

Pour half of mixture in blender container or food processor bowl using metal blade; cover. Blend at high speed or process until smooth. Repeat with remaining mixture. Pour blended mixture back into same casserole.

Microwave, uncovered, at medium setting (50% power) 5 to 8 minutes or until heated through, stirring after 3 minutes.

Serve as directed.

AIOLI SAUCE

Serve over hot or cold potatoes, or use as a dressing. For a milder flavor, use just one garlic clove.

1 slice firm bread, crust removed
3 tblsp. milk
1 to 3 cloves garlic, quartered
2 egg yolks
¼ tsp. salt
1½ c. olive oil
3 tblsp. lemon juice
Hot water

In small bowl soak bread in milk for 5 minutes. Squeeze out milk.

In blender container or in food processor bowl using metal blade, place bread and garlic; cover. Blend at high speed or process until mixture forms a rough paste.

Add egg yolks and salt. Blend or process until well mixed. With blender at high speed or processor running, gradually pour oil in steady stream through center of cover or through feed tube until mixture is thick. (Mixture should look like mayonnaise.)

With blender or processor running, add lemon juice, 1 tblsp. at a time. Then blend or process in enough hot water, about 3 tblsp., to make a thick sauce.

Pour sauce into bowl. Cover and refrigerate 2 hours to blend flavors.

Keeps up to 2 weeks in refrigerator. Makes 2 c.

TOMATO SAUCE CUBES

A savory sauce that's meant to be frozen, then used as needed.

¼ c. butter or regular margarine
2 tblsp. flour
1 (6-oz.) can tomato paste
1 tblsp. olive or vegetable oil
2 tsp. onion powder
1 tsp. sugar
1 tsp. salt
1 tsp. Dijon-style mustard
½ tsp. dried basil leaves
¼ tsp. garlic powder
¼ tsp. pepper
1 c. water

In 1-qt. saucepan over medium-high heat, melt butter. Remove from heat. Stir in flour until smooth. Stir in tomato paste and remaining ingredients except water until well blended. Gradually stir in water until well blended.

Pour into 8x8x2" baking pan. Cover and freeze until firm. Cut into 16 cubes; place in freezer container. Store in freezer up to 1 year. Makes 16.

Saucy Vegetables: In 2-qt. saucepan over low heat, place 1½ c. cooked fresh vegetables, drained, or 1 (10-oz.) pkg. frozen vegetables, cooked and drained, ¼ c. water and 2 Tomato Sauce Cubes. Over low heat cook, stirring constantly, until vegetables are coated and sauce thickens. Makes 1½ c.

PESTO

(see photo facing page 182)

Freeze this herb sauce to enjoy year 'round over pasta, or blend it with butter to spread over corn.

2 c. tightly packed fresh basil leaves
¾ c. olive or vegetable oil
½ c. grated Parmesan cheese
½ c. lightly packed fresh parsley sprigs
¼ c. pine nuts or walnuts
2 cloves garlic, quartered

In food processor bowl using metal blade, place all ingredients; cover. Process until mixture is finely chopped but not mushy. Spoon into container, covering with a thin coat of oil to prevent from darkening. Cover and refrigerate 2 hours to blend flavors.

Keeps up to 2 weeks in refrigerator. Makes 1¼ c.

TO FREEZE: Line large baking sheet with plastic wrap. Drop Pesto by tablespoonfuls onto plastic wrap. Cover with another sheet of plastic wrap. Freeze until firm, about 2 hours.

Remove pesto cubes and place in freezer container. Cover and store in freezer up to 1 year.

Blender Pesto: Use same ingredients.

In blender container place all ingredients; cover. Blend at high speed until mixture is finely chopped, stopping several times to scrape down sides of blender.

Refrigerate or freeze as directed.

Pesto Butter: In small bowl using mixer at high speed, beat ½ c. softened butter or regular margarine until light and fluffy. Beat in ¼ c. Pesto until well blended. Makes ⅔ c.

SALSA VERDE

A no-cook garlic sauce that's great for new potatoes or broiled fish. Makes a good salad dressing, too.

½ c. lightly packed parsley sprigs
2 tblsp. drained capers
1 tblsp. lemon juice
¼ tsp. dried oregano leaves
⅛ tsp. salt
⅛ tsp. pepper
4 anchovy fillets
2 green onions, sliced
1 clove garlic, quartered
¾ c. olive or vegetable oil

In blender container place all ingredients except oil; cover. Blend at high speed until smooth.

With blender at high speed, gradually pour oil in steady stream through center of cover into parsley mixture. Continue blending until sauce is thick, stopping several times to scrape down sides of blender.

Serve immediately. Makes 1¼ c.

MIXED HERB BUTTER

A blend of basil, dill and tarragon — a good seasoning for green beans.

¼ c. butter or regular margarine, softened
2 tsp. finely chopped onion
2 tsp. chopped fresh basil or ½ tsp. dried basil leaves
2 tsp. chopped fresh dill or ½ tsp. dried dill weed
¼ tsp. dried tarragon leaves, crushed
⅛ tsp. salt

In small bowl using mixer at high speed, beat butter until light and fluffy. Beat in onion and remaining ingredients until well blended. Cover and refrigerate at least 2 hours to blend flavors.

Keeps up to 2 weeks in refrigerator. Makes ¼ c.

DILL BUTTER

Season boiled potatoes with a little of this butter, or serve it melted as a dipping sauce for artichokes.

¼ c. butter or regular margarine, softened
1 tblsp. finely chopped onion
2 tsp. chopped fresh dill or ½ tsp. dried dill weed
⅛ tsp. salt

In small bowl using mixer at high speed, beat butter until light and fluffy. Beat in onion, dill and salt until well blended. Cover and refrigerate at least 2 hours to blend flavors.

Keeps up to 2 weeks in refrigerator. Makes ¼ c.

GARLIC BUTTER

Perfect for topping baked potatoes, and for making garlic bread, too.

¼ c. water
2 cloves garlic, peeled
¼ c. butter or regular margarine, softened

In 1-qt. saucepan over medium heat, bring water and garlic to a boil; boil 2 minutes. Remove garlic and put through garlic press. Set aside.

In small bowl using mixer at high speed, beat butter until light and fluffy. Beat in garlic until well blended. Cover and refrigerate at least 2 hours to blend flavors.

Keeps up to 2 weeks in refrigerator. Makes ¼ c.

BROWN BUTTER

Whether you call it brown butter or buerre noire, this clarified butter tastes great over most vegetables.

6 tblsp. butter

In small saucepan over low heat, slowly melt butter so that the milk solids (white reside) sink to bottom of pan. Gradually pour off yellow liquid (clarified butter) into another small saucepan. Discard milk solids.

Over low heat continue cooking butter until it turns light brown (do not burn).

Serve immediately. Makes ¼ c.

LEMON-PARSLEY BUTTER

Complements the flavor of cooked vegetables as well as broiled fish.

¼ c. butter or regular margarine, softened
1 tblsp. chopped fresh parsley
1 tsp. lemon juice
⅛ tsp. salt
⅛ tsp. pepper

In small bowl using mixer at high speed, beat butter until light and fluffy. Beat in parsley, lemon juice, salt and pepper until well blended. Cover and refrigerate at least 2 hours to blend flavors.

Keeps up to 2 weeks in refrigerator. Makes ¼ c.

BLUE CHEESE TOPPING

Blend just two ingredients—then spread over tomato halves and broil.

1 c. dairy sour cream
¼ c. crumbled blue cheese (2 oz.)

In small bowl stir together sour cream and blue cheese. Cover and refrigerate at least 2 hours to blend flavors.

Keeps up to 2 weeks in refrigerator. Makes 1 c.

SOUR CREAM-DILL TOPPING

A few spoonfuls of this topping will make mashed potatoes special.

1 c. dairy sour cream
2 tblsp. chopped fresh dill or 2 tsp. dried dill weed

In small bowl stir together sour cream and dill. Cover and refrigerate at least 2 hours to blend flavors.

Keeps up to 2 weeks in refrigerator. Makes 1 c.

CHEDDAR-ONION TOPPING

For an easy appetizer, dollop this topping over slices of zucchini.

1 c. shredded sharp Cheddar cheese (4 oz.)
½ c. dairy sour cream
¼ c. butter or regular margarine, softened
2 tblsp. chopped green onions

In small bowl using mixer at medium speed, beat together all ingredients until well blended. Cover and refrigerate at least 2 hours to blend flavors.

Keeps up to 2 weeks in refrigerator. Makes 1¼ c.

FRENCH DRESSING

Light and elegant, this all-purpose dressing should suit anyone's taste.

⅔ c. vegetable oil
⅓ c. red wine vinegar
1 tblsp. water
1 tsp. sugar
1 tsp. Dijon-style mustard
¼ tsp. salt
⅛ tsp. paprika
⅛ tsp. pepper
1 hard-cooked egg, chopped

In blender container place all ingredients; cover. Blend at high speed until smooth. Cover and refrigerate at least 2 hours to blend flavors.

Keeps up to 2 weeks in refrigerator. Makes 1¼ c.

PIQUANT FRENCH DRESSING

Flavored with garlic—a dressing to enliven any mix of greens.

⅔ c. vegetable oil
⅓ c. red wine vinegar
1 tsp. sugar
¾ tsp. dry mustard
½ tsp. salt
Dash pepper
1 clove garlic, minced

In jar with tight-fitting lid place all ingredients. Cover; shake until well mixed. Refrigerate at least 2 hours to blend flavors.

Keeps up to 1 month in refrigerator. Makes 1 c.

SWEET 'N' SOUR DRESSING

To make a relish, combine this dressing with shredded carrots, chunks of pineapple and raisins.

⅔ c. vegetable oil
⅓ c. cider vinegar
3 tblsp. sugar
¼ tsp. salt
¼ tsp. dry mustard

In jar with tight-fitting lid place all ingredients. Cover; shake until well mixed. Refrigerate at least 2 hours to blend flavors.

Keeps up to 1 month in refrigerator. Makes 1 c.

CARAWAY DRESSING

A delicate dressing made with parsley, mustard and caraway seed.

⅓ c. vegetable oil
¼ c. white wine or rice vinegar
2 tblsp. dairy sour cream or plain yogurt
2 tblsp. chopped fresh parsley
1 tblsp. soy sauce
½ tsp. caraway seed
⅛ tsp. dry mustard
1 clove garlic, crushed

In jar with tight-fitting lid place all ingredients. Cover; shake until well mixed. Refrigerate at least 2 hours to blend flavors.

Keeps up to 2 weeks in refrigerator. Makes ⅔ c.

ITALIAN DRESSING

Marinate vegetable kabobs with this herb dressing, then grill or broil.

1⅓ c. vegetable oil
⅔ c. white wine vinegar
½ tsp. salt
½ tsp. dried oregano leaves
½ tsp. dried basil leaves
½ tsp. dried marjoram leaves
¼ tsp. pepper

In blender container place all ingredients; cover. Blend at high speed until smooth. Cover and refrigerate at least 12 hours to blend flavors.

Keeps up to 1 month in refrigerator. Makes 2 c.

CELERY SEED DRESSING

This tangy mixture is a natural with coarsely shredded cabbage.

½ c. vegetable oil
⅓ c. cider vinegar
2 tblsp. sugar
1 tblsp. Dijon-style mustard
1½ tsp. celery seed
¼ tsp. salt
⅛ tsp. pepper
⅛ tsp. paprika

In jar with tight-fitting lid place all ingredients. Cover; shake until well mixed. Refrigerate at least 2 hours to blend flavors.

Keeps up to 1 month in refrigerator. Makes 1 c.

HONEY-ORANGE DRESSING

Good for sliced orange salads, or as a sauce for cooked sliced parsnips.

⅔ c. vegetable oil
⅓ c. honey
3 tblsp. frozen orange juice concentrate, thawed
3 tblsp. lemon juice
½ tsp. dry mustard
¼ tsp. celery salt
¼ tsp. paprika

In blender container place all ingredients; cover. Blend at high speed until smooth. Cover and refrigerate at least 2 hours to blend flavors.

Keeps up to 2 weeks in refrigerator. Makes 1⅓ c.

DECIDEDLY DILL DRESSING

For a simple salad, pour this over sliced cucumbers and onions.

⅔ c. vegetable oil
⅓ c. white wine vinegar
2 tblsp. chopped fresh dill or 2 tsp. dried dill weed
1 tsp. sugar
½ tsp. salt
¼ tsp. pepper
⅛ tsp. garlic powder

In jar with tight-fitting lid place all ingredients. Cover; shake until well mixed. Refrigerate at least 2 hours to blend flavors.

Keeps up to 1 month in refrigerator. Makes 1 c.

GINGER DRESSING

Soy sauce, horseradish and fresh grated ginger create a unique flavor.

¼ c. chili sauce or ketchup
2 tblsp. dry sherry
2 tblsp. water
1 tblsp. soy sauce
2 tsp. dark molasses
1 tsp. grated fresh ginger root
½ tsp. prepared horseradish
⅛ tsp. dry mustard

In jar with tight-fitting lid place all ingredients. Cover; shake until well mixed. Refrigerate at least 2 hours to blend flavors.

Keeps up to 1 month in refrigerator. Makes ¾ c.

ITALIAN TOMATO DRESSING

For a more intense garlic flavor, refrigerate two days before using.

1 (8-oz.) can tomato sauce
½ c. vegetable oil
⅓ c. cider vinegar
¼ c. finely chopped celery
2 tblsp. mayonnaise or salad dressing
1 tsp. sugar
1 tsp. instant minced onion
1 tsp. dry mustard
1 tsp. paprika
½ tsp. salt
½ tsp. dried oregano leaves
½ tsp. Worcestershire sauce
1 small clove garlic, minced

In blender container place all ingredients; cover. Blend at high speed until smooth. Cover and refrigerate at least 2 hours to blend flavors.

Keeps up to 1 month in refrigerator. Makes 2 c.

LOW-CALORIE TOMATO DRESSING

To add even more zip to this recipe, use spicy tomato juice.

1 c. tomato juice
2 tblsp. red wine vinegar
1½ tsp. chopped fresh dill or ½ tsp. dried dill weed
¼ tsp. dry mustard
¼ tsp. salt
¼ tsp. dried basil leaves
¼ tsp. Worcestershire sauce
⅛ tsp. pepper
1 small clove garlic, crushed

In jar with tight-fitting lid, place all ingredients. Cover; shake until well mixed. Refrigerate at least 12 hours to blend flavors.

Keeps up to 1 month in refrigerator. Makes 1¼ c.

FRENCH DRESSING MIX

This mix of dry ingredients will keep up to a year. Add a dash of it to sautéed onions and green peppers.

1 (2-oz.) jar onion powder (¼ c.)
2 tblsp. garlic powder
2 tblsp. sugar
1 tblsp. pepper
2 tsp. paprika
1½ tsp. salt

In jar with tight-fitting lid place all ingredients. Cover; shake until well mixed.

Store, covered, up to one year. Makes enough mix for 12⅔ c. dressing.

French Salad Dressing: In blender container place 1 c. mayonnaise or salad dressing, ½ c. buttermilk, ½ c. ketchup, 2 tblsp. French Dressing Mix, 2 tblsp. vegetable oil and 2 tblsp. red wine vinegar; cover. Blend at high speed until smooth, stopping several times to scrape down sides of blender. Serve immediately or cover and refrigerate at least 2 hours to blend flavors.

Keeps up to 2 weeks in refrigerator. Makes 2⅓ c.

LOW-CALORIE CREAMY FRENCH DRESSING

Less fattening than most, because yogurt replaces the high-calorie oil.

1 (8-oz.) container plain yogurt (1 c.)
⅓ c. tomato juice
1½ tsp. French Dressing Mix (see preceding recipe)
1 tsp. sugar

In small bowl using a wire whisk, beat together all ingredients. Cover and refrigerate at least 12 hours to blend flavors.

Keeps up to 2 weeks in refrigerator. Makes 1⅓ c.

EAST INDIES DRESSING

Turn this creamy curry dressing into a dip by adding ½ c. sour cream.

1 beef bouillon cube
¼ c. boiling water
1 tsp. instant minced onion
½ tsp. curry powder
1 c. mayonnaise or salad dressing

In small bowl dissolve bouillon cube in boiling water. Stir in onion and curry powder. Using wire whisk, gradually beat in mayonnaise until smooth. Cover and refrigerate at least 2 hours to blend flavors.

Keeps up to 1 month in refrigerator. Makes 1¼ c.

BUTTERMILK DRESSING

From Texas, a ranch-style dressing that's one of our favorites.

1 c. buttermilk
1 c. mayonnaise or salad dressing
1 tblsp. chopped fresh dill or 1 tsp. dried dill weed
1 tblsp. chopped fresh parsley
½ tsp. dried basil leaves
¼ tsp. dried tarragon leaves
¼ tsp. Worcestershire sauce
⅛ tsp. garlic powder
⅛ tsp. onion powder

In small bowl using wire whisk, beat together all ingredients. Cover and refrigerate at least 12 hours to blend flavors.

Keeps up to 2 weeks in refrigerator. Makes 2 c.

VINAIGRETTE DRESSING MIX

Keep this mix of seasonings on hand to make fast, fresh dressings.

4 tsp. instant minced onion
2 tsp. salt
1¼ tsp. dried minced garlic
1 tsp. sugar
1 tsp. paprika
1 tsp. pepper
½ tsp. dry mustard

In jar with tight-fitting lid, place all ingredients. Cover; shake until well mixed.

Store, covered, up to one year. Makes enough mix for 5 c. dressing.

Vinaigrette Dressing: In jar with tight-fitting lid, place ⅔ c. olive or vegetable oil, ¼ c. red wine vinegar, 1 tblsp. water and 1½ tsp. Vinaigrette Dressing Mix. Cover; shake until well mixed. Serve immediately or refrigerate at least 2 hours to blend flavors.

Keeps up to 2 weeks in refrigerator. Makes 1 c.

LOW-CALORIE VINAIGRETTE

For a cheesy dressing, just add 2 tblsp. grated Parmesan cheese.

1 c. tomato juice
2 tblsp. lemon juice
2 tblsp. red wine vinegar
1½ tsp. Vinaigrette Dressing Mix (see previous recipe)

In jar with tight-fitting lid place all ingredients. Cover; shake until well mixed. Refrigerate at least 2 hours to blend flavors.

Keeps up to 1 month in refrigerator. Makes 1¼ c.

HOT BACON DRESSING

Toss shredded romaine or spinach in this dressing to make a hot salad.

6 slices bacon, diced
⅓ c. cider vinegar
3 tblsp. sugar
2 tblsp. water
¼ tsp. salt
¼ tsp. dry mustard

In 10″ skillet over medium-high heat, cook bacon until browned. Drain bacon on paper towels. Pour off all but ¼ c. bacon drippings.

Add vinegar, sugar, water, salt and mustard to bacon drippings. Over medium-high heat cook, stirring constantly, until sugar is dissolved. Stir in bacon. Serve hot. Makes ¾ c.

CITRUS DRESSING

Grapefruit juice, ginger and sour cream make a sweet, tangy dressing.

½ c. dairy sour cream
6 tblsp. grapefruit juice
2 tsp. sugar
¼ tsp. ground ginger

In small bowl using wire whisk, beat together all ingredients. Cover and refrigerate at least 2 hours to blend flavors.

Keeps up to 2 weeks in refrigerator. Makes 1 c.

CREAMY FRENCH DRESSING

A basic dressing for greens, this is good on mixed fruits, too!

1 c. mayonnaise or salad dressing
2 tblsp. lemon juice
1 tblsp. sugar
1 tblsp. milk
1 tsp. paprika
½ tsp. salt
½ tsp. dry mustard
⅛ tsp. pepper

In small bowl using wire whisk, beat together all ingredients. Cover and refrigerate at least 2 hours to blend flavors.

Keeps up to 1 month in refrigerator. Makes 1¼ c.

Creamy Garlic French Dressing: Prepare as directed, adding 1 small clove garlic, minced. Makes 1¼ c.

RUSSIAN DRESSING

Add bean sprouts or sauerkraut to make a super sandwich topping.

1 c. mayonnaise or salad dressing
⅓ c. chili sauce or ketchup
2 tsp. lemon juice
1 tsp. sugar
⅛ tsp. onion powder
3 drops hot pepper sauce

In small bowl using wire whisk, beat together all ingredients. Cover and refrigerate at least 12 hours to blend flavors.

Keeps up to 1 month in refrigerator. Makes 1⅓ c.

CRUNCHY THOUSAND ISLAND DRESSING

This vegetable and mayonnaise dressing is ideal for a chef's salad.

1 c. mayonnaise or salad dressing
½ c. chili sauce
⅓ c. finely chopped celery
2 tblsp. sweet pickle relish
2 tblsp. chopped pimiento-stuffed olives
1 tsp. instant minced onion
1 tsp. Worcestershire sauce
¼ tsp. paprika
3 drops hot pepper sauce
1 hard-cooked egg, chopped

In small bowl using wire whisk, beat together all ingredients. Cover and refrigerate at least 12 hours to blend flavors.

Keeps up to 2 weeks in refrigerator. Makes 2¼ c.

COUNTRY CREAM DRESSING

An easy dressing for macaroni salad or for carrot or cabbage slaw.

2 c. dairy sour cream
½ c. sugar
6 tblsp. cider vinegar
1 tblsp. milk
1 tsp. salt
½ tsp. dry mustard
¼ tsp. onion powder
⅛ tsp. pepper

In small bowl using wire whisk, beat together all ingredients. Cover and refrigerate at least 2 hours to blend flavors.

Keeps up to 1 month in refrigerator. Makes 2¼ c.

CREAMY HORSERADISH DRESSING

This dressing makes a good spread for sliced roast beef or ham.

1 c. mayonnaise or salad dressing
3 tblsp. milk
4½ tsp. prepared horseradish
¼ tsp. salt
¼ tsp. dry mustard
Dash pepper

In small bowl using wire whisk, beat together all ingredients. Cover and refrigerate at least 12 hours to blend flavors.

Keeps up to 1 month in refrigerator. Makes 1 c.

CREAMY CAESAR DRESSING

Ladle this garlic-cheese dressing on lettuce; garnish with croutons.

1 c. mayonnaise or salad dressing
3 tblsp. grated Parmesan cheese
3 tblsp. milk
2 tblsp. red wine vinegar
½ tsp. sugar
1 small clove garlic, minced

In small bowl using wire whisk, beat together all ingredients. Cover and refrigerate at least 12 hours to blend flavors.

Keeps up to 1 month in refrigerator. Makes 1¼ c.

CREAMY ITALIAN DRESSING

This is a creamy version of the classic oil-and-vinegar dressing.

1 c. mayonnaise or salad dressing
¼ c. grated Parmesan cheese
2 tblsp. red wine vinegar
1 tblsp. sugar
¼ tsp. salt
¼ tsp. dried oregano leaves
¼ tsp. dried basil leaves
¼ tsp. dried marjoram leaves
⅛ tsp. onion powder
⅛ tsp. pepper
1 small clove garlic, minced

In small bowl using wire whisk, beat together all ingredients. Cover and refrigerate at least 12 hours to blend flavors.

Keeps up to 1 month in refrigerator. Makes 1¼ c.

CREAMY GARLIC DRESSING

You can use your blender to make this; let it mince the garlic for you.

1 c. mayonnaise or salad dressing
3 tblsp. milk
2 tblsp. red wine vinegar
½ tsp. sugar
¼ tsp. salt
¼ tsp. onion powder
⅛ tsp. black pepper
1 small clove garlic, minced

In small bowl using wire whisk, beat together all ingredients. Cover and refrigerate at least 12 hours to blend flavors.

Keeps up to 1 month in refrigerator. Makes 1⅓ c.

SWEET-SOUR BACON DRESSING

For a German-style salad, toss this with macaroni twists and celery.

4 slices bacon, diced
1 small onion, finely chopped
3 tblsp. sugar
3 tblsp. white wine vinegar
1⅓ c. mayonnaise or salad dressing
2 tblsp. milk

In 10″ skillet over medium-high heat cook bacon until browned. Drain bacon on paper towels. Pour off all but 1 tblsp. bacon drippings.

Over medium heat cook onion in bacon drippings until tender. Add sugar and vinegar. Cook, stirring frequently, until sugar dissolves. Cool.

In small bowl using wire whisk, beat onion mixture into mayonnaise and milk; stir in bacon. Cover and refrigerate at least 2 hours to blend flavors.

Keeps up to 1 month in refrigerator. Makes 1½ c.

COTTAGE-BLUE CHEESE DRESSING

To make this dressing extra-smooth, prepare it in a food processor.

⅔ c. mayonnaise or salad dressing
⅓ c. large-curd cottage cheese
2 tblsp. milk
2 tblsp. cider vinegar
⅛ tsp. salt
3 drops hot pepper sauce
1 (4-oz.) pkg. blue cheese, crumbled

In small bowl using wire whisk, beat together all ingredients except blue cheese. Fold in blue cheese. Cover and refrigerate at least 12 hours to blend flavors.

Keeps up to 2 weeks in refrigerator. Makes 1⅔ c.

HERBED YOGURT DRESSING

In this herb-garlic dressing, yogurt replaces some of the mayonnaise.

2 c. plain yogurt
¼ c. mayonnaise or salad dressing
¼ c. chopped fresh dill or 4 tsp. dried dill weed
¼ c. chopped fresh parsley
2 green onions, chopped
1 small clove garlic, minced
2 tblsp. lemon juice
2 tsp. sugar

In small bowl using wire whisk, beat together all ingredients. Cover and refrigerate at least 12 hours to blend flavors.

Keeps up to 2 weeks in refrigerator. Makes 2⅓ c.

CRUNCHY COTTAGE CHEESE DRESSING

Chopped green pepper and radishes give this relish-style dressing extra crunch. Great over baked potatoes!

½ c. mayonnaise or salad dressing
½ c. large-curd cottage cheese
¼ c. finely chopped green pepper
¼ c. finely chopped radishes
2 tblsp. minced onion
1 tblsp. milk
½ tsp. sugar
½ tsp. salt
⅛ tsp. paprika
⅛ tsp. pepper
4 drops hot pepper sauce

In small bowl stir together all ingredients until well blended. Cover and refrigerate at least 12 hours to blend flavors.

Keeps up to 2 weeks in refrigerator. Makes 1⅔ c.

CUCUMBER DRESSING

A mayonnaise-based dressing, dotted with bits of cucumber and onion.

1 large cucumber, cut up
1 small onion, cut up
2 c. mayonnaise or salad dressing
3 tblsp. milk
2 tblsp. lemon juice
1 clove garlic, minced

Using coarse blade of food grinder grind cucumber and onion. Drain well.

Place cucumber mixture in small bowl. Stir in mayonnaise and remaining ingredients until well blended. Cover and refrigerate at least 2 hours to blend flavors.

Keeps up to 2 weeks in refrigerator. Makes 3 c.

CREAMY CUCUMBER-DILL DRESSING

(see photo facing page 182)

Naturally delicious — a marriage of dill, cucumbers and sour cream!

1 c. dairy sour cream
½ c. chopped, seeded cucumber
2 tblsp. chopped fresh dill or 2 tsp. dried dill weed
1 tblsp. minced onion
1 tblsp. lemon juice
2 tsp. sugar
⅛ tsp. garlic salt

In bowl stir together all ingredients until well blended. Cover and refrigerate at least 12 hours to blend flavors.

Keeps up to 2 weeks in refrigerator. Makes 1⅓ c.

GREEN GODDESS DRESSING

Use your blender to prepare this classic dressing in a jiffy.

1 c. mayonnaise or salad dressing
¾ c. lightly packed fresh parsley sprigs
3 anchovy fillets
2 green onions, cut up
1 small clove garlic, quartered
3 tblsp. milk
2 tblsp. lemon juice
1 tsp. dried tarragon leaves
½ tsp. sugar
¼ tsp. salt
⅛ tsp. pepper
½ c. dairy sour cream

In blender container place all ingredients except sour cream; cover. Blend at high speed until smooth, stopping several times to scrape down sides of blender.

Pour into bowl; fold in sour cream. Cover and refrigerate at least 12 hours to blend flavors.

Keeps up to 2 weeks in refrigerator. Makes 1¾ c.

CUCUMBER-BLUE CHEESE DRESSING

This one-step salad dressing makes a good topping for hamburgers.

2 c. mayonnaise or salad dressing
1 (4-oz.) pkg. blue cheese, crumbled
1 c. peeled, seeded, grated cucumbers (about 1½ cucumbers)
2 tblsp. lemon juice
1 tblsp. milk
1 tsp. sugar
½ tsp. onion powder
¼ tsp. salt

In medium bowl stir together all ingredients until well blended. Cover and refrigerate at least 12 hours to blend flavors.

Keeps up to 2 weeks in refrigerator. Makes 3 c.

9

Goodies with Goodness

There's nothing like the aroma that fills the house when you're baking, and anyone who finds it hard to resist homemade breads, cookies and cakes will appreciate baked goods made with carrots, squash and pumpkin—even those who claim that they really don't care for vegetables.

It's hard to imagine anyone turning down a slice of coffee bread the likes of Whole-wheat Carrot and Walnut Twists. The recipe makes two large twists—one just isn't enough. Unless you make a point of it, your children probably won't notice that the tea bread they love so much is made with zucchini or butternut squash. The Raised Corn Muffins pictured following page 86 are made with whole-kernel corn, and you can use leftover mashed potatoes to make a beautiful batch of Potato Cinnamon Rolls.

Some good things just don't change, and your grandmother may have made loaves of potato bread from a recipe similar to the one in this chapter. You can shape the dough into balls and bake them as dinner rolls, then freeze them and reheat as needed. Crunchy Onion Twists, made with lots of chopped onion, are crisp-crusted and chewy, like little loaves of French bread. They're great for dunking, so serve them with soup or stew.

Easy drop cookies can be made with shredded carrots, zucchini or cooked pumpkin. The cookie jar will empty in a flash when you fill it with Chocolate Carrot Krinkles and Zucchini-Nut Chip Cookies. Pumpkin-Pecan Cupcakes are a good choice for a lunch box dessert because they need no frosting; they're light, tender and sweetly delicious.

Rich, tender-crumbed cakes made with various vegetables and flavored with chocolate have long been common treats in country kitchens. The sampling in this chapter includes an assortment of truly delicious cakes that contain mashed potatoes, pumpkin, beets and even sauerkraut.

At holiday time, consider serving spicy Winter Squash Pie, Sweet Potato Pie or Puffed Pumpkin Custard for dessert. Even if you still prefer pumpkin pie, try cooking it in the microwave oven or baking the filling in individual tart shells. You'll also find recipes for Pumpkin Swirl Cheesecake and Carrot Cheesecake, each one a perfect example of creamy cheesecake at its best.

SQUMPKIN BREAD

An Iowa woman invented this recipe when she substituted squash for pumpkin in her sister's recipe.

3½ c. sifted flour
3 c. sugar
1½ tsp. salt
1½ tsp. baking soda
1 tsp. ground cinnamon
1 tsp. ground nutmeg
1 c. vegetable oil
4 eggs
2 c. mashed, cooked butternut squash
⅔ c. water

Into large bowl sift together first 6 ingredients; set aside.

In medium bowl stir oil and remaining ingredients until well blended. Stir into dry ingredients, mixing just until moistened.

Pour batter into 2 greased and waxed paper-lined 9x5x3″ loaf pans.

Bake in 350° oven 1 hour 15 minutes, or until toothpick inserted in center comes out clean.

Cool in pans 10 minutes. Remove; cool completely on racks. Makes 2 loaves.

ZUCCHINI NUT BREAD

To vary the flavor, you can stir in chopped peanuts in place of pecans.

2 c. sifted flour
1 tsp. ground cinnamon
½ tsp. salt
½ tsp. baking soda
¼ tsp. baking powder
2 eggs
1⅓ c. sugar
⅔ c. vegetable oil
2 tsp. vanilla
1⅓ c. shredded zucchini
½ c. chopped pecans
Confectioners' sugar

Into large bowl sift together first 5 ingredients; set aside.

In another large bowl using mixer at medium speed, beat eggs until foamy. Gradually add sugar and then oil, mixing well after each addition. Beat in vanilla.

Reduce speed to low; beat in dry ingredients until well blended. With spoon stir in zucchini and pecans. Pour batter into greased 9x5x3″ loaf pan.

Bake in 350° oven 1 hour 15 minutes, or until toothpick inserted in center comes out clean.

Cool in pan 10 minutes. Remove; cool completely on rack.

Sprinkle with confectioners' sugar. Makes 1 loaf.

WHEAT GERM-ZUCCHINI BREAD

A crunchy loaf made with walnuts, sesame seed and wheat germ.

2½ c. sifted flour
2 tsp. salt
2 tsp. baking soda
½ tsp. baking powder
1 c. granulated sugar
1 c. packed brown sugar
1 c. vegetable oil
1 tsp. maple flavoring
3 eggs
2 c. shredded zucchini
1 c. chopped walnuts
½ c. wheat germ
½ c. sesame seed

Into large bowl sift together flour, salt, baking soda and baking powder; set aside.

In medium bowl using mixer at medium speed, beat granulated sugar, brown sugar, oil, maple flavoring and eggs until thick and foamy.

Reduce speed to low; beat in dry ingredients until moistened. With spoon stir in zucchini and remaining ingredients. Pour batter into 2 greased and waxed paper-lined 9x5x3″ loaf pans.

Bake in 350° oven 1 hour, or until toothpick inserted in center comes out clean.

Cool in pans 10 minutes. Remove; cool completely on racks. Makes 2 loaves.

WHOLE-WHEAT ZUCCHINI BREAD

Mildly spiced, these loaves are a good choice for holiday giving.

3 c. shredded zucchini
2 c. sifted flour
1 c. stirred whole-wheat flour
1 tsp. baking soda
1 tsp. ground cinnamon
½ tsp. salt
¼ tsp. baking powder
3 eggs
2 c. sugar
1 c. vegetable oil
1 tsp. vanilla
1 c. chopped walnuts

Place zucchini in dish towel; wrap and twist to squeeze out as much liquid as possible; set aside.

In large bowl stir together flour, whole-wheat flour, baking soda, cinnamon, salt and baking powder; set aside.

In another bowl using mixer at medium speed, beat eggs, sugar, oil and vanilla until well mixed.

Reduce speed to low and beat in zucchini and dry ingredients. With spoon stir in walnuts.

Spread batter in 2 greased 8½x4½x2⅝" or 9x5x3" loaf pans.

Bake in 350° oven 1 hour, or until loaves are golden brown and toothpick inserted in center comes out clean.

Cool in pans 10 minutes. Remove; cool completely on racks. Makes 2 loaves.

GREEN ONION BISCUITS

These tender and flaky biscuits have a delicate onion flavor.

1 tblsp. butter or regular margarine
1 c. sliced green onions
2 c. sifted flour
4 tsp. baking powder
2 tsp. sugar
½ tsp. onion salt
½ tsp. cream of tartar
½ c. shortening
⅔ c. milk

In small skillet over medium heat, melt butter. Add green onions; cook until barely tender. Set aside.

Into large bowl sift together flour, baking powder, sugar, onion salt and cream of tartar. With pastry blender cut in shortening until mixture forms coarse crumbs.

Add green onions and milk. With fork quickly mix just until mixture forms soft dough and leaves side of bowl.

Turn dough out onto lightly floured surface and knead 10 strokes to mix thoroughly. Roll dough ¾" thick. With floured 2" biscuit cutter cut dough.

On ungreased baking sheet place biscuits 1" apart. Bake in 450° oven 12 minutes or until golden brown. Serve warm. Makes 14 biscuits.

CARROT-RAISIN TEA MUFFINS

(see photo on back jacket)

Firm, even-textured muffins that bake to a rich brown color.

3 c. sifted flour
1 tsp. baking soda
½ tsp. salt
½ tsp. ground cinnamon
1¾ c. sugar
1 c. vegetable oil
¼ c. milk
1 tblsp. vanilla
3 eggs
2½ c. shredded carrots
1 c. raisins
1 c. chopped walnuts (optional)

Into large bowl sift together flour, baking soda, salt and cinnamon; set aside.

In another large bowl using mixer at medium speed, beat sugar, oil, milk, vanilla and eggs 2 minutes.

Reduce speed to low; beat in dry ingredients until well blended. With spoon stir in carrots, raisins and walnuts until blended.

Spoon batter into 28 paper-lined 2½" muffin-pan cups, filling two-thirds full.

Bake in 375° oven 20 to 25 minutes or until toothpick inserted in center comes out clean. Remove from pans. Serve warm or cold. Makes 28 muffins.

Carrot-Raisin Tea Bread: Prepare batter as directed.

Spoon batter into 2 greased and floured 8½x4½x2⅝" loaf pans.

Bake in 325° oven 1 hour 10 minutes or until toothpick inserted in center comes out clean.

Cool in pans 10 minutes. Remove; cool completely on racks. Serve warm or cold. Makes 2 loaves.

RAISED CORN MUFFINS

(see photo following page 86)

Doubly good, because they're studded with kernels of corn.

2 c. milk
1½ c. yellow corn meal
½ c. shortening
¼ c. sugar
¼ c. honey
1 tsp. salt
1 pkg. active dry yeast
¼ c. warm water (105-115°)
2 eggs
4¾ c. sifted flour
1½ c. cooked corn

In 2-qt. saucepan over medium heat scald milk. Pour into large bowl. Stir in corn meal, shortening, sugar, honey and salt. Cool to lukewarm.

In small bowl dissolve yeast in warm water. Add to corn meal mixture with eggs and 2 c. flour. Using mixer at medium speed beat 2 minutes. With spoon stir in remaining flour until smooth. Stir in corn.

Cover with towel and let rise in warm place until doubled, about 45 minutes.

With spoon stir down batter; spoon into 36 greased 2½" muffin-pan cups. Let rise, uncovered, until doubled, about 45 minutes.

Bake in 400° oven 15 minutes or until golden brown. Serve warm. Makes 36 muffins.

BACON-ONION STICKS

An "old-country" favorite passed down through a Latvian farm family.

2 pkg. active dry yeast
2 c. lukewarm milk (105-115°)
½ c. butter or regular margarine, melted
1 tsp. salt
1 tsp. sugar
1 tsp. ground cardamom
5½ to 6 c. sifted flour
1 lb. bacon, diced
1¼ c. chopped onions
1 egg, beaten
Coarse salt

In large bowl dissolve yeast in warm milk. Add butter, salt, sugar, cardamom and 2½ c. flour to milk mixture. Using mixer at medium speed beat 2 minutes.

With spoon stir in enough remaining flour to make a soft dough. Turn dough out onto lightly floured surface. Knead about 8 to 10 minutes or until smooth and elastic.

Place in greased large bowl, turning dough over so that top is greased. Cover with towel; let rise in warm place until doubled, about 1 hour and 15 minutes.

Meanwhile, in 12" skillet over medium heat, cook bacon and onions until bacon is browned and onions are tender. Drain on paper towels. Cool completely.

Punch down dough. Cover and let rest 10 minutes.

On lightly floured surface knead bacon mixture into dough. Roll dough into 14" square. Brush dough with egg and sprinkle with coarse salt.

Cut dough in half to make 2 rectangles. Cut each rectangle into thirds crosswise to make smaller rectangles. Cut each small rectangle into 6 sticks about 4½" long.

Place sticks 2" apart on greased baking sheets. Cover and let rise until doubled, about 30 to 45 minutes.

Bake in 375° oven 15 minutes or until golden brown. Serve warm. Makes 36 sticks.

CRUNCHY ONION TWISTS
(see photo following page 86)

Similar in texture to French bread, these rolls stay crisp when reheated.

1 pkg. active dry yeast
1 c. warm water (105-115°)
2 tsp. sugar
1 tsp. salt
2¾ to 3¼ c. sifted flour
3 tblsp. butter or regular margarine
1½ c. chopped onions
3 tblsp. butter or regular margarine, melted
Paprika

In large bowl dissolve yeast in warm water. Add sugar, salt and 1½ c. flour. Using mixer at medium speed beat 2 minutes.

With spoon stir in enough remaining flour to make a soft dough. Turn dough out onto lightly floured surface. Knead about 5 minutes or until smooth and elastic.

Place in greased large bowl, turning dough over so that top is greased. Cover with towel; let rise in warm place until doubled, about 1 hour.

Meanwhile, in 10" skillet over medium heat, melt 3 tblsp. butter. Add onions; cook until tender but not brown. Remove from heat; set aside.

Punch down dough. Cover and let rest 10 minutes.

On lightly floured surface roll dough into 16x12" rectangle. Spread half of the onions in a 3" lengthwise strip down center of dough. Fold one-third of dough over onions. Spread remaining onions on top, then fold over remaining third of dough. Pat gently to flatten.

Cut dough crosswise into 16 strips. Twist each strip twice and place strips 2" apart on greased large baking sheet.

Cover and let rise until doubled, about 30 minutes. Brush twists with half of the melted butter. Sprinkle with paprika.

Bake in 375° oven 25 minutes or until golden brown. Brush with remaining melted butter. Serve warm. Makes 16 twists.

QUICK GARLIC LOAVES
(see photo following page 86)

A pretty pull-apart biscuit bread that bakes up quickly and easily.

3¼ c. sifted flour
2 tblsp. sugar
4 tsp. baking powder
1 tsp. salt
1 (3-oz.) pkg. cream cheese
¼ c. butter or regular margarine
1 c. milk
1 egg
1 tblsp. butter or regular margarine, melted
4 cloves garlic, minced
¼ tsp. paprika
1 egg yolk
2 tsp. water

Into large bowl sift together flour, sugar, baking powder and salt. With pastry blender cut in cream cheese and ¼ c. butter until mixture forms coarse crumbs.

In small bowl beat together milk and egg. Add to flour mixture. With fork quickly mix just until mixture forms soft dough and leaves side of bowl.

Turn dough onto lightly floured surface and knead 15 strokes to mix thoroughly. Divide dough in half.

Roll each dough half into 12x6" rectangle.

Brush each rectangle with melted butter, then sprinkle with garlic and paprika. Make 2" cuts at 1" intervals along both long sides of each rectangle. Fold strips alternately from each side, over center of dough.

Carefully transfer each loaf to a greased large baking sheet. In small bowl beat together egg yolk and water; brush over loaves.

Bake in 375° oven 20 minutes or until golden brown. Serve warm. Makes 2 loaves.

POTATO CINNAMON ROLLS

Make a batch of two dozen spicy buns drizzled with a simple icing.

2 pkg. active dry yeast
1 c. warm water (105-115°)
¾ c. warm unseasoned mashed potatoes
½ c. packed brown sugar
⅓ c. nonfat dry milk
1 tsp. salt
2 eggs
½ c. butter or regular margarine, softened
5 to 5½ c. sifted flour
2 to 3 tblsp. butter, melted
¾ c. granulated sugar
2 tsp. ground cinnamon
Confectioners' Sugar Icing (recipe follows)

In large bowl dissolve yeast in warm water. Add potatoes, brown sugar, dry milk, salt, eggs, ½ c. butter and 2 c. flour. Using mixer at medium speed beat 2 minutes.

With spoon stir in enough remaining flour to make a soft dough. Turn dough out onto lightly floured surface. Knead about 5 minutes or until smooth and elastic.

Place in greased large bowl, turning dough over so that top is greased. Cover with towel; let rise in warm place until doubled, about 1 hour.

Punch down dough. Cover and let rest 10 minutes. Divide dough in half.

On lightly floured surface roll each half into 18x12" rectangle. Brush each half with melted butter.

In small bowl stir together sugar and cinnamon; sprinkle over buttered dough. Starting with one short side, roll up each rectangle, jelly-roll fashion. Pinch seams to seal.

Cut each roll into 12 (1") slices. Place slices cut-side down in 24 greased 3" muffin-pan cups. Cover with towel; let rise in warm place until doubled, about 30 minutes.

Bake in 350° oven 20 minutes or until golden brown. Remove from pans. Cool on racks 10 minutes.

Meanwhile, prepare Confectioners' Sugar Icing.

Drizzle rolls with icing. Serve warm. Makes 24 rolls.

Confectioners' Sugar Icing: In bowl stir 1½ c. sifted confectioners' sugar, 2 tblsp. milk and ¼ tsp. vanilla until smooth.

BRIOCHE MUSHROOM BRAID

(see photo following page 86)

This big, beautiful ring of braided yeast bread has a mushroom filling.

1 pkg. active dry yeast
Water
4 tsp. sugar
1 tsp. salt
½ c. butter or regular margarine
3 eggs
3¼ to 3½ c. sifted flour
Mushroom Filling (recipe follows)
1 tblsp. butter or regular margarine, melted
1 egg yolk

In small bowl dissolve yeast in ½ c. warm water (105-115°); set aside.

In large bowl using mixer at medium speed, beat sugar, salt and ½ c. butter until light and fluffy. Beat in eggs until well blended. Reduce speed to low; beat in yeast mixture and 1 c. flour until well blended.

Stir in enough remaining flour to make a soft dough. Turn dough out onto lightly floured surface. Knead about 5 minutes or until smooth and elastic.

Place in greased large bowl, turning dough over so that top is greased. Cover with towel; let rise in warm place until doubled, about 1½ hours.

Punch down dough. Cover with plastic wrap; refrigerate overnight.

Prepare Mushroom Filling; set aside.

Again, punch down dough. Divide dough in half. On lightly floured surface roll each half into 18x10" rectangle. Brush each rectangle with melted butter.

Spread half of the Mushroom Filling on each rectangle, to within ½" of sides. Starting with one long side, roll up each rectangle, jelly-roll fashion. Pinch seams to seal.

Twist dough rolls together. On greased baking sheet shape twisted rope into a ring. Pinch ends to join. Cover with towel; let rise in warm place until doubled, about 1 hour.

In small bowl beat together egg yolk and 1 tblsp. water. Brush egg yolk mixture over ring.

Bake in 350° oven 40 minutes or until golden brown. Serve warm. Makes 1 (12") loaf.

Mushroom Filling: In 10" skillet over medium-high heat, melt ¼ c. butter or regular margarine. Add 1 lb. mushrooms, chopped, ½ c. chopped onion, ¼ c. chopped fresh parsley, ½ tsp. dried marjoram, ¼ tsp. salt and ⅛ tsp. pepper.

Cook until vegetables are tender and all liquid is evaporated. Remove from heat. Cool completely.

POTATO BREAD

You can use this versatile recipe to make either rolls or loaves.

1 large potato, peeled and diced
Water
2 pkg. active dry yeast
⅓ c. nonfat dry milk
3 tblsp. sugar
3 tblsp. shortening
1 tblsp. salt
6½ to 7 c. sifted flour

In 2-qt. saucepan place potato and 2 c. water. Cover; over medium heat cook until potato is tender. Remove from heat. Drain potato, reserving liquid. Mash potato.

Add enough water to reserved liquid to make 2 c. Cool to 105-115°.

Pour liquid into large bowl. Dissolve yeast in liquid.

Add dry milk, sugar, shortening, salt, 3 c. flour and mashed potato. Using mixer at medium speed beat 2 minutes.

With spoon stir in enough remaining flour to make a soft dough. Turn dough out onto lightly floured surface. Knead about 8 minutes or until smooth and elastic.

Place in greased large bowl, turning dough over so that top is greased. Cover with towel; let rise in warm place until doubled, about 1 hour.

Punch down dough. Cover and let rest 10 minutes. Divide dough in half.

On lightly floured surface roll each half into 12x8" rectangle. Starting with long end, tightly roll dough, jelly-roll fashion; pinch seam and ends to seal. Place seam-side down into 2 (9x5x3") greased loaf pans.

Cover and let rise until doubled, about 45 minutes. Dust tops of loaves with flour.

Bake in 375° oven 35 minutes, or until loaves are golden and sound hollow when tapped with fingers. Remove from pans; cool on racks. Makes 2 loaves.

Potato Pan Rolls: Prepare dough as directed and let rise.

Punch down dough. Cover and let rest 10 minutes. Shape dough into 48 balls. Dip balls into ¼ c. melted butter or regular margarine. Place in greased 15½x10½" open roasting pan.

Cover; let rise until doubled, about 30 minutes. Do not dust with flour. Bake in 425° oven 15 to 20 minutes or until golden brown. Remove from pan. Serve warm. Makes 48 rolls.

WHOLE-WHEAT CARROT AND WALNUT TWISTS

For a warm snack, pop a slice in the toaster-oven for 5 minutes or for 30 seconds in the microwave oven.

2 pkg. active dry yeast
1 c. warm water (105-115°)
2 c. stirred whole-wheat flour
¾ c. mashed or puréed, cooked carrots
½ c. sugar
½ c. butter or regular margarine, softened
⅓ c. nonfat dry milk
1 tsp. salt
2 eggs
3½ to 4 c. sifted flour
1 c. raisins
Nut Filling (recipe follows)
Confectioners' Sugar Icing (see Index)

In large bowl dissolve yeast in warm water. Add whole-wheat flour, carrots, sugar, butter, dry milk, salt and eggs.

Using mixer at medium speed, beat carrot mixture 2 minutes, until smooth and well blended.

Stir in enough flour to make soft dough. Turn dough out onto lightly floured surface. Knead 5 minutes. Knead in raisins; continue kneading until smooth and elastic.

Place in greased large bowl, turning dough over so that top is greased. Cover with towel; let rise in warm place until doubled, about 1 hour.

Meanwhile, prepare Nut Filling.

Punch down dough. Cover and let rest 10 minutes. Divide dough in half.

On lightly floured surface roll out each half into 16x12″ rectangle. Sprinkle each rectangle with half of the filling.

Starting with one long side, roll up each rectangle, jelly-roll fashion. Pinch seams and ends to seal.

Place each roll diagonally on greased baking sheet, seam-side down. With kitchen scissors cut each roll almost through at ¾″ intervals. Gently pull slices alternately to the left and to the right.

Cover with towel; let rise in warm place until doubled, about 30 minutes.

Bake in 350° oven 20 minutes or until golden brown. Remove from baking sheets. Cool on racks 10 minutes.

Meanwhile, prepare Confectioners' Sugar Icing.

Drizzle icing over twists. Serve warm. Makes 2 large twists.

Nut Filling: In small bowl stir together 1 c. sugar, 1 c. chopped walnuts, ¼ c. butter or regular margarine, melted, and 4 tsp. ground cinnamon.

CHOCOLATE CARROT KRINKLES

A sugar topping adds a snowy contrast to these chocolaty morsels.

2½ c. sifted flour
2 tsp. baking powder
½ tsp. salt
4 (1-oz.) squares unsweetened chocolate
½ c. butter or regular margarine
2 c. sugar
1 tsp. vanilla
4 eggs
1 c. shredded carrots
1 c. chopped pecans
Confectioners' sugar

Into large bowl sift together flour, baking powder and salt; set aside.

In small saucepan over low heat, melt chocolate and butter.

In another large bowl using mixer at medium speed, beat chocolate mixture, sugar, vanilla and eggs 2 minutes. Reduce speed to low; beat in dry ingredients. With spoon stir in carrots and pecans.

Cover and refrigerate dough 4 hours or until firm.

Shape rounded teaspoonfuls of dough into 1¼″ balls. Roll in confectioners' sugar. Place 2″ apart on greased baking sheets.

Bake in 375° oven 15 minutes or until slight imprint remains on top of cookie when touched with finger. Remove from baking sheets; cool completely on racks. Makes about 5 doz. cookies.

CARROT-GINGER COOKIES_____

Gingersnap cookies with crunchy outsides and soft, chewy insides.

2¼ c. sifted flour
2 tsp. baking soda
1½ tsp. ground ginger
1 tsp. ground cinnamon
½ tsp. ground cloves
¼ tsp. salt
1 c. packed brown sugar
¾ c. shortening
¼ c. molasses
1 egg
1 c. tightly packed shredded carrots

Into large bowl sift together first 6 ingredients; set aside.

In another large bowl using mixer at medium speed, beat brown sugar and shortening until light and fluffy. Beat in molasses and egg. Reduce speed to low; beat in dry ingredients. With spoon stir in carrots.

Cover and refrigerate 3 hours or until firm.

Drop dough by rounded teaspoonfuls 2″ apart on greased baking sheets.

Bake in 375° oven 12 minutes or until lightly browned. Remove from baking sheets; cool completely on racks. Makes 3½ doz. cookies.

PUMPKIN-RAISIN COOKIES_____

Tuck a few of these goodies into your children's lunch boxes.

2 c. sifted flour
2 tsp. ground cinnamon
½ tsp. baking powder
½ tsp. baking soda
½ tsp. ground allspice
½ tsp. ground nutmeg
¼ tsp. salt
1 c. sugar
½ c. butter or regular margarine, softened
1 c. mashed, cooked pumpkin
1 egg
1 c. raisins
1 c. chopped walnuts

Into large bowl sift together first 7 ingredients; set aside.

In another large bowl using mixer at medium speed, beat sugar and butter until light and fluffy. Beat in pumpkin and egg. Reduce speed to low; beat in dry ingredients. With spoon stir in raisins and nuts.

Drop dough by heaping teaspoonfuls 2″ apart on greased baking sheets.

Bake in 375° oven 14 minutes or until golden brown. Remove from baking sheets; cool completely on racks. Makes 3 doz. cookies.

ZUCCHINI-NUT CHIP COOKIES_____

A Michigan grandmom bakes these for her grandchildren's camp-outs.

4 c. sifted flour
1 tsp. baking soda
¼ tsp. salt
1 c. butter or regular margarine, softened
1 c. granulated sugar
1 c. packed brown sugar
2 eggs
2 tsp. vanilla
2 c. shredded zucchini
1 c. chopped pecans
1 (12-oz.) pkg. semisweet chocolate pieces

Into large bowl sift together flour, baking soda and salt; set aside.

In another large bowl using mixer at medium speed, beat butter, granulated sugar and brown sugar until light and fluffy. Beat in eggs and vanilla. Reduce speed to low; beat in zucchini, then dry ingredients. With spoon stir in pecans and chocolate pieces.

Drop rounded teaspoonfuls of dough 2″ apart on greased baking sheets.

Bake in 350° oven 15 minutes or until golden brown. Remove from baking sheets; cool completely on racks. Makes 7 doz. cookies.

CHOCOLATE ZUCCHINI SQUARES

This is a great cake to tote on an outing—it's served from the pan.

2½ c. sifted flour
¼ c. unsweetened cocoa
2 tsp. baking soda
½ tsp. ground allspice
½ tsp. ground cinnamon
¼ tsp. salt
½ c. butter or regular margarine, softened
1 c. packed brown sugar
½ c. granulated sugar
½ c. vegetable oil
½ c. buttermilk
1 tsp. vanilla
3 eggs
2 c. shredded zucchini
1 c. semisweet chocolate pieces

Into large bowl sift together first 6 ingredients; set aside.

In another large bowl using mixer at medium speed, beat butter, brown sugar, granulated sugar and oil 2 minutes, or until light and fluffy. Beat in buttermilk, vanilla and eggs.

Reduce speed to low; beat in dry ingredients until well blended. With spoon stir in zucchini. Spread batter in greased 13x9x2″ baking pan. Sprinkle with chocolate pieces.

Bake in 325° oven 45 minutes or until toothpick inserted in center comes out clean. Cool completely in pan on rack. Cut into 24 squares. Makes 24 servings.

PUMPKIN-PECAN CUPCAKES

Light and spicy, and sweet enough to be served without frosting.

2 c. sifted flour
4 tsp. baking powder
½ tsp. salt
½ tsp. pumpkin pie spice
⅔ c. granulated sugar
⅔ c. packed brown sugar
½ c. shortening
1 c. mashed, cooked pumpkin
¼ c. milk
2 eggs
1 c. chopped pecans

Into large bowl sift together flour, baking powder, salt and pumpkin pie spice; set aside.

In another large bowl using mixer at medium speed, beat granulated sugar, brown sugar and shortening until light and fluffy. Beat in pumpkin, milk and eggs until blended.

Reduce speed to low; beat in dry ingredients until well blended. With spoon stir in pecans.

Spoon batter into 24 paper-lined 2½″ muffin-pan cups, filling two-thirds full.

Bake in 350° oven 30 minutes or until toothpick inserted in center comes out clean. Serve warm or cold. Makes 24 cupcakes.

ZUCCHINI SPICE CAKE

"One of my favorite recipes," wrote an Iowan—and no wonder!

2 c. sifted flour
1 tblsp. ground cinnamon
2 tsp. baking soda
½ tsp. baking powder
½ tsp. salt
1 c. granulated sugar
1 c. packed brown sugar
1 c. vegetable oil
1 tblsp. vanilla
3 eggs
2 c. shredded zucchini
1 c. chopped walnuts
Cream Cheese Frosting (recipe follows)

Into large bowl sift together first 5 ingredients; set aside.

In another large bowl using mixer at medium speed, beat granulated sugar, brown sugar, oil, vanilla and eggs until well blended. Reduce speed to low; beat in dry ingredients, zucchini and walnuts. Spread batter in greased 13x9x2" baking pan.

Bake in 350° oven 45 minutes or until toothpick inserted in center comes out clean. Cool completely in pan on rack.

Meanwhile, prepare Cream Cheese Frosting.

Frost top of cake. Makes 16 servings.

Cream Cheese Frosting: In bowl using mixer at low speed, beat ½ (8-oz.) pkg. cream cheese, softened, ⅓ c. butter or regular margarine, softened, 3 c. sifted confectioners' sugar and 1 tsp. vanilla until creamy. Makes 1½ c.

GOLDEN CARROT RING

Serve this ring alone as a dinner bread, or fill it with sauced vegetables for a terrific side dish.

3 c. shredded carrots
2 c. sifted flour
2 tsp. baking powder
1 tsp. baking soda
1 tsp. salt
1 tsp. ground cinnamon
1¼ c. butter or regular margarine, softened
1 c. packed brown sugar
4 eggs, separated
2 tblsp. water
2 tblsp. lemon juice
⅛ tsp. cream of tartar

Into large bowl stir together first 6 ingredients; set aside.

In another large bowl using mixer at medium speed, beat butter and brown sugar until light and fluffy. Beat in egg yolks until light and fluffy.

Reduce speed to low. Gradually beat carrot mixture into butter mixture alternately with water and lemon juice.

In small bowl with clean beaters using mixer at high speed, beat egg whites and cream of tartar until stiff, but not dry, peaks form.

With rubber spatula gently fold egg whites into carrot mixture just until combined. (Do not overmix.) Spoon batter into greased and floured 3-qt. ring mold.

Bake in 350° oven 1 hour or until toothpick inserted in center comes out clean.

Cool in pan 5 minutes. Turn out onto serving platter. Serve warm. Makes 10 to 12 servings.

TO MICROWAVE: *Change ingredients as indicated.*

Grease 3-qt. microwave-safe ring mold, using *1 tblsp. butter or regular margarine.* (To make a ring mold, grease 3-qt. microwave-safe casserole and outside of 2½" drinking glass. Place glass in center of casserole.) Sprinkle inside of ring mold with ⅓ *c. finely chopped nuts.*

Prepare batter as directed, using *1 tsp. baking powder and omitting water.* Beat egg whites as directed, using ½ *tsp. cream of tartar.*

Spoon batter into prepared ring mold. Microwave at low setting (30% power) 25 minutes, rotating dish one-quarter turn every 6 minutes.

Microwave at medium setting (50% power) 3 to 7 minutes, rotating dish one-quarter turn every 2 minutes, until cake begins to pull away from edge and the moist top reveals dry cake below when touched.

Let stand, covered loosely with waxed paper, 5 minutes. Place on rack and cool completely. Turn out onto serving platter.

Carrot Ring with Peas: Cook 2 c. fresh peas. Prepare Onion Sauce (see Index). Stir peas into sauce. Spoon creamed peas into center of ring. Makes 10 to 12 servings.

CHOCOLATE SAUERKRAUT CAKE

The chopped sauerkraut in this cake looks and tastes like coconut.

2¼ c. sifted flour
½ c. unsweetened cocoa
1 tsp. baking powder
1 tsp. baking soda
¼ tsp. salt
1½ c. sugar
⅔ c. butter or regular margarine, softened
3 eggs
1 tsp. vanilla
1 c. water
⅔ c. sauerkraut, rinsed, drained and chopped
Confectioners' sugar

Into large bowl sift together first 5 ingredients; set aside.

In another large bowl using mixer at medium speed, beat sugar and butter until light and fluffy. Add eggs, one at a time, beating well after each addition. Beat in vanilla.

Reduce speed to low; add dry ingredients alternately with water to egg mixture, beating well after each addition. With spoon, stir in sauerkraut. Pour batter into greased 10" fluted tube pan.

Bake in 350° oven 45 minutes or until toothpick inserted in center comes out clean. Cool in pan 20 minutes. Remove from pan; cool completely on rack.

Sprinkle cake with confectioners' sugar. Makes 12 servings.

CHOCOLATE POTATO CAKE

For a richer chocolate color, add a little red food color to the batter.

2 c. sifted flour
2 c. sugar
3 tsp. baking powder
1 tsp. salt
1 tsp. baking soda
1 c. cold mashed potatoes
¾ c. buttermilk or sour milk
½ c. butter or regular margarine, softened
1 tsp. vanilla
⅛ tsp. red food color (optional)
4 eggs
2 (1-oz.) squares unsweetened chocolate, melted and cooled
Whipped Chocolate Frosting (recipe follows)

Into large bowl sift together first 5 ingredients. Add potatoes, buttermilk, butter, vanilla, food color and eggs.

Using mixer at low speed beat until well blended. Increase speed to medium; beat 4 minutes. Beat in melted chocolate. Pour batter into 2 greased and waxed paper-lined 9" round cake pans.

Bake in 350° oven 35 minutes or until toothpick inserted in center comes out clean.

Cool in pans 10 minutes. Remove from pans; cool completely on racks.

Meanwhile, prepare Whipped Chocolate Frosting.

Fill and frost top of cooled cake. Makes 12 servings.

Whipped Chocolate Frosting: In 1-qt. saucepan over low heat, melt 2 (1-oz.) squares unsweetened chocolate and 2 tblsp. butter or regular margarine. Cool slightly.

In medium metal bowl place chocolate mixture, 1 c. sifted confectioners' sugar, ¼ c. milk, 1 tsp. vanilla and 1 egg. Set bowl in another bowl filled with ice cubes and water.

Using mixer at high speed, beat until soft peaks form, about 5 minutes. Makes about 2 c.

PUMPKIN-CHOCOLATE TORTE

This torte would make an elegant finale to Thanksgiving dinner.

2 c. sifted flour
2 tsp. baking powder
1 tsp. baking soda
½ tsp. salt
1½ tsp. ground cinnamon
½ tsp. ground cloves
¼ tsp. ground ginger
¼ tsp. ground allspice
Sugar
4 eggs
2 c. mashed, cooked pumpkin or 1 (1-lb.)
   can pumpkin
1 c. whole bran cereal
1 c. vegetable oil
1 (6-oz.) pkg. semisweet chocolate pieces
1 c. chopped walnuts
1½ c. heavy cream
½ tsp. vanilla

Into large bowl sift together first 8 ingredients and 2 c. sugar; set aside.

In another large bowl using mixer at high speed, beat eggs until foamy. Beat in pumpkin, cereal and oil.

Reduce speed to low; beat in dry ingredients until moistened. With spoon stir in chocolate pieces and walnuts. Spread batter in 3 greased and waxed paper-lined 9″ round cake pans.

Bake in 350° oven 25 minutes or until toothpick inserted in center comes out clean.

Cool in pans 10 minutes. Remove from pans; cool completely on racks.

In chilled bowl with mixer at high speed, beat cream, vanilla and 2 tblsp. sugar until soft peaks form.

Spread whipped cream on top of each cake layer. Stack layers frosting-side up.

Refrigerate 3 hours before serving. Makes 12 servings.

RED BEET CHOCOLATE CAKE

A bountiful beet crop challenged a Missouri woman to create this cake.

1¾ c. sifted flour
1½ tsp. baking soda
½ tsp. salt
1½ c. sugar
1 c. vegetable oil
3 eggs
1½ c. puréed, cooked beets
2 (1-oz.) squares unsweetened chocolate,
   melted and cooled
1 tsp. vanilla
White Mountain Frosting (recipe follows)

Into large bowl sift together flour, baking soda and salt; set aside.

In another large bowl using mixer at medium speed, beat sugar, oil and eggs 2 minutes. Beat in beets, melted chocolate and vanilla.

Reduce speed to low; gradually beat in dry ingredients, beating until well mixed. Pour batter into 2 greased and waxed paper-lined 9″ round cake pans.

Bake in 350° oven 25 minutes or until toothpick inserted in center comes out clean.

Cool in pans 10 minutes. Remove from pans; cool completely on racks.

Meanwhile, prepare White Mountain Frosting.

Fill and frost cooled cake. Makes 12 servings.

White Mountain Frosting: In 2-qt. saucepan over medium heat, cook ½ c. sugar, ¼ c. light corn syrup and 2 tblsp. water until temperature reaches 242° on candy thermometer.

Meanwhile, in large bowl using mixer at high speed, beat 2 egg whites until stiff peaks form.

With mixer at high speed gradually pour hot syrup in a thin stream into egg whites. Continue beating until stiff glossy peaks form. Beat in 1 tsp. vanilla. Makes 3½ c.

CARROT-ZUCCHINI CAKE ROLL

Airy sponge cake, wrapped around a filling of cinnamon whipped cream.

¾ c. shredded zucchini
1 c. sifted flour
½ tsp. baking powder
½ tsp. baking soda
½ tsp. ground cinnamon
¼ tsp. salt
¼ tsp. ground cloves
3 eggs
¾ c. sugar
¾ c. shredded carrots
Confectioners' sugar
Cinnamon Whipped Cream (recipe follows)

Wrap zucchini in dish towel and twist to squeeze out as much liquid as possible; set aside.

Into large bowl sift together flour, baking powder, baking soda, cinnamon, salt and cloves; set aside.

In another large bowl using mixer at high speed, beat eggs and sugar until thick and lemon-colored.

With rubber spatula, fold in dry ingredients, zucchini and carrots. Spread batter in greased and waxed paper-lined 15½x10½x1" jelly-roll pan.

Bake in 350° oven 20 minutes or until top springs back when touched.

Loosen edges with metal spatula. Turn out on dish towel sprinkled with confectioners' sugar. Trim crusts from edges.

Starting at one narrow end, roll up cake and towel, jelly-roll fashion. Cool completely on rack.

Meanwhile, prepare Cinnamon Whipped Cream.

Unroll cooled cake; spread Cinnamon Whipped Cream to within ½" of edges. Reroll and place seam-side down on serving plate. Refrigerate until ready to serve. Makes 8 to 10 servings.

Cinnamon Whipped Cream: In chilled bowl using mixer at high speed, beat 1 c. heavy cream, 2 tblsp. sugar, ½ tsp. vanilla and ¼ tsp. ground cinnamon until soft peaks form.

PUMPKIN SWIRL CHEESECAKE

Real cheesecake, beautifully marbleized with swirls of pumpkin.

1 c. graham cracker crumbs
½ tsp. ground cinnamon
¼ c. butter or regular margarine, melted
3 (8-oz.) pkg. cream cheese, softened
1 c. sugar
5 eggs
1 tsp. vanilla
1 c. mashed, cooked pumpkin
¼ c. packed brown sugar
2 tblsp. flour
1 tsp. pumpkin pie spice
1 tsp. grated orange rind

In bowl mix together graham cracker crumbs, cinnamon and melted butter. Press into bottom of 9" springform pan. Refrigerate.

In large bowl using mixer at medium speed, beat cream cheese and sugar until smooth and creamy. Beat in 4 eggs and vanilla. Remove 2½ c. cheese mixture; set aside.

To remaining cheese mixture in bowl add 1 egg, pumpkin and remaining ingredients. Using mixer at medium speed, beat until smooth.

Alternately spoon plain cheese mixture and pumpkin mixture into chilled graham cracker crust. Swirl with spatula for marbled effect.

Bake in 325° oven 55 minutes, or until edge is set but center is still soft. Cool completely on rack.

Refrigerate at least 6 hours or until well chilled. Makes 12 servings.

CARROT CHEESECAKE

Walnuts in the graham cracker crust contrast with the creamy filling.

1⅔ c. graham cracker crumbs
1 c. finely chopped walnuts
½ c. butter or regular margarine, melted
Ground cinnamon
4 c. carrots (cut into 1" chunks), cooked
  and drained
6 eggs
3 (8-oz.) pkg. cream cheese, softened
1 c. packed brown sugar
¼ c. flour
Vanilla
Ground nutmeg
1 c. sour cream
2 tblsp. granulated sugar

In large bowl mix together graham cracker crumbs, walnuts, melted butter and ½ tsp. cinnamon.

Press crumb mixture into bottom and two-thirds of the way up sides of 9" springform pan. Refrigerate.

In food processor bowl with metal blade, place cooked carrots and eggs; cover. Process until smooth.

In large bowl using mixer at medium speed, beat cream cheese and brown sugar until smooth and creamy.

Beat in flour, 1 tsp. cinnamon, ½ tsp. vanilla, ⅛ tsp. nutmeg and carrot-egg mixture until smooth. Pour batter into graham cracker crust.

Bake in 325° oven 1 hour and 5 minutes, or until edge is set but center is still soft.

In small bowl stir together sour cream, granulated sugar and ¼ tsp. vanilla. Carefully spread on top of cake. Sprinkle with nutmeg. Cool completely on rack.

Refrigerate at least 6 hours or until well chilled. Makes 12 servings.

Pumpkin Cheesecake: Prepare as directed, but substitute 2 c. mashed, cooked pumpkin, or 1 (1-lb.) can pumpkin for carrots.

Squash Cheesecake: Prepare as directed, but substitute 2 c. puréed, cooked butternut or acorn squash for carrots.

PIE SHELL

This pastry is nice and pliable, so it's easy to form into a fluted edge.

1⅓ c. sifted flour
½ tsp. salt
½ c. shortening
3 tblsp. iced water

In large bowl place flour and salt. Using a pastry blender cut in shortening until coarse crumbs form.

Sprinkle iced water over crumb mixture a little at a time, tossing with fork until dough forms. Press dough firmly into a ball.

On lightly floured surface roll out dough to 13" circle. Loosely fit into 8" or 9" pie plate. Using your fingertips, gently press out air pockets. Trim edge to 1" beyond rim of pie plate. Fold under edge of crust and form a ridge. Flute ridge.

Use as directed in recipe. Makes 1 (8" or 9") pie shell.

Baked Pie Shell: Cover and refrigerate shell for 30 minutes. With fork prick entire surface of pie shell.

Bake in 450° oven 10 to 15 minutes or until golden brown. Cool on rack.

Herbed Pie Shell: Use same ingredients and prepare pastry as directed, except add one of the following to flour-and-salt mixture: 1 tblsp. chopped fresh parsley; or ½ tsp. dried dill weed, dried basil leaves, dried oregano leaves, dried rubbed sage, dried thyme leaves or caraway seed.

Spiced Pie Shell: Use same ingredients and prepare pastry as directed, except add ¼ tsp. ground cinnamon or ground nutmeg to flour-and-salt mixture.

Nut Pie Crust: Use same ingredients and prepare pastry as directed, except add one of the following to flour-and-salt mixture: 1 tblsp. toasted sesame seed; or 2 tblsp. finely ground walnuts, peanuts or toasted almonds.

MICROWAVED PIE SHELL

Margarine is the secret of the golden color of this crust.

1¼ c. unsifted flour
Dash of salt
½ c. regular margarine
2 to 3 tblsp. iced water

In large bowl place flour and salt. Using a pastry blender cut in margarine until coarse crumbs form.

Sprinkle iced water over crumb mixture a little at a time, tossing with fork until dough forms. Press firmly into a ball.

On lightly floured surface roll out dough to 13" circle. Loosely fit into 9" pie plate. Using your fingertips, gently press out air pockets. Trim edge to 1" beyond rim of pie plate. Fold under edge of crust and form a ridge. Flute ridge.

Refrigerate 30 minutes. Prick surface of pie shell with fork.

Microwave at high setting (100% power) 3 minutes. Rotate plate one-half turn. Microwave 3 to 4 minutes or until pastry is dry and opaque, covering any brown spots that appear with small flat pieces of aluminum foil. (Check your oven's use-and-care manual before using foil.) Cool on rack.

Fill as directed in recipe. Makes 1 (9") baked pie shell.

PASTRY FOR 2-CRUST PIE

The key ingredient — shortening — makes this pie crust extra-flaky.

2 c. sifted flour
¾ tsp. salt
⅔ c. shortening
4 to 5 tblsp. iced water

In large bowl place flour and salt. Using a pastry blender cut in shortening until coarse crumbs form.

Sprinkle iced water over crumb mixture a little at a time, tossing with fork until dough forms. Press firmly into a ball.

Use as directed in recipe. Makes pastry for 1 (2-crust) 8" or 9" pie.

PUMPKIN PIE

This American classic tastes every bit as good when you microwave it — and it's ready in half the time.

1 unbaked 9" Pie Shell with fluted edge (see page 245)
2 c. mashed, cooked pumpkin or 1 (1-lb.) can pumpkin
1 c. packed brown sugar
2 eggs
1 tsp. ground cinnamon
1 tsp. ground ginger
¼ tsp. salt
¼ tsp. ground allspice
¼ tsp. ground cloves
1½ c. evaporated milk
½ c. boiling water

Prepare Pie Shell; set aside.

In large bowl using mixer at low speed, beat pumpkin and next 7 ingredients until smooth. Beat in evaporated milk and boiling water. Pour into unbaked pie shell.

Bake in 375° oven 55 minutes or until knife inserted in center comes out clean. Cool completely on rack. Makes 6 to 8 servings.

Pumpkin Tarts: Prepare Pastry for 2-Crust Pie.

Divide pastry into 18 equal pieces and shape into balls. Roll each ball into 4¼" circle. Line 18 (3") muffin-pan cups with pastry.

Prepare Pumpkin Pie filling as directed. Pour some of the filling into each tart shell.

Bake in 400° oven 25 minutes or until knife inserted in center comes out clean. Cool completely on racks. Makes 18 tarts.

TO MICROWAVE: *Change ingredients as indicated.*

Prepare *Microwaved Pie Shell* (see facing page).

In 1-qt. microwave-safe bowl with electric mixer at low speed, beat *1⅔ c. mashed, cooked pumpkin, 1 c. evaporated milk* and remaining ingredients except pie shell, *omitting boiling water.*

Microwave at medium setting (50% power) 5 to 8 minutes or until filling is very hot and slightly thickened, stirring every 2 minutes. Pour into Microwaved Pie Shell.

Microwave at medium setting 10 to 15 minutes or until knife inserted 1″ from center and edge comes out clean, rotating one-quarter turn every 2 minutes. Cool completely on rack.

SWEET POTATO PIE

Pecans add crunch to the smooth, light texture of this pie.

1 unbaked 9″ Pie Shell with fluted edge
    (see page 245)
1 lb. sweet potatoes or yams
1¾ c. light cream
½ c. packed brown sugar
1 tsp. ground cinnamon
1 tsp. vanilla
¼ tsp. salt
3 eggs
½ c. chopped pecans

Prepare Pie Shell; set aside.

In 3-qt. saucepan over medium heat, bring 1″ water to a boil. Add sweet potatoes. Cover and cook until tender. Drain. Peel and mash. (There should be 1½ c. mashed sweet potatoes.)

In blender container place mashed sweet potatoes, cream and remaining ingredients except pie shell and pecans; cover. Blend at high speed until smooth.

Sprinkle pecans on bottom of pie shell. Pour sweet potato mixture into pie shell. Stir gently to evenly distribute pecans.

Bake in 400° oven 35 minutes or until knife inserted in center comes out clean. Cool on rack. Makes 6 to 8 servings.

ZUCCHINI PIE

A scrumptious dessert that'll please even the most avid apple-pie lovers.

6 c. sliced, halved, peeled, zucchini or
    yellow summer squash
½ tsp. salt
¾ c. sugar
¼ c. lemon juice
3 tblsp. quick-cooking tapioca
¾ tsp. ground cinnamon
¾ tsp. ground allspice
¾ tsp. vanilla
Pastry for 2-Crust Pie (see facing page)
1 tblsp. butter or regular margarine

If using large zucchini or summer squash, peel; halve lengthwise and scoop out seeds, then slice.

In 3-qt. saucepan place zucchini and salt. Add boiling water to cover. Over high heat bring to a boil. Remove from heat; let stand 5 minutes.

Meanwhile, in large bowl stir together sugar, lemon juice, tapioca, cinnamon, allspice and vanilla.

Drain zucchini. Add to sugar mixture. Toss until zucchini is well coated; set aside.

Prepare pastry. Divide pastry almost in half. On lightly floured surface roll larger half into 13″ circle. Line 9″ pie plate with pastry. Trim edge to ½″ beyond rim of pie plate. Spoon zucchini mixture into pastry-lined plate. Dot with butter.

Roll remaining pastry into 11″ circle. Place circle on top of zucchini mixture. Trim pastry to 1″ beyond rim of pie plate.

Fold top crust under lower crust and form a ridge; flute ridge. Cut slits in top crust of pie to vent steam.

Bake in 425° oven 30 minutes. Reduce temperature to 350°. Bake 30 minutes more or until crust is golden brown. Makes 6 to 8 servings.

PARSNIP PIE

Tastes a lot like sweet potato pie.
A blender makes the filling easy.

1 unbaked 9″ Pie Shell with fluted edge
  (see Index)
1 lb. parsnips, peeled and cut into 1″ pieces
1 c. milk
⅓ c. sugar
¼ c. ground almonds
¼ c. butter or regular margarine, melted
1 tsp. grated orange rind
½ tsp. vanilla
2 eggs
¼ c. strained orange marmalade
2 tblsp. sliced almonds

Prepare Pie Shell; set aside.
In 3-qt. saucepan over medium
heat, bring 1″ water to a boil. Add
parsnips.
Cover and cook until tender.
Drain.
In blender container place parsnips, milk, sugar, ground almonds,
melted butter, orange rind, vanilla
and eggs; cover. Blend at high speed
until smooth. Pour into pie shell.
Bake in 375° oven 50 minutes or
until knife inserted in center comes
out clean.
While pie is still warm, spread top
with strained marmalade. Sprinkle
with sliced almonds. Cool completely
on rack. Makes 6 to 8 servings.

TO MICROWAVE: *Change ingredients as
indicated.*
Prepare *Microwaved Pie Shell*
(see page 246).
In 2-qt. microwave-safe casserole
place parsnips and *½ c. water.* Cover with lid or plastic wrap, turning
back one section to vent steam.
Microwave at high setting (100%
power) 12 to 14 minutes or until tender, stirring every 3 minutes. Drain.
In blender container place parsnips, milk, sugar, ground almonds,
melted butter, orange rind, vanilla
and eggs. Cover. Blend at high
speed until smooth. Pour into 1-qt.
microwave-safe bowl.
Microwave at high setting 3 to 4
minutes or until very hot, stirring
each minute.

Pour into Microwaved Pie Shell.
Microwave at medium setting (50%
power) 10 to 15 minutes or until
knife inserted 1″ from center comes
out clean, rotating one-quarter turn
every 2 minutes. Let stand
5 minutes.
Spread top with strained marmalade. Sprinkle with sliced almonds.
Cool completely on rack.

NAVY BEAN PIE

*A cousin to pumpkin pie in its
spicy flavor and its appearance.*

1 unbaked 9″ Pie Shell with fluted edge
  (see page 245)
2 c. mashed, cooked navy beans (about
  ½ lb. dried beans)
1 (13-oz.) can evaporated milk
½ c. packed brown sugar
½ c. honey
1½ tsp. ground cinnamon
½ tsp. ground allspice
½ tsp. ground ginger
½ tsp. ground nutmeg
2 eggs

Prepare Pie Shell; set aside.
In blender container place all ingredients except pie shell; cover.
Blend at high speed until smooth.
Pour into pie shell.
Bake in 425° oven 15 minutes.
Reduce temperature to 350°; bake
45 minutes or until knife inserted
in center comes out clean. Cool
completely on rack. Makes 6 to 8
servings.

MOCK APPLE CRISP

*One Minnesota woman surprises
friends at pot-luck suppers with her
apple crisp—it's made with zucchini.*

6 c. sliced, peeled zucchini
½ c. sugar
⅓ c. quick-cooking tapioca
1½ tsp. ground cinnamon
¼ tsp. salt

¾ c. water
⅓ c. lemon juice
Crumb Topping (recipe follows)

If using large zucchini, peel, halve lengthwise and scoop out seeds, then slice.

In 3-qt. saucepan over high heat, bring all ingredients except Crumb Topping to a boil. Reduce heat to medium. Simmer 10 minutes, stirring frequently.

Meanwhile, prepare Crumb Topping.

Pour zucchini mixture into greased 12x8x2" (2-qt.) baking dish. Sprinkle with topping.

Bake in 350° oven 40 minutes or until golden brown.

Cool slightly and serve warm. Makes 8 servings.

Crumb Topping: In small bowl mix 1 c. sifted flour, ½ c. packed brown sugar, ½ tsp. baking powder and ½ tsp. ground cinnamon. Using a pastry blender cut in ⅓ c. butter or regular margarine until crumbly.

WINTER SQUASH PIE

This can be made with acorn squash, too. The Illinois cook who shared this recipe serves it with ice cream.

1 unbaked 9" Pie Shell with fluted edge (see page 245)
1 (2½-lb.) butternut squash
3 eggs
1 c. sugar
½ c. dark corn syrup
1 tsp. vanilla
½ tsp. ground cinnamon
¼ tsp. salt
1 c. chopped pecans
¼ c. pecan halves

Prepare Pie Shell; set aside.

Cut squash into quarters; scoop out stringy flesh and seeds.

In 3-qt. saucepan over medium heat, bring 1" water to a boil; add squash. Cover and cook until tender. Drain and peel squash.

In food processor bowl using metal blade, place peeled squash; cover. Process until smooth. (There should be 2 c. puréed squash.) Return to processor bowl.

Add eggs and remaining ingredients except pecans and pie shell. Cover and process until well blended. Add chopped pecans. Cover and process just until mixed.

Pour into pie shell. Arrange pecan halves on top of filling.

Bake in 425° oven 15 minutes. Reduce temperature to 350°; bake 35 to 40 minutes or until knife inserted in center comes out clean.

Cool slightly on rack. Serve warm or cool completely. Makes 6 to 8 servings.

PUFFED PUMPKIN CUSTARD

To make this soufflé-like dish extra-special, serve with heavy cream.

6 eggs
½ c. heavy cream
½ tsp. ground cinnamon
¼ tsp. ground nutmeg
½ c. packed brown sugar
1 c. mashed, cooked pumpkin
1 (8-oz.) pkg. plus 1 (3-oz.) pkg. cream cheese, cut up

In blender container place all ingredients except cream cheese; cover. Blend at high speed until smooth.

Remove center of cover on blender. Blending at high speed, add cream cheese, a few pieces at a time, through center of cover. Continue blending until mixture is smooth, stopping several times to scrape down sides of blender.

Pour pumpkin mixture into 8 greased 6-oz. custard cups.

Bake in 375° oven 20 to 25 minutes or until centers are set. Serve immediately. Makes 8 servings.

10

After
Your Garden Grows

Preserving summer's bounty of fresh vegetables will reward you with an assortment of pickles, relishes and jams that you can savor long after the warm days of summer are over.

In this chapter you'll find recipes to refrigerate, freeze and can, plus basic information on both canning and freezing. A chart on pages 254-255 tells which vegetables freeze well, along with their blanching times.

CANNING BASICS

There are two methods of canning, and all the processed pickle and relish recipes in this chapter make use of the boiling water canner. This method is completely safe for high-acid recipes, and each one of our recipes has been double-checked as to its acid content.

If you wish to can fresh vegetables other than tomatoes (not pickles and relishes), you *must* use a pressure canner. For more tomato canning information, see Tomatoes on page 36. Be sure to process the full length of time suggested. (For more information about pressure-canning vegetables, ask your county extension agent or see *Farm Journal's Freezing & Canning Cookbook.*)

A boiling water canner is a deep kettle fitted with a tight cover and has a rack to hold jars. The rack keeps jars evenly spaced and off the bottom of the canner, out of direct contact with heat, so they won't crack or break.

Use a boiling water canner or any deep saucepot with a rack to keep jars at least ½" from the bottom of the pan. The canner should be deep enough so that the rim of the canner is at least 4" above the jars and large enough so jars do not touch the side of the canner or each other.

Use only tempered glass jars made especially for canning.

Then follow these steps.

1. *Check jars,* new or used, to be sure they're free of cracks and chips that will prevent an airtight seal.

2. *Wash jars,* caps or lids and bands in hot, soapy water; then rinse. Leave jars and caps in clean hot water until ready to fill. If the processing

time in the boiling water canner is *less* than 15 minutes, the empty jars *must* be sterilized before filling.

To sterilize jars: Place them right-side up on a rack in the boiling water canner. Fill canner and jars with water to a level at least 1″ above tops of jars. Over high heat bring the water to a *full, rolling boil,* and boil 15 minutes. Keep the jars in the water until ready to fill.

3. *Before packing jars,* fill the canner half full with water. Over high heat bring water to a boil.

4. *Pack and seal jars* one at a time, using cold or hot pack methods.

Raw or cold pack: Firmly pack raw, cold food into jars, then cover with a boiling liquid to within a specific space at the top of the jar. (Each recipe tells the amount of space that is needed; this space often is called head space.)

Hot pack: Loosely pack hot foods into jars and cover with a boiling liquid to within a specific space at the top of the jar. (Each recipe tells the amount of space needed.)

After filling each jar, gently run a plastic spatula or knife up and down around the inside of jar to remove air bubbles. Wipe top rim of jar with damp cloth and cover with cap, following manufacturer's directions. Repeat with remaining jars.

Do not pack more jars than your canner can hold at one time.

5. *Place packed jars in boiling water* on rack in canner. Add hot, boiling water to raise the level at least 1″ — preferably 2″ — above jar tops. Cover canner and quickly bring water to a full, rolling boil.

Start counting processing time when water in canner comes to a boil. Add more boiling water if needed to keep jars covered with at least 1″ boiling water while canning.

Water bath processing times given in recipes are for altitudes of less than 1,000 feet. If you are canning at a higher altitude, check with your county extension agent or see *Farm Journal's Freezing and Canning Cookbook.*

6. *Remove jars and cool.* As you lift each processed jar from canner, stand it upright on a folded towel or rack, leaving 1″ between jars so they will cool evenly. Retighten caps (or screw bands) *only* if recommended by lid manufacturer. Cool jars in a place free of drafts at least 12 to 24 hours.

7. *Check seals* when jars are cool. If using a two-piece cap, remove screw band. If the lid is depressed or concave and will not move when pressed, and if it gives a clear ring when tapped with a spoon, jar is sealed. If the lid sounds dull when tapped, it may not be sealed. Check by turning jar on its side and rolling it; if it doesn't leak, the jar is airtight.

Jars with zinc caps and rubber rings are sealed if caps are low in the center.

If you find an unsealed jar, refrigerate the food and use within a week.

8. *Store jars* up to 1 year in a clean, cool, dark, dry area.

FREEZING BASICS

Be sure to select the freshest, most tender vegetables you can find. Pick vegetables from your garden early in the morning, before they have been warmed by the sun. It's best to blanch and freeze vegetables immediately after they're harvested. If this is impractical, then you *must* cool them as soon as possible in cold water and keep them in cold water, or drain and refrigerate.

1. *Shell or cut* vegetables just before blanching and freezing. Otherwise, vegetables will lose flavor and nutrients, and their texture will change.

2. *Blanch.* It's essential to blanch most vegetables before freezing. Blanching helps preserve the fresh-picked quality by deactivating enzymes.

To blanch, place water in large saucepot with lid. Use *at least* 1 gal. water for each pint of vegetables except leafy greens. For these, use 2 gal. water for each pint of greens. Bring water to a rolling boil.

Place prepared vegetables in a wire basket and submerge in *vigorously boiling water.* Cover saucepot with lid and start counting time immediately (see chart). If the blanching time is brief, water may not return to a boil.

Each vegetable requires a certain blanching time; check the chart and count time precisely.

The same hot water may be used to blanch more vegetables, but add more water occasionally to keep it at the correct level during blanching.

At high elevations, blanching times must be increased: from 2,000 to 4,000 feet, add 30 seconds; above 4,000 to 6,000 feet, add 1 minute; above 6,000 feet, add 2½ minutes to blanching times.

It's important to blanch thoroughly. A good test is to cut a few pieces of the vegetable in half to see if it's hot in the center. Don't overblanch; this will result in poor texture, inferior flavor and loss of nutrients.

3. *Chill vegetables immediately* after blanching by plunging them in iced water or placing them under cold running water. It will take about as long to chill the vegetables as it did to blanch them. Rapid chilling stops the cooking process, retains nutrients and helps keep vegetables at peak quality.

Test for sufficient cooling by biting into a few pieces of vegetables to see if they are cold to the tongue.

4. *Drain* chilled vegetables.

5. *Pack* chilled, drained vegetables in rigid pint or quart freezer containers, leaving ½" space at the top. Pack vegetables firmly, but not tightly. Vegetables that pack loosely, like broccoli, need no head space.

Vegetables also may be packed in a flat, uniform layer in plastic freezer bags. Spread packages in a single layer in freezer. *Do not stack packages until vegetables are thoroughly frozen.*

6. *Serve* within 9 to 12 months.

BLANCHING AND FREEZING VEGETABLES

Vegetable	Selection and Preparation	Size	Blanching Time
Asparagus	Use young asparagus that snap when broken. Break off woody stems; rinse tips and scales to remove sand.	whole stalks up to 1½" in diameter; or 2" pieces	3 min.
		larger stalks	4 min.
Beans: Green and Wax	Use tender beans that snap when broken. Wash and trim ends. If possible, blanch and freeze immediately after picking.	whole beans or 1" pieces	3 min.
Lima	Wash and shell beans, discarding any white or blemished ones. Do not wash after shelling. Blanch and freeze immediately after shelling.	small to medium beans	3 min.
		large beans	4 min.
Beets	Use small to medium-size beets. Cook beets until tender (see page 5); peel. Freeze whole, sliced or diced.		
Broccoli	Use firm stalks with compact heads. Wash and cut broccoli into stalks with flowerets 1" in diameter. Cut lengthwise through stalks for even blanching. Soak in 1 qt. water and ¼ c. salt 30 min. to remove insects. Rinse.	stalks with 1" flowerets	4 min.
Brussels Sprouts	Use sprouts with compact heads. Wash and trim. As for broccoli, soak in 1 qt. water and ¼ c. salt 30 min. Rinse.	small or medium	4 min.
		large	5 min.
Carrots	Trim tops; wash and peel.	¼" slices	3½ min.
Cauliflower	Use compact heads. Wash and cut cauliflower into flowerets 1" in diameter. As for broccoli, soak in 1 qt. water and ¼ c. salt 30 min. Rinse.	stalks with 1" flowerets	4 min.
Corn	Use mature, tender corn. Husk ears, remove silk and trim ends. If possible, blanch and freeze immediately after picking. For whole-kernel corn: Blanch ears 4½ min. and cool; then cut from cob and freeze.	corn on cob: small ears up to 1½" in diameter at large end	8 min.
		large ears	11 min.
Eggplant	Best if thoroughly cooked (see page 14) before freezing.		
Greens	Use young, tender leaves. Trim tough stems. Wash well under cold running water.	most greens collards and stems of Swiss chard	2 min. 4 min.

BLANCHING AND FREEZING VEGETABLES

Vegetable	Selection and Preparation	Size	Blanching Time
Kohlrabi	Trim tops; wash and peel.	½" cubes	2½ min.
Mushrooms	Use young, firm mushrooms. Wash; cut a thin slice from end of each stem. Blanch as directed. Or, cut into ¼" slices; sauté in butter 2 min.; cool and freeze.	small or medium / large (quartered or sliced)	4 min. / 3 min.
Okra	Use tender okra. Trim stems; scrub with soft brush under cold running water.	2 to 4"-long pods / larger pods	4 min. / 5 min.
Onions: Yellow	Peel and chop. (Do not store frozen onions longer than 6 months.)	chopped	1½ min.
Parsnips	Trim tops; wash and peel.	¼" slices	3 min.
Peas: English	Use well-filled pods; shell. (If peas are difficult to shell, blanch 1 min.) Place peas in 1 gal. water and ½ c. salt for 10 min. Use only the peas that float to the top.		2 min.
Sugar Snap and Snow	Use young, tender pods. Wash; remove stem ends and string.	whole pods	3 min.
Peppers	Wash, remove stems and seed. Cut into halves. Blanch as directed. Chopped peppers need no blanching; just freeze.	halves	3 min.
Potatoes: Sweet	Cook thoroughly (see Chapter 1). Cool and peel. Slice or mash; freeze.		
Potatoes: White	Scrub with stiff brush under cold running water; peel.	¼ to ½" cubes	5 min.
Pumpkin	*See* Potatoes: Sweet.		
Rutabagas	Use young, tender rutabagas. Trim tops; wash and peel.	slices or ¼" cubes	3 min.
Spinach	*See* Greens.		1½ min.
Squash: Summer	Use small, tender squash, 5 to 7" long. Wash. Do not peel. Trim.	¼" slices / 1½" slices	3 min. / 6 min.
Squash, Winter	*See* Potatoes: Sweet		
Tomatoes	Wash, wrap and freeze whole (no blanching needed). Use within 2 months. Cool and freeze.		
Turnips	Trim tops; wash and peel.	½" cubes	2½ min.

CUCUMBER REFRIGERATOR PICKLES

(see photo facing page 183)

So easy—just slice cucumbers and marinate in a dill and garlic brine.

4 lb. cucumbers, sliced (1 gal.)
1 qt. 5% acid-strength white vinegar
3 c. sugar
1 c. chopped fresh dill
1 tblsp. pickling spice
1 tblsp. whole black pepper
8 cloves garlic, sliced

In clean 1-gal. glass jar with tight-fitting lid place cucumber slices.

In large bowl stir together vinegar and remaining ingredients until well mixed. (Sugar need not dissolve.) Pour over cucumbers. Cover.

Refrigerate 3 days, carefully inverting jar once each day. Store in refrigerator up to 3 months. Makes 1 gal.

PICKLED SNOW PEAS

Slightly sweet and slightly sour; a tangy pickle with lots of crunch.

Water
Iced water
1 lb. snow peas with strings removed
1½ c. white vinegar
½ c. sugar
1 tblsp. pickling spice
½ tsp. salt

In 3-qt. saucepan over high heat, bring 2 qt. water to a boil.

Meanwhile, fill a large bowl with iced water.

Add snow peas to boiling water; blanch 20 seconds (snow peas will turn bright green). Immediately drain snow peas in colander. Plunge colander into iced water and let stand until snow peas cool, about 5 minutes. Drain well.

In 2 clean, hot 1-pt. jars, tightly pack snow peas, standing them on end.

In same saucepan over high heat, bring vinegar, sugar, pickling spice, salt and ⅓ c. water to a boil. Boil 2 minutes.

Pour boiling liquid over snow peas. Cover jars; cool.

Refrigerate at least 2 days before serving. Store in refrigerator up to 3 weeks. Makes 2 pt.

BREAD-AND-BUTTER CUCUMBER CHUNKS

Chunks of cucumber with the flavor of classic bread-and-butter pickles.

6 lb. cucumbers
½ c. pickling salt
3 qt. ice cubes
1 qt. 5% acid-strength cider vinegar
2 c. granulated sugar
2 c. packed brown sugar
4 tsp. mustard seed
1 tblsp. ground ginger
2 tsp. whole black pepper
1 tsp. ground allspice
½ tsp. ground turmeric
2 cloves garlic, minced
2 lb. onions, sliced (6 c.)

Trim ends from cucumbers. Cut cucumbers into 1" chunks. In very large bowl toss together cucumber chunks and pickling salt. Cover with ice cubes.

Refrigerate 3 hours. Drain well. Set aside.

In 8-qt. stainless-steel or enamel saucepot over medium heat, bring vinegar and remaining ingredients except cucumbers and onions to a boil. Boil 10 minutes.

Add cucumbers and onions; return mixture to a boil.

Immediately ladle boiling mixture into 9 clean, hot 1-pt. jars, leaving ¼" space at top. Wipe rims of jars with damp cloth. Cover with lids and seal according to jar manufacturer's directions.

Process in boiling water bath 15 minutes from time water in canner returns to a boil.

Remove jars. Cool on racks 12 to 24 hours. Check jars for airtight seal. Makes 9 pt.

GREEN TOMATO PICKLES

Pungent with mustard, these spicy pickles use end-of-season tomatoes.

8 qt. sliced green tomatoes (13 to 14 lb.)
6 medium onions, sliced
1 c. pickling salt
6 c. 5% acid-strength cider vinegar
4½ c. sugar
⅔ c. mustard seed
2 tblsp. ground cinnamon
2 tblsp. whole cloves
2 tblsp. dry mustard
2 tblsp. ground nutmeg

In very large bowl gently toss together tomatoes, onions and pickling salt. Cover loosely with plastic wrap and let stand overnight.

Drain tomatoes and onions well.

In 16-qt. stainless-steel or enamel saucepot over high heat, bring tomatoes, onions, vinegar and remaining ingredients to a boil. Reduce heat to medium-high; boil 30 minutes, stirring occasionally.

Immediately ladle boiling mixture into 11 clean, hot 1-pt. jars, leaving ¼" space at top. Wipe rims of jars with damp cloth. Cover with lids and seal according to jar manufacturer's directions.

Process in boiling water bath 15 minutes from time water in canner returns to a boil.

Remove jars. Cool on racks 12 to 24 hours. Check jars for airtight seal. Makes 11 pt.

CARROT PICKLES

Cinnamon and cloves flavor these quick and easy refrigerator pickles.

4 c. sliced carrots (about 2 lb.)
1 c. cider vinegar
¾ c. sugar
1 tsp. salt
10 whole cloves
2 (3") cinnamon sticks, broken into small pieces

In 2-qt. saucepan over medium heat, bring 1" water to a boil. Add carrots. Cover and cook until tender-crisp; drain.

In clean, hot 1-qt. jar, pack carrots.

In same saucepan over high heat, bring vinegar and remaining ingredients to a boil. Reduce heat and simmer, uncovered, 3 minutes.

Pour simmering mixture over carrots. Cover jar; cool.

Refrigerate at least 2 days before serving. Store in refrigerator up to 2 weeks. Makes 1 qt.

PICKLED BEETS

When you've finished the beets, use the juice to marinate a mixture of sliced onions and hard-cooked eggs.

2 c. small whole beets, cooked and drained, or 1 (16-oz.) can small whole beets, drained
¾ c. white vinegar
⅓ c. sugar
¼ c. water
3 whole cloves
1 (1") cinnamon stick
1 lemon slice
1 onion slice

In 2-qt. stainless-steel or enamel saucepan over high heat, bring all ingredients to a boil. Boil 1 minute.

In clean, hot 1½-pt. jar ladle beet mixture. Cover with lid; cool.

Refrigerate at least overnight before serving. Store in refrigerator up to 3 weeks. Makes about 1 pt.

PICKLED HOT PEPPERS

Seed and chop these fiery peppers for use in Mexican-style dishes.

2 lb. whole jalapeno peppers
5 tsp. vegetable oil
2½ tsp. pickling salt
5 cloves garlic
2¼ c. water
2¼ c. 5% acid-strength cider vinegar

Wash peppers. In 5 clean, hot 1-pt. jars tightly pack peppers. To each jar add 1 tsp. oil, ½ tsp. pickling salt and 1 clove garlic.

In 2-qt. stainless-steel or enamel saucepan over high heat, bring water and vinegar to a boil.

Ladle boiling liquid over peppers, leaving ½" space at top. Wipe rims of jars with damp cloth. Cover with lids and seal according to jar manufacturer's directions.

Process in boiling water bath 15 minutes from time water in canner returns to a boil.

Remove jars. Cool on racks 12 to 24 hours. Check jars for airtight seal. Makes 5 pt.

DILLY BEANS

Add these tender morsels to an antipasto platter; serve well chilled.

2 lb. green beans, trimmed
1 tsp. ground red pepper
4 cloves garlic
4 large heads dill
2 c. 5% acid-strength vinegar
2 c. water
¼ c. pickling salt

In 4 hot, sterilized 1-pt. jars, tightly pack green beans, standing them on end. To each jar add ¼ tsp. red pepper, 1 clove garlic and 1 head dill.

In 2-qt. stainless-steel or enamel saucepan over high heat, bring vinegar, water and pickling salt to a boil.

Pour boiling liquid over beans, leaving ¼" space at top. Wipe rims of jars with damp cloth. Cover with lids and seal according to jar manufacturer's directions.

Process in boiling water bath 5 minutes from time water in canner returns to a boil.

Remove jars. Cool on racks 12 to 24 hours. Check jars for airtight seal. Makes 4 pt.

DILLED OKRA PICKLES

Chop some of these pickles to use as a piccalilli topping for burgers.

3 lb. small whole young okra
10½ tsp. dill seed
3½ tsp. celery seed
7 cloves garlic
3½ c. water
3½ c. 5% acid-strength cider vinegar
½ c. pickling salt

Wash okra and prick each one once with point of sharp knife to allow pods to absorb pickling brine.

In 7 hot, sterilized 1-pt. jars, pack okra. To each jar add 1½ tsp. dill seed, ½ tsp. celery seed and 1 clove garlic.

In 3-qt. stainless-steel or enamel saucepan over high heat, bring water, vinegar and pickling salt to a boil.

Ladle boiling liquid over okra, leaving ¼" space at top. Wipe rims of jars with damp cloth. Cover with lids and seal according to jar manufacturer's directions.

Process in boiling water bath 5 minutes from time water in canner returns to a boil.

Remove jars. Cool on racks 12 to 24 hours. Check jars for airtight seal. Makes 7 pt.

ZUCCHINI SPEARS

Use that bumper crop of zucchini to make some crunchy curried pickles.

10 medium zucchini (7½ lb.)
2 large onions, diced
½ c. pickling salt
3 qt. ice cubes
1 (1-lb.) pkg. brown sugar
6 c. 5% acid-strength cider vinegar
3⅔ c. granulated sugar
3 tblsp. whole allspice
1 tsp. curry powder
½ tsp. ground turmeric
½ tsp. ground ginger
3 cloves garlic, minced
2 (3") cinnamon sticks

Cut each zucchini lengthwise into 8 strips, then cut strips in half crosswise.

In very large bowl alternately layer zucchini, onions and pickling salt. Cover with ice cubes. Refrigerate 4 to 5 hours.

Drain zucchini and onions well. In 10 clean, hot 1-pt. jars tightly pack zucchini spears and onions, standing spears on end.

In 4-qt. stainless-steel or enamel Dutch oven over high heat, bring brown sugar and remaining ingredients to a boil. Reduce heat to low. Cover and simmer 15 minutes.

Remove cinnamon sticks. Pour simmering mixture over zucchini, leaving ¼" space at top. Wipe rims of jars with damp cloth. Cover with lids and seal according to jar manufacturer's directions.

Process in boiling water bath 15 minutes from time water in canner returns to boil.

Remove jars. Cool on racks 12 to 24 hours. Check jars for airtight seal. Makes 10 pt.

THREE-BEAN SALAD
(see photo facing page 183)

In the wintertime, serve this in place of a high-cost green salad.

Water
3 c. green beans, cut into 1½" pieces
3 c. wax beans, cut into 1½" pieces
3 c. shelled lima beans
3 c. sliced onions
3 c. sliced carrots
1½ c. sliced celery
1½ c. diced sweet red peppers
2 tblsp. pickling spice
2 tsp. whole black pepper
3¾ c. 5% acid-strength white vinegar
3 c. sugar
2 tblsp. pickling salt
4 tsp. mustard seed
3 cloves garlic, minced

In 8-qt. stainless-steel or enamel saucepot over medium heat, bring 1½" water to a boil. Add green beans, wax beans, lima beans, onions, carrots, celery and red peppers. Cover and cook until tender, about 10 minutes. Drain well; set aside.

Tie pickling spice and whole black pepper in cheesecloth. In same 8-qt. saucepot over medium heat bring spice bag, 1½ c. water, vinegar and remaining ingredients except vegetables to a boil. Boil 10 minutes. Remove spice bag. Add cooked vegetables; return mixture to a boil.

Immediately ladle boiling mixture into 7 clean, hot 1-pt. jars, leaving ¼" space at top. Wipe rims of jars with damp cloth. Cover with lids and seal according to jar manufacturer's directions.

Process in boiling water bath 15 minutes from time water in canner returns to a boil.

Remove jars. Cool on racks 12 to 24 hours. Check jars for airtight seal. Makes 7 pt.

TOMATO-APPLE CHUTNEY

(see photo facing page 183)

*Serve this spicy accompaniment
with roast pork, poultry or lamb.*

5 lb. ripe tomatoes, peeled and diced
   (about 9 c.)
2 lb. tart apples, peeled, cored and diced
   (about 4 c.)
1 (1-lb.) pkg. brown sugar
2 c. 5% acid-strength cider vinegar
2 c. chopped onions
1½ c. chopped green peppers
1½ c. raisins
1 tblsp. pickling salt
1 tblsp. ground ginger
1 tblsp. ground cinnamon
2 tsp. whole cumin seed (optional)
1 tsp. ground allspice
½ tsp. ground cloves
2 cloves garlic, minced

In 8-qt. stainless-steel or enamel
saucepot over medium heat, bring all
ingredients to a boil, stirring often.

Simmer, uncovered, 1½ hours or
until thick, stirring occasionally.

Immediately ladle simmering mixture into 11 clean, hot ½-pt. jars,
leaving ¼" space at top. Wipe rims
of jars with damp cloth. Cover with
lids and seal according to jar manufacturer's directions.

Process in boiling water bath
15 minutes from time water in canner returns to a boil.

Remove jars. Cool on racks 12 to
24 hours. Check jars for airtight
seal. Makes 11 half-pints.

CARROT CITRUS MARMALADE

*This golden-colored marmalade
makes a good glaze for poultry.*

1½ c. thinly sliced lemons (about 2 large)
1 c. thinly sliced orange (about 1 medium)
2 c. finely ground carrots
Water
2⅓ c. sugar

Cut lemon and orange slices into
quarters.

In 4-qt. Dutch oven stir together
lemons, orange, carrots and 3 c.
water; cover. Over high heat bring
to a boil and cook 25 minutes, stirring occasionally. Measure mixture;
there should be 3½ c. Add water if
necessary. Return to Dutch oven.

Stir in sugar and 3½ c. water.
Boil rapidly, uncovered, 20 to 30
minutes until mixture thickens,
stirring frequently.

Immediately ladle boiling mixture
into 4 hot, sterilized ½-pt. jars, leaving ¼" space at top. Wipe rims of
jars with damp cloth. Cover with
lids and seal according to jar manufacturer's directions.

Process in boiling water bath 5
minutes from time water in canner
returns to a boil.

Remove jars. Cool on racks 12 to
24 hours. Check jars for airtight
seal. Makes 4 half-pints.

SUMMER SQUASH RELISH

(see photo facing page 183)

*One Texas farm woman prefers this
to any green tomato relish.*

5 lb. yellow summer squash, cut into
   chunks
4 large onions (1½ lb.), quartered
4 large green peppers, quartered and
   seeded
2 (4-oz.) jars sliced pimiento, drained
5 tblsp. pickling salt
2 tsp. pickling spice
5 c. sugar
3½ c. 5% acid-strength cider vinegar
2½ tsp. celery salt
1½ tsp. ground turmeric

With food grinder using coarse
blade, grind together squash, onions
and green peppers.

In very large bowl stir together
ground vegetables, pimiento and
pickling salt.

Cover and let stand at room
temperature overnight. Rinse and
drain well.

Tie pickling spice in cheesecloth. In 8-qt. stainless-steel or enamel saucepot over medium heat, bring spice bag, sugar, vinegar, celery salt and turmeric to a boil. Boil 5 minutes. Remove spice bag.

Add drained vegetables; return mixture to a boil.

Immediately ladle boiling mixture into 7 clean, hot 1-pt. jars, leaving ¼ " space at top. Wipe rims of jars with damp cloth. Cover with lids and seal according to jar manufacturer's directions.

Process in boiling water bath 15 minutes from time water in canner returns to a boil.

Remove jars. Cool on racks 12 to 24 hours. Check jars for airtight seal. Makes 7 pt.

RED PEPPER RELISH

Pepper relishes are at their peak served within 6 months of canning.

12 medium sweet red peppers, halved
   and seeded
Boiling water
4 tsp. whole allspice
2 c. chopped onions
2 c. 5% acid-strength white vinegar
3 c. sugar
4 tsp. pickling salt
1 lemon, sliced
½ tsp. ground ginger

In very large bowl place peppers and enough boiling water to cover. Let stand 5 minutes; drain.

With food grinder using coarse blade, grind peppers.

Tie allspice in cheesecloth.

In 4-qt. stainless-steel or enamel Dutch oven over medium heat, bring peppers, spice bag, onions and remaining ingredients to a boil. Cook 30 minutes.

Pour into glass bowl. Let stand overnight.

Return mixture to same Dutch oven and bring to a boil. Remove spice bag.

Immediately ladle boiling mixture into 3 hot, sterilized 1-pt. jars, leaving ¼ " space at top. Wipe rims of jars with damp cloth. Cover with lids and seal according to jar manufacturer's directions.

Process in boiling water bath 10 minutes from time water in canner returns to a boil.

Remove jars. Cool on racks 12 to 24 hours. Check jars for airtight seal. Makes 3 pt.

BEET CHUTNEY

A crimson-colored relish that's spiced with ginger and cumin.

1 lb. beets, cooked, peeled and quartered
2 large apples, peeled, cored and quartered
2 large onions, quartered
1 large green pepper, quartered and
   seeded
1 (1-lb.) pkg. brown sugar
3 c. 5% acid-strength cider vinegar
1 c. golden raisins
1 tblsp. ground ginger
1 tsp. salt
⅛ tsp. ground red pepper
¼ tsp. ground cumin

With food grinder using coarse blade, grind together beets, apples, onions and green pepper.

In 4-qt. stainless-steel or enamel Dutch oven over medium heat, bring ground mixture, brown sugar and remaining ingredients to a boil, stirring often. Simmer, uncovered, 30 minutes or until thick, stirring frequently.

Immediately ladle simmering mixture into 8 clean, hot ½-pt. jars, leaving ¼ " space at top. Wipe rims of jars with damp cloth. Cover with lids and seal according to jar manufacturer's directions.

Process in boiling water bath 15 minutes from time water in canner returns to a boil.

Remove jars. Cool on racks 12 to 24 hours. Check jars for airtight seal. Makes 8 half-pints.

GREEN PEPPER GEL

Use as an appetizer, drizzled over crackers spread with cream cheese.

5 to 6 chili peppers, seeded and quartered
4 to 5 large green sweet peppers, seeded
  and quartered
6½ c. sugar
1½ c. 5% acid-strength white vinegar
¼ tsp. pickling salt
1 (6-oz.) pkg. liquid fruit pectin
1 tsp. red food color

With food grinder using coarse blade, grind chili peppers. Drain ground peppers and measure ½ c. Grind green peppers. Drain and measure 1 c.

In 6-qt. enamel or stainless-steel saucepot over high heat, bring ground chili and green peppers, sugar, vinegar and pickling salt to a boil, stirring constantly. Boil 1 minute.

Remove from heat. Stir in pectin and food color. Continue stirring 3 minutes so that pectin is evenly distributed.

Immediately ladle mixture into 8 hot, sterilized ½-pt. jars, leaving ¼" space at top. Wipe rims of jars with damp cloth. Cover with lids and seal according to jar manufacturer's directions.

Process in boiling water bath 5 minutes from time water in canner returns to a boil.

Remove jars. Cool on racks 12 to 24 hours. Check jars for airtight seal. Makes 8 half-pints.

FROZEN CUKE AND ONION RELISH

Stock your freezer with this frosty relish; it makes a great salad, too.

8 large cucumbers, sliced (4 qt.)
4 c. sliced onions
1⅓ c. sugar
1⅓ c. vinegar
3 tblsp. salt

In large bowl toss together all ingredients. Let stand 10 minutes.

In 4 (1-qt.) freezer-safe containers, pack relish. Cover and freeze. Store in freezer up to 6 months.

Thaw at room temperature 3 hours before serving. Makes 4 qt.

WINTER SALAD RELISH

Cabbage and cucumbers make this relish crunchy and mild-flavored.

2 qt. sliced green tomatoes (about 3½ lb.)
Pickling salt
2 tsp. mustard seed
1 tsp. whole allspice
1 qt. 5% acid-strength vinegar
2 c. sugar
2 tsp. ground turmeric
2 qt. shredded cabbage
2 qt. sliced, seeded, peeled cucumbers
1 qt. chopped onions
1⅓ c. chopped red sweet peppers
1 c. chopped green sweet peppers

In large bowl toss together tomatoes and ¼ c. pickling salt. Cover loosely with plastic wrap and let stand overnight at room temperature. Rinse and drain well.

Tie mustard seed and allspice together in cheesecloth.

In 16-qt. stainless-steel or enamel saucepot over medium heat, bring spice bag, vinegar, sugar, turmeric and 2 tblsp. pickling salt to a boil. Boil 10 minutes.

Add tomatoes, cabbage and remaining ingredients; cook until mixture returns to a boil. Remove spice bag.

Pour boiling mixture into 10 hot, sterilized 1-pt. jars, leaving ¼" space at top. Wipe rims of jars with damp cloth. Cover with lids and seal according to manufacturer's directions.

Process in boiling water bath 10 minutes from time water in canner returns to a boil.

Remove jars. Cool on racks 12 to 24 hours. Check jars for airtight seal. Makes 10 pt.

TOMATO JUICE COCKTAIL

Serve this low-calorie refresher over ice and garnish with a rib of celery.

18 lb. ripe tomatoes, peeled
2 c. chopped celery
1 c. chopped carrots
¼ c. chopped onion
⅓ c. sugar
4 tblsp. pickling salt
1 tblsp. celery seed
⅛ tsp. ground red pepper
Lemon juice

Place 12-qt. enamel or stainless-steel saucepot over medium heat. Quarter tomatoes directly into saucepot, a few at a time, to maintain a boil. (This procedure helps keep the canned juice from separating.)

Gradually add chopped celery, carrots and onion, always maintaining a boil. Add sugar and remaining ingredients except lemon juice. Simmer, uncovered, 20 minutes. Cool slightly.

Put vegetable mixture through sieve or food mill. Return to saucepot; bring to a boil.

Into each of 7 clean, hot 1-qt. jars pour 4 tsp. lemon juice.

Ladle tomato juice into jars, leaving ½" space at top. Wipe rims of jars with damp cloth. Cover with lids and seal according to jar manufacturer's directions.

Process in boiling water bath 35 minutes from time water in canner returns to a boil.

Remove jars. Cool on racks 12 to 24 hours. Check jars for airtight seal. Makes 7 qt.

ZUCCHINI JAM

Vary the flavor of this jam by varying the flavor of the gelatin.

About 2¾ lb. zucchini, cut into 1" chunks
4 c. sugar
½ c. lemon juice
1 (8-oz.) can crushed pineapple, drained
1 (6-oz.) box fruit-flavored gelatin (lemon, peach, apricot or other fruit flavor)

With food grinder using coarse blade, grind zucchini. Measure 6 c. ground zucchini with its liquid.

In 4-qt. Dutch oven over medium-high heat, bring zucchini and its liquid to a boil. Cook, uncovered, 15 minutes, stirring occasionally.

Stir in sugar, lemon juice and drained pineapple; return to a boil. Cook 6 minutes, stirring occasionally. Remove from heat.

Stir in gelatin until dissolved.

Ladle into 8 (½-pt.) freezer jars or freezer-safe containers. Cover and cool.

Store in refrigerator up to 3 weeks or in freezer up to 1 year. Makes 8 half-pints.

CARROT RELISH

A marinated sweet and sour relish that's stored in the freezer.

2 c. sugar
1 c. cider vinegar
2 tsp. salt
1 tsp. celery seed
7 c. shredded, pared carrots
1 c. chopped onion

In large bowl stir together sugar, vinegar, salt and celery seed. Add carrots and onion; toss to mix well.

In 3 (1-pt.) freezer-safe containers, pack relish. Cover and freeze. Store in freezer up to 6 months.

Thaw at room temperature 3 hours before serving. Makes 3 pt.

GREEN BEANS AND CARROTS WITH WALNUT BUTTER

Packages of frozen vegetables with butter sauce needn't be expensive—not when you prepare them yourself.

¾ c. butter or regular margarine
1⅓ c. coarsely chopped walnuts
4 cloves garlic, minced
⅓ c. chopped fresh parsley
1 tsp. salt
Water
3 lb. green beans, trimmed and cut into 2" pieces
Iced water
2 lb. carrots, sliced ⅛" thick

In 10" skillet over medium heat, melt butter. Add walnuts and garlic; cook until butter and walnuts are golden brown. Remove from heat. Stir in parsley and salt.

Into 9x5x3" loaf pan, pour walnut butter. Freeze until firm enough to cut, about 20 minutes.

Cut into quarters. Refrigerate until ready to use.

Into large stainless-steel or enamel saucepot, pour 1 gal. water. Cover; over high heat bring to a rolling boil.

Place one-third of the beans in wire basket. Submerge in boiling water and blanch 3 minutes (start counting time immediately, without waiting for water to return to a boil). Plunge basket into iced water and cool beans, about 3 minutes. Drain well. Repeat twice more with remaining beans, adding ice to iced water as needed.

Place half of the carrots in wire basket. Blanch 2 minutes and cool, using same method as for beans. Repeat with remaining carrots.

In large bowl mix together beans and carrots.

In 4 plastic freezer bags pack beans and carrots. To each bag add one-quarter of the chilled walnut butter. Seal bags.

Freeze. Store in freezer up to 12 months.

To serve, in 10" skillet place frozen contents of 1 bag. Add 2 tblsp. water. Cover. Over medium-high heat, cook 6 to 8 minutes or to desired degree of doneness, stirring occasionally.

Uncover and cook 1 to 2 minutes more to allow excess liquid to evaporate. Makes 4 (1-lb.) bags or 4 servings per bag.

FREEZER TOMATO SAUCE

For a spicier sauce, use 1 lb. hot peppers in place of green peppers.

20 lb. ripe tomatoes
1 bunch celery, cut into 1" pieces
4 large onions, coarsely chopped
3 large green peppers, each cut into eighths
8 cloves garlic, quartered
3 tblsp. salt
3 tblsp. dried basil leaves

Quarter tomatoes, cutting away any soft spots and blemishes.

In 18-qt. stainless-steel or enamel saucepot place all ingredients except salt and basil. Cover; over medium heat cook until tender. Cool slightly.

In blender container place 1 qt. vegetable mixture; cover. Blend at high speed about 3 seconds, until smooth. Put through food mill or sieve. Pour into bowl. Repeat with remaining vegetable mixture. Rinse saucepot.

Return tomato mixture to saucepot. Stir in salt and basil. Over high heat bring to a boil, stirring occasionally. Reduce heat to medium-low and simmer, uncovered, 1 hour 15 minutes or until sauce reaches desired thickness, stirring occasionally.

In 10 (1-pt.) freezer-safe containers, ladle sauce; cool. Cover and freeze. Store in freezer up to 12 months. Makes 10 pt.

Index

A

acorn squash, 34-35
  stuffed, 127
Aioli Sauce, 218
alfalfa sprouts, 32
anise, 2
  Sautéed Tomatoes and, 172
Anna, Potatoes, 168
Antipasto Platter, 63
appetizer(s), 59-69
  Eggplant, 62
  Zucchini-Shrimp, 64
Apple
  Chutney, Tomato-, 260
  Crisp, Mock, 248
  Skillet, Cabbage and, 166
artichoke(s), 2-3. *See also* Jerusalem
    artichokes
  Salad, Tuna, 113
  Saucy, 180
  Stuffed, 195
arugala, 20-21
asparagus, 3
  Citrus, 160
  Pie, Country, 150
  Soup, Cream of, 84
  Stir-fried, 183
  Sunny, 123
au Gratin
  Potatoes, 186
  Salsify, 191

B

bacon
  dressings, 226, 228
  Omelet, Potato-, 118
  -Onion Sticks, 234

Bake(d). *See also* beans
  Brussels Sprouts Cheese, 189
  Corn, Spicy, 188
  Creamy Lasagne, 137
  goods, 231-249
  Layered Pepper-Chili, 142
  Pie Shell, 245
  Potatoes, Twice-, 194
  Vegetable-Chicken, 139
baking potatoes, 27-28
Ball(s)
  Crispy Squash, 69
  French-fried Potato, 198
  Pecan-Sweet Potato, 196
  Vegetable-Cheese, 65
  with Pasta, Vegetable, 133
banana squash, 34-35
Barbecued Lima Beans, 181
Basil Beans and Tomatoes, 172
Basil Beans, Savory, 177
Basil Tomato Sauté, 173
Batter, Beer, 198
Batter, Tempura, 126
bean(s), 4, 14. *See also* lentils; peas
  and Tomatoes, Basil, 172
  baked
    Old-fashioned, 193
    Super, 194
    Sweet-and-Sour, 193
  black, 14
    -eyed, 14
    Soup, 95
  Dilly, 258
  dried, 13-14
  green, 4
    and Carrots with Walnut Butter, 264
    and Peanut Salad, 101
    Best-Ever, 163
    Festive, 164
    Marinated, 163
    Oriental, 184

bean(s) (continued)
  green
    Sesame, 171
    Sunny, 123
  lima, 4
    Barbecued, 180
    Chowder, 88
    dried, 14
    Skillet, Mexican, 148
    Stew, Chicken and, 145
  navy, 14
    Pie, 248
  Salad, Five-, 102
  Salad, Three-, 259
  Savory Basil, 177
  Soup, Pasta and, 94
  sprouts, mung, 32
  Sprouts, Tabouli with, 110
  Sweet-Sour, 193
Béarnaise Sauce, 215
  Blender, 216
Beef
  and Potato Casserole, 140
  Casserole, Harvest, 140
  Soup with Pastry Cap, Vegetable, 89
  Stew, Chunky, 146
  with Vegetables, Stir-fried, 124
Beer Batter, 198
beet(s), 5
  and Greens, 176
  and Orange Salad, 101
  and Turnip Calla Lilies, 53
  Chocolate Cake, Red, 243
  Chutney, 261
  Flowers, 50
  greens, 5
  Hot Spiced, 165
  Mum, 54
  Pickled, 257
Belgian endive, 6
bell peppers, 26
Bermuda onions, 23-24
Best-Ever Green Beans, 163
bibb lettuce, 20-21
Big-Batch Macaroni Salad, 109
Biscuits, Green Onion, 233
Biscuit Topping, 148
Bisque, Curried Squash, 81
Bisque, Tomato-Dill, 73
black beans. See beans
Black-eyed Susans, 54
black salsify, 30
Blanching and Freezing (chart), 254-255
Blender
  Béarnaise Sauce, 216
  Hollandaise Sauce, 216

Blender (continued)
  Pesto, 219
  Spinach Soufflé, 121
B.L.T. Salad, 98
Blue Cheese
  Dressing, Cottage-, 228
  Dressing, Cucumber-, 229
  Topping, 221
Blue Devil Onions, 100
Boiled Dinner, New England, 155
bok choy, 11
  Salad, 106
Borscht, Continental, 72
Boston lettuce, 20-21
Bouquet, Garnish, 57
Braid, Brioche Mushroom, 236
Braised Greens with Red Pepper, 175
Braised Leeks and Carrots, 174
Bread(s), 231. See also Muffins
  -and-Butter Cucumber Chunks, 256
  Carrot-Raisin Tea, 234
  Potato, 237
  Potato Cinnamon Rolls, 236
  Squmpkin, 232
  Stuffing, Zucchini Corn, 206
  Tex-Mex Stuffed, 65
  Topping, Corn, 148
  Wheat Germ-Zucchini, 232
  Whole-Wheat Zucchini, 233
  Zucchini Nut, 232
Brioche Mushroom Braid, 236
broad beans, 4
broccoli, 6-7
  -Cheese Squares, 190
  di rape, 16-17
  Flowerets, Oven-fried, 67
  Quiche, 121
  Salad, 100
  Soufflé, 120
  Soup, Curried, 80
Brown Butter, 221
Brussels sprouts, 7
  Cheese Bake, 189
  Tangy, 164
Bundles, Saucy Cabbage, 128
butter
  beans, 4
  Brown, 221
  Cucumber Chunks, Bread-and-, 256
  Dill, 220
  Garlic, 220
  Green Beans and Carrots with Walnut, 264
  Lemon-Parsley, 221
  Mixed Herb, 220
  Pesto, 219
Butterflies, Zucchini, 56

Buttermilk Dressing, 225
butternut squash, 34-35
    Whipped, 169
Buttery Onions and Turnips, 179

C

cabbage, 8
    and Apple Skillet, 166
    Bundles, Saucy, 128
    Casserole, 187
    celery, 11
    Chinese, 11
    Chow Mein, 183
    Napa, 11
    Patch Soup, 75
    Rolls, Creole, 129
    Roses, 55
    Salad, Fruited, 104
    Savoy, 8
    Slaw, Farmhouse, 104
    Sweet-Sour Red, 166
    turnip, see kohlrabi
    with Cheese Sauce, Stuffed, 128
Caesar Dressing, Creamy, 227
Caesar Salad, 98
Cake(s)
    Chocolate Potato, 242
    Chocolate Sauerkraut, 242
    Red Beet Chocolate, 243
    Roll, Carrot-Zucchini, 244
    Zucchini Spice, 240
California chilies, 26
Calla Lilies, 53
Canapés, 65
Canning basics, 251
    recipes, 257, 258-261, 262, 263
Cantonese Vegetables, 185
Caraway Dressing, 222
carrot(s), 8-9
    and Walnut Twists, Whole-Wheat, 238
    Braised Leeks and, 174
    -Celery Stuffing, 206
    Cheesecake, 245
    Citrus Marmalade, 260
    Fritters, 199
    -Ginger Cookies, 239
    Hot Spiced, 165
    Krinkles, Chocolate, 238
    Lily, 53
    Molds, Individual, 111
    Mousse, 112
    Pasta, 204
    Patties, Miniature, 69
    Phyllo Roulades, Spinach-, 68
    Pickles, 257

Carrot(s) (continued)
    Purée, 161
    -Raisin Salad, 105
    -Raisin Tea Bread, 234
    -Raisin Tea Muffins, 233
    Ravioli with Spinach Filling, 135
    Relish, 263
    Ring, Golden, 241
    Sauté, Zucchini and, 173
    Soup, 82
    Supreme, Golden, 167
    with Walnut Butter, Green Beans and, 264
    -Zucchini Cake Roll, 244
Casserole(s)
    Beef and Potato, 140
    Cabbage, 187
    Harvest Beef, 140
    Ranch-style Lentil, 141
cauliflower, 9
    Mold, 111
    Salad, 100
    Soup, Creamy, 82
celeriac, 10
celery, 10-11.
    and Cheese Rosettes, 66
    cabbage, 11
    Seed Dressing, 223
    Soup, Cream of, 83
    Stuffing, Carrot-, 206
    Three-Cheese Stuffed, 64
Chain, Vegetable, 48
chard
    Chinese, 11
    in Mornay Sauce, Swiss, 189
    Swiss, 16-17
chayote squash, 32-33
Cheddar-Onion Topping, 221
Cheddar Sauce, 214
Cheese. See also dressings;
        sauces; Toppings
    Bake, Brussels Sprouts, 189
    Ball, Vegetable-, 65
    cake
        Carrot, 245
        Pumpkin, 245
        Pumpkin Swirl, 244
        Squash, 245
    Dip, Chili-, 60
    Frosting, Cream, 240
    Grilled Eggplant and, 131
    Potatoes, Gourmet, 186
    Rosettes, Celery and, 66
    Salad in Pepper Cups, Confetti, 103
    Squares, Broccoli-, 190
    Stuffed Celery, Three-, 64
Cheesy Corn Chowder, 88

cherry tomato(es), 36
  Sauté, 173
Chicken
  and Lima Bean Stew, 145
  and Vegetable Tempura, 126
  Bake, Vegetable-, 139
  Chowder, Parslied, 87
  Gumbo, 89
  Jambalaya Soup, 90
  Julienne Salad, Curried, 115
  Liver Vegetable Pie, Deep-dish, 152
  Noodle Salad, Chinese, 112
  Pot Pies, 151
  with Vegetables, Chinese, 125
chick pea(s), 14
  Spread, 61
chicory, 20-21
  root, 6
Chili
  Bake, Layered Pepper-, 142
  -Cheese Dip, 60
  Texas-style, 142
  Vegetarian, 143
chilies, 26
Chilled Cucumber Soup, 72
Chinese
  cabbage, 11
  chard, 11
  Chicken Noodle Salad, 112
  Chicken with Vegetables, 125
  mustard, 11
  Pepper Steak, 124
Chip Cookies, Zucchini-Nut, 239
Chocolate
  Cake, Red Beet, 243
  Carrot Krinkles, 238
  Potato Cake, 242
  Sauerkraut Cake, 242
  Torte, Pumpkin-, 243
  Zucchini Squares, 240
Chowder(s). See also soups; Stews
  Cheesy Corn, 88
  Lima Bean, 88
  Manhattan Clam, 87
  Parslied Chicken, 87
  Vegetable, 76
  Vegetable-Lentil, 86
Chow Mein Cabbage, 183
Chunks, Bread-and-Butter Cucumber, 256
Chunky Beef Stew, 146
Chunky Lentil Soup, 92
Chutney, Beet, 261
Chutney, Tomato-Apple, 260
Cinnamon Rolls, Potato, 236
Cinnamon Whipped Cream, 244

Citrus
  Asparagus, 160
  Dressing, 226
  Marmalade, Carrot, 260
Clam Chowder, Manhattan, 87
Cocktail, Tomato Juice, 263
Coleslaw, Tangy, 104
collard greens, 16-17
Confectioners' Sugar Icing, 236
Confetti Cheese Salad in Pepper Cups, 103
Confetti Salad, 105
Continental Borscht, 72
Cookies
  Carrot-Ginger, 239
  Pumpkin-Raisin, 239
  Zucchini-Nut Chip, 239
corn, 12
  Bread Stuffing, Zucchini, 206
  Bread Topping, 148
  Chowder, Cheesy, 88
  Creamed, 170
  Fritters, 199
  Muffins, Raised, 234
  on the Cob, Herbed, 162
  Quiche, 122
  Rarebit, 170
  Spicy Baked, 188
Cottage-Blue Cheese Dressing, 228
Cottage Cheese Dressing, Crunchy, 228
Country Asparagus Pie, 150
Country Cream Dressing, 227
Cracked Wheat Pilaf, 206
Cream Cheese Frosting, 240
Creamed
  Corn, 170
  Kale and Onions, 187
  Spinach, 170
Cream
  of Asparagus Soup, 84
  of Celery Soup, 83
  of Mushroom Soup, 84
  of Tomato Soup, 80
  Sauce, 137
Creamy
  dressings, 224, 226, 227, 229
  Lasagne Bake, 137
  Mashed Potatoes and Turnips, 169
  soups, 79, 81, 82
Creole
  Cabbage Rolls, 129
  onions, 23-24
  Sauce, 217
Crisp, Mock Apple, 248
Crispy Squash Balls, 69
Crispy Vegetables, 197
crookneck squash, 32-33

Croutons, Toasted, 115
Crunchy
  Cottage Cheese Dressing, 228
  Onion Twists, 235
  Thousand Island Dressing, 226
Crust. See Pastry
Cubes, Tomato Sauce, 219
Cucumber(s), 12-13
  and Tomato Skillet, 178
  -Blue Cheese Dressing, 229
  Canapés, 65
  Chunks, Bread-and-Butter, 256
  -Dill Dressing, Creamy, 229
  Dip, 60
  Dressing, 229
  Mold, Dilly, 110
  Refrigerator Pickles, 256
  Soup, Chilled, 72
  -Sour Cream Salad, 100
  -Yogurt Sauce, 216
Cuke and Onion Relish, Frozen, 262
Cupcakes, Pumpkin-Pecan, 240
Cup(s)
  Confetti Cheese Salad in Pepper, 103
  Flowers, Radish, 50
  Macaroni in Green Pepper, 127
  Mushroom, 50
curly-leafed endive, 20-21
Curried
  Broccoli Soup, 80
  Chicken Julienne Salad, 115
  Egg and Zucchini Rounds, 63
  Sour Cream Dip, 60
  Squash Bisque, 81
Curry, Venison, 147
Custard, Puffed Pumpkin, 249
Cutlets, Vegetable, 203
Cutouts, Flower, 48, 49

D

Dahlia, Onion, 57
Daikon radish, 29
Daisy Cutouts, 49
dandelion greens, 16-17
  Salad, 99
Decidedly Dill Dressing, 223
Deep-dish Chicken Liver Vegetable Pie, 152
Deep-fried Ravioli, 135
Deep-fried Vegetables, 198
delicious squash, golden, 34-35
Dill(ed)
  Bisque, Tomato, 73
  Butter, 220
  Dip, 61

Dill(ed) (continued)
  Dressing, Creamy Cucumber-, 229
  Dressing, Decidedly, 223
  Okra Pickles, 258
  Topping, Sour Cream, 221
Dilly Beans, 258
Dilly Cucumber Mold, 110
Dinner, New England Boiled, 155
dips, 60-61
dressings, 209, 222-229. See also Toppings
dried beans, peas and lentils, 13-14
Duchess-style Potatoes, 198
Dumplings
  Parslied, 91
  Shortcut, 145
Dutch Pancake, Vegetable-Filled, 123
Dutch Potato Soup, 78

E

East Indies Dressing, 225
Egg and Zucchini Rounds, Curried, 63
Eggciting Potato Salad, 107
Egg Foo Yong, Pork, 119
eggplant, 14
  and Cheese, Grilled, 131
  Appetizer, 62
  Parmesan, 130
  Patties, 202
  Sandwiches, 202
  Sauce, Rigatoni with, 134
  -Sesame Spread, 61
  Slices, Oven-fried, 197
  Stuffed, 130
  with Tomatoes, 181
endive, Belgian, 6
endive, curly-leafed, 20-21
English peas, 25-26
enoki mushrooms, 21-22
escarole, 20-21
  Soup, 77

F

Falafel, 67
Fans, Roasted Potato, 168
Farmhouse Cabbage Slaw, 104
fava beans, 4
Favorite Potato Salad, 106
Feathers, Radish, 51
fennel. See anise
Festive Green Beans, 164
Fettucini Noodles, 204

Filling(s)
  Carrot Ravioli with Spinach, 135
  Herb, 67
  Mushroom, 236
  Nut, 238
finocchio. *See* anise
fish. *See also* Salmon; Shrimp; Tuna
  Roulades with Onion-Lemon Sauce, 156
Five-Bean Salad, 102
Flannel Hash, Red, 157
Flower(s)
  Beet, 50
  Cutouts, 48, 49
  Radish Cup, 50
  Tomato, 51
Fluted Mushrooms, 50
Franks, Potato, 157
Freezer Tomato Sauce, 264
freezing, 251
  basics, 253
  chart, 254-255
  recipes, 262, 263, 264
French Dressing, 222
  Creamy, 226
  Low-Calorie Creamy, 224
  Mix, 224
  Piquant, 222
French-fried Potato Balls, 198
French Onion Soup, 74
French Salad Dressing, 224
Fried
  Green Tomatoes and Okra, 177
  Potato Balls, French-, 198
  Potato Skins, 68
  Rice, Spinach-, 205
  Tomatoes with Sour Cream Sauce, 176
  Vegetables, Deep-, 198
  Vegetables, Stir-, 184
Frittata, Spinach-Tomato, 118
Fritters, 199
Frosting, Cream Cheese, 240
Frozen Cuke and Onion Relish, 262
fruit(ed). *See also individual names of fruit*
  Cabbage Salad, 104
  Salad, Yam, 107

G

garbanzo beans. *See* chick peas
Garden Row Soup, 77
garlic, 14-15
  Butter, 220
  Dressing, Creamy, 227
  Loaves, Quick, 235
garnishes, 47-57
  Bouquet, 57

Gazpacho, Souper, 73
Gel, Green Pepper, 262
Ginger Cookies, Carrot-, 239
Ginger Dressing, 223
Gnocchi, Potato, 205
Golden
  Carrot Ring, 241
  Carrots Supreme, 167
  delicious squash, 34-35
  Harvest Onions, 166
  Parsnips Supreme, 167
  Rutabagas Supreme, 167
Gourmet Cheese Potatoes, 186
Great Northern beans, 14
Greek Salad, 98
Greek-style Marinated Tomatoes, 103
green. *See* beans; onions; peppers
  Goddess Dressing, 229
greens, 16-17
  beet, 5, 176
  in Spicy Peanut Sauce, Rice and, 122
  turnip, 37
  with Red Pepper, Braised, 175
Green Salad, Tossed, 99
green squash, 34-35
Green Tomatoes and Okra, Fried, 177
Green Tomato Pickles, 257
Grilled Eggplant and Cheese, 131
Gumbo, Chicken, 89

H

Harvest Beef Casserole, 140
Harvest Onions, Golden, 166
Hash, Red Flannel, 157
Herb(ed)
  and spice chart, 210-213
  Butter, Mixed, 220
  Corn on the Cob, 162
  -filled Snow Peas, 64
  Filling, 67
  Pie Shell, 245
  Tomato Stars, 67
  Yogurt Dressing, 228
Hollandaise Sauce, 216
Honey-Orange Dressing, 223
horse beans, 4
Horseradish Dressing, Creamy, 227
Hot
  Bacon Dressing, 226
  Lettuce and Peas, 175
  Peppers, Pickled, 258
  Pot, Oriental, 125
  Spiced Beets, 165
  Spiced Carrots, 165

Hot (continued)
Spiced Parsnips, 165
Spinach Salad, 98
hubbard squash, 34-35

I

iceberg lettuce, 20-21
Icing, Confectioners' Sugar, 236
Idaho potatoes, 27-28
Indies Dressing, East, 225
Individual Carrot Molds, 111
Italian
Dressing, 222, 224, 227
onions, red, 23-24
plum tomatoes, 36
Roasted Peppers, 62
-style Marinated Tomatoes, 103

J

Jacks, Vegetable, 48
jalapeno chilies, 26
Jambalaya Soup, Chicken, 90
Jam, Zucchini, 263
Jerusalem artichoke(s), 17
Parmesan, 160
Slaw, 105
jicama, 18
Salad, 101
Jonquil, Turnip or Rutabaga, 55

K

Kabobs, Vegetable, 171
kale, 16-17
and Onions, Creamed, 187
Katahdin potatoes, 27-28
kidney beans, 14
Knishes, Potato, 201
kohlrabi, 18-19
Krinkles, Chocolate Carrot, 238

L

Lamb Pie Supreme, 148
Lasagne
Bake, Creamy, 137
Noodles, 204
Spaghetti Squash, 137
Turkey-Zucchini, 136

Layered
Pepper-Chili Bake, 142
Salmon Salad, 113
Tuna Salad, 113
leaf lettuce, 20-21
leek(s), 19-20
and Carrots, Braised, 174
Soup, Potato-, 78
Lemon-Parsley Butter, 221
Lemon Sauce, 126
Fish Roulades with Onion-, 156
lentil(s), 13-14. *See also* beans; peas
Casserole, Ranch-style, 141
Chowder, Vegetable-, 86
Soup, Chunky, 92
sprouts, 32
lettuce, 20-21
and Peas, Hot, 175
Lilies, 52, 53
lima beans. *See* beans
Loaf, Vegetable, 203
Loaves, Quick Garlic, 235
long white potatoes, 27-28
Low-Calorie
Creamy French Dressing, 224
Tomato Dressing, 224
Vinaigrette, 225

M

Macaroni
in Green Pepper Cups, 127
Salad, Big-Batch, 109
main dish(es), 117-157
Potato Salad, 113
Manhattan Clam Chowder, 87
Marinara Sauce, 218
Marinated
Green Beans, 163
Mushrooms, 62
Tomatoes, 103
Vegetable Platter, 63
Marmalade, Carrot Citrus, 260
Mashed
Potatoes, Creamy, 169
Swedish Rutabagas, 161
Turnips, Creamy, 169
meat. *See* Beef; Chicken; Pork; Turkey
Meatball(s), 90, 91
and Pasta Soup, 90
Medium White Sauce, 214
Medley, Zucchini Skillet, 179
Mexican
Lima Bean Skillet, 148
Topping, 68

Microwaved Pie Shell, 246
Microwave Tips, 38
Microwaving (chart), 39-45
Minestrone, Vegetarian, 93
Miniature Carrot Patties, 69
Mixed Herb Butter, 220
Mixed Vegetable Salad, 111
Mix, French Dressing, 224
Mix, Vinaigrette Dressing, 225
Mock Apple Crisp, 248
molds, 110, 111
Mornay Sauce, Swiss Chard in, 189
Moussaka, 138
Mousse, Carrot, 112
Mousse, Spinach and Salmon, 66
Muffins, Carrot-Raisin Tea, 233
Muffins, Raised Corn, 234
Mum, Turnip or Beet, 54
mung bean sprouts, 32
mushroom(s), 21-22
    Braid, Brioche, 236
    Cups, 50
    Fluted, 50
    Marinated, 62
    Sauce, Sour Cream, 215
    Soup, Cream of, 84
mustard greens, 16-17
    Chinese, 11

N

Napa cabbage, 11
navy bean(s), 14
    Pie, 248
Nectarine Salad, Watercress and, 99
New England Boiled Dinner, 155
New England-style Sweet Potatoes, 188
new potato(es), 27-28
    Canapés, 65
Nicoise, Salad, 114
Noodle(s). See also Pasta
    Fettucini, 204
    Lasagne, 204
    Salad, Chinese Chicken, 112
Northern Plains Rabbit, 145
Nut
    Bread, Zucchini, 232
    Chip Cookies, Zucchini-, 239
    Filling, 238
    Pie Crust, 245

O

oak mushrooms, 21-22
okra, 23
    and Rice Skillet, Tomato, 178
    Fried Green Tomatoes and, 177
    Fritters, 199
    Pickles, Dilled, 258
Old-fashioned Baked Beans, 193
Omelet, Potato-Bacon, 118
onion(s), 23-24
    and Turnips, Buttery, 179
    Blue Devil, 100
    Creamed Kale and, 187
    Creole, 23-24
    Dahlia, 57
    Dip, Sour Cream, 60
    Golden Harvest, 166
    green, 15
        Biscuits, 233
        Lily, 52
    -Lemon Sauce, Fish Roulades with, 156
    Relish, Frozen Cuke and, 262
    Salad, Tomato-, 102
    Sauce, 214
    Soup, French, 74
    Sticks, Bacon-, 234
    Topping, Cheddar-, 221
    Twists, Crunchy, 235
Orange Dressing, Honey-, 223
Orange Salad, Beet and, 101
Oriental
    Green Beans, 184
    Hot Pot, 125
    Salad, 99
    Sauce, 119
    Snow Peas, 182
    Vegetable Soup, 79
Oven-fried Broccoli Flowerets, 67
Oven-fried Eggplant Slices, 197
oyster mushrooms, 21-22
oyster plant. See salsify

P

Pancake(s)
    Potato, 200
    Salsify, 201
    Swiss Potato, 199
    Vegetable-filled Dutch, 123
    Zucchini, 200
Pan Rolls, Potato, 237
Parmesan
    Eggplant, 130
    Jerusalem Artichokes, 160
    Topping, 68

Parsley Butter, Lemon-, 221
Parslied
  Chicken Chowder, 87
  Dumplings, 91
parsnip(s), 24-25
  and Tomato Soup, Creamy, 81
  Hot Spiced, 165
  Pie, 248
  Supreme, Golden, 167
Pascal celery, 10
pasilla chilies, 26
Pasta. See also Noodles; Pizza
  and Bean Soup, 94
  and Snow Pea Salad, 108
  and Vegetable Salad, 108
  Carrot, 204
  Primavera, 132
  Soup, Meatball and, 90
  Spinach, 204
  Vegetable Balls with, 133
Pastry. See also Pies; Phyllo
  Cap, Vegetable Beef Soup with, 89
  Crust, Nut, 245
  for 2-Crust Pie, 246
  Sage, 151
  Shells, 245, 246
Patties
  Eggplant, 202
  Miniature Carrot, 69
  Salmon Squash, 155
pattypan squash, 32-33
pea(s), 25-26. See also beans; chick peas; lentils
  and Shrimp Salad, 115
  Carrot Ring with, 241
  dried, 13-14
  Hot Lettuce and, 175
  Salad, seafood and, 115
  snow, 25-26
    Salad, Pasta and, 108
    Herb-filled, 64
    Oriental, 182
    Pickled, 256
    Shrimp-filled, 64
  Soup with Meatballs, Split, 91
  Vegetable Soup, Split, 92
Peanut
  -Pepper Sauce, 217
  Salad, Green Bean and, 101
  Sauce, Rice and Greens in Spicy, 122
pearl onions, 23-24
Pecan Cupcakes, Pumpkin-, 240
Pecan-Sweet Potato Balls, 196
Peony, Turnip, 56
pepper(s), 26
  Braised Greens with Red, 175
  -Chili Bake, Layered, 142

pepper(s) (continued)
  Cups, Confetti Cheese Salad in, 103
  green, 26
    Cups, Macaroni in, 127
    Gel, Green, 262
  Italian Roasted, 62
  Pickled Hot, 258
  red
    Braised Greens with, 175
    Poinsettia, 48
    Relish, 261
  Sauce, Peanut-, 217
  Steak, Chinese, 124
  Vegetarian Stuffed, 126
Pesto, 219
Phyllo Roulades, Spinach-Carrot, 68
Pickled
  Beets, 257
  Hot Peppers, 258
  Snow Peas, 256
Pickles
  Carrot, 257
  Cucumber Refrigerator, 256
  Dilled Okra, 258
  Green Tomato, 257
Pie(s). See also Pastry
  Chicken Pot, 151
  Country Asparagus, 150
  Deep-dish Chicken Liver Vegetable, 152
  Navy Bean, 248
  Parsnip, 248
  Pumpkin, 246
  Russian, 153
  Shepherd's, 149
  Supreme, Lamb, 148
  Sweet Potato, 247
  Winter Squash, 249
  Zucchini, 247
Pilaf, Cracked Wheat, 206
pink beans, 14
pinto beans, 14
Piquant French Dressing, 222
Pitawiches, Vegetable, 66
Pizza
  Potato, 132
  Topping, 68
  Zucchini, 131
Plain Roasted Potato Fans, 168
Platter, Antipasto, 63
Platter, Marinated Vegetable, 63
plum tomatoes, Italian, 36
poblano chilies, 26
Poinsettia, Red Pepper, 48
Pompons, Radish, 51
Pork
  Egg Foo Yong, 119

Pork (continued)
  Meatballs, 91
  Roast, Stuffed, 154
  Skillet, Savory, 152
Potato(es), 27-28. *See also* sweet potatoes; yams
  Anna, 168
  au Gratin, 186
  -Bacon Omelet, 118
  Balls, French-fried, 198
  Bread, 237
  Cake, Chocolate, 242
  Canapés, New, 65
  Casserole, Beef and, 140
  Cinnamon Rolls, 236
  Creamy Mashed, 169
  Duchess-style, 198
  Fans, 168
  Franks, 157
  Gnocchi, 205
  Gourmet Cheese, 186
  Knishes, 201
  -Leek Soup, 78
  Pancakes, 199, 200
  Pan Rolls, 237
  Pizza, 132
  Salad
    Eggciting, 107
    Favorite, 106
    Main-Dish, 113
    Skillet, 107
    Sour Cream, 106
  Sauté, Two-, 174
  Scalloped, 185
  Skins, Fried, 68
  Soup, Dutch, 78
  Twice-Baked, 194
  Wedges, Roasted, 168
Primavera, Pasta, 132
Pudding, Yam, 192
Pudding, Zucchini, 192
Puffed Pumpkin Custard, 249
Puffs, Spinach, 69
pumpkin, 28
  Cheesecake, 245
  -Chocolate Torte, 243
  Custard, Puffed, 249
  -Pecan Cupcakes, 240
  Pie, 246
  -Raisin Cookies, 239
  seeds, how to roast, 28
  Soup, 86
  Swirl Cheesecake, 244
  Tarts, 246
Purée, Carrot, 161
Purée, Spinach, 162
purple onions, red-, 23-24

Q

Quiche(s)
  Broccoli, 121
  Corn, 122
  Zucchini, 122
Quick Garlic Loaves, 235

R

Rabbit, Northern Plains, 145
radish(es), 29
  Cup Flowers, 50
  Daikon, 29
  Feathers, 51
  Lilies, 52
  Pompons, 51
Raised Corn Muffins, 234
Raisin
  Cookies, Pumpkin-, 239
  Salad, Carrot-, 105
  Tea Bread, Carrot-, 234
  Tea Muffins, Carrot-, 233
Ranch-style Lentil Casserole, 141
Rarebit, Corn, 170
Ratatouille, 182
Ravioli, Deep-fried, 135
Ravioli with Spinach Filling, Carrot, 135
red. *See also* peppers
  beans, 14
  Beet Chocolate Cake, 243
  Cabbage, Sweet-Sour, 166
  Flannel Hash, 157
  Italian onions, 23-24
  potatoes, round, 27-28
  -purple onions, 23-24
Refrigerator Pickles, Cucumber, 256
Relish(es)
  Carrot, 263
  Frozen Cuke and Onion, 262
  Red Pepper, 261
  Summer Squash, 260
  Winter Salad, 262
Rice. *See also* Risotto
  and Greens in Spicy Peanut Sauce, 122
  Salad, 109
  Skillet, Tomato, Okra and, 178
  Spinach-Fried, 205
Rigatoni with Eggplant Sauce, 134
Ring(s)
  Golden Carrot, 241
  Molded Vegetable, 110
  with Peas, Carrot, 241
Risotto, 207
Roast, Stuffed Pork, 154

Roasted
  Peppers, Italian, 62
  Potato Fans, 168
  Potato Wedges, 168
Roll(s). *See also* Bread; Roulades
  Carrot-Zucchini Cake, 244
  Creole Cabbage, 129
  Stuffed Turkey, 154
romaine, 20-21
root chicory, 6
Roses, Cabbage and Tomato, 55
Rosettes, Celery and Cheese, 66
Roulades, Spinach-Carrot Phyllo, 68
Roulades with Onion-Lemon Sauce, Fish, 156
round red potatoes, 27-28
Rounds, Curried Egg and Zucchini, 63
round white potatoes, 27-28
russet potatoes, 27-28
Russian Dressing, 226
Russian Pie, 153
rutabagas, 29-30
  Jonquil, 55
  Mashed Swedish, 161
  Supreme, Golden, 167
  Swedish, 161

S

Sage Pastry, 151
Salad(s), 97-115. *See also* Relishes
  Five-Bean, 102
  Three-Bean, 259
Salmon
  and Pea Salad, 115
  Mousse, Spinach and, 66
  Salad, Layered, 113
  Squash Patties, 155
Salsa, Tomato, 217
Salsa Verde, 220
salsify, 30
  au Gratin, 191
  Pancakes, 201
  Scorzonera, 30
  Soup, 85
Sandwiches, Eggplant, 202
sauces, 209, 214-220. *See also* Toppings
  Cheese, 128
  Cream, 137
  Freezer Tomato, 264
  Lemon, 126
  Mornay, 189
  Onion-Lemon, 156
  Oriental, 119
  Rigatoni with Eggplant, 134
  Sesame Yogurt, 67

Sauce(s) (continued)
  Sour Cream, 176
  Spicy Peanut, 122
  Sweet-Sour, 126
Saucy
  Artichokes, 180
  Cabbage Bundles, 128
  Vegetables, 219
Sauerkraut Cake, Chocolate, 242
Sauté(ed)
  Basil Tomato, 173
  Cherry Tomato, 173
  Tomatoes and Anise, 172
  Two-Potato, 174
  Zucchini, 173
  Zucchini and Carrot, 173
Savory
  Basil Beans, 177
  Pork Skillet, 152
Savoy cabbage, 8
Scalloped Potatoes, 185
scallop squash, 32-33
Scorzonera salsify, 30
seasonings, 209
  chart, 210-213
serrano chilies, 26
Sesame
  Green Beans, 171
  Spread, Eggplant-, 61
  Yogurt Sauce, 67
shallots, 30-31
shells, pie, 245, 246
Shepherd's Pie, 149
shiitake mushrooms, 21-22
Shortcut Dumplings, 145
Shrimp
  Appetizers, Zucchini-, 64
  -filled Snow Peas, 64
  Salad, Pea and, 115
side dishes, 159-207
Skillet
  Cabbage and Apple, 166
  Cucumber and Tomato, 178
  Medley, Zucchini, 179
  Mexican Lima Bean, 148
  Potato Salad, 107
  Savory Pork, 152
  Tomato, Okra and Rice, 178
Skins, Fried Potato, 68
Slaw, Farmhouse Cabbage, 104
Slaw, Jerusalem Artichoke, 105
Slices, Oven-fried Eggplant, 197
small white onions, 23-24
snap beans, 4
snap peas, sugar, 25-26
snow peas. *See* peas

Soufflé
  Blender Spinach, 121
  Broccoli, 120
  Spinach, 120
soups, 71-95. *See also* Chowders; Stews
Sour Cream
  -Dill Topping, 221
  Dip, Curried, 60
  Mushroom Sauce, 215
  Onion Dip, 60
  Potato Salad, 106
  Sauce, 176
  Salad, Cucumber-, 100
soybeans, 14
spaghetti squash, 34-35
  Lasagne, 137
  Tuna-stuffed, 114
Spanish onions, 23-24
Spanish radishes, 29
Spears, Zucchini, 259
Spice Cake, Zucchini, 240
Spice(d). *See also* Hot
  chart, 210-213
  Pie Shell, 245
Spicy Baked Corn, 188
Spicy Peanut Sauce, Rice and Greens in, 122
spinach, 31
  and Salmon Mousse, 66
  -Carrot Phyllo Roulades, 68
  Creamed, 170
  Filling, Carrot Ravioli with, 135
  -Fried Rice, 205
  Pasta, 204
  Puffs, 69
  Purée, 162
  Salad, Hot, 98
  Soufflé, 120, 121
  Stuffing, 207
  -Tomato Frittata, 118
split
  dried peas, 14
  Pea Soup with Meatballs, 91
  Pea Vegetable Soup, 92
Spread, Chick Pea, 61
Spread, Eggplant-Sesame, 61
Spring, Zucchini, 57
sprout(s), 32
  Brussels, 7
  Cheese Bake, Brussels, 189
  Salad, 102
  Tabouli with Bean, 110
  Tangy Brussels, 164
Squares, Broccoli-Cheese, 190
Squares, Chocolate Zucchini, 240
squash, 32-35
  Balls, Crispy, 69

squash (continued)
  Bisque, Curried, 81
  Cheesecake, 245
  Lasagne, Spaghetti, 137
  Patties, Salmon, 155
  Pie, Winter, 249
  Relish, Summer, 260
  Stuffed Acorn, 127
  Stuffed Turban, 196
  Tulip, 54
  Tuna-stuffed Spaghetti, 114
  Whipped Butternut, 169
  zucchini, 32-33
Squmpkin Bread, 232
Stars, Herb Tomato, 67
Steak, Chinese Pepper, 124
Stew(s). *See also* Chowders; soups
  Chicken and Lima Bean, 145
  Chunky Beef, 146
  Vegetable, 144
Stewed Tomatoes, 170
Sticks, Bacon-Onion, 234
Stir-fried
  Asparagus, 183
  Beef with Vegetables, 124
  Vegetables, 184
Stock, Vegetable, 72
straightneck squash, 32-33
straw mushrooms, 21-22
Stuffed
  Acorn Squash, 127
  Artichokes, 195
  Bread, Tex-Mex, 65
  Cabbage with Cheese Sauce, 128
  Celery, Three-Cheese, 64
  Eggplant, 130
  Peppers, Vegetarian, 126
  Pork Roast, 154
  Sweet Potatoes, 195
  Turban Squash, 196
  Turkey Roll, 154
Stuffing
  Carrot-Celery, 206
  Spinach, 207
  Zucchini Corn Bread, 206
Succotash, 167
Sugar Icing, Confectioners', 236
sugar snap peas, 25-26
summer squash, 32-33
  Relish, 260
sunchokes. *See* Jerusalem artichokes
Sunny Asparagus, 123
Sunny Green Beans, 123
Super Baked Beans, 194
Susans, Black-eyed, 54
Swedish Rutabagas, 161

Sweet-and-Sour. *See* Sweet-Sour
sweet peppers, 26
sweet potato(es), 35-36. *See also* yams
  Balls, Pecan-, 196
  New England-style, 188
  Pie, 247
  Stuffed, 195
Sweet-Sour
  Bacon Dressing, 228
  Baked Beans, 193
  Dressing, 222
  Green Beans, 180
  Red Cabbage, 166
  Sauce, 126
Swirl Cheesecake, Pumpkin, 244
Swiss chard, 16-17
  in Mornay Sauce, 189
Swiss Potato Pancake, 199

T

Tabouli with Bean Sprouts, 110
Tangy Brussels Sprouts, 164
Tangy Coleslaw, 104
Tarts, Pumpkin, 246
Tea Bread, Carrot-Raisin, 234
Tea Muffins, Carrot-Raisin, 233
Tempura, Chicken and Vegetable, 126
Texas-style Chili, 142
Tex-Mex Stuffed Bread, 65
Thousand Island Dressing, Crunchy, 226
Three-Bean Salad, 259
Three-Cheese Stuffed Celery, 64
Toasted Croutons, 115
tomato(es), 36
  and Anise, Sautéed, 172
  and Okra, Fried Green, 177
  -Apple Chutney, 260
  Basil Beans and, 172
  -Dill Bisque, 73
  Dressing, Italian, 224
  Dressing, Low-Calorie, 224
  Eggplant with, 181
  Flowers, 51
  Fried, with Sour Cream Sauce, 176
  Frittata, Spinach-, 118
  Greek-style Marinated, 103
  Italian-style Marinated, 103
  Juice Cocktail, 263
  Okra and Rice Skillet, 178
  -Onion Salad, 102
  Pickles, Green, 257
  Rose, 55
  Salsa, 217
  Sauce Cubes, 219

tomato(es) (continued)
  Sauce, Freezer, 264
  Sauté, Basil, 173
  Sauté, Cherry, 173
  Skillet, Cucumber and, 178
  Soup, Cream of, 80
  Soup, Creamy Parsnip and, 81
  Stars, Herb, 67
  Stewed, 170
Topping(s)
  Biscuit, 148
  Blue Cheese, 221
  Cheddar-Onion, 221
  Corn Bread, 148
  Mexican, 68
  Parmesan, 68
  Pizza, 68
  Sour Cream-Dill, 221
Torte, Pumpkin-Chocolate, 243
Tossed Green Salad, 99
Tulip, Squash, 54
Tuna
  and Pea Salad, 115
  Artichoke Salad, 113
  Salad, Layered, 113
  -stuffed Spaghetti Squash, 114
turban squash, 34-35
  Stuffed, 196
Turkey
  Roll, Stuffed, 154
  Soup with Parslied Dumplings, 91
  -Zucchini Lasagne, 136
turnip(s), 37
  Buttery Onions and, 179
  Calla Lily, 53
  Creamy Mashed, 169
  greens, 37
  Jonquil, 55
  Mum, 54
  Peony, 56
Twice-Baked Potatoes, 194
Twists, Crunchy Onion, 235
Twists, Whole-Wheat Carrot and Walnut, 238
Two-Crust Pie, Pastry for, 246
Two-Potato Sauté, 174

V

Valencia Soup, 76
Vegetable(s). *See also individual names of
  vegetables*
  Balls with Pasta, 133
  Beef Soup with Pastry Cap, 89
  Cantonese, 185
  Chain, 48

Vegetable(s) (continued)
-Cheese Ball, 65
-Chicken Bake, 139
Chinese Chicken with, 125
Chowder, 76
Crispy, 197
Cutlets, 203
Deep-fried, 198
-filled Dutch Pancake, 123
Jacks, 48
Kabobs, 171
-Lentil Chowder, 86
Loaf, 203
Pie, Deep-dish Chicken Liver, 152
Pitawiches, 66
Platter, Marinated, 63
Ring, Molded, 110
Salad, Mixed, 111
Salad, Pasta and, 108
Saucy, 219
Soup
Creamy, 79
Oriental, 79
Split Pea, 92
Stew, 144
Stir-fried, 184
Stir-fried Beef with, 124
Stock, 72
Tempura, Chicken and, 126
Vegetarian
Chili, 143
Minestrone, 93
Stuffed Peppers, 126
Venison Curry, 147
Verde, Salsa, 220
Vichyssoise, 74
Vinaigrette Dressing, 225
Low-Calorie, 225
Mix, 225

W

Walnut Butter, 264
Walnut Twists, Whole-Wheat Carrot and, 238
watercress, 20-21
and Nectarine Salad, 99
Soup, 78
Water Lilies, 52
wax beans, 4
Wedges, Roasted Potato, 168
Wheat Germ-Zucchini Bread, 232
Wheat Pilaf, Cracked, 206
Whipped Butternut Squash, 169
Whipped Cream, Cinnamon, 244

White
Mountain Frosting, 243
onions, small, 23-24
potatoes, 27-28
Sauce, Medium, 214
Whole-Wheat Carrot and Walnut Twists, 238
Whole-Wheat Zucchini Bread, 233
Winter Salad Relish, 262
winter squash, 34-35
Pie, 249

Y

yam(s), 35. *See also* sweet potatoes
Fruit Salad, 107
Pudding, 192
yellow beans, 4
yellow onions, 23-24
Yogurt
Dressing, Herbed, 228
Sauce, Cucumber-, 216
Sauce, Sesame, 67
Yong, Pork Egg Foo, 119

Z

zucchini, 32-33
and Carrot Sauté, 173
Bread, Wheat Germ-, 232
Bread, Whole-Wheat, 233
Butterflies, 56
Cake Roll, Carrot-, 244
Corn Bread Stuffing, 206
Fritters, 199
Jam, 263
Lasagne, Turkey-, 136
Nut Bread, 232
-Nut Chip Cookies, 239
Pancakes, 200
Pie, 247
Pizza, 131
Pudding, 192
Quiche, 122
Rounds, Curried Egg and, 63
Sauté, 173
-Shrimp Appetizers, 64
Skillet Medley, 179
Soup, 76
Spears, 259
Spice Cake, 240
Spring, 57
Squares, Chocolate, 240